THE THEORY OF WAGE DETERMINATION

Other Symposia published for the International Economic Association

THE BUSINESS CYCLE IN THE POST-WAR WORLD
Edited by ERIK LUNDBERG

CLASSICS IN THE THEORY OF PUBLIC FINANCE
Edited by R. A. MUSGRAVE and A. T. PEACOCK

THE ECONOMIC CONSEQUENCES OF THE SIZE OF NATIONS
Edited by E. A. G. ROBINSON

ECONOMIC DEVELOPMENT FOR LATIN AMERICA
Edited by HOWARD S. ELLIS assisted by HENRY C. WALLICH

THE ECONOMICS OF INTERNATIONAL MIGRATION
Edited by BRINLEY THOMAS

THE ECONOMICS OF TAKE-OFF INTO SUSTAINED GROWTH
Edited by W. W. ROSTOW

INFLATION
Edited by D. C. HAGUE

INTERNATIONAL TRADE THEORY IN A DEVELOPING WORLD
Edited by ROY HARROD and D. C. HAGUE

STABILITY AND PROGRESS IN THE WORLD ECONOMY
Edited by D. C. HAGUE

THE THEORY OF CAPITAL
Edited by F. A. LUTZ and D. C. HAGUE

THE THEORY OF WAGE DETERMINATION

Proceedings of a Conference held by the International Economic Association

EDITED BY

JOHN T. DUNLOP

LONDON
MACMILLAN & CO LTD
NEW YORK · ST MARTIN'S PRESS
1964

First Edition 1957
Reissued 1964

MACMILLAN AND COMPANY LIMITED
St Martin's Street London WC 2
also Bombay Calcutta Madras Melbourne

THE MACMILLAN COMPANY OF CANADA LIMITED
70 Bond Street Toronto 2

ST MARTIN'S PRESS INC
175 Fifth Avenue New York 10 NY

PRINTED IN GREAT BRITAIN

CONTENTS

IV

THE WAGE STRUCTURE

V

THE NATURE OF BARGAINING

VI

LABOUR MARKET AND LABOUR SUPPLY

VII

REPORT ON THE PROCEEDINGS

LIST OF PARTICIPANTS

M. T. Bagiotti, Bocconi University, Milan, Italy

Professor H. Brochier, University of Grenoble, France

Professor E. H. Phelps Brown, The London School of Economics, London, England

Professor J. T. Dunlop, Harvard University, Cambridge, Massachusetts, U.S.A.

Professor L. H. Dupriez, University of Louvain, Belgium

M. I. Gasparini, Bocconi University, Milan, Italy

Mr. Douglas Hague, University College, London, England

Professor H. Haller, University of Kiel, Germany

Dr. Bent Hansen, University of Uppsala, Sweden

Professor F. H. Harbison, University of Chicago, U.S.A.

Mr. H. G. Johnson, King's College, Cambridge, England

Professor W. A. Jöhr, Handelshochschule, St. Gallen, Switzerland

Professor Clark Kerr, Chancellor, University of California, Berkeley, California, U.S.A.

Dr. W. Krelle, University of Heidelberg, Germany

Mr. K. Laffer, University of Sydney, Australia

Professor E. Lindahl, University of Uppsala, Sweden

Professor Jean Marchal, Sorbonne, Paris, France

Dr. R. Meidner, Landsorganisationen, Stockholm, Sweden

Professor Charles A. Myers, Massachusetts Institute of Technology, Cambridge, Massachusetts, U.S.A.

Professor Kazuo Okochi, University of Tokyo, Japan

Mr. A. Peacock, The London School of Economics, London, England

Dr. S. D. Punekar, Employees' State Insurance Corporation, Bombay, India

Dr. Gösta Rehn, Konjunkturinstitutet, Stockholm, Sweden

Professor Lloyd G. Reynolds, Yale University, New Haven, Conn., U.S.A.

Mr. E. J. Riches, International Labour Office, Geneva, Switzerland

Mr. B. C. Roberts, The London School of Economics, London, England

Professor E. A. G. Robinson, Sidney Sussex College, Cambridge, England

Dr. Melvin Rothbaum, Harvard University, Cambridge, Massachusetts, U.S.A.

Mr. K. Rothschild, Oesterreichisches Institut für Wirtschaftsforschung, Vienna, Austria

Mr. G. Rottier, Institut de Science Économique Appliquée, Paris, France

Professor D. B. Schouten, University of Tilburg, Netherlands

Professor F. Sellier, University of Aix-en-Provence et Marseille, France

Professor G. L. S. Shackle, University of Liverpool, England

Mr. H. A. Turner, University of Manchester, England

Professor V. Wagner, University of Basel, Switzerland

PROGRAMME COMMITTEE

Professor Dunlop (Chairman)
Professor Phelps Brown
Professor Demaria
Professor Marchal
Professor Robinson (representing the Executive Committee of I.E.A.)

INTRODUCTION

BY JOHN T. DUNLOP

THE International Economic Association was founded under the auspices of Unesco at a meeting held in Monaco in September 1950. Each year since then a round-table conference has been held with papers and discussion centred upon a single major topic or a sector of the discipline. Succeeding conferences have been devoted to The Problem of Long-Term International Balance (1950), Monopoly and Competition and their Regulation (1951), The Business Cycle in the Post-War World (1952), and The Determinants of Economic Progress (1953).

For the 1954 Round Table Conference the topic of Wage Determination was chosen. It was held September 4-13 at Seelisberg, Switzerland, in the Hotel Kulm overlooking Lake Lucerne. There were 35 participants from 13 countries ; 22 papers were discussed during 16 half-day sessions. The final day was spent in a general review of the work as a whole. A summary of this discussion, in the final part of this volume, indicates the main issues of the conference, the degree to which a consensus was developed, and the questions on which a spectrum of ideas remained.

The conference brought together economists with a wide variety of professional experience, as a glance at the list of participants will show. The group included a number of general economists interested in pure theory, monetary and fiscal policy, as well as specialists in labour economics and the institutions of the wage market. Some had been solely academics ; others had extensive experience in the planning and administration of public policies, and still others had been practitioners in labour organizations, managements, and governments, or arbitrators in the making of wage decisions and in the settlement of other disputes. As might be expected wherever 35 economists are gathered together, the discussion also reflected a range of political and social convictions and programmes for public policy. The sessions were much enriched by the wide diversity of these experiences and talents ; in such a group general principle and stubborn fact could not long be kept apart.

The participants were drawn from quite different environments with diverse wage practices and institutions in the labour market.[1]

[1] See John T. Dunlop and Melvin Rothbaum, 'International Comparisons of Wage Structures', *International Labour Review* (April 1955).

In some countries wage decisions are relatively centralized through a labour court (Australia), or through confederation-wide bargaining (Sweden, Holland, and to a lesser extent Italy), or through the influence of a government determined minimum wage (France). In other countries there is considerable industry-wide bargaining but relatively little central co-ordination of these negotiations, except in war-time (England, Belgium, Germany). In still other instances (United States), plant or locality bargaining is the dominant form, although instances of industry-wide bargaining are significant. In some countries the direct wage constitutes a comparatively high proportion (85 per cent) of total compensation and labour costs, while in other countries supplementary benefits, family allowances, and social security payments of all kinds make direct wages a comparatively smaller percentage (60 per cent). In some countries these supplementary benefits are paid largely under government auspices and have immediate fiscal significance, while in other cases these payments are made by employers in the same way as direct wages.

The economic position of a country has important impacts on its wage policies. Some economies are relatively isolated while others are keenly sensitive to changes in the volume of world trade and to the terms of trade. Some economies are highly industrialized, while others are at the early stages of economic development. Some have had chronic underemployment (Italy) ; others have had long periods of overemployment (Sweden) ; others have apparently been able to exert some measure of control over the labour market through the flow of immigration (Switzerland) ; still others are said to reflect a structural tendency towards long-run inflation (France). Some have had extreme price and wage increases since the late 'thirties (thirty- to fortyfold in France and Italy), while others reflect relatively little inflation (doubling in England and Sweden). Further, political and social factors may be expected to play a rôle. Thus, some of these countries have had labour governments for significant periods while others have had predominantly conservative governments. Wage developments and wage structures are shaped by these diverse wage-setting institutions and by these differences in economic position.

There is a deep-seated intellectual habit, none the less, for writers on wage determination to generalize from the experience of their own country. They tend to assume the unique validity of their native institutions, be they Americans, British, Swedish, or French. The Seelisberg papers clearly reflect this tendency. The varied descriptions and explanations of wages proffered by economists puts one in mind of the conflicting impressions of the elephant developed by a group of blind men, each of whom explored a different sector of its anatomy.

The discussion at Seelisberg helped to provide an antidote to such parochialism in two ways. (1) A comparative view places wage determination in the context of a wide spectrum of experience. This diversity among countries quickly leads to questions of theoretical interest: how do wage movements in economies with centralized wage determination compare with those in which wage decisions are more widely diffused? What has happened to wage structures under extreme inflation, compared to relatively modest increases in wages and prices? Are there significant differences in the wage structures of relatively static as compared to highly dynamic economies, or in the wage differentials of underdeveloped as compared to highly industrialized economies? How is one to account for the fact that payments above contract scales, the wage drift or wage slide, are significant in some countries and unimportant in others? A comparative view may also highlight the particular constellation of factors which has created a unique national wage determination pattern. The chapters by Marchal and Perroux, for instance, provide much illumination on the distinctive features of the French experience.

(2) By bringing together specialists in labour economics and general theorists,[1] the round-table conference aspired towards a more general theory of wages, towards a framework of analysis of wage experience applicable to a wider range of economies. Labour specialists have a contribution to make on such matters as the behaviour of labour organizations and managements, the degree of flexibility of the wage structure in response to relative changes in employment and other factors, and the impact of labour organizations on the operation of otherwise unorganized labour markets. General theorists, in turn, emphasize the common elements in the experience among countries: the rôle of wages in inflation, the relations between wage policy and monetary and fiscal policy, the relations between wages and transfer payments, and the factors determining the structure of wage differentials. The labour specialist sees the unique features of the labour market and the internal interdependencies within the wage structure. The general theorist is a constant reminder of the larger interactions between the labour factor of production and money flows of compensation, on the one hand, and the total economy, including an international system of markets, on

[1] See Joseph A. Schumpeter, *History of Economic Analysis* (1954), pp. 946-947, n. 6, for comments on the relative lack of 'co-operation and consequent cross-fertilization' between labour economists and theorists in an earlier period.

the other hand. The interchange between labour specialists and general theorists [1] lifts attention from the features of a single country at a given time and presents the challenge of a more general analysis in which the experience of separate countries become special cases.

The focus of attention at the Seelisberg conference was wage theory. The original choice of this subject was made by the Executive Committee of the International Economic Association. The primary interest was not the comparative description of wage-determining institutions [2] nor an evaluation of wage or pay-roll statistics,[3] nor even an appraisal of alternative wage policies [4] under varying economic conditions. Indeed, the growth in our knowledge of the operation of these institutions and the improvements in the quantity and quality of wage data, despite many deficiencies, impose a heavier standard upon wage theory. While questions of wage-setting institutions, source of wage data and wage measures, and issues of wage policy necessarily entered the discussion at Seelisberg at many points, still the central purpose was wage theory: the general explanation of the wage level, the complex structure of wage differentials which comprises the wage structure, and the process of wage determination.

Ten topics were originally suggested for papers. When the authors had been chosen and their individual interests and inclinations were known, the emphasis and distribution among topics was shifted in some degree. None the less, these ten topics and associated questions are set forth below, since they help to explain the genesis of the chapters which follow, and at the same time they may be of interest as sub-topics within the field of wage theory.

SUGGESTED PROGRAMME FOR ROUND TABLE ON WAGE DETERMINATION

1. *The Requirements of a Theory of Wages*

What questions is a theory of wages required to answer? What data should it seek to explain? How have the questions, and

[1] By way of contrast, see David McCord Wright (ed.), *The Impact of the Labor Union* (1951).

[2] See International Labour Office, *Wages*, (*a*) *General Report*, International Labour Conference, Thirty-First Session (1948).

[3] See International Labour Office, various reports of the international conferences of labour statisticians.

[4] See Barbara Wootton, *The Social Foundations of Wage Policy* (1955), pp. 161-190; The Swedish Confederation of Trade Unions; *Trade Unions and Full Employment* (1953); International Labour Office, *Report of the Director-General* (1951); Allan Flanders, *A Policy for Wages*, Fabian Tract 281 (July 1950).

the scope of wage theory, changed over the past hundred years? What is the relation between wage theory and distribution theory? How does one integrate questions of real and money wages? wage level and wage structure?

2. *The Determination of the General Level of Wage Rates*

Is this subject to be within the scope of economics, or is it to be assumed that the money wage level is given for purposes of economic discussions? What are the determinants of the wage level in various economic systems: classical, Walras, Keynes, Tinbergen, Klein? What do econometric models teach about wage level determination? It is sometimes said that in the nineteenth century money supply determined prices and wages were then adjusted accordingly, while in the twentieth century wages are first determined by collective bargaining and then money supply permits prices to be adjusted. How valid is this caricature?

3. *Wage Policy and Full Employment in the Short Run*

What are the range of choices between full employment and inflation? What conclusions are to be drawn from the experience since 1945? How much unemployment is required for wage stability? What factors determine this point or level? What are the consequences of the fact that labour supply varies with employment levels? Are wage and price controls inevitable for practical full employment? What 'responsibility' can be expected from the parties in collective bargaining?

4. *The Long-term Movement of the Wage Level*

The problem of dividing the gains in productivity in the form of lower prices or higher wage rates. The problem of adjustment in wage structure and differentials and piece-rates is easier with a rising wage level. Cost-of-living escalation as a wage policy. Adjustments within the community to long-run inflation.

5. *The Impact of Bargaining on the Wage Structure*

Compare wage setting in pure theory, under non-union or unorganized conditions, and under collective bargaining. A restatement of the theory of wage differentials by occupation, sex, area, industry. How extensive are autonomously induced 'distortions' in the wage structure?

6. *A Review and Appraisal of the Theory of Bargaining*

Review of Edgeworth, Pigou, Shackle, etc. Has the theory of games any contribution to make? What are the limits of 'bargaining' or 'indeterminacy'? What contribution has the theory of oligopoly to make to wage determination?

7. *The Concept of Labour Supply*

   Is the amount of labour supplied a function uniquely of price (wage rate)? Supply to the firm? Locality supply? Supply in the country? What can be said about the shape of these functions? Is it possible to develop a classification of labour market competitive conditions to parallel product market classes and types? What is a labour market?

8. *The Union as an Economic Institution*

   Can any assumptions of rational behaviour be developed? What about conflicting theories of union behaviour as 'political' or 'economic'? Are there any significant degrees of difference in rationality in the behaviour of businesses and unions? What behaviouristic assumptions are warranted?

9. *Relation between Wage Rate Changes and Variations in the Size and Share Distribution of Income*

   What have been the effects of changes in wage rates on size distribution of income? What models? Changes in income within labour income and between factor incomes? Where do we stand on the share distribution problem?

10. *The Impact of Inflation on Wage Differentials*

    In the light of European inflations, and comparisons between countries, what can be said about relation of inflation to wage structure? Are differentials measured in percentage or absolute terms? What models can be developed to explain developments?

A preliminary committee at Seelisberg grouped the papers into major headings and arranged the sequence of their presentation. This order has been modified here only in minor respects.

Part I is introductory and seeks to present the task and problems of contemporary wage theory against the background of a brief review of the development of wage theory since the early nineteenth century.

Part II (Chapters 2-7) is concerned with the general level of wages. These chapters consider in turn the determination of the general level of money wages, the relation between the level of wages and the level of employment, the movement of real wages, and the general interrelation between wage rates and other economic variables. These chapters consider the wage level in macro-economics.

Part III (Chapters 8-11) is oriented toward the impact on wages of labour organizations and other organized groups in the labour market. In modern industrial societies wage rates are not set as abstracted under the conditions of pure competition, but rather the price of labour services is determined, at least in part, by negotiations between organized labour and managements. The government may also play an active rôle. These chapters explore the consequences for wage determination of these institutional features of the labour market and the community.

Part IV (Chapters 12-17) is devoted to the important subject of the wage structure, considered as a complex of wage differentials. Chapter 12, by Kerr, is a general treatment of the problem ; the chapters which follow are primarily concerned with the evidence drawn from particular countries : the United States, Sweden, France, and England. While it is possible to develop a great many classifications of differentials, these chapters recognize the following types : interpersonal, interfirm within the same product market, interoccupational, interindustrial, and interregional. These chapters are concerned with explanations for the structure of wages and their changes in recent years.

Part V (Chapters 18-19) surveys the contribution of bargaining theory to an explanation of wage determination. If wage rates are determined in negotiations between labour and management organizations, the theory of wages must draw from the pure theory of bargaining.

Part VI (Chapters 20-21) is concerned with the operation of the labour market and with the difficult subject of labour supply. There has been considerable growth in recent years in our knowledge of the detailed operation of the labour market in the United States, and Chapter 20 seeks to summarize these results and to indicate their implications for wage theory.

Part VII constitutes a summary of the discussion at Seelisberg and seeks to draw together some of the principal areas of consensus of views and to indicate some of the major divisions of opinion.

Finally, may I express the gratitude not only of the Programme Committee, but also that of all those who took part in the Conference, to some of those who contributed to its success and its smooth hearing : to Mme Berger Lieser, the indefatigable Secretary of the Association ; to Mrs. Henderson, who was chiefly responsible for the translation of papers written in languages other than English ; to M. Jacob and Miss Hélène Heroys, who translated our discussions and helped to make our often incoherent contributions intelligible to our colleagues ; to Douglas Hague, who has reduced to order and summarized the record of the debate ; and to the friendly and helpful management and staff of the Hotel Kulm.

PART I

THE SETTING FOR THE DISCUSSION

Chapter 1

THE TASK OF CONTEMPORARY WAGE THEORY

BY

JOHN T. DUNLOP
Harvard University, U.S.A.

THE high purpose of these sessions is symbolized by a passage from Michael Polanyi :

> Science is not conducted by isolated efforts like those of the chess players or shellers of peas and could make no progress that way. If one day all communications were cut between scientists, that day science would practically come to a standstill. . . . The co-ordinative principle of science . . . consists in the adjustment of each scientist's activities to the results hitherto achieved by others. In adjusting himself to the others each scientist acts independently, yet by virtue of these several adjustments scientists keep extending together with a maximum efficiency the achievements of science as a whole.[1]

In matters of wage theory we have all been too much concerned with domestic chess and shelling of peas ; there has been too little international adjustment of ideas.

THE HERITAGE OF WAGE THEORY

An appraisal of the current state of wage theory needs historical perspective. A brief treatment of a hundred and fifty years of wage discussion runs the dangers of superficiality and dogmatism ; it has the advantage, however, of compelling attention to fundamentals.

The task of wage theory — the questions which have concerned successive generations of economists — has not always been the same. Indeed, the wage theory of a period can be interpreted as a product of (1) the economic developments and quantities of the time and place, including the movement of wage rates ; (2) the

[1] *The Logic of Liberty, Reflections and Rejoinders* (1951), pp. 34-35.

wage-setting institutions ; (3) the dominant economic theory of the period ; and (4) the policy issues of the day. An understanding of the wage discussions of the past must seek to recreate these features of the context.

A review of the history of wage theory suggests a division into three broad periods : [1] the first is the classical period ending around 1870 in which the wages fund symbolized wage thinking ; the second period may be dated to end with the Great Depression of 1929 and is characterized by marginal productivity ; the third period is the contemporary one.

I. The Classical Period

The economic developments of the first half of the nineteenth century which were most decisive in shaping reflection on wage problems were as follows. Reference is made to English experience, for, as Schumpeter says, the 'period was the specifically English period in the history of our science'.[2] The population increased very rapidly, primarily as a consequence of a decrease in the death rate. The extent and the nature of the increase was not accurately known at the time. Real wages showed no marked trend for the period, although it was evident to a contemporary that some groups of workers (the classic case of hand weavers) suffered marked deterioration in their position with mechanization. The best evidence seems to suggest a small decline on the average in real wages during the period of price increases associated with the Napoleonic wars and a gradual rise recouping these losses thereafter.[3] Despite growing industrialization by mid-century there appeared only small real wage benefits and some spectacular new real social costs. The marked differences in real wages among countries, despite the absence of accurate statistics, was a fact of frequent comment; wages were higher in the New World and generally lower on the Continent, and much lower in Asia. The agricultural sector of the economy, even in England, provided the largest part of employment. This sector was seen to be characterized by the law of diminishing returns.

[1] For a discussion of the problems of dating periods, see Joseph A. Schumpeter, *History of Economic Analysis* (1954), pp. 379-380.

[2] Schumpeter, *Economic Analysis*, p. 382.

[3] See T. S. Ashton, *The Industrial Revolution, 1760–1830* (1948) ; 'Some Statistics of the Industrial Revolution in Britain', *Manchester School*, May 1948 ; 'The Standard of Life of Workers in England, 1790–1830', *Tasks of Economic History*, supplement ix (1949) ; Arthur D. Gayer, W. W. Rostow, Anna Jacobson Schwartz, *The Growth and Fluctuation of the British Economy, 1790–1850* (1953), 2 vols., pp. 657-658. Also see F. A. Hayek (ed.), *Capitalism and the Historians* (1954).

Labour unions were not regarded as significant wage-setting institutions of the period. Indeed, the combination laws were not repealed until 1824. While there is some discussion of the impact of 'combination' on wages, the problem does not appear as urgent. The administration of the poor laws prevented their being used as a minimum support for cash wages.

The central problem of classical theory was that of distribution, the division of the national dividend among the recipients of rents, profits, and wages. As Ricardo stated : 'To determine the laws which regulate this distribution, is the principal problem in Political Economy'.[1] If the central problem of economics was distribution, the keystone in the theoretical system was the determination of wages. The theory of wages was at the very heart of economics.

The policy issues of the period that concerned wage determination and labour policy were whether the combination laws against trade unions should be eliminated, whether the poor laws should provide only maintenance in the workhouse or outright assistance, the effects of the introduction of machinery on the working class, and the corn law controversy.[2] In the later years of this period the question of the effects of unions received more attention.

The theory of wages of the period was developed as follows :[3] The use of land according to the theory of rent is not a factor in the pricing process, and the distribution problem becomes the division between capital and labour. The amount of capital used is assumed to be proportional to the amount of labour, and accordingly prices of products are proportional to the amount of labour employed in them. Capital ceases to be regarded as an independent factor of production. Then all types and grades of labour are reduced to multiples of 'normal labour' with the result that the analysis dispenses with relative wages and concerns a single wage rate. Wage determination by these steps becomes the key question of price determination and distribution.

In the short run, population is given and uniquely determines the labour supply. The wages fund is the amount of wage goods, the means of subsistence, or variable capital which capitalists have decided to spend on labour. If the wage rate is fixed in the market above the rate indicated by the wages fund and population, then unemployment will result. If the wage rate is fixed below this

[1] See David Ricardo, Preface to *Principles*, Piero Sraffa, ed., *The Works and Correspondence of David Ricardo* (1951), vol. i, p. xlviii.

[2] See Lionel Robbins, *The Theory of Economic Policy in English Classical Political Economy* (1953).

[3] See T. W. Hutchison, *A Review of Economic Doctrines, 1870–1929* (1953), ch. 1 ; Gustav Cassel, *The Theory of Social Economy*, translated by S. L. Barron (1932), pp. 298-370.

average rate, then there will be unfulfilled demand. In the long run, the wages fund will change as savings change in the community. Population will vary according as wages are above or below the subsistence level, in accordance with the strict Malthusian doctrine. In the long run, through the variation in population, wages tend to be fixed at the minimum of subsistence level. The theory of wages briefly outlined was a tool of analysis for the period. 'It was an analytical tool that, within the analytical structure of its time, was distinctly useful. . . .' (Schumpeter, p. 669.)

The long-run wages fund in its strict formulation requires that the minimum of subsistence be given by physical necessity outside the system. The theory frequently recognized, however, that it was a customary or a social standard to which population would adjust wages. As a consequence, in the long run wages cease to be 'determined' within an economic system but come to be given outside the economic system by social convention. Wage rates in the long run are taken as a datum ; only a short-run wages theory logically remained. In this case supply (population) was given and wages were determined by variations in the demand (wages fund). For a variety of reasons later economists were to agree that the wages fund is not given in the short run as a unique sum. When confronted with the problems of a later day the wages fund theory was abandoned.

In this brief sketch it is to be noted that the theory of wages started at the core of the central theoretical problems of the classical system. There was little or no concern with the structure of wage rates since the theoretical system was developed around a single rate. The social or customary minimum tended to remove the determination of wages from the theoretical system and to take the wage as datum given outside the system. The theory was found wanting on the supply side. Finally, the wages fund theory was abandoned as inadequate to the problems of a new day before an alternative theory was developed. It was not abandoned in the face of a competitor. This history of the wages fund doctrine was to be repeated almost sixty years later with marginal productivity as a theory of wages.

II. Marginal Productivity Distribution Theory

The second period of wage theorizing is not concentrated in a single country ; the ideas of marginal productivity sprang up quite widely : England, Austria, United States, Sweden, Italy, and

Switzerland.[1] Indeed, these widespread and somewhat independent developments suggest that similar environmental conditions, intellectual and practical, were at work.

Economic theory, which included wage theory as an integral part, was to be rebuilt after 1870 by specialists as university economists. The earlier writings had been largely the product of practitioners and political and moral philosophers. The principal economic developments of the period which were to be most influential in conditioning reflection on wage problems were as follows : The birth rates of western Europe had shown evidence of decline under urban conditions, and the population problem ceased to be of overwhelming significance. More accurate census data helped to place the population movements in perspective.

It became increasingly evident that industrialization was creating an increase in real wages and living standards. The pessimism of the early part of the century had given way to optimism for rising living standards. New marvels of the urban industrial age were everywhere apparent. It is true that the industrial age created pressing 'social questions' : factory conditions, working women and children, and slums. But the intellectual problem could not be escaped as to how the benefits of the new era were to be shared. Moreover, the strong challenge of the Marxian analysis of capitalism sharply high-lighted this problem.

In this period the labour union emerges as a significant and continuing institution. In England by the 'sixties there were strong unions whose impact on wages was a challenging intellectual and policy problem. In the 'nineties there was an outburst of 'new unionism', and the same problem appeared the more urgent as collective bargaining became the more widespread. Each outburst of union growth has brought a renewed interest in these theoretical questions. The contemporary United States is no exception, where wage discussions are again interpreting the effects of the rapid growth in union membership from 1933 to 1945. The government in various countries began to affect the wage bargain in some respects by factory legislation regulating hours and later wages, particularly for women and children, and, still later, wages of all employees in some 'sweated trades'.

The central theoretical problem of economics was still distribution. In the words of John Bates Clark : 'For practical men, and hence for students, supreme importance attaches to one economic problem — that of the distribution of wealth among different

[1] See George J. Stigler, *Production and Distribution Theories* (1941), and T. W. Hutchison, *Economic Doctrines*.

claimants.'[1] It was no longer a problem of distribution among social classes, rather distribution of a rising national product among competing and substitutable factors of production.

In the case of some writers, particularly Clark, the distribution problem carried strong moral overtones. The following quotation is instructive :

> The welfare of the laboring classes depends on whether they get much or little ; but their attitude toward other classes — and, therefore, the stability of the social state — depends chiefly on the question, whether the amount that they get, be it large or small, is what they produce. If they create a small amount of wealth and get the whole of it, they may not seek to revolutionize society ; but if it were to appear that they produce an ample amount and get only a part of it, many of them would become revolutionists, and all would have the right to do so. The indictment that hangs over society is that of 'exploiting labour'.[2]

The period sought a theory of distribution which got beyond residuals. Professor Knight has said of the classical period that, apart from rent, 'the only sense in which the treatment gets beyond the circle of each claimant getting what the other does not get lies in the idea that labor gets what it has to have'. The new professional economists, many with some mathematical training, were interested in a more elegant and more formal solution to the problem of distribution.

The policy issues of the day that seemed to have shaped wage discussions most significantly were as follows : (a) What are the effects of union action, including strikes, upon the distribution of the national product ? Can the share of labour be increased by these actions ?[3] (b) Can the existing social order and the functional distribution of income be defended against the Marxist charge of exploitation ?

In this setting the 'marginal productivity' theory of wages developed. Historically, the central notions of marginal productivity had been stated earlier than this period, for instance by Longfield and Thunen. But the ideas gained hold when marginal 'utility' had been advanced to explain the behaviour of consumers and the

[1] *The Distribution of Wealth: A Theory of Wages, Interest and Profits* (1900), p. 1. The quotation is the first sentence of the book.

[2] *Distribution of Wealth*, p. 4.

[3] See, for example, Eugen von Böhm-Bawerk, 'Macht oder ökonömisches Gesetz', *Zeitschrift für Volkswirtschaft, Sozialpolitik und Verwaltung* (December 1914), pp. 205-271, translated by J. R. Mez (1931), mimeographed ; A. C. Pigou, *Principles and Methods of Industrial Peace* (1905) ; Alfred Marshall, *Elements of Economics of Industry* (1893), pp. 374-411. This last chapter is an analysis of 'Trade Unions'.

prices of final products. Marginal productivity emerges as an extension of marginal utility analysis to the problem of the pricing of the factors, an 'imputation' of value to the factors from the price of finished products. The firm combines and 'co-ordinates' factors so as to maximize profit as the consumer varies the combination of expenditures to maximize utility.

Maximization of profits by the firm requires, simply as a logical deduction, that as an equilibrium condition the price of each factor of production be proportional to marginal physical productivity and that the marginal value productivity of each factor be equal to its price.[1] This is true of any factor of production, including labour services, and holds regardless of the character of competition.

But the prices of factors are not 'determined' by marginal productivity. Marginal productivity establishes demand schedules, but factor pricing also requires supply schedules. The original formulators of marginal productivity distribution theory regarded the supply of labour as set by a 'pain-cost explanation'. The amount of labour services offered would be set at the point where the marginal utility of the wage equalled the marginal disutility of labour. Later developments recast the supply function in terms of individual choices between income and leisure at varying wage rates. The operation of the labour market would determine a wage rate and the actual quantities of labour services sold and purchased.

The theory of wages just sketched probably never enjoyed the same measure of acceptance as the wages fund doctrine. Strictly, marginal productivity is not a theory of wages, but only a statement of the demand side. From the outset the supply schedule has been a weak tool. The element of convention has been recognized as strong in setting the length of the work day and in decisions whether and where to work. A reservation price dictated by custom or trade union action limited the pure theory. Inquiry into the actual operation of the labour market suggested many imperfections. In time, many writers came close to the position that the wage rate was determined outside the system, and marginal productivity indicated how much labour would be employed at that wage. As in the classical period, wage determination came to be pushed outside the system of formal theory.

Expanding industrialization creates an increasing number of occupations and jobs. A great deal of interest in the world of affairs is centred on the structure of wage rates or the differentials among these jobs in various firms, industries, and regions. Marginal

[1] See Paul A. Samuelson, *Foundations of Economic Analysis* (1947), pp. 57-89.

productivity theory, with some notable exceptions, has not been widely applied to the complexities of wage structures.

There was another complication to marginal productivity. The classical wage scheme was clearly designed for the total system. While the distinction was not often explicitly made for the particular firm, the wage fund could be applied, and with a single grade of labour and a perfect labour market the theory as a whole could be used in the particular case. The marginal productivity writers ordinarily fail to make this distinction. They do not distinguish in their system between particular wages and the general wage level. In a model with Say's law and full employment the distinction is perhaps not crucial. But where changes in the price of labour as a whole may have significant income effects, particular equilibrium is inadequate to a theory of the general level of wages. T. W. Hutchison has said :

> But nothing replaced or supplemented the analysis of the Wages Fund doctrine, or that of its critics. Not merely did the doctrine itself die away, but the whole problem it sought to deal with was in the main shelved or abandoned. The marginal productivity analysis of distribution which emerged a quarter of a century later, was an explanation of relative wages. . . .[1]

The marginal productivity analysis of distribution remains at the heart of distribution theory, but the theory of wage rate determination erected at the same time has involved a retreat to a position largely outside economic theory. True, 'wages tend to measure the marginal productivity of labour',[2] but this is not a theory of wage rate determination. It does not explain particular wages nor the general wage level. The supply side has again substantially collapsed. Like the wages fund doctrine before it, marginal productivity, including historically related labour supply notions, was not displaced by an alternative or competing theory. Its popularity has declined because of dissatisfaction with it as a tool of analysis.

III. The Contemporary Setting

The contemporary discussion of wage theory likewise needs to be placed in the perspective of economic developments, for instance,

[1] *Economic Doctrines*, p. 27 and p. 319. Also see Joseph A. Schumpeter, *Economic Analysis*, p. 942.

[2] Dennis H. Robertson, 'Wage Grumbles', reprinted in *Readings in the Theory of Income Distribution* (1946), pp. 221-236.

since the Great Depression.[1] The chronic depression in England of the 'twenties and the world-wide unemployment of the early 'thirties compelled attention to the question: To what extent is unemployment to be attributed to wage policy? The major economic literature since the Great Depression has very substantially been concerned with models of the total system which attempt to provide more adequate explanations for unemployment and fluctuation in the total system. In 1932, in his presidential address before the Royal Economic Society, Edwin Cannan said: 'But general unemployment is in reality to be explained almost in the same way as particular unemployment. . . . General unemployment appears when asking too much is a general phenomenon'.[2] It is a measure of the change in thinking since 1932, wrought by events and by further analysis, that wages and employment for the total system are thought to be interrelated in a vastly more complex manner than can be fruitfully portrayed in a Marshallian demand curve.

The period is characterized by great expansion in organized statistical and quantitative data relevant to economic problems and particularly to measures for the total economy. Even though each generation has noted the same development, the improvements in quantity and quality of economic data in the current period are truly outstanding. Wage rate and labour market data are no exception. Moreover, many studies have been made of the operation of labour organizations, managements, and the collective bargaining process.[3] Theoretical analysis of wage setting can be tested against a vast body of empirical material as never before.

Indeed, one of the consequences of improved and enlarged data is that we become less and less satisfied with existing theoretical systems. The ever-enlarging data challenge the theory at new points and impose new strains on theory. Part of the current dissatisfaction with wage theory arises from ever increasing factual knowledge of wage rates and the labour market.[4] The new danger of the period is that we shall be so weighted down and made timid by unique facts and complexity that we fail to discern boldly the general relationships.

The passage of time has afforded the opportunity better to

[1] See Lloyd G. Reynolds, 'Economics of Labor', in *A Survey of Contemporary Economics*, Howard S. Ellis, ed. (1948), pp. 255-287.

[2] 'The Demand for Labour', *Economic Journal*, xlii (1932), p. 367.

[3] See National Planning Association, *Fundamentals of Labor Peace, A Final Report* (December 1953); Allan Flanders and H. A. Clegg, editors, *The System of Industrial Relations in Great Britain* (1954).

[4] See Gladys L. Palmer, *Labor Mobility in Six Cities: A Report on the Survey of Patterns and Factors in Labor Mobility, 1940–1950* (1954).

appraise the potentialities of modern industrialization and its consequence for living standards and wage rates. In the period 1896–1917 there was apparently a relative plateau in real hourly earning in many countries. The current perspective permits the judgment that real wages have been increasing substantially over time. Data for the United States suggests that real wages are actually rising at an increasing rate ; their rate of increase since 1914 is materially above the rates for any extended portion of the nineteenth century.[1]

In wage-setting institutions the period has seen collective bargaining become the method by which the most significant wage rates are set in Western countries. Instead of treating unions as an aberration to the usual market determination, it is clear that collective bargaining must be taken as the normal case. Moreover, governmental action has impinged on wage-setting forces very generally. There are minimum-wage laws. In many European countries important components of compensation, such as vacations with pay, various insurance schemes, and family allowances are fixed by government. In France and Italy such components amount to 30 and 40 per cent, respectively, of total labour costs. In a number of Western countries, for varying periods, the political parties created or supported by the unions have been the responsible government. Wage-setting arrangements have been made more complex by these governmental relations.

In contemporary economic analyses a rather sharp distinction has been drawn between total system problems and particular equilibrium analysis. In wage discussions this is reflected in separate concern with the general wage level and the wage structure. One of the tasks of analysis is to relate the two areas of theory more adequately.

In setting the intellectual context of contemporary wage discussion, it should be noted that there has developed a degree of specialization, at least in the United States, in which general economic model builders are not familiar with labour market developments and in which labour market specialists are inadequately familiar with central theoretical developments.[2] It should also be reported as a fact that labour market or wage specialists have all been most uncomfortable with 'received' theory. There have been no unabashed defenders in this group. This dissatisfaction arises in

[1] See Leo Wolman, 'Wages in the United States since 1914', Industrial Relations Research Association, *Proceedings of the Sixth Annual Meeting* (December 28-30, 1953), pp. 40-46.

[2] See, for example, the reception and reviews of *The Impact of the Union*, David McCord Wright, ed. (1951).

part from expecting too much from any theoretical analysis, in part from a lack of application of the most advanced theoretical analysis, particularly dealing with the total system, and partly from the inadequacy of the theoretical analysis itself.

The preceding brief review suggests that the developments in wage theory have been related to the economic events of the period, to wage-setting institutions, and to the central body of analytical economics. In the contemporary period there is need for the formulation of a body of wage analysis suitable to the labour market developments and to the wage-setting institutions of the day, drawing upon the central body of economic analysis.

A theory of wages must first identify the questions it seeks to answer or the particular features of the economy and labour market it desires to explain. The classical period was concerned with these questions : How is the national dividend divided between the three social classes ? To what level do wages normally or naturally tend ? In the period of marginal productivity discussion these questions were to the fore : How is the product distributed between the factors which produce it ? Is the product exactly exhausted by this distribution ? Can there be widespread exploitation of labour ? How is the rising product of industry distributed ?

In the main these questions are of little contemporary interest ; wage discussions are now more concerned with other problems. What determines the general level of real wage rates ? the money level ? What determines the structure of wage rates among firms, industries, and occupations ? The 'share' question is discussed in specialized articles, but it is not the core of wage theory.

It should not be presumed that there are no common threads in wage discussions over these periods. Indeed, there are. But the common questions arise on a less grand scale : What are the effects of machinery on wages ? What impact do unions have on wages ? Are wages determined relatively more by economic law or by power and political action ? Do higher wages lead to higher efficiency ? These questions are not new ; [1] they run through the whole period of wage discussion.

[1] Consider one illustration. 'The strong pressure of unions for higher wages, however, has undoubtedly helped to raise the standard of living because this pressure has forced management to work harder to keep down labor costs and has thereby accelerated technological progress.' — Sumner H. Slichter, *What's Ahead for American Business* (1951), p. 13. Compare this statement with a long chain of precedents : J. W. F. Rowe, *Wages in Practice and Theory* (1928), pp. 215-225 ; H. L. Moore, *Laws of Wages, An Essay in Statistical Economics* (1911), p. 189. The history of this idea is interrelated with the effects of a wage change on the efficiency of labour. Refer to Alfred Marshall, *Elements of Economics of Industry* (1893), pp. 408-410 ; Francis A. Walker, *The Wages Question* (1886), pp. 387-388, and many earlier writers.

BEGINNINGS ON A REFORMULATION

The brief review of the heritage of wage discussions has provided a setting in which to make a few suggestions on the future course of speculation on wages. The topic requires a book, but the five sections which follow are designed to sketch a few major concepts.

IV. Preliminary Observations

All wage theory is in a sense demand and supply analysis. A wage is a price, and the wage structure is a sub-system of prices. Prices and price systems are fruitfully to be interpreted in terms of demand and supply. There is no special or peculiar 'demand and supply' theory of wages.

The notion of a 'political' theory of wages involves confusion. In the absence of unions, firms or groups of managements make wage decisions, and under conditions of collective bargaining the parties reach agreement on wage scales. It is indeed appropriate to study the processes, procedures, and influences which determine decisions in these organizations and their agreement making processes. But it does not advance understanding of decision-making in organizations to label the process as either 'political' or 'economic'. The decisional process internal to a management organization or a union is an appropriate area of research, but this subject does not pre-empt the theory of wages. Moreover, a large part of the institutional study of decisions should seek to show the impact of external, including market developments, on internal decisions.

It has been a problem in wage discussions from the earliest years to define and to indicate the independent effect of a strike, or power, or political action upon wage determination.[1] It is not a new issue. It is this old question which is revived under the guise of a 'political' theory of wages.[2] The appropriate question is still what differences, if any, do unions make on wage determination? Are the net effects large or small? Are the effects different for various components of compensation and on different types of wage rates in the total wage structure? [3]

[1] See, for instance, Eugen von Böhm-Bawerk, *Zeitschrift für Volkswirtschaft*, 'Nor could any sensible person deny that the existence of labour organizations with their weapon of strikes has been of pronounced influence on the fixation of wages of labour. . . . The great problem, not adequately settled so far, is to determine the exact extent and nature of the influence of both factors. . . .' ('purely economic' and 'social' categories).

[2] See Arthur M. Ross, *Trade Union Wage Policy* (1948).

[3] See below, Clark Kerr, 'Wage Relationships — The Comparative Impact of Market and Power Forces'.

Wage theory has tended historically to disintegrate on the supply side. As has been noted, in the course of refinement of the wage fund theory and the supply function associated with marginal productivity, the supply function tended to be pushed outside the analytical system. The amount of labour supplied and the wage rate came to be determined by social custom or institutional considerations. The wage rate came to be given for purposes of economic analysis. In a sense, the pivotal task of wage theory is to formulate an acceptable theory on the supply side.

It is not satisfactory to treat wage determination in terms of a single rate. In the past there have been various devices to reduce wage setting to the problem of a single rate. A single unskilled or common labour rate is envisaged into which all skilled labour may be translated as consisting of so many 'units' of unskilled labour. This classical convention was followed by both Marx and Keynes. A single wage rate, out of the whole structure, is regarded as an index or barometer for all other rates. But all wage rates do not move together either in the short run nor in the long period. The wage structure is not completely rigid over time. Moreover, the determination of the wage level and the wage structure are closely interrelated.

Wage theory must operate with the concept of wage structure — the complex of rates within firms differentiated by occupation and employee and the complex of interfirm rate structures. The concept of wage structure for the purpose of the present analysis is a central concept; the analysis of wage determination will be approached through the wage structure. Indeed, instead of reducing wage setting to the problem of a single rate, the task of analysing wage determination is rather the problem of the setting and variation in the whole structure or complex of rates. While the general level of wage rates can be thought of changing apart from variations in structure, in fact they are not dissociated. Changes in the wage level, associated with changes in output levels in the system, are necessarily associated with changes in wage structure. The interrelations between the wage level and the wage structure is itself a major area of inquiry.

A distinction is to be made between the wage structure within a plant, firm, or other grouping in which wage differentials are set by the same authority and the complex of interfirm or group structures set by a number of different agencies. From the point of view of the individual decision makers, the first wage structure is internal while the second is external. One of the central problems of wage analysis is to indicate the interrelations between the internal and external wage structure.

The Setting for the Discussion

The analysis that follows utilizes two concepts which require explanation: job clusters and wage contours.

V. Job Clusters and Wage Contours

A job cluster is defined as a stable group of job classifications or work assignments within a firm (wage determining unit) which are so linked together by (a) technology, (b) by the administrative organization of the production process, including policies of transfer and promotion, or (c) by social custom that they have common wage-making characteristics. In an industrial plant which may literally have thousands of jobs, each wage rate is not equally related and dependent upon all other wage rates. The internal wage structure, the complex of differentials, is not rigidly fixed for all time. Neither do relative rates change in random relation to each other. The internal wage rate structure is to be envisaged as divided into groups of jobs or job clusters. The wage rates for the operations and jobs within a cluster are more closely related in their wage movements than are rates outside the cluster.

Thus a tool-room in a plant would ordinarily constitute a job cluster. The training and skill of the machinists are similar who operate the various specialized machines — lathes, shapers, cutters, and so on. Their work is closely interrelated in the productive process. They may work apart from others. They may have a common promotion and transfer pattern. The wage rates within the tool-room are more closely related with each other than they may be with the rates for other employees in the power plant, on production lines, in the maintenance crew, in the office, or in the sales force. The wage structure of a plant is to be envisaged as comprised of a limited number of such job clusters, each with a number of rates.

From the analytical point of view these job clusters are given in the short period by the technology, the managerial and administrative organization of the wage determining unit, and by the social customs of the work community. Thus, the employees on a furnace or mill may constitute a job cluster (technology); so may employees in a department (administrative organization) or the women in an office (social custom). Wage theory, for the short period, does not seek to explain these job clusters. For the longer period, it is essential to show that the scope of a job cluster within a rate structure may be expanded, restricted, or divided as a consequence of changes in the technology, administrative organization, or social customs in the plant.

The job cluster can be examined in more detail. Ordinarily, a job cluster will contain one, or in some cases several, key rates. The cluster consists of the key rate(s) and a group of associated rates. The key rate may be the highest paid, or the top step in a promotion ladder, or the job at which a large number of workers are employed. Typically, these key rates show relatively less change in job content over time. They are often relatively more standardized as between firms than other jobs. These key rates are those which managements and unions typically have in mind and explicitly discuss in considering the internal wage structure.

The smallest building block in the wage structure is thus the job cluster comprised of a key rate, or several such rates in some cases, and a group of associated rates. The internal wage structure of the plant (wage-determining unit) consists of a number of job clusters. Such is the anatomy of the internal wage structure.

It is not to be presumed that the forces which determine the wage rate for a group of jobs in a cluster are confined within a firm. The 'exterior' plays a very important rôle. The 'exterior', including the 'market', cannot operate directly on a thousand slightly differentiated jobs. The key rates play a decisive rôle in relating the exterior to the internal rate structure. Indeed, the key rates are affected by the exterior, and adjustments in these rates are transmitted to other rates within the plant, cluster by cluster.

A wage contour is defined as a stable group of firms (wage determining units) which are so linked together by (a) similarity of product markets, (b) by resort to similar sources for a labour force, or (c) by common labour market organization (custom) that they have common wage-making characteristics. The wage rates of a particular firm are not ordinarily independent of all other wage rates ; they are more closely related to the wage rates of some firms than to others. A contour for particular occupations is to be defined both in terms of the product market and the labour market. A contour thus has three dimensions : (a) particular occupations or job clusters, (b) a sector of industry, and (c) a geographical location. The firms which comprise a contour constitute a particular product market ; they also may be located in one labour market or scattered throughout a region or the country as a whole.

Thus, in the United States, the basic steel contour for production jobs consists of the producers of basic steel products scattered in various communities throughout the country. The wage rates of the jobs in these firms, in their blast furnace, steel works, and rolling mill operations move together. Some other operations and occupations of the same companies, such as cement mills or shipping, are typically excluded from the basic steel contour. While there are a variety of submarkets, and each basic steel producer may have some specialized features to its product market or locality in which it hires labour, none the less the basic steel wage contour is sharply defined and distinguishable from others.

A contour may be confined to a locality in its labour market dimension. Thus, newspapers in New York City constitute a contour for wage-setting purposes. The rates for various occupations in one newspaper are closely related to those in other newspapers in that city. Specialized product markets, for other types of printing or publishing, are a part of still other wage contours.

A contour refers to particular ranges of skill, occupations, or job clusters. Not all types of labour hired by a firm will have wage rates determined in the same contour. Thus, a firm employing a professional chemist, a pattern-maker, and a clerk may be expected to be part of three quite different contours. A construction firm hiring boilermakers, operating engineers, and labourers will be a part of the construction product market in each instance, but three separate wage contours are involved. The boilermaker's rate is set over the largest geographical area while the labourer's rate is likely to be confined to a single locality.

A wage contour can be explored in further detail. In the ordinary case a wage contour contains one, or in some instances several key bargains. The contour is comprised of the rates for the key firm(s) and a group of associated firms. The key bargain may be set by the largest firm, the price leader, or the firm with labour relations leadership. Thus, in the basic steel contour, the wages determined by the U.S. Steel Company generally have been followed by all other firms in the contour. In this case the other basic steel producers have customarily followed the 'pattern' almost immediately. In other cases more time may elapse before a change by the followers. Some firms may follow only at a distance, altering even the terms of the key settlement in some minor respects.

A wage contour then can be envisaged as a grouping of firms, for a given range of occupations, in which some firms are very closely related to the leaders. Other firms are less directly associated. At the exterior of the contour, furthest from the key rates, the firms may only remotely follow the leadership.

A variety of devices have been developed which relate wages determined by the key bargain to those other firms in the contour. The existence of a common expiration date or the sequence of anniversary dates is reflective of the relations within a wage contour.

Some firms commit themselves in advance to pay the wages of others ; many commit themselves to consider a change when a 'wage movement' has developed in the industry (contour). Specialized product markets or sources of labour supply or skill requirements may mean that a particular firm, remote from the 'centre' of the contour, will modify the 'pattern' established at the key bargain in some respects.

The firms which comprise a wage contour may be organized into a formal employers' association rather than appear to make wage decisions without a common organization. In an association not all firms actually have equal weight in making decisions ; wage leaders exercise their same functions, although an association may mean that all wages are changed at the same time. In many instances an association constitutes only a formal difference from wage leadership conditions that would be evident without an employer's organization.[1]

Wage-making forces are envisaged as concentrated on the key rates in the job clusters. These rates 'extend' out from the internal structure of the firm to the 'exterior' and constitute the focal points for wage-setting forces among firms within the contour. The key rates in the job clusters constitute the channels of impact between the exterior developments in the contour and the interior rate structure of the firm. Moreover, in an analogous way, the key bargains constitute the focal point of wage-setting forces within the contour and constitute the points where wage-making forces converge that are exterior to the contour.

A theory of wages is not required to treat each wage rate in the system as of equal importance. The view of the wage structure outlined above singles out a limited number of key rates and key bargains for analysis. These particular rates are selected, at least in the short run, by the anatomy of the wage structure which is given by (a) the technology and administrative arrangements of firms ; (b) by competitive patterns in product markets ; and (c) the sources of labour supply.

The concepts of job cluster and wage contour are analogous. In each case a group of rates surrounds a key rate. The concepts seek to relate the internal and the external wage structure ; they focus attention on the mechanics by which the internal structure through job clusters are influenced by external developments in

[1] While the impact of labour organization upon wage rates is frequently discussed in current literature, the question of the effect of employer organization upon wage rates is seldom explored. Frequently, a formal employer organization only sharpens relations already apparent. The wage contour is more sharply defined at the 'edges'.

the wage contour. Wage theory cannot reduce all structure to a single rate ; the limited number of strategic rates depicted by the job clusters and wage contours are to be the focus of wage theory.[1]

VI. Wage Structure in the Short Run

The concepts developed in the preceding section can be applied to a particular case. The attached table shows the union scale for motor-truck drivers in Boston for July 1951. Each rate shows the wage scale established between the union and an association or group of employers engaging in selling transportation services. Some small part of the differences in wages may be attributed to variations in the skill or work performed ; some small differences may be related to differences in the length of the work week and the timing of contract expiration during a year. But the teamsters who work at these various rates are essentially similar and substitutable. Essentially the same disparity in rates is found in most other cities, with a high similarity in the relative ranking of rates for various branches of the trade.

In a significant sense, the case constitutes a kind of critical experiment. One type of labour performing almost identical work, organized by the same union, is paid markedly different rates by different associations of employers in the truck transportation industry. Why the wide range in wage rates ? Are the disparities temporary ? Do they arise from 'friction' or 'immobilities' in the labour market ? Are they primarily the consequence of a monopolistic seller of labour discriminating among types of employers ? I believe the answer to these several questions is in the negative.

Basically each rate reflects a wage contour. Each is a reflection of the product market. Within any one contour the wage rates will tend to be equal. As among beer distributors, construction firms, ice deliverers, or scrap iron and metal haulers, there will tend to be few differences in rates. But there are sharp differences in rates as among contours. Fundamentally the differences in the product market are reflected back into the labour market.

But what are the mechanics ? Why do not teamsters all move to the higher paying contours ? Or, why do not the employers in the higher paying contours set a lower wage rate since similar labour

[1] For an imaginative discussion on the concept of labour market, see Clark Kerr, 'The Balkanization of Labor Markets', *Labor Mobility and Economic Opportunity* (1954), pp. 92-110. The present discussion would add to that of Professor Kerr the emphasis that the scope of product markets is reflected back into the labour market defining the scope of wage setting.

seems to be available to other contours at lower rates? In a perfect labour market (a bourse) such changes toward uniformity would tend to take place.

Part of the explanation is to be found in the historical sequence of growth of the trucker's wage scale as indicated in the preceding

TABLE 1

UNION SCALE FOR MOTOR-TRUCK DRIVERS *

(Boston, July 1, 1951)

	$
Magazine	2·25
Newspaper, day	2·16
Oil	1·985
Building construction	1·85
Paper handlers, newspaper	1·832
Beer, bottle and keg	1·775
Grocery, chain store	1·679
Meat-packing house, 3-5 tons	1·64
Bakery, Hebrew	1·595
Wholesale	1·57
Rendering	1·55
Coal	1·518
Garbage disposal	1·50
General hauling	1·50
Food service, retail	1·475
Ice	1·45
Armored car	1·405
Carbonated beverage	1·38
Waste paper	1·38
Linen supply	1·342
Movers, piano and household	1·30
Scrap, iron and metal	1·20
Laundry, wholesale	1·20

* Bureau of Labor Statistics, *Union Wages and Hours: Motortruck Drivers and Helpers* (July 1, 1951), Bulletin 1052, pp. 9-10.

section. Newer and expanding industries or contours, such as oil, have had to pay higher wages to attract labour in the evolution of wage scales. Part of the explanation is derived from the fact that this historical structure of wages has conditioned the labour supply so that the relative rates among contours are regarded as proper. A minor part of the explanation lies in the fact that these wage rates are influenced by the wages of the group of workers these employees tend to be associated with in work operations. Teamsters hauling oil and building materials come in contact with high-paid employees in their work operations, while laundry and scrap drivers have more direct contact with lower-paid employees. A larger emphasis is to be placed on the fact that competitive conditions permit higher pay at the top end of the list. Demand is more inelastic and wages tend to be a lower proportion of the sales revenue. But why do the firms pay more, simply because they can afford to do so ? If the union is brought into the explanation as a decisive factor, then an explanation can simply be made in terms of the union acting as a discriminating seller as among different industries. While this factor may be significant in some cases, the type of wage spread is so general, apart from the union, that the principal explanation should lie elscwhere.

In periods of tightness in the labour market the various contours are able to bid for labour, and a differentiated structure of rates reflecting the product market contours and competitive conditions tends to be established. For a variety of reasons these differentials are not readily altered in a looser labour market. There are costs involved in making a wage change or changing a differential among sectors. Newer and expanding employers using the same type of labour have to pay more to attract a labour force, and a differential once established by a contour is not easily abolished.

For these various reasons the structure of the product market tends to be mirrored in the labour market. The differentials are not transitory ; they are not to be dismissed as imperfections. The differentials are not basically to be interpreted as a range of indefinite or random rates, although a community with a wide variety of firms in different product markets may present the impression of random rates. The wage contours and their relative rates reflect the basic nature of product and labour markets.

The arguments developed above can be applied to most of the cases of interfirm wage differentials that have been reported. There are some differences in wage rates which reflect differences in job content ; there are differences in costs and earnings in the way firms administer the same wage structure, and there are differences in methods of compensation (incentive and time rates). These factors account for some of the statistically observed variations in wage rates. The theoretically significant differences for similar grades of labour are those which reflect different product market competitive conditions.

VII. Wage Determination : the General Level

The sketch which follows is designed to highlight relationships significant to the determination of the general level of money wage rates.

Start with the identity that the total national income of the economy can be divided into wage income and non-wage income. If W = wage rate, E = employment, P = product price, O = output, and N = non-wage income, then

$$WE/PO + N/PO = 1 \quad . \quad . \quad . \quad (1)$$
$$W = PO/E - N/E \quad . \quad . \quad . \quad (2)$$

It is proposed to develop a system of equations highlighting the determination of wages based upon: wage rates (W), employment (E), product prices (P), output (O), and N (non-wage income) which will be construed to be equivalent to profits (π). For some problems the difference between profits and non-wage income is, of course, important.

In the system developed below,[1] there is no attempt to determine output (O). That will be presumed to be given by a more general system, say the Keynesian scheme or similar formulations which concentrate upon the determination of total income. Then

$$O = \bar{O} \text{ (output is given)} \quad . \quad . \quad . \quad (3)$$
$$WE + N = PO \text{ (by definition)} \quad . \quad . \quad . \quad (4)$$
$$O/E = (E) \text{ (production function)} \quad . \quad . \quad (5)$$
$$W = F(E, N) \text{ or } W = F(E, \pi) \quad . \quad . \quad (6)$$
$$P = f(O/E, W_t) \quad . \quad . \quad . \quad . \quad (7)$$

It is on equations (6) and (7) that attention is to be concentrated. The general level of wages is a function of employment levels (E) and profits (π), and the price level is another function of past wages and productivity.

These relationships can be placed in a form to indicate the process of change over time.

$$W_t - W_{t-1} = F(E_{t-1}, \pi_{t-1}) \quad . \quad . \quad . \quad (8)$$

That is, the change in wages from last year to this year is a function of last year's employment (or unemployment) and last year's profit levels. Also,

$$P_t - P_{t-1} = f(W_t - W_{t-1}, O/E_t - O/E_{t-1}) \quad . \quad . \quad (9)$$

That is, the change in prices from last year to this year is a function of the change in the same period in the wage level and productivity.

These equations can be subjected to extensive statistical inquiry. The following equations are illustrative for the United States in the period 1929–1952:

$$\bar{Y} = 194 - 3X_1 + 17X_2 \quad . \quad . \quad . \quad (10)$$

[1] I am indebted to Professor James Duesenberry for his discussions with me on this subject.

$\bar{Y}$ is estimated $W_t - W_{t-1}$, statistically the change in average hourly earnings; X_1 is employment of the preceding year represented by the percentage of the labour force unemployed; and X_2 is profits of the preceding year represented by the ratio of corporate profits before taxes to corporate sales. The correlation between the actual course of wages and the estimated values was 0·76. The negative value of X_1 is theoretically disturbing in some respects.

$$\bar{P} = -26{\cdot}866 + 1{\cdot}1987X_1 - 0{\cdot}2604X_2 \quad . \quad . \quad (11)$$

$\bar{P}$ is estimated $P_t - P_{t-1}$, statistically the change in the consumer's price index; X_1 is the change in wages represented by average hourly earnings; and X_2 is the change in productivity. The correlation between the actual course of prices and the estimated values was 0·91.

There are a great variety of statistical measures of the equations (8) and (9) that are possible. Lags of varying lengths can be used. Monthly data rather than annual data are possible. Wholesale prices can be substituted for the consumer's price index. A critical level of unemployment may be introduced (say 2 or 3 per cent of the labour force) at which it is the level of unemployment rather than the change in unemployment which affects wage rates.

A general scepticism should be maintained about statistical fits among variables that are so highly interrelated. Such varied computations can be instructive, however, on the interrelations between wages and other elements of the system. The significant question is whether such equations and statistical computation organize and systematize insight into the wage determination process.

The equations above (8) and (9) can be applied to particular sectors of the system, as well as to aggregates of the whole. Indeed, in testing the relations in various sectors is most insight to be gained. Statistical computations are quite feasible. Thus a comparison of the reaction of wage rates in the steel contour and in the cotton textile contour to changes in output is highly illuminating to wage determination. A fall in textile demand, given the character of textile product markets, reduces prices, which in turn push wages down. In steel, given the character of competition, prices do not fall and there is no comparable pressure on wage rates, even though unemployment may be greater.

In more generalized form, the structural determinants of wage changes in particular contours in response to changes in demand are seen to be: (a) the character of competition in the contour, (b) the proportion of labour costs to total costs, and (c) the rate of change in labour productivity in its pure rather than statistical sense.

In any given contour where these elements are given in the short period the size of the response of wage rates to changes in demand will depend upon the change in profits and the level of unemployment.

This approach is designed to relate the determination of the general level of wage rates and particular sectors. The general level of wages is only determined at particular key bargains in strategic contours. The relations outlined above affecting the general level operate at these points.

VIII. The Long-Term Development of Wage Structure

The structure of wage rates of a country can be conceived as reflecting the course of its industrialization and economic development. The supply of labour and the rate and pattern of industrialization are the crucial factors. A country with a scarcity of labour will likely require and establish larger wage differentials for skill than one with an abundant labour supply. A rapid rate of industrialization will produce larger skill differentials than a slow rate. The sequence in the development of industries in the industrialization process will affect to some degree the structure of wage rates as differentials are used to attract labour force to these industries from agriculture or from other industrial activity. A comparative study of the wage structures of various countries today reflects these imprints of the path of economic development.[1]

A study of the sequence in the development of the wage structure is instructive. Starting with an agrarian society, relatively small differentials are required to attract a labour force away from agrarian pursuits. The first industries historically required simpler skills, and the levels of rates over agriculture were slight. As successive industries develop, higher rates are required to draw a work force, not primarily directly from agriculture, but from lower-paid industries. Successive industries appear to require more specialized skills and higher wages result. The structure of wages thus reflects the pattern of industrialization.

Some of the same phenomena can be seen in a particular community today with the introduction of new plants. There are a variety of circumstances which may result in new employers setting higher rates. These factors will be stronger, the higher the general level of employment. The new industries may require higher standards of skill. They may be employed in plants with a minimum

[1] See John T. Dunlop and Melvin Rothbaum, 'International Comparisons of Wage Structures', *International Labour Review* (April 1955).

number of employees of several thousands. A higher rate is needed to attract that number than if the plant were to grow gradually from a small figure. The labour costs are frequently a small fraction of total costs, and the product markets are often oligopolistic. These factors permit or encourage the enterprise to set a higher rate for the key jobs in comparison to others in the community. The oil, chemical, atomic, and television industries would be current examples. The discussion suggests that for comparable levels of skill there is a tendency for new industries to give the wage level a drift upwards.

The wage structure is to be approached as a reflex of the larger pattern of industrialization. The wage structure of an agricultural economy is largely undifferentiated by skill or product market divisions. Increasing industrialization creates increasing differentiation by skill, thereby creating many new occupations and job operations. Some of these occupations or jobs are key jobs and provide the basis for interfirm comparisons. Increasing industrialization also creates new groupings of products within which are unique types of competition. These product market characteristics, combined with some features of the labour market, create wage contours within which wages tend to move under common forces, relatively to wages outside the contour.

When a wage structure has been established, the labour supply tends to adapt itself to the relative structure of rates, as reflected in key rates, in a variety of ways. Preferences and relative ratings given to jobs by workers are not autonomous ; they reflect the broad outlines of the established wage structure. The long established relative rate structure created as envisaged above itself influences the choice of workers and may even take on normative elements. The labour force in general, for most occupations, would appear to be highly pliable over a generation. The established wage structure comes to shape labour supply over the long run. This is not to deny that supply may not adapt readily in the short period to changes in relative demand. Nor does it deny that relative wage rates may affect long-run supply for some occupations within some limits. But the point is that the labour supply over a generation is clearly highly adaptable to the great variety of jobs created by modern industrialization, and the work force tends in important respects to adapt itself to a long-established rate structure of key jobs.

The questions which are posed for contemporary wage theory are quite different from those which challenged the wages fund and marginal productivity periods. The analysis of wage determination was in each doctrine at the very centre of economics. As these doctrines declined in popularity, a tendency developed to treat wage rates as determined outside the system and given for economic problems. Wage theory has shown a tendency to break down, particularly on the supply side.

A few suggestions have been made for future wage discussions. A single wage rate or average concept is inadequate. The structure of wages, the whole complex of differentials, needs to be explained. Moreover, the determination of the level and structure of wage rates are interrelated. In the analysis of wage structure the concepts of job clusters and wage contours define the points at which wage-making forces are concentrated. The anatomy of the wage structure is to be understood if one is to explain changes in response to demand and supply factors. These concepts help to focus attention upon the operation of demand and supply. They suggest that product market competition and conditions decisively influence the structure of wage rates. In the longer run, the wage structure is to be depicted as a reflex of the pattern and speed of industrialization.

PART II

THE GENERAL LEVEL OF WAGES

Chapter 2

THE DETERMINATION OF THE GENERAL LEVEL OF WAGE RATES

BY

HARRY G. JOHNSON
King's College, Cambridge, England.

MONETARY theorists have not taken much explicit interest in the determination of the general level of wage rates. By and large, the 'classical' monetary theorists were concerned with the determination of the price level, taken to be the focal point of analysis of the trade cycle and the mechanism of international adjustment. Money wage rates, like the prices of particular goods, were left to be inferred from the price level by the application of value and distribution theory. On the other hand, modern theorists, following Keynes, have been chiefly concerned with the determination of the level of output and employment, and of the rate of interest. In their analysis, the money wage level has tended to be placed outside the range of economic analysis, being treated either as a datum or as an exogenous variable.

In neither case has the money wage level been the explicit object of analysis, and consequently the theory of its determination has to be inferred or constructed ; it cannot be simply digested from the literature on monetary theory. Moreover, the stimulus of Keynesian theory has prompted a great deal of critical revision of 'classical' monetary theory, which has its implications for the determination of money wage rates in that system. For both these reasons I do not propose to discuss the work of the classical monetary theorists in detail ; instead, I shall begin by discussing the determination of the wage level in a 'modernized' classical model, and the rôle of money wages in the Keynesian system, and proceed via a discussion of some limitations of monetary theory to the determination of the wage level under modern conditions of collective bargaining.

I. THE CLASSICAL THEORY

Classical economic theory postulated a dichotomy between 'real' and 'monetary' theory. In the former, relative prices, including the real wages of various types of labour or of 'labour' as a homogeneous factor, were determined by the interaction of tastes, technology, and factor supplies, on the assumption of individual maximizing behaviour in competitive markets. In the latter, the level of prices was determined by the quantity of money, either in crude terms of a fixed velocity of circulation and quantum of transactions, or in more refined terms of equality of the market rate of interest with the rate required to maintain full-employment equilibrium of the system. The quantity of money determined the level of prices, but had no influence on relative prices. The implication for the determination of money wage rates was that money wages would be fixed at whatever level would yield the real wage rate consistent with full-employment equilibrium, but that this real wage rate would be independent of the quantity of money ; a doubling of the money supply, for example, would lead to a doubling of all wages and prices, leaving the real situation unchanged. The complete separation between the theories of relative and absolute prices assumed in this mode of thought is highly convenient for applied economic analysis ; but it is logically invalid, as the work of Patinkin [1] and others has shown. In a society which uses money as more than a mere unit of account, the holding of stocks of money implies a demand for money and substitutability between money and goods, which in turn implies that the quantity of money influences the determination of relative prices as well as absolute prices. The real and monetary theories are inseparable : relative and absolute prices are codetermined. This was in fact the position ultimately adopted by Walras, who shifted from a 'velocity' approach to monetary theory to a formulation in terms of a 'desired cash-balance' based on the convenience of holding command over goods and services in monetary form, and assimilated his monetary theory to his general theory of fixed-capital formation and inventory holding. A similar approach to the demand for money is of course characteristic of the Cambridge school, but its implications for the determination of relative prices were not appreciated, probably as a corollary of the habit of partial equilibrium analysis.

In a logically consistent theory of the classical type, relative prices and real wages will be determined by the real quantity of money and the demand for it, as well as by the demand and supply of goods and services. Such a system retains the property that a change in the nominal amount of money (or a shift of demand between goods and monetary assets) leads to an equiproportionate change in absolute prices, leaving relative prices unchanged. How-

[1] See D. Patinkin, 'Further Considerations of the General Equilibrium Theory of Money', *Review of Economic Studies*, xix, 3 (1952–1953), pp. 186-195.

ever, a change in the amount of money brought about by security purchases or sales by the banking system (or a change of preferences as between holdings of money and other credit instruments) will produce a change in relative as well as absolute prices. For example, an increase in the money supply brought about by open market operations would reduce the interest rate and probably raise real wages.

The bearing of the modern revision of classical monetary theory on the determination of the level of money wage rates may be summarized in the proposition that, though money wage rates will be fixed at the level yielding the real wage rate consistent with full-employment equilibrium, this real wage rate will not in general be independent of the quantity of money. Consequently the movement of money wage rates cannot be simply deduced from changes in the quantity of money, as the dichotomous classical theory would imply, although there will be a determinate relationship between the two.

II. The Keynesian Theory

The classical theory of wage determination rests on the assumption of maximizing behaviour by individuals in their capacity as suppliers of labour. While the theory assumed this behaviour to be carried on in a framework of perfectly competitive markets, no essential difference would be made to the analysis by the assumption of market imperfections and collective bargaining, so long as the assumption of maximizing behaviour were retained and the assumed market situations were such as to yield determinate results. However, it is on this very assumption of maximizing behaviour that Keynesian theory diverges from the classical, for the mainstay of the whole Keynesian analysis of underemployment equilibrium is the assumption of rigid money wages, built into the Keynesian model by the device of measuring the monetary magnitudes in wage units, and justified by the contention that wage earners are interested in their money wages rather than their real wages.

The dependence of Keynesian underemployment equilibrium on the assumption of rigid wages has often been denied, usually as a result of the mistaken belief that Keynesian policy recommendations stand or fall by this argument. The point is a purely logical one. In the Keynesian system the level of employment and output is determined by the propensity to save, the marginal efficiency of capital, liquidity preference, and the quantity of money, measured in wage units. Given the quantity of nominal money, the lower the wage rate, the greater will be the quantity of money in wage units, and the more fully satisfied the demand for money. This in turn implies a lower rate of interest, a higher level of investment, and possibly a lower propensity to save, and therefore a higher level of effective demand and employment. The reduction of the rate of interest may be blocked by a lower limit set by liquidity preference, or by the fact that the rate of interest cannot become negative (since cash can always be held instead of lent) ; but further wage reduction would still increase the real value of cash balances, and eventually increased wealth would induce the holders of cash to reduce their saving and increase consumption—the so-called Pigou effect.[1]

The fundamental difference, therefore, between Keynesian and classical monetary theory lies in the Keynesian assumption of rigid wages, which in turn rests on an assumption of economic irrationality on the part of wage earners. Without this assumption, the determination of the level of wages in Keynesian theory would be qualitatively the same as in classical theory (although with differences of detail arising from Keynes's development of the theory of demand for money) and the money wage level would be deducible from the quantity of money. With this assumption, the determination of the wage level is placed outside the purview of economic analysis, except to the extent that an economic rationale can be found for wage rigidity as a long-run phenomenon.

The assumption, of course, is unacceptable as a generally valid empirical observation : the most that can be said for it is that it was a justifiable approximation for the policy problem with which Keynes was concerned for many years before the publication of the

[1] See, for example, A. C. Pigou, *Lapses from Full Employment* (1945), p. 24. The Pigou effect operates only on that part of the money supply which is not created against debts of various kinds, a limitation which restricts its practical as opposed to its theoretical significance. In the case of financial obligations other than money, and of money backed by debt, the increased wealth of creditors is counterbalanced by the decreased wealth of debtors, and there is no presumption as to the net effect, although it might be argued that in the case of government debt the increased real value of the obligations would not influence the government's behaviour, so that the Pigou effect would extend to private holdings of public debt and of money backed by it. In so far as private debt held by banks is redeemable, the money supply will tend to fall *pari passu* with the wage-price level, as the demand for bank accommodation falls.

The Pigou effect assumes a money supply partly consisting of coins and of notes and deposits backed by gold or foreign currency ; to the extent that these assets can be produced (e.g. by mining or exports), the Pigou effect is reinforced by the increased profitability of their production.

The argument implies neither that these effects are large or rapid enough to make wage reduction a practicable antidepression policy nor that wage reduction is preferable to expansionary fiscal and monetary policies. Its most important limitation in this connection is that it is a static argument, and does not consider the effects of falling (as distinct from lower) wages and prices ; that is, it ignores dynamic expectational problems.

General Theory — that of prolonged mass unemployment in Great Britain — and that its use as the basic assumption of his monetary theory permitted him to elucidate the operation of those forces which have the most important influence on the level of output and employment in the relatively short run. Outside the range of 'depression economics', however, the approximation of rigid wage rates becomes seriously restrictive, and the interaction of effective demand and the wage level has to be brought back into the analysis.

So far, we have been discussing what pure monetary theory has to say about the determination of the general level of wage rates. The conclusion which emerges from the argument is the rather obvious one that the level of money wages is a proper subject for economic analysis, unless we are prepared to reject the assumption that wage earners (and other economic units) are in some sense economically rational; and that the level of money wages will be governed by the quantity of money, though not in the simple way postulated by classical monetary theory in its unsophisticated form.

III. Practical Limitations

The practical applicability of this conclusion, however, is rather limited by the fact that the form of the argument excludes two important considerations:

(1) While theory indicates the direction of change of the wage level in conditions of unemployment or inflationary pressure, the important practical problem is usually the rate at which this change occurs. This, in a sense, is the crucial problem of depression policy on which Keynes focused attention; more recently, it has been a crucial problem in the economics of inflation and of exchange devaluation; and it is a problem which turns on the prevalence and characteristic processes of collective bargaining. If, for example, the possible degree of wage adjustment is narrowly restricted by long intervals between negotiations and conventional limits on the magnitudes of the changes that can be negotiated, money wages will in practice be largely beyond the range of theoretical analysis.

This is a subject on which some econometric evidence is available, though its precise interpretation is susceptible to a number of difficulties. In his *Economic Fluctuations in the United States, 1921–1941* (1950) Professor Klein presents, but does not discuss, a wage-adjustment equation estimated by least-squares from the 1920–1941 data. This equation confirms the hypothesis that money wages will fall more rapidly, the greater the amount of unemployment and the longer its duration.[1] But the equation is set up on this hypothesis, and no others are tested; the method of estimation, as Klein himself emphasizes, is open to various economic and statistical objections; and the form of the equation is such as to make extrapolation a rather dubious procedure.[2] It is therefore doubtful how much significance can be attached to the magnitude and the stability of the estimated relationship between wage rate adjustment and unemployment.

Similar reservations apply to Tinbergen's finding[3] that the money wage rate in the United States in the period 1919–1932 was determined by the amount of employment, the cost of living, and a trend factor, with a lag of approximately five months.[4]

Experience of inflation since the second World War also throws some light on the problem, though countries differ and in each case there are difficulties of interpretation. In Britain, wage adjustments seem to have been significantly influenced by conventionally long intervals between demands for new negotiations, conventional limits on the increases that can reasonably be asked for, and conventions

[1] Klein, *Economic Fluctuations*, p. 121, equation (3.4.9.):

$$\Delta w = 1056{\cdot}20 - 25{\cdot}08(N_L - N_E) - 7{\cdot}90(N_L - N_E)_{-1} - 0{\cdot}64w_{-1} + 9{\cdot}76(t - 1931) + u'_3$$
$$(R = 0{\cdot}93)$$

In the equation, w is the average annual wage in current dollars, $N_L - N_E$ millions unemployed, t the year, u'_3 the error term, and the subscript -1 indicates the figure for the previous year. The equation shows that the average annual wage tends to fall by about 1·75 per cent of its average during the period ($1427·81) for every million unemployed during the year, and by about 0·5 per cent of its average for every million unemployed during the previous year. (One million unemployed represents about 2·3 per cent of the average labour force during the period.)

[2] The equation makes the annual change in the wage rate depend on the absolute amount of unemployment, though the labour force was growing during the period and one might expect the wage adjustment to depend on the proportion rather than the amount of unemployment. The numerical coefficients imply that if unemployment were constant, at no matter what level, the annual average wage would settle down (after a number of years varying with the amount of unemployment) to increasing by $15·25 per annum.

[3] J. Tinbergen, *Business Cycles in the United States of America, 1919–1932* (1939), p. 55, equation (3.1):

$$l_{+0{\cdot}42} = 0{\cdot}30(u + v) + 0{\cdot}39p + 0{\cdot}51t$$

where $1_{+0{\cdot}42}$ is an index of hourly earnings in twenty-five manufacturing industries, lagged 0·42 years, $u + v$ is quantity of output in milliards of 1929 dollars, and p is a cost-of-living index. According to this equation, the earnings index tends to fall by 0·30 points for every reduction of output by 1·24 per cent of its average during the period, and by 0·39 points for every point reduction in the cost-of-living index. A wage determination equation for the British economy is presented in the same author's *Business Cycles in the United Kingdom*.

[4] Tinbergen's equation implies that the trend of wages is independent of the level of employment, Klein's that it is independent of the level of unemployment, in the long run; in both equations the trend element is relatively small. If the equations could be assumed to represent fundamental characteristics of wage determination in the United States, it could be inferred from them that the maintenance of full employment there would not result in a rapid increase in wages.

against competition for labour via wage increases. On the other hand, the persistence of these conventions may have been a transitional phenomenon intimately associated with the ethos of economic planning in the face of chronic crises inherited from the war. In the United States and other countries, trade unions seem to have been much quicker to appreciate the effects of inflation and to adapt their bargaining techniques and demands accordingly.

In general, one would expect that while collective bargaining by its large-scale institutional nature would tend to operate in terms of various conventions which would restrict the degree of response of wages to sudden and large-scale changes in the general economic situation, these conventions would in time be revised to suit new circumstances, and be revised in ways amenable to economic analysis. To put the point in a way relevant to recent economic problems, while inflation economics may be able to assume that the pace of inflation is set by the conventions of collective bargaining, the conventions will themselves be influenced by the degree and duration of inflation.

(2) The second consideration is the more fundamental. While monetary theory takes the quantity of money as an autonomous variable, there is no necessary empirical reason for doing so. Since countries no longer depend on precious metals for circulating media, and are not obliged to maintain fixed exchange rates and invariant commercial policies, the money supply is more or less a matter of governmental policy; and the money supply and the wage-price level must be regarded as jointly determined by the economic policy pursued by the government.

This does not, however, imply what is sometimes suggested: that in modern economies the wage rate is autonomously determined by collective bargaining and the money supply is automatically adjusted to it. Such would be the case if the government were firmly committed to the maintenance of full employment, whatever happened: it would then have to accept the wage-price level determined by bargaining, and adjust the money supply so as to prevent unemployment. But governments have not in fact been prepared to accept this sort of unlimited commitment; they have instead been prepared to tolerate a varying amount of unemployment, both in the aggregate and in particular trades, and they have been prepared to apply monetary restriction and other deflationary measures rather than allow rising wages and prices to create internal and external problems. Alternatively, it could be said that though governments have been prepared to adjust the money supply to the wage level in the interests of high employment, the accommodation has been conditional on the fulfilment of other policy objectives, and the determination of the level of wages through collective bargaining has been influenced directly or indirectly by this fact.

In a modern economy, therefore, the money supply and the wage level are jointly determined by the balancing of full employment against other policy objectives such as internal price stability, or the maintenance of the balance of payments without devaluation or intensification of import and exchange controls. While economic theory cannot predict the balance that will be struck between these objectives in any particular country at any particular time, it can usefully be applied to the analysis of the choices which have to be made, and the implications of and possible inconsistencies between various policy objectives, including the implications for the wage level.

Given the assumption of rational maximizing activity, the level of money wage rates will tend towards the level required for full employment ; but the implied real wage level will be influenced by, and not independent of, monetary factors. The essential difference between Keynesian and classical monetary theory is the Keynesian assumption of rigid money wages, which is untenable as a general assumption. For practical application, the rate of change of money wages and the policy of the monetary authorities are important considerations ; but these matters are themselves susceptible of economic analysis. The argument is admittedly highly formal, and leaves the determination of the level of money wages dependent at crucial points on sociological and political factors such as the capacity of collective bargaining institutions to adapt their methods to changing circumstances, and the willingness of governments to tolerate rising prices. But this is a limitation common to all economic theory, which is concerned primarily with consequences and not the explanation of preferences.

Chapter 3

APPROACHES TO THE DETERMINATION OF THE GENERAL LEVEL OF WAGE RATES

BY

INNOCENZO GASPARINI
Bocconi University, Milan, Italy

THREE approaches can be adopted towards the formulation of a theory of wages: (1) distribution theory; (2) employment theory; and (3) noneconomic theories such as those of the German historical school, Commons, the Webbs, and some recent American labour economists. Only theories of the first and the second types will be considered in this discussion.

Wage theories, as for instance the distribution theory, present many approaches, but they all may be classified either as they seek to determine the income per unit of the labour factor, or as they determine the share of the same factor in the national income. The marginal productivity theory takes into consideration both problems with the same tools, and the results of the determination of the price per unit of the labour factor are, more or less correctly, expanded to the determination of the distribution by shares of the national income.

In the group of theories which determine the income per unit of the labour factor, special theories are to be distinguished from general theories. A theory may be called special if wages are determined by a few variables or if only a single form of the market is taken into consideration (perfect competition, oligopoly, and so on). A wage theory may be defined as general if two conditions are fulfilled: (a) if it takes into consideration at the same time either all the forces at work within the economic system according to Pareto's approach, or the economic system as a whole, that is, all the possible market forms; and (b) if it explains the variables and forces which are known or constant for the static definition of the general equilibrium.

Economic reality is open also to exogenous original changes (in the sense that no *a priori* forecast is possible), which are particularly significant for wage theory. Changes in the social and political framework, in the trends of economic policy, in the bargaining power of labour and employers ; the effects of innovations ; the structural changes of the national income, for instance, are problems whose effects on the level of wage rates can only be investigated with the help of a general theory. It may also be pointed out that there will always be a certain amount of logical and dynamic indetermination.

I. The Classical Approach

The wage fund theory is a test case of the limitations of the special or causal type of theory. The classical approach can be presented in macro-economic terms : Assuming the money supply as given and the stock of capital constant,[1] the system is described by :

$$M = kpy$$
$$S(i) = I(i)$$
$$y = y(N)$$
$$\frac{dy}{dN} = \frac{w}{p}$$
$$N = f\left(\frac{(w)}{p}\right)$$

where M is the money supply ; S, savings ; I, investment ; i, the money interest rate ; p, and w, the price and the wage level ; y, the output, and N, employment.

Labour supply and demand determine the rate of real wages and the employment level ; the technical input-output relationships determine the output level, since the stock of capital is constant and employment has already been determined ; the rate of interest is dependent upon the level of savings and investment, and the price level is determined by the exchange velocity of money, taken as constant and constituting the given supply. As a variant, we may assume that when the level of output and the rate of interest are determined, the money supply determines the price level.

We are not going to criticize this approach *per se* but will make only a few remarks concerning the general thesis of this paper. It is to be emphasized that the relationships of the classical approach are all unidirectional. Labour demand is inversely correlated with only one variable, the rate of real wages. This function, criticized by Malthus, cannot be admitted even under conditions of static equilibrium. It is further to be criticized not only as to the determina-

[1] L. R. Klein, 'Theories of Effective Demand and Employment', *Journal of Political Economy* (April 1949).

tion of the rate of interest, but also on the grounds that the prices of inputs, complementary or competitive to labour in a combination, are not variables of the functions of labour demand. For the classics, the supply function is very inelastic and negatively inclined, if population is unchanged, and the supply function is positively inclined, if population is dynamic. However, as in the neoclassic approach (Keynes and Robinson, for instance), there is still an unidirectional dependence from one variable : the wage rate. There are two basic assumptions : the standard of life of the working classes is more or less constant ; a wage increase decreases the marginal utility of income and the wage earners are thus induced to work less. Experience does not confirm the first assumption, and it may be opposed to the second in that even for the isolated worker we cannot say *a priori* that the individual labour supply curve is always negatively inclined.[1] The criticism applies not only to labour demand and supply considered for the economic system as a whole, but also to the more correct way of dealing with collective curves, labour market by labour market, by taking homogeneous groups of workers.

The classical theoretical framework is undoubtedly a fascinating formulation, relatively simple for operative purposes, but as a consequence of the unidirectional relationships upon which it is built, it allows only for limited application.

II. The Keynesian Approach

Labour demand is formulated as a function of income and thus of the aggregate effective demand :

$$N = F(D_1 + D_2)$$

where D_1 is consumer's goods and D_2 producer's goods demand. The aggregate demand and its basic components are determined by other equations of the system, upon which the general theory of employment is built. The theory of labour demand and the determination of the general level of wage rates is thus taken into consideration within this larger framework, as N is a function of income.

The income determination, and with it the determination of the level of employment, is carried out from a macro-economic approach, which is undoubtedly a stimulating and useful tool. As Pigou has

[1] G. Demaria, *Logica della produzione e dell' occupazione* (1950), pp. 162-163.

pointed out: 'Keynes . . . brought all the relevant factors, real and monetary at once, together in a single formal scheme, through which their interplay could be coherently investigated'.[1] It is thus easy to understand how a flow of econometric investigations was promoted as a result of the choice of national income as the strategic variable of the system — in addition to the special investigations on the marginal propensity to consume, the liquidity preference and the multiplier.[2] These studies are significant not only because of the new tools and the quantitative approach to the problems of economic policy, but also for the developments in economic theory which they induced.

There are, however, many objections both to the approach and to the studies themselves which have their theoretical background in employment theory. As against the classics, it can be said that the relationships of the Keynesian system are unidirectional. Labour demand depends upon income, the dynamics of which depend upon investment (the multiplier has to be taken into account); investment is a function of the prospective rate of interest, and the demand for money is a function of income and money interest. As to the Keynesian concept of investment, it may be pointed out that the changes in the rate of interest have significant direct and indirect effects on its level; the *quantum* of these effects depends upon the duration of the production cycles, upon the demand elasticity of the input and output, and on the elasticity of substitution of capital invested during these cycles. These effects must not be overlooked, even in the short run.[3]

Further, such variables as stock exchange speculation, the supply of entrepreneurial factors, and the degree of monopoly on the side of the investors are also significant and may cause multidirectional responses in investment and employment. As for the multiplier, there may be a negative multiplier due to a decrease in investment or, more probably, to an increase in the price level. The production functions are not necessarily homogeneous of the first degree and there may be limitations in the opportunities for an expansion of investment in the very short run in which the Keynesian analysis is interested.[4]

These remarks limit and qualify the determination of the general

[1] A. C. Pigou, *Keynes's General Theory* (1952), p. 65.

[2] See, for instance, J. Tinbergen, 'The Significance of Keynes's Theory from the Econometric Point of View' in *The New Economics*, Seymour E. Harris, ed. (1948), pp. 219-231.

[3] G. Demaria, pp. 454-494.

[4] Demaria, pp. 205-209; V. Dominedo, 'Investimenti di capitale e tendenze cicliche' in *Acta Seminarii*, Department of Economics, Bocconi University, (1942), pp. 94-104.

level of wage rates in the Keynesian system. There is also a direct criticism: the investment multiplier and Kahn's employment multiplier are not identical.[1] National income may increase more than employment, while the increase in non-labour income is more than proportional to that in labour incomes. The increase in output will be smaller than the increase in employment, if decreasing returns are prevailing.

The response depends thus on the starting position. However, it is more probable that the increase in non-labour incomes will be larger, even if the effects on the distributive shares are to a certain degree corrected by a higher level of employment, while the rôle of decreasing returns is not very significant if the system is not under full employment. Also, for employment, we cannot dismiss the play of a negative multiplier.

From a general point of view, it is to be emphasized that employment theories do not take into consideration the effects of changes in relative prices and costs upon the volume of aggregate output and employment. The criticism of the limited rôle of the effects of changes in interest rates upon investment may be extended to the prices of all the inputs and to the changes in the productive function. Supply and demand of labour and, indeed, of every input have, market by market, different elasticities and technological relationships.

Production functions are different, and responses of employment to an increase in effective demand, even reasoning in Keynesian terms, are different market by market or by types of markets. The problem cannot, therefore, be approached in terms of wage levels alone, either for purposes of economic theory or economic policy.

The criticism of the Keynesian system is not so much directed at the conclusions as at the type of aggregative theory which emphasizes the level of wage rates instead of the structure of wages. To avoid this difficulty, the Keynesian system would have to be extended to a general equilibrium approach or shifted to a period or sequence analysis. Its operative advantages have a cost, if we may say so, as employment theory must be integrated into value theory.

III. The Econometric Formulation

Klein introduced models based on algebraic equations for the American economic system during the period 1921–1941.[2] The

[1] J. M. Keynes, *General Theory of Employment, Interest and Money* (1936), p. 114; A. Hansen, *A Guide to Keynes* (1953), pp. 86-88.

[2] L. R. Klein, *Economic Fluctuations in the United States, 1921–1941* (1950).

wage-salary bill (W_1) is one of the endogenous variables. The labour demand equation is :

$$W_1 = 4{\cdot}70 + 0{\cdot}47(pX - E) + 0{\cdot}12(pX - E)_{-1} + 0{\cdot}19(t - 1931) + u_1$$

pX being the value of output, E the excess and u_1 the random disturbance : all data are in billion dollars. There is also an adjustment equation for the labour market, making the rate of change of the wage rate a function of excess supply of labour :

$$\triangle W = 1056{\cdot}20 - 25{\cdot}08(N_L - N_E) - 7{\cdot}90(N_L - N_E)_{-1} - 0{\cdot}64W_{-1} + 9{\cdot}76(t - 1931) + u'_3$$

N_L being the labour force and N_E the effective employment.

When comparing computed values with observed values, the models yield satisfying results. These studies give interesting information not only for the choice of measures of economic policy, but also for checking the assumptions in economic theories. The 'Klein models' take into consideration other significant variables which have been pointed out in the preceding discussion. However, the formulation of labour demand in this approach and in other econometric investigations makes it clear that the questions raised concerning the macro-economic approach and its integration cannot be answered.

This conclusion may be checked with the results of a recent article by Tinbergen on the effects of wage level fluctuations on employment.[1] An increase in the wage level would lead to an increase in the price level equal to the percentage of wage costs in the product prices. In the Dutch economic system, a 1 per cent increase in wages would lead to a 0·3 per cent increase of the price level. The volume of imports would increase by 0·1 per cent, exports would decrease by 0·6 per cent, and their value by 0·3 per cent, while the balance of payment would deteriorate by 0·37 per cent of the value of imports. A decrease in employment of 0·37 per cent would be necessary to restore equilibrium. However, non-labour groups would try to increase prices more than wages, and thus the cut in employment might be larger (about 0·85 per cent).

Professor Tinbergen's analysis is very stimulating, but only as a first approximation is the increase in the price level equal to the wage costs in product prices. Even if we do not consider the reaction of non-labour interests to the cut in the volume of output,

[1] J. Tinbergen, 'The Significance of Wage Policy for Employment', *International Economic Papers*, 1 (1951), pp. 186-194.

the problem must be examined market by market. Only in a simplified model can the equilibrium of the balance of payments be re-established by a cut in imports, and it is also doubtful if this target can be reached through a reduction in the employment level.

Professor Tinbergen also discusses the case of an increase in wages arising from an increase in labour productivity, and the consequences for the balance of payments.[1] The effects on employment would be negative if the increase in wages is equal to the increase in labour productivity. Prices, owing to the assumed wage increase, cannot be cut down ; the sales on foreign markets cannot be expanded while the inland sales depend upon national income, which cannot be higher if exports, prices, and inland sales are constant. There would be no negative effects on employment in two cases only : if the economic resources are fully employed but there is a backlog of orders and the foreign demand is increased through a devaluation, or if the increase in wages is less than the increase in labour productivity.

Some remarks are again necessary in regard to the limits and characteristics of the macro-economic approach. The starting-point, the increase in labour productivity, is very far from reality if it is assumed that there is the same increase in productivity for every firm in every industry. We may, instead, assume an average increase in labour productivity ; some firms and some industries will expand their production while others will contract it, and the chain of effects may be different from the one described by Professor Tinbergen, as the demand elasticities for the inputs and outputs of the two groups of firms and industries are different.

If it is assumed, instead, that the increase in productivity, though equal industry by industry, applies to the marginal firm, then the supply curve would become more inelastic, but neither the output nor the price would change. There would be a lower level of employment and an increase in profits which, being spent, would reduce the negative effect on employment. Under monopolistic competition, there would be a downward shifting of the marginal cost curve and an increase in output and employment. The marginal revenue curve would also show later a downward shift, and the increase in output and employment would be reduced and partly cancelled.

However, the central fact — the difference in reaction from firm to firm and from industry to industry — cannot be examined by applying a macro-economic or an aggregative method.

[1] J. Tinbergen, 'The Significance of Wage Policy', pp. 192-193.

IV. The General Equilibrium Approach

The Walras-Pareto approach deals with the problems of capital raised by the wage-fund theory and explains the supply of those quantities, which were assumed as given by the marginal productivity theory. It does not determine a general level of wage rates, but considers the different inputs of labour, and at the same time, the prices of all the inputs and outputs.

The theory is doubtless a general wage theory since it can explain, within its time horizon, all the variables which are significant for the determination of wages and employment, and it does not explain merely some variables with unidirectional relationships. However, this theory is to be supplemented in two ways : wage determination under conditions of imperfect competition and the effects of non-economic forces, which are at work in shaping the unions and their policies.

Pareto used differential equations, which cannot always be solved, and which cause logical indeterminancy. This system is satisfying from a logical point of view but not from an operative one.

A different formulation is proposed by Professor Demaria [1] for the problem of the determination of the general level of wages.

The collective available labour supply is written :

$$O_1 = F(s, V_2 \ . \ . \ . \ V_{10})$$

where s is the wage rate, including the fringe benefits, while $V_2 \ldots V_{10}$ are : the increase in population ; the distribution of population by age groups ; the internal and international migrations ; the degree of efficiency of the labour force ; the distribution of the labour force by job, industry, and labour market ; labour mobility ; policies adopted by workers or imposed by government ; length and intensity of the labour effort ; the disutility of labour. The variables of the labour supply equation are affected not alone by economic forces, and there is multidirectionality even if s and not all the ten variables are taken into consideration. The labour supply will tend to be perpendicular to the abscissa if the change in wages is general, while, if it is localized, the supply will be an S-shaped curve. A low transfer cost for labour is a necessary condition.

The labour demand function is :

$$D_1 = F(p_t, s, p_k, \ . \ . \ ., p_A, p_B \ . \ . \ ., f, S)$$

where p_t, p_k, and p_A, p_B are input and output prices ; f is the employer's bargaining power, including the degree of monopoly

[1] G. Demaria, *Logica della produzione*, pp. 344-348.

and S the social interests, that is, the non-economic motivations in entrepreneurial behaviour. The labour demand equation is thus an integration of the general equilibrium approach.

Wages are also a function of β, which is the effect of government action and institutional factors, according to the historical framework under which an economic system is operating. Two types of indeterminancy may be at work : the logical, h, and the dynamic indeterminancy, σ : the former is due to a lack of knowledge in determining on *a priori* basis the movements of labour supply and demand while the latter is due to original changes.

The wage rate function will be :

$$s = F(O_1, D_1, \beta, h, \sigma).$$

This approach is a general theory, in the sense already discussed, of the determination of the wage level. Its theoretical background is that of general equilibrium, with the supplements already mentioned. It is not a macro-economic or aggregative approach. The prices of inputs and outputs, for instance, are taken into consideration, but not as variables depending upon the national income or the volume of output. The study of changes of labour demand localized in some parts of the economic system, within the limits of general interdependence, is one approach to an analysis of change and innovation.

Chapter 4

THE LONG-TERM MOVEMENT OF REAL WAGES[1]

BY

E. H. PHELPS BROWN

The London School of Economics and Political Science, England.

THE following pages present some provisional hypotheses to account for apparent features of the movement of real wages in the past eighty years.[2] They await the test of critical discussion, and also of the production of more evidence, for though in part they rest upon estimates of wages and income in five Western economies, the explanation of shifts in distribution has been worked out for the United Kingdom alone.

I. THE RELATION BETWEEN REAL WAGES AND PRODUCTIVITY

We can think of the movement of real wages in an economy as dependent on two groups of factors : those which govern the movement of real income per head of the whole occupied population, which is the broadest measure of productivity ; and those which decide the division of that income between wages and other shares. The first group, among which capital accumulation and technical advance are the chief factors, shall be taken as given here, and this discussion will be concerned mainly with the factors of the second group. We shall find that real wages per wage earner have for the most part moved in step with productivity, but sometimes have gone somewhat ahead, and sometimes fallen behind. This is illustrated by Table 1, which shows how the rise of real wages, in

[1] I am indebted to my colleagues Dr. S. A. Ozga and Mr. J. Wiseman for great help given me by comment on a draft of this paper.

[2] The studies specially drawn upon here have been published over my name as follows : (with S. V. Hopkins), 'The Course of Wage-Rates in Five Countries, 1860-1939', *Oxford Economic Papers*, ii (June 1950) ; (with P. E. Hart) 'The Share of Wages in National Income', *Economic Journal*, lxii (June 1952) ; (with S. J. Handfield-Jones), 'The Climacteric of the 1890's', *Oxford Economic Papers*, iv (October 1952) ; (with B. Weber), 'Accumulation, Productivity, and Distribution in the British Economy, 1870–1938', *Economic Journal*, lxiii (June 1953) ; (with S. A. Ozga), 'Economic Growth and the Price Level', *Economic Journal*, (March 1955).

certain countries and periods, can be divided conceptually between the rise which would have come about if real wages had simply kept

TABLE 1

PROPORTIONATE RISE IN REAL OUTPUT PER HEAD OF THE OCCUPIED POPULATION, AND IN WAGE RATES (RECKONED IN UNITS OF OUTPUT), WITH INFERRED DISTRIBUTIVE SHIFT BETWEEN WAGES AND OTHER SHARES

All figures are percentages of the average wage rate (reckoned in units of output) in the base period shown

	GERMANY Base, 1872–1880			SWEDEN Base, 1870–1878		
	1886–1894	1905–1913	1924–1928	1886–1894	1905–1913	1924–1928
1. Rise in output per occupied person	24	44	22	23	85	109
2. Distributive shift	−3	−14	+12	+13	+2	+84
3. Rise in wage rate (in units of output)	21	30	34	36	87	193
	U.K. Base, 1870–1878			**U.S.A. Base, 1869**		
	1886–1894	1905–1913	1924–1928	1886–1894	1905–1913	1924–1928
1. Rise in output per occupied person	32	55	41		33	55
2. Distributive shift	nil	−23	+6		nil	+23
3. Rise in wage rate (in units of output)	32	32	47		33	78

step with the general rise of output per occupied person, and a distributive shift through which the actual rise became greater or less. Our task is to explain this kind of observed behaviour by providing an account of the distributive process in its setting of economic development.

The Wage/Income Ratio

It is usual to approach the distributive process by considering the share of wages in national income, but in the movements of this share the effects of changes in the relative factor price of labour are combined with those of changes in the proportion of wage earners within the occupied population. As a consequence 'a fall in the share of wages' will come about, even though there has been no fall in the relative remuneration of wage-earners' work, if there has been a reduction in the proportion of the occupied population which is classified as wage earning. There is reason to believe that such a reduction generally occurs in the course of the development of an industrial economy. According to the definitions followed here, the boundary between wage earners and other employees is set by the line commonly drawn in factories between 'operatives' and 'staff', which is then projected, though with some arbitrariness, through other sorts of employment.

This leaves outside the ranks of the wage earners and among the salaried, all clerical, administrative, and technical employees, and there seems clearly to have been a tendency in the last half century for the relative number of these salaried employees to grow. This raises the question whether the separation of wages from other sorts of payment to employees is significant, especially when nowadays many of the salaried earn less than many wage earners: probably the distinction is now too blurred to be useful, but before 1914 it was more clearly marked, in social status as well as pay, and perhaps as far even as 1938 we can use it to mark off a body of workers whose members had much more in common with each other than with other employees. But because the relative size of this body was shrinking, for a study of distribution we want to be able to disentangle the effects of relative numbers from those of relative factor prices.

This can be done if it is noted that the share of wages in national income is the product of the proportion of wage earners in the occupied population, with the ratio which the average wage bears to the average income of all occupied people.[1] This ratio may be designated the wage/income ratio. The term will be used here as a means of tracing the changing relation between wages and other factor prices, without admixture of the arithmetic consequences of changes in the deployment of the occupied population between wage earning and other sorts of job. If, between one year and another, the average money wage and the average money income

[1] Let the total wage bill be W, and the national income Y: then the share of wages in national income is W/Y. Let us regard W as received by l wage earners with an average wage w, and Y as received by n occupied persons with an average income y. Then the share of wages in national income

$$= \frac{W}{Y}$$

$$= \frac{lw}{ny} = \frac{l}{n} \times \frac{w}{y}.$$

per occupied person both rose by, say, 4 per cent, then it can be said that there was no change in the wage-income ratio, whatever the course of prices meanwhile. The course of the wage income ratio has been estimated by dividing an index of money wages by one of national money income per head of the occupied population.

Some estimates of this kind are shown in Fig. 1. For lack of sufficient records of earnings, it has been necessary to derive all these ratios from index of recorded wage rates. Since 1938, in various countries, actual earnings have risen above recorded rates, fringe benefits have risen relatively to the money wage, and a substantial part of the wage-earner's compensation has come to him through social benefits ; but these factors were generally of minor account before 1938. It is more serious, for the comparability of our series over time, that the hourly and weekly wage rates used are not adjusted for the effects of changes in the normal week, nor is any allowance for such effects made in the series showing output per occupied person. But with this reservation, these ratios can be used for broad comparisons : and what comes out here is their similarity. They seem to be composed on the same plan, in which periods of little change are interrupted by fairly wide displacements fairly quickly completed. There is also much resemblance between the course of the series, period by period. So much agreement between different economies would hardly be anticipated as a matter of course and cannot arise merely from the way in which the figures have been compiled. It is likely to mark the working of common processes and may help us to understand them.

Movements of the Wage Rate/Income Ratio without Distributive Significance

Two of the movements of these series can be accounted for readily and do not mark trends in distribution. The first is the cyclical movement which appears clearly in Sweden and the United Kingdom down to 1914, and in all five countries is strongly marked from the beginning of the great depression in 1929. In all these instances, the wage rate/income ratio rises in depression and falls back in recovery. But this is only an example of the familiar 'elbow-joint' or 'ratchet' effect : money wage rates offer strong resistance to downward pressures (this was true long before 1914, and does not seem to depend on trade unionism) so that at a time when national money income falls away quickly, the wage rate/income ratio rises. When national income recovers, it takes this rise back again. A wage earnings/income ratio would show less movement, and the share of aggregate wage earnings in national income, at least in the United Kingdom, has shown remarkably little

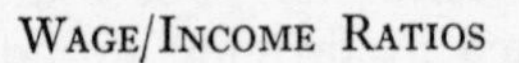

WAGE/INCOME RATIOS

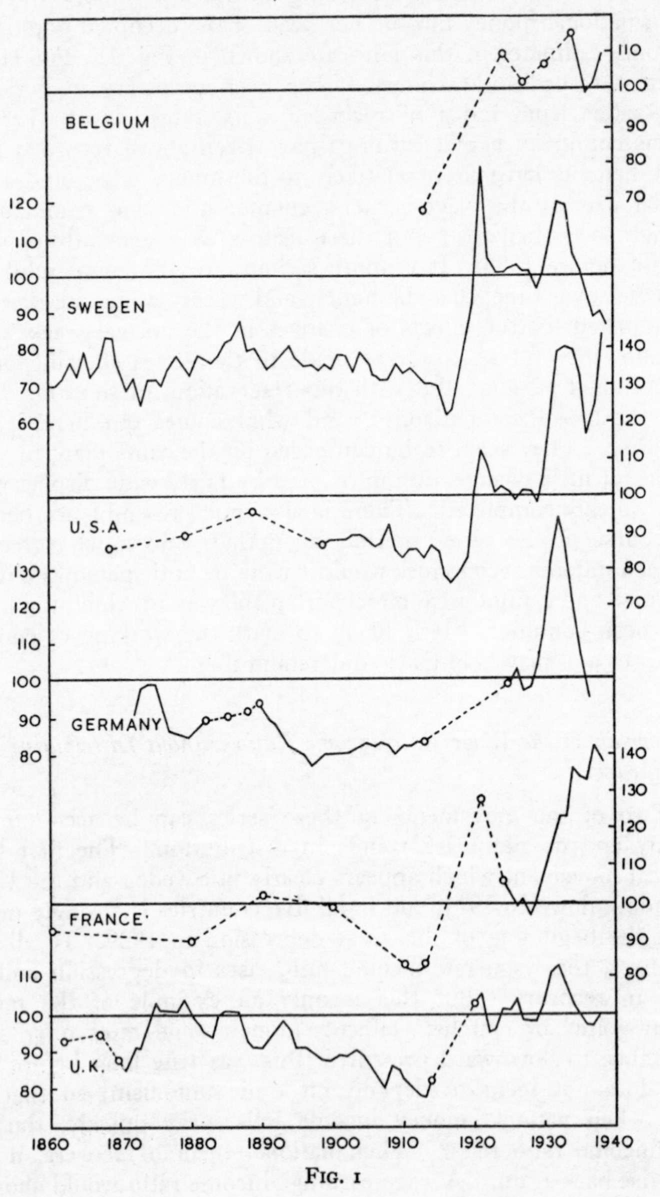

FIG. 1

sign of the trade cycle: in the depression wage earnings fall less than profits, but wages and profits together fall more than salaries and rents, and the two movements have about offset one another.

The second kind of movement which we can probably dispose of is the progressive, if gentle downward movement, of the wage rate/income ratio which goes on till 1914 from a starting-point which may be put at about 1879 for the United Kingdom, 1887 for Sweden, 1889 for the United States, and perhaps 1890 for France. If the United Kingdom is representative here, this is rather an example of the limitations of our indexes of wage rates than evidence of a distributive change. For during this period there took place in the United Kingdom a rise in the relative wages of the unskilled, who tend to be underweighted because of the lack of negotiated and published rates for them; and at the same time a substantial change was taking place in the deployment of labour, as a higher proportion of the wage earners came to be employed in the better paid jobs.[1] These are the reasons why — to state the disparity at its extreme — the index of money wage rates for the United Kingdom shows a rise of only 24 per cent between 1886 and 1913, when average wage earnings, even after some correction for cyclical movement, rose by around 40 per cent. In the wage earnings/income ratio shown in Fig. 2, the downward trend no longer appears.

Inertia and Displacement in the Wage Rate/Income Ratio

These observations increase the extent of the stability revealed in Fig. 1, and this stability is one of the main features which must be accounted for in the working of the distributive process: there have been long periods during which the changes in real wages due to distributive shifts have been very small compared with those associated with the movements of productivity. That this has been so is, in a sense, common knowledge, and yet it is not something we can naturally expect and readily explain, for the course of development made many openings for distributive change. There were big movements in the general level of prices and money incomes. There was a great rise in productivity; in the seventy years before the second World War, productivity seems to have risen by three-quarters in the United Kingdom and France, and by about a half in Germany and the United States, while in Sweden it trebled. This increase would have made possible a big rise in the relative size of one distributive share or other without any cutting back of

[1] A. L. Bowley, *Wages and Income in the United Kingdom since 1860* (1937), Appendix B.

the absolute size of the rest. The growth of productivity went on at different rates in successive periods. It came about, moreover, through great changes in technique and increases in equipment : these might well have set their mark on distribution, and in particular the growth of capital per head might well have resulted in capital getting a bigger share of the product. Yet the wage rate/income ratio shows no propensity to change cumulatively. This demands explanation.

Besides this element of stability, Fig. 1 shows two kinds of displacement which are important for our present inquiry. The

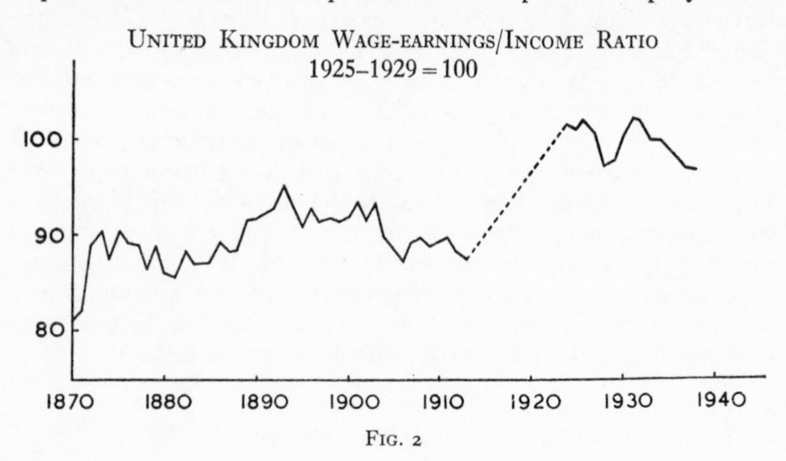

FIG. 2

first, a minor displacement in which within two or three years the general level of wages is shifted relatively to other factor prices, is better seen, for the United Kingdom alone, in the wage earnings ratio of Fig. 2. We notice here the upward shifts of 1870–1873 and 1888–1891, and the downward shifts of 1903–1906 and 1926–1928 : these were not reversible cyclical swings, but moved the wage earnings/income ratio to a new level. The second kind of displacement is that which took place in five countries of Fig. 1 within the gap in our records during and after the first World War. By 1925 the wage rate/income ratio stood at the following percentages above its value in 1913 :

France	22	U.K.	29	Sweden	45
Germany	19	U.S.A.	22		

There are thus three features of the wage rate/income ratio which call for explanation : it shows a predominant stability, interrupted by some minor and some major displacements. Since the series do not react to these displacements by returning to a normal level, but stay about the new level as steadily as they did about the old, it is better to refer to inertia rather than to stability. The problem is to account for both the inertia and the displacements, and this naturally leads to the markets in which factors are priced and to the body of economic analysis which accounts for the division of a given product, in various conditions of competition, between the participant factors. But the proposal to apply this analysis to a long run of years, in Fig. 1, encounters a serious difficulty: this analysis usually supposes a given state of technique, whereas in such a long period technique has changed radically. This is an obstacle which we must now try to remove.

II. The Distributive Process in the Course of Economic Development

Any useful account of distribution must be set in a context of development. Throughout our period, population was growing, most often rapidly; the amount of equipment was increasing faster than population; technique was changing. We cannot provide an explanation which derives a certain distribution of the product from given amounts of productive factors combined under a given technique, but will be upset, or be liable to give a very different answer, when those amounts and the technique are substantially changed.

This requirement is basic, and it is the main reason for not being able to accept in the present application those accounts of the distribution of the national product which consist in a generalization of the static theory of the combination of productive factors or of the firm. One such is Douglas's application [1] to the statistics of labour, capital, and product over a period of years in the whole economy of a production function of the type which shows the quantities of product that will result from various alternative sets of productive factors combined always under the same technique. It is unlikely that such a structure can be significantly fitted to the records of a growing, changing economy. A similar difficulty exists in Kalecki's theory,[2] which derives the distribution of the national

[1] C. W. Cobb and P. H. Douglas, 'A Theory of Production', *American Economic Review*, Supplement (March 1928). P. H. Douglas, *The Theory of Wages* (1934). P. H. Douglas, 'Are There Laws of Production?' *American Economic Review* (March 1948).

[2] M. Kalecki, 'The Distribution of the National Income', *Essays in the Theory of Economic Fluctuations* (1939); 'Long Run Theory of Distribution', *Oxford Economic Papers* (1941); 'Costs and Prices', *Studies in Economic Dynamics* (1943).

product by aggregation from the distribution of the net product within the firm. The problem is to fit in the changes which have actually occurred in the proportion of factors and in technique. In the United Kingdom, for example, the quantity of capital per occupied person in 1914 seems to have been nearly double what it had been in 1870, but the rate of return per unit of capital seems to have continued close to 11 per cent throughout.[1] How can we put this sort of change into a diagram showing the revenue and cost curves of a firm ? A quantitative increase in equipment per worker must shift the marginal cost curve, and in practice it will be accompanied by technical change which will also change its shape and position. The framework twists in our hands.

An account is needed which combines the forces which govern the distribution of the net product of the firm at any one time with one which shows how the relation between intake and output proceeds under the play of accumulation and technical change. A suggestion to this end has occurred to me through finding that in the United Kingdom, over the whole span between 1870 and 1938, both real capital per head and real income per head nearly doubled. If we define as capital coefficient the ratio which at any one time the stock of capital bears to the current annual outflow of product, it can be said that over this span the capital coefficient hardly changed. Estimates for the intervening years suggest that it was, in fact, fairly stable : it seems to have declined from about 3·7 in the 1870's to 3·3 in the 1890's and risen again to about 3·9 in 1912 ; in the inter-war years it may have moved from about 4·0 to 3·6.[2] In the United States the capital coefficient seems to have risen from 3 to 3·5 between the late 1870's and the mid 1890's but thereafter to have remained about 3·5, though in the inter-war years its cyclical movements about this level were wide.[3] It is natural to ask whether such stability is only the chance outcome of the interplay of a number of perhaps conflicting tendencies in the course of growth, or whether there are equilibrating forces which tend to check too wide a divergence from a norm. Here let us only accept the comparative stability as a fact of history.

As such, it provides an opportunity to solve the problem of tracing the change in the production function in the course of growth. If it be assumed, as a first approximation, that the capital

[1] 'Accumulation, Productivity and Distribution in the British Economy, 1870–1938', *Economic Journal*, lxiii (June 1953).

[2] 'Accumulation, Productivity and Distribution in the British Economy, 1870–1938', p. 266.

[3] B. Weber and S. J. Handfield-Jones, 'Variations in the Rate of Economic Growth in the U.S.A., 1869–1939', *Oxford Economic Papers* (June 1954), Fig. 6.

coefficient is constant, then there is a direct relation between the rate of return on capital and the share of labour of all kinds in the national income, whatever the state of technique and accumulation. The following identity may help to make this clear, provided that it is not mistaken for a functional relation. Consider an economy whose national product Y is divided exhaustively between L, the compensation of all kinds of labour, and a rate of return r on a stock of capital C. Then $Y \equiv L + rC$. If now the capital coefficient is k, that is, $C \equiv kY$, we have $Y \equiv L + rkY$, and the proportionate share of labour of all kinds in national income, L/Y, is identically equal with $1 - rk$. (For the United Kingdom in the later nineteenth century this can be roughly evaluated as $56\% \equiv 1 - 11\% \times 4$.) We see that so long as k is constant, there is a direct relation between L/Y and r: steadiness of the one will go with steadiness of the other. A rise in the share of labour in national income will go with a fall in the rate of return on capital, whatever changes in technique or in the proportion of capital to labour may have been taking place meanwhile. Thus, the actual complex course of development seems to have had in the aggregate a fairly simple outcome: capital and income have grown at about the same rate. So long as this is so, the distribution of income can be studied by a kind of static analysis even in the midst of change and growth, for the shares of capital and labour prove to be related in much the same way as if technique were unchanging and income constant.

This direct relation is between the rate of profit and the share in the national income of the earnings of the whole occupied population. Between this share and the wage/income ratio which we have been using as the most compendious index of the relative factor price of the wage-earners' work, there are two steps. First, wages are only a part of all earnings, and it has already been noticed that because of the growth of the clerical, administrative, and technical employments, they will have been a decreasing part, so that a constant rate of profit would go with a falling share of wages proper in national income. But second, to arrive at the wage/income ratio we have to divide this share of wages by the proportion of wage earners in the whole occupied population, and this proportion has also been diminishing, so there has been some compensation. The compensation will not be complete, because since wages are lower than most other earnings, a given transfer from the number of wage earners to other occupations tends to make a more than proportional decrease in the share of wages in all earnings. But here again there is some compensation, because this kind of transfer has been promoted by the extension of education which, by raising the relative supply of those qualified for non-manual jobs and decreasing that of the merely manual workers, has depressed the rates of pay in these other jobs relatively to wage rates. So, broadly, the kind of direct relation found between the rate of profit and the share of wages is likely to hold also with the wage/income ratio; though some reservations must be made.

III. The Rate of Profit

The inquiry into the inertia and displacement of the wage/income ratio leads to an examination of the rate of profit. Estimates of the generally prevailing rate are few and hazardous, but Fig. 3

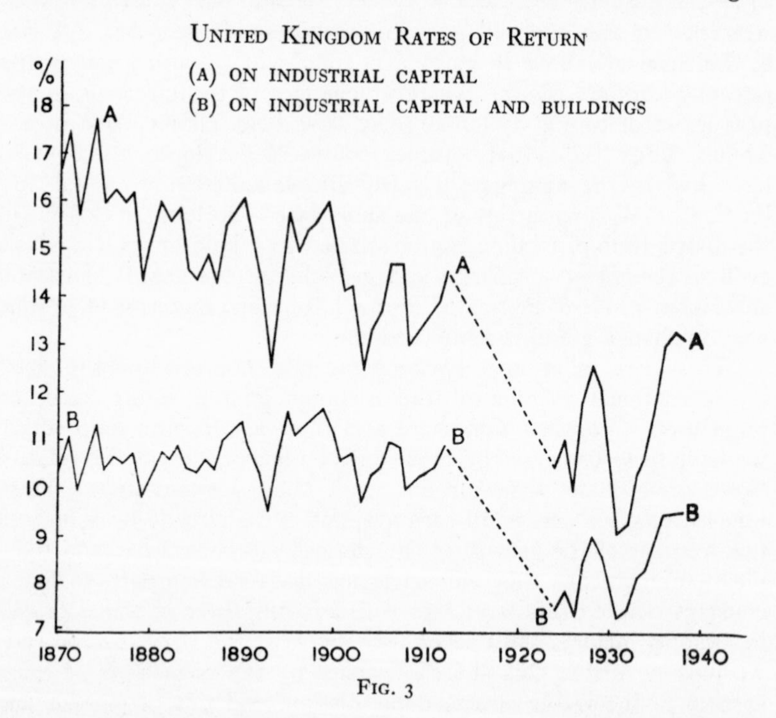

Fig. 3

shows some which have been attempted for the United Kingdom. Here we have all non-agricultural profits expressed as a percentage of the aggregate current replacement value of industrial capital; and these profits, together with rents of buildings, are shown as a percentage of the combined total of industrial capital and revenue-yielding buildings, both again taken at their estimated replacement value. The first of these rates of profit is fairly steady around

15 per cent between 1878 and 1900, but seems to have been around 17 per cent in the earlier 1870's and around 14 per cent between 1901 and 1913 ; it undergoes a big displacement through the first World War, and its fluctuations afterwards are around 11 per cent. The second and broader rate of return shows greater stability before 1914, when it generally lies between 10 and 11 per cent ; like the first, it is sharply displaced after 1914, and its fluctuations in the inter-war years are around a central value between 8 and 9 per cent. This evidence, though limited, strongly suggests a behaviour of the rate of profit which is interesting because it shows the same elements as the wage/income ratio : inertia and displacement. What explanation can be offered for it ?

It is customary to suppose that behind the realized rate of profit lies a long-run supply price of enterprise, or risk capital, and also that the workings of the market will maintain some rough equivalence between this supply price and the net contribution which enterprise or risk-capital make to output. The present evidence gives no ground to doubt the ultimate importance of these forces, but the characteristics of inertia and displacement are not readily explicable by them, and suggest the presence of a further factor, operative in the determination of the rate of profit realized from day to day, within limits set by the long-run forces. This further factor may be found if we can regard the day-to-day decisions of firms about adjustments of price and output as guided by a working rule which for the time being firms tacitly accept in concert, and which indicates the rate of profit at which it is reasonable to aim.

This is a convention of the kind which grows up whenever the outcome of one man's decisions depends on the similar decisions of other men, and he does not know what these are going to be. A manufacturer whose selling prices yield him for a time profits so big as to attract greater competition brings much trouble on himself ; but if he sets his prices low he may be leaving too little margin for contingencies, or failing to earn as much as shareholders expect, or stirring up a price-cutting war. Any one of a number of firms bidding for a contract can very likely get the contract, if it goes low enough, but only to make a loss ; if it allows itself a good profit it may not get the contract. In these circumstances a convention is likely to arise, even where there is no collusion, to regulate competition by the general acceptance of a certain profit margin as reasonable. Keynes [1] has described how we try to give definition

[1] J. M. Keynes, 'The General Theory of Employment', *Quarterly Journal of Economics*, li (February 1937). See also R. F. Harrod, 'Price and Cost in Entrepreneurs' Policy', *Oxford Economic Papers* (May 1939).

and stability to our decisions when they have to be taken in ignorance of the future. In uncertainty we are driven to conformity.

> Knowing our own individual judgment is worthless, we endeavour to fall back on the judgment of the rest of the world which is perhaps better informed. That is, we endeavour to conform with the behaviour of the majority or the average. The psychology of a society of individuals each of whom is endeavouring to copy the other leads to what we may strictly term a *conventional* judgment.

If such a conventional judgment coalesces about what is a reasonable or normal rate of profit, pricing and output decisions will be based on it and tend to provide it. They cannot do so, of course, in isolation from other economic forces ; agreement upon a rate is not always enough to achieve it : but at any one time the rate depends immediately not on supply and demand, but on convention, and the workings of economic forces may leave sufficient latitude for the conventional rate to persist unchanged for some time. At least it appears that in the United Kingdom the realized rate did so persist.

Finding the proximate determinant of the rate of profit in convention provides an explanation not only for the observed stability, but also for the observed displacements. It is the nature of a convention that it can collapse. Once a twist of events carries people away from it willy-nilly, they can no longer believe that in following it they are doing what everyone is doing. But if after a time the rates actually being obtained settle down, let their level be within fairly wide limits what you will, then a new convention can coalesce, and a new period of stability ensues. A displacement of this kind, a sharp movement from one sustained level to another, seems more likely to appear if the variable depends immediately on convention than if it emerges from a running interplay of demand and supply.

With this hypothesis about the factors governing the rate of profit, let us turn to the interplay between profits, wages, and other factor incomes.

IV. Inertia and Displacement in the Relation between Wages and Other Factor Receipts

The Rigid and Flexible Sectors of Income

Our study of this interplay will be made with the following framework. Factor receipts are divided into two groups : the first contains the receipts of those factors whose prices change slowly, and follow general movements only with resistances and lags, namely, rents and salaries : this we may call the rigid sector. The second group contains wages and profits, which change more readily in the short run, and make up the flexible sector. The main distributive shifts can be conveniently divided into those between the two sectors, and those within the second or flexible sector, though some shifts have partaken of both sorts of movement.

Throughout both sectors there is a resistance to downward movement, a resistance which is strongest where factor prices enter into long-term contracts, but which is strong also among wage earners, even when they are not organized, so that the main pressure of a contraction of total effective demand falls on profits. An upward movement of factor prices may follow, as notably it does in war-time, upon a rise in total effective demand ; but we shall also assume here that factor prices can, so to speak, take the initiative, and raise costs before product prices have risen. In either kind of upward movement there are familiar forces at work to enable each factor to take part : in the rigid sector there will be an endeavour to keep up, even though at some distance ; in the flexible sector there will be pressure from wage earners, unorganized as well as organized, while firms, as we have seen them, will try to maintain a conventional rate of profit. At times these various pressures will be in balance, but at others, whether or not the initiative comes from the side of effective demand, the balance will be upset, and distributive shifts will occur.

At any such time of disturbed balance, it is an important question whether there is an effective limit to total money income : can one factor obtain more only by transfer from others, or may its successful endeavour to get more be matched by similar increases in the receipts of other factors, so that total money income is raised ? The assumption that is made here requires argument at length,[1] but must be boldly stated. It is assumed that the price level, and hence, with given real output, the size of monetary income, is not the passive outcome of a monetary equation, but can itself take the initiative, under the impulse of changes initiated among factor prices and the price-setting decisions of firms, the quantity of money required to mediate the resultant flow of payments being, with more or less resistance, adapted to it. It is further assumed that so far as this process goes on, a major influence on the course of prices lies in the consensus of opinion among firms about the practicability of passing rises in costs on in higher product prices.

[1] Brown and Ozga, 'Economic Growth and the Price Level', *Economic Journal* (March 1955).

This consensus will be based partly on facts of the market, such as the pressure of foreign competition, but will also, so far as such facts are not mandatory, be a matter of convention. If we pass on a rise in costs by putting up prices, or refrain from passing on some reduction in costs, are we likely to find ourselves isolated and under competitive fire, or shall we be only keeping step with the main body ? The prevalent answer which firms find to this sort of question, and use in their decisions on price and output, may be said to constitute a market environment. When the general view is that price rises are impracticable, and reductions in cost must be matched by lower selling prices, the market environment may be said to be hard. When the general view is that price rises, for due cause, are unlikely to recoil on the seller, because they are part of a general tendency, the market environment may be said to be soft. In a hard market environment a rise in the monetary receipts of one factor cannot be easily passed on in higher selling prices by the firms whose costs they raise, and there must be some squeeze of other shares ; but in a soft market environment all can go up together.

Shifts between the Two Sectors

Within the framework outlined in the last two paragraphs let us now consider the different sorts of distributive shift. Of these the first is a shift between the rigid and the flexible sectors. This is the general outcome of large and rapid changes in the total monetary income. We have already noted the swing between the two sectors as such changes occur in the course of the trade cycle. A bigger change of this kind may come about through war : in the United Kingdom, for instance, the combined share of profits and wages in the national income was about 66 per cent on the eve of the second World War, but about 72 per cent between 1947 and 1950. Movements of this kind have often not been reversed, but there seems to have been such a reversal in the United Kingdom, in the deflation which followed the boom after the first World War. The combined share of wages and profits in national income was rather lower in 1925 than it had been in 1913. The share of wages alone was raised through both wars : but whereas in the more recent period this rise came about only by transfer from the rigid sector, in the earlier it had been possible only by a reduction in the share of profits. This brings us to our second class of shifts, those internal to the flexible sector.

Inertia and Displacement within the Flexible Sector

In trying to account for these, the discussion envisages a typical firm whose decisions from day to day about price and output are guided by two conventions, one prescribing the reasonable or normal rate of profit which the firm will endeavour to realize, the other guiding its opinion on the probable consequences of a change in selling price, and so constituting a market environment. This hypothesis of a market environment is developed to explain why the distributive shifts affecting wages in the United Kingdom which are shown in Fig. 2 are sometimes correlated as might be expected with trade union activity or weakness, but not always. 'If union strength tends to raise the share of wages in national income, we have to explain why it did this in 1870–1872 and 1888–1889, but not in 1909–1913 and 1946–1950. If union weakness tends to lower the share, we have to explain why it did so in 1903–1905 and 1926–1928, but not in 1879–1881.'[1] Let us now consider in turn the cases of inertia, minor shifts, and major shifts within the flexible sector.

There have been some notable examples of inertia in the relation between wages and profits, notable because of the extent of the change in wage rates through which the inertia persisted. In the United Kingdom the successful trade union pressure for higher money wages in the five years before the first World War is one instance, the virtual trebling of money wage earnings between 1938 and the present day another. Probably the same process was at work in two instances of combined action by government and trade unions to raise money wages, which seems to have had as its main effect only a raising of the general level of costs and prices: New Zealand, after the return of a labour government in 1936,[2] and France, in 'l'expérience Blum'.[3] The essential factor in these cases seems to have been a soft market environment: firms generally felt able to pass on rises in costs. But inertia may appear also when the market environment is hard. The United Kingdom in 1879–1881 may provide an instance of this: the prostration of the trade unions then was not accompanied by any shift adverse to

[1] Brown and Hart, 'The Share of Wages in National Income', *Economic Journal* (June 1952), p. 269.

[2] A. E. C. Hare, *Report on Industrial Relations in New Zealand* (1946), p. 109. In factory industry a rise of 50 per cent in total wages in two years went with a rise only from 66·1 to 70·7 per cent in the share of wages in the net product.

[3] M. Kalecki, 'The Lessons of the Blum Experiment', *Economic Journal* (March 1938); R. Marjolin, 'Reflections on the Blum Experiment', *Economica* (May 1938).

wages, perhaps because a hard market environment kept selling prices pressed down on costs.

The minor shifts between wages and profits seem to have arisen out of the conjuncture of trade union activity and the market environment. In the United Kingdom profit margins were squeezed between strong union pressure and a hard market environment, conceivably though doubtfully in 1870–1873, more probably in 1889–1891. Profit margins widened when a market environment soft enough not to enforce the passing on of cost reductions went with trade union inactivity, in 1903–1905 and 1926–1928. In both kinds of change the convention governing the normal rate of profit is modified by the conjuncture of the condition of the unions with the market environment.

It may be suggested that this mechanism tends to hasten or check the rise of real wages in two ways at once. For there is reason to believe that a major factor in the formation of the conventional element in the market environment is the observed trend of the prices of primary products : so that periods in which these products are becoming more abundant relatively to the demand of the industrial world, and so falling in price, will tend to be periods of hard market environment, and conversely. But in that case the times when the supply of primary product to the industrial wage earner is improving more rapidly will also be times in which successful pressure for higher money wages can squeeze profit margins against a general reluctance to raise selling prices : the position being reversed in both respects at times when primary products are becoming scarcer. The period which began probably with the end of the American Civil War, and continued to the mid-'nineties, seems to be an example of the first type ; that from the mid-'nineties to 1914 of the second.

The mark of a major shift in the relation between wages and profits is that the prevailing level of profits is widely displaced, and does not move back again. In the explanation offered here this must be associated with a complete change, as distinct from a temporary modification, of the convention concerning the normal rate of profit : in a period of great and rapid changes the old landmarks have been lost, and as stability is recovered, a new convention forms. This must be our account of the great shift which Figs. 2 and 3 show in the United Kingdom between 1914 and 1924, and perhaps something of the same kind may have come about in other countries which also show over this interval a marked rise in their wage rate/income ratio. What seems to have happened in the United Kingdom is that a general inflationary rise of profits and wages during and immediately after the war was met by a sharp deflationary movement which, wherever it may have begun, was carried on by a general belief that present values were 'artificial'. But this strong downward pressure encountered trade unions whose membership had doubled since 1914, and who put up strong resistance to wage cuts. Though in one sense generally defeated, they succeeded in keeping the fall in money wage rates less than the fall in product prices. Thus a market environment pressing downwards against a trade union floor had much the same effect as trade unions pressing upwards against a market environment ceiling. But the distinctive mark of the first process was that it was powerful enough to carry the business community away from its old landmarks and usher in a new convention concerning normal profit.

The main ideas which have been put forward to account for the observed long-term movement of real wages may be summarized as follows. The rise of real wages has been connected with that of general productivity by a relation made up both of inertia and displacement. An opportunity to simplify the analysis of this relation is provided by the comparative stability observed in the capital coefficient, which allows us to treat the distribution of income in the setting of growth by methods which otherwise would be sufficient only in a stationary state. We divide distributive processes into those governing the division of income between the rigid and flexible sectors of factor receipts and those which are internal to the flexible sector. The former depend mainly on big changes in national money income. In the latter we find a direct relation between wage costs, profit margin, and selling price, in which the profit margin is subject to varying pressure between trade union activity and the market environment. This mechanism includes the guidance of the decisions of firms by two conventions, which may be in conflict with one another, one concerning the normal rate of profit, the other concerning the advisability of changes in selling prices.

Chapter 5

FULL EMPLOYMENT AND WAGE STABILITY

BY

BENT HANSEN

University of Uppsala, Sweden

IN the discussion of the problems of a full employment economy many more-or-less different definitions of the precise content of 'full employment' have been given. Of these definitions, the following deserve special attention.

(1) Starting out from a social view-point, Beveridge [1] argued that full employment ought to mean a situation in which there exists 'more vacant jobs than unemployed men'. An unemployment figure of 3 per cent on the average was mentioned in this context.

(2) There is the price stabilization view-point towards full employment. Wage stability is a *conditio sine qua non* for price stability.

Wage stability does not necessarily imply constant money wages but rather a movement of the money wage level compatible with a constant price level. Money wages cannot remain stable, it is argued, if employment is too high. The bargaining power of workers is assumed to increase with increasing employment. A certain volume of unemployment is, accordingly, necessary to deprive workers of their power continuously to push up money wages at a rate incompatible with price stability. This argument, first put forward by Joan Robinson [2] as early as 1937, has been repeated over and over again, and it has often been taken to imply a higher average percentage of unemployment than that mentioned by Beveridge. Figures of 5 and 10 per cent have been mentioned.

(3) There is the general welfare view-point towards full employment. The main object of economic policy ought to be to obtain as high a national product as possible. This view-point has been vigorously stressed by Ohlin.[3] Absenteeism, excessive mobility of labour, bottlenecks in production, and other phenomena supposed to accompany very high employment make it likely, it is maintained, that the highest possible national product is not necessarily attained

[1] W. Beveridge, *Full Employment in a Free Society* (1944).
[2] J. Robinson, *Essays in the Theory of Employment* (1937).
[3] B. Ohlin, *The Problem of Employment Stabilization* (1949).

at the highest possible employment level. This general welfare view-point may also lead to a higher average level of unemployment than indicated by Beveridge.

I. The Wage Level in an Unorganized Labour Market

Consider the case of a labour market with no organizations, neither organizations of employers nor employees. If there are large numbers of both employers and employees, this market corresponds to a perfect competition market. This abstract case is useful as a starting-point, partly because the mechanism of the market is relatively simple, and also partly because the perfect competition case tells us something essential about the dynamics of labour markets, which is by no means irrelevant when organizations are introduced into the picture.

If the labour force of a community is completely homogeneous with respect to skill, ability, and so on, and also in space, no serious difficulties arise when we try to define full employment. *Ceteris paribus*, we can, under this assumption of homogeneity, describe the total demand for, and the total supply of labour in the community as functions of the money wage rate. If the demand and supply curves cut each other at a point with a certain money wage and a certain quantity of labour bought and sold, this point may be said to determine a situation of full employment. For here demand and supply of labour are equal ; no unemployment and no scarcity of labour exists. If the demand and the supply curves cut several times, all such cutting points may be said to be situations of full employment. If the *ceteris paribus* assumptions behind the demand and supply functions are changed, the functions will change, and the full employment point will change too. But this does not give rise to difficulties. The crucial thing is that demand and supply in the labour market are equal.

Fig. 1 shows a *ceteris paribus* demand curve, D, and supply curve, S, for labour, with money wage rate, w, on the ordinate and quantity of labour, q, on the abscissa. The full employment point is $(\bar{q}, \bar{w})$.

If the money wage rate was as high as w_1, supply would exceed demand and the money wage might be expected to tend to fall ; if the money wage rate was fixed below $\bar{w}$, demand would exceed supply and the money wage would tend to increase. This seems quite generally to be accepted as the law of motion of prices in general and of money wage rates in particular under the conditions specified.

This law of motion seems to be reasonable both when the market is of the 'bourse' type and of the 'quotation' type.[1] We hardly have a better hypothesis.[2] More precisely this hypothesis can be formulated in the following well-known way. Let w^1 and w^0 be money wage rates at the time points 1 and 0 respectively. Wage rates are assumed to change only at the time points 0, 1, etc. So, for the period between 0 and 1 the money wage is constant and equal to w^0. Then $\Delta w = w^1 - w^0$. Let D^0 and S^0 be demand and supply for the period between time points 0 and 1 at the wage rate w^0 given for the period. $X^0 = D^0 - S^0$ then is the excess demand for labour during the period. With this notation, our hypothesis of the dynamics of money wages is

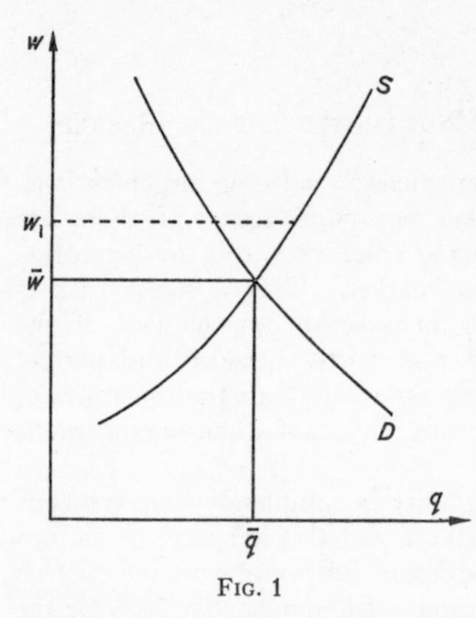

FIG. 1

$$\frac{\Delta w}{w^0} = k . \frac{X^0}{S^0}, \text{ } k \text{ being a positive constant.} \qquad (1)$$

This equation says that the relative change of the money wage rate, $\Delta w/w^0$, from time point 0 to time point 1, is determined by the relative excess demand for labour, X^0/S^0, during the period, multiplied by a certain constant, k, the coefficient of money wage flexibility. For the change of the money wage rate from time point 1 to 2, (1) may again be applied, *mutatis mutandis* ; needless to say, at time point 1 X and S will have changed, not only because w has changed, but also because both the demand and the supply curve may shift as a result of other changes in the system.

From (1) it follows immediately that if the excess demand for labour equals zero, money wage will not be changed at time point 1. So the definition of full employment given in connection with the figure also secures a constant money wage rate. It is not clear how Beveridge would define full employment under these abstract conditions. The general tenor of his book makes it likely that he

[1] J. T. Dunlop, *Wage Determination Under Trade Unions* (1950), ch. ii.

[2] See, for instance, J. R. Hicks, *Value and Capital* (1939), ch. v, and P. A. Samuelson, *Foundations of Economics* (1947), ch. xi.

would have chosen a definition like the one just given. If, however, his actual formulation be accepted — more jobs than men — this would mean that demand exceeds supply so that a positive excess demand exists. This again would imply a tendency for money wages to increase.

If we turn to the last one of the three definitions of full employment, employment at which the maximum national product is obtained, with our assumptions, maximum production must be expected to arise when money wages are such that demand equals supply. For if, in the figure, money wages are fixed below $\bar{w}$, the supply and also employment will be smaller than $\bar{q}$. (As a rule it can be assumed that if $D < S$, employment is equal to demand, and if $S < D$, it is equal to supply. In a seller's market sellers' plans are carried out ; in a buyer's market buyers' plans are carried out.) This conclusion is, however, dependent upon the way in which we have drawn the curves. If, for instance, the supply curve had a negative slope (absolutely greater than that of the demand curve), employment and national product would be greater at a wage below the equilibrium level $\bar{w}$, that is, in a state with excess demand. But if, on the other hand, both curves had a positive slope and the demand curve were steeper than the supply curve, employment and national product would be greater at a wage above the equilibrium level $\bar{w}$, that is, in a state with excess supply and unemployment.

All this is elementary and well known. We shall now drop the assumption of a homogeneous labour force and instead we shall assume that the labour market is split up into, say, n submarkets. It is assumed that in the very short run it is difficult for a worker to move from one submarket to another. So, in each period each submarket has its own money wage rate w_i, supply S_i, demand D_i, and excess demand X_i.[1] Furthermore, it is assumed that for each submarket a law of motion exists corresponding to (1) :

$$\frac{\Delta w_i}{w_i^0} = k_i \cdot \frac{X_i^0}{S_i^0}. \qquad (2)$$

The money wage flexibilities, k_i, need not be the same for all submarkets.

If demand and supply are made equal in each single submarket, that is, all $X_i = 0$, this case of non-homogeneity will not differ from the case of complete homogeneity. The interesting problems arise,

[1] The period is assumed to be the period of the Stockholm School. It can be shown that this period has the virtue of being so short that all interdependencies are ruled out ; see R. Bentzel and B. Hansen, 'On Recursiveness and Interdependency in Economic Models', paper read at the 16th European Meeting of the Econometric Society, 1954 (to be published).

however, as soon as it is recognized that in reality all submarkets cannot in general be assumed to be in equilibrium at the same point of time. Some markets may have an excess demand with over-employment, and some markets an excess supply with unemployment.[1] This could not happen when labour was homogeneous. With homogeneity the total market must exhibit either excess demand or excess supply ; not both simultaneously. With non-homogeneity this still holds within individual submarket, but not between submarkets. For the total labour market, excess demand and excess supply, vacant jobs and unemployed men, may now be coexistent. Beveridge no doubt had in mind a non-homogeneous labour market when he formulated his definition of full employment.

Now, let us try to formulate the condition for the average money wage level to be constant from one period to the next, the money wage rates of the submarkets being assumed to move up and down according to whether excess demand or supply exist in the individual submarkets. Define the wage level, W^1, at time point 1, as

$$W^1 = \frac{\Sigma w_i^1 \,.\, S_i^0}{\Sigma w_i^0 \,.\, S_i^0}. \qquad (3)$$

This money wage index is a moving Laspeyres index with the supplies of the submarkets in the base period (the preceding period) as weights. Probably a wage index with the employment of the submarkets in the base period as weights would better correspond to practical index-making, but for the sake of simplicity the above index was chosen. The main argument is not dependent upon this special choice of index. The change of this index from time point 0 to time point 1, i.e. $W^1 - W^0 = \Delta W$, may now be written as

$$\Delta W = \frac{\Sigma \Delta w_i \,.\, S_i^0}{\Sigma w_i^0 \,.\, S_i^0}. \qquad (4)$$

Inserting (2) in (4) we get

$$\Delta W = \frac{\Sigma k_i \,.\, w_i^0 \,.\, X_i^0}{\Sigma w_i^0 \,.\, S_i^0}. \qquad (5)$$

It follows immediately from (5) that the condition for the money wage level to be constant, that is for $\Delta W = 0$, is that

$$\Sigma k_i \,.\, w_i^0 \,.\, X_i^0 = 0. \qquad (6)$$

If all X_i^0 are zero, this condition is satisfied. If not all $X_i^0 = 0$, some of them must be positive and some negative, k_i and w_i^0 being

[1] In this paper excess demand and overemployment and excess supply and unemployment are used as synonyms.

positive. So (6) states that for the average wage level to be constant, a weighted sum of all money values of excess demands (excess supplies are taken as negative excess demands) must be zero, the weights being the money wage flexibility coefficients of the submarkets. If the flexibilities are the same for all submarkets, (6) reduces to $\Sigma w_i^0 . X_i^0 = 0$, that is, a simple sum of the money values of the excess demands in the submarkets shall be zero. The sum $\Sigma w_i^0 . X_i^0$ is well known from 'gap' analyses and has been called the 'factor-gap'.

Write all positive excess demands in (6) as $^+X_i^0$ and all negative excess demands (i.e. excess supplies) as $^-X_i^0$. Then the total unemployment existing when (6) is satisfied is

$$\Sigma\, ^-X_i^0 \quad . \quad . \quad . \quad . \quad (7)$$

and the percentage of unemployment is $100 . \Sigma ^-X_i^0 / \Sigma S_i^0$. In the same way the total number of vacant jobs existing when (6) is satisfied is

$$\Sigma\, ^+X_i^0 \quad . \quad . \quad . \quad . \quad (8)$$

and the 'percentage of overemployment' may be expressed by

$$100 . \Sigma\, ^+X_i^0 / \Sigma S_i^0 .$$

From (5) it is also seen that

$$\Delta W \gtreqless 0 \text{ according to whether } \Sigma k_i . w_i^0 . X_i^0 \gtreqless 0. \quad . \quad (9)$$

If the money wage flexibilities of all submarkets are the same, and if the factor gap is positive, the wage level, as defined in (3), will tend to increase; if the factor gap is negative, the wage level will tend to fall. If the money wage flexibilities are not the same in all submarkets, the wage index can, of course, always be reconstructed in such a way (the weights in the index, S_i^0, should then be multiplied by the inverted values of the money wage flexibilities) that this statement still holds. The wage index derived in this way may, however, be uninteresting from a policy point of view. So, if the money wage flexibilities are not equal in all submarkets, it will as a rule be necessary to consider a weighted and not an unweighted factor gap.[1] These relationships seem to be the central point in all types of gap analysis, including saving-investment analysis.[2]

Two propositions of interest now follow:

First, there is no one-to-one correspondence between the percentage of unemployment and the movements of the money

[1] This result should be compared with the attempts of L. R. Klein, *Economic Fluctuations in the United States, 1921–1941* (1950), p. 121, to explain money wage movements by the volume of unemployment, that is, by $\Sigma - X_i$.

[2] See Bent Hansen, *A Study in the Theory of Inflation* (1951), chs. i and ix.

wage level. The average wage level may be constant with high unemployment or with low unemployment, if only the number of vacant jobs existing at the same time is high or low respectively. The average wage level may be increasing when unemployment is large, and falling when unemployment is low. But there is a simple correspondence between the total 'gap' in the labour market (that is, between the total weighted money value of all excess demands and supplies in the submarkets) and the movements of the wage level. This seems to suggest that gap analysis and not mere unemployment analysis is the appropriate type of analysis in the study of changes of the wage level.

Second, the satisfaction of (6) with constancy of the wage level as a consequence may be consistent with the condition that

$$\Sigma^{+}X_i^0 > \Sigma^{-}X_i^0, \qquad \qquad (10)$$

that is, with the number of vacant jobs being greater than the number of unemployed men. A glance at (6) shows that if the positive excess demands (the vacant jobs) are especially to be found in submarkets with relatively low money wage rates and with low money wage flexibilities, and if the negative excess demands (the unemployed men) are especially to be found in submarkets with relatively high money wage rates and high money wage flexibilities, then full employment in the sense of Beveridge may be compatible with a constant, and even with a falling average money wage level. So, it is by no means generally true that full employment in Beveridge's sense leads to smaller unemployment figures than full employment in the sense that a constant average wage level be preserved. (If the price stability policy allows a certain increase in the money wage level, it is still more likely that full employment in Beveridge's sense is compatible with the stabilization policy.) Nor is it generally true that full employment in Beveridge's sense necessarily implies increasing money wage level.

The relation between Beveridge's definition of full employment and the wage stabilization definition of full employment has now been clarified in the case where the labour force is not homogeneous. We turn to the importance of non-homogeneity for the last full employment definition, maximum national product. The phenomenon of bottlenecks is intimately connected with the lack of homogeneity of labour. If excess demand arises in a certain submarket, this may also mean that a bottleneck has arisen. Such bottlenecks may mean disorganization in other branches of production and perhaps a decrease of total production. This is one of the reasons proponents of the welfare view-point have found it wise to keep total effective demand and employment at such a level that no bottlenecks appear, rather than to keep employment at a higher level with the risk of excess demand and bottlenecks in certain sectors. It follows that maximum production requires a higher unemployment than Beveridge advocated. A distinction must be made, however, between excess demands for labour in lower and higher stages of production. If bottlenecks appear in raw material or production equipment sectors, the effects may be disastrous for total national product. But if the excess demand for labour appears in the final production of consumer goods, this will not in itself have adverse effects on other branches of production. It follows that we cannot say in general that excess demands are harmful to production and that maximum national product should necessarily require that no excess demands exist and that unemployment be substantial.

The general conclusion of this section is that it is not possible in general to say which one of our three definitions of full employment imply the highest amount of unemployment. Everything seems to depend upon the precise nature of the partial disequilibria of the submarkets of the labour market.

II. The Organized Labour Market

The argument of the preceding section was based on the assumption that there were no labour market organizations. Does it follow that when organizations are assumed to exist, the results of the preceding section lose all significance? On the contrary, very likely all the results from the analysis of the unorganized labour market can in the main be carried over to the case of the organized market. This should not be taken to imply that nothing is changed when employers and employees become organized. It only means that the general state of demand and supply, as summarized in expressions like (6), is of full relevance as a determinant for the tendencies of money wage changes, even if both parties in the labour market are organized. It is not maintained that the state of demand and supply is the only circumstance which influences money wages when organizations exist. Furthermore, it should be stressed that the discussion only concerns money wage determination in cases where the general level of employment is relatively high; when unemployment is widespread and of overwhelming magnitude, things may perhaps be otherwise.

When the labour market is organized, wage determination takes place at regular intervals through agreements, perhaps every year or every second year. All wage determination, however, is not confined to the agreements. Between agreements wage determination takes place on a more individual level. Indeed, each time a worker gets a new job, the worker and the entrepreneur must agree upon the wage rate to be applied. It may be that they take it for granted that the wage rate shall be in accordance with the specifications of a general agreement between their respective organizations ; but they may also agree upon a different wage rate. So, it is useful to distinguish between wage determination through general agreements and individual wage determination during the interval between agreements.

First, consider wage determination through general agreements between organizations. The discussion of wage determination under conditions of full employment has on the whole been concentrated on this type of wage determination ; this is true, at least, for the European discussion. The standard assumption that the bargaining power of labour increases with increasing employment refers to the bargaining power of the trade unions in making wage agreements with the employers' organizations. This standard assumption can also be expressed by stating that the bargaining power of the trade unions is inversely dependent upon the volume of unemployment : the smaller the unemployment, the greater the bargaining power of the trade unions. This relationship seems to be the crucial point in the debate ; it is the existence of such a relationship which leads to the idea that a certain volume of unemployment is necessary for money wages to be constant. It may be true that such a relationship exists between unemployment and the trade unions' bargaining power. But this is not the whole story.

Agreements are made between trade unions and employers' unions. The bargaining power of employers' unions is just as important for the outcome of wage negotiations as is the bargaining power of the trade unions.[1] For the sake of simplicity, consider only the case where top organizations agree upon all money wages. It seems obvious that in the same way that unemployment, the excess supplies, is of importance for the trade unions' bargaining power (toughness), so the overemployment, the excess demands, is of importance for the bargaining power (toughness) of the employers' unions in such a way that the higher overemployment the less resist-

[1] The concept of 'bargaining power' so widely used in the literature seems to suffer from a serious lack of precision. It is used here in an absolute sense to describe the general attitude and 'fighting spirit' of the parties of a bargaining process. The word 'toughness' would perhaps be better.

ance will employers' unions make to money wage increases. One important reason is that the profits of the industries are in general directly correlated with the level of overemployment. Schematically, it should be possible to use total unemployment, $\Sigma\, {}^{-}X_i$, or perhaps, the percentage of unemployment, $100\,.\,\Sigma\, {}^{-}X_i/\Sigma S_i$, as an expression for the bargaining power of the trade unions, as is usually done, and total overemployment, $\Sigma\, {}^{+}X_i$, or perhaps, the percentage overemployment, $100\,.\,\Sigma\, {}^{+}X_i/\Sigma S_i$, as an expression for the bargaining power of the employers' unions. The smaller $\Sigma\, {}^{-}X_i$ is, the greater is the bargaining power of the trade unions ; the smaller $\Sigma\, {}^{+}X_i$ is, the greater is the bargaining power of employers' unions. For each given $\Sigma\, {}^{-}X_i$ there is a certain corresponding $\Sigma\, {}^{+}X_i$, so that the bargaining powers of the two parties are the same, with the result that the average level of money wages is left unchanged in the agreements concluded.

From this it follows that it is wrong to say that when organizations exist, constant (average) money wages require a certain level of unemployment. The level of unemployment coexistent with agreements on unchanged money wages may be high or low if the simultaneously existing overemployment (excess demands) is high or low respectively. The condition for money wages to be constant on the average is that a certain weighted sum of excess demands and excess supplies in the labour market shall be zero. So we are led to a condition for constant money wage level of much the same character as the condition (6) in the case without organizations. The whole difference consists in the weighting. It is true that the balance between excess demands and supplies may be changed in the direction of relatively more excess supply or relatively more excess demand ; it seems impossible, however, to say in what direction, if any, the balance will be changed.

It is not realistic to assume that the trade unions' bargaining power should depend only upon the excess supplies and that the bargaining power of employees' unions should depend only upon the excess demands. Trade unions also observe and take into account eventual excess demands, and employers' unions are certainly influenced by the existence of unemployment. So it seems reasonable to assume that the lower the unemployment and the higher the overemployment, the greater the bargaining power of the trade unions and the smaller the bargaining power of the employers' unions. But this does not disturb our conclusion : that it is the relation between excess supplies (unemployment) and excess demands (overemployment), and not the unemployment alone which is decisive for the tendency of the money wage level to move in an upward or downward direction when organizations agree upon money wages.

If these ideas are accepted as a correct description of the way in which the general state of demand and supply in the labour market influences money wage determination when organizations exist, all the results with respect to the relationships between the three definitions of full employment in the case with no organizations can be carried over to the case with organizations.

Second, consider wage determination during the interval between the making of general agreements. If such wage determination results in money wage rates different from those agreed upon by the organizations, we can refer to 'black-market wage changes' or better, 'wage slide' (a literal translation of the Swedish term for the phenomenon).[1] Since a wage slide is called forth by the same forces as are at work in an unorganized market, we should expect that in submarkets with excess demand an upward wage slide will take place with the result that the wage rates tend to become higher than those agreed upon by the organizations. In submarkets with excess supply a downward wage slide should be expected to take place. In the experience of the Scandinavian countries in the 'forties the wage slide was of great quantitative importance. This is true especially for wage increases, but downward wage adjustments are also to be found, although they seem to be less significant.[2] This lack of symmetry may have its explanation in the fact that workers are more loyal to their organizations than employers ; it may also be explained in part by the nature of wage agreements : agreements stipulate minimum wage rates.

The existence of such an asymmetry may be taken as a point in favour of the idea that full employment, in the wage stability sense, implies a higher volume of unemployment than Beveridge's definition of full employment.

III. Induced and Spontaneous Wage Changes

In *A Treatise on Money* Lord Keynes ventured upon a distinction between 'induced' and 'spontaneous' income inflation.[3] Keynes had in mind changes in factor prices (Keynes's *E*). Induced factor

[1] See Chapter 17 by Gosta Rehn, *infra*.

[2] An interesting study of the Danish wage-slide phenomenon is given by A. Lund, 'Spontan og autooom lönstigning', *Festskrift til Jörgen Pedersen* (1951).

[3] J. M. Keynes, *A Treatise on Money* (1930), vol. i, ch. 11.

price changes are in Keynes's terminology such factor price changes as are called forth by the existence of a difference between investment and saving, by excess demand or supply. Spontaneous factor price changes are all other factor price changes. If trade unions for political reasons started an action for higher wages in a situation with general unemployment and succeeded in obtaining an agreement on higher wages, this should be called a spontaneous money wage increase.

This Keynesian distinction which had been largely overlooked is useful from the view-point of monetary theory.[1] It must be admitted, however, that sometimes it is very difficult to discern what type of wage change is taking place. All wage changes in a labour market without organizations and without legislative interference must be of the induced type. The same holds for all wage changes 'between agreements', the wage slide in an organized labour market. The difficulties arise when we try to split up wage changes through agreements made by organizations into induced and spontaneous changes. The outcome of wage negotiations cannot always be explained simply by referring to demand and supply. But, on the other hand, agreements on wage changes can very often be regarded as a simple result of the general state of demand and supply in the labour market.

To accept the distinction between induced and spontaneous money wage changes implies that only part of the changes in money wages is explained endogenously within the economic model; the other part of money wage change is the consequence of exogenous disturbances. The exogenous part of the money wage changes may again be explained (outside the economic model) by 'sociological' or 'institutional' factors; so there seems to be no ground for a controversy between 'economic' and 'sociological' explanations of the movements of money wages. Whether or not Keynes's distinction is satisfactory will, of course, depend on the purpose of the analysis. From the view-point of monetary theory, the distinction is useful and, probably, indispensable. The procedure of splitting a certain economic phenomenon into two parts, one of which is explained within the model at hand, the other being taken as a datum is well known from other fields of economic theory in its econometric applications. In the theory of investments, for instance, the concepts of 'induced' and 'spontaneous' (or 'autonomous') investments have exactly the same meaning as the Keynesian concepts of induced and spontaneous wage changes.

[1] B. Hansen, *A Study in the Theory of Inflation*, chs. i and vii.

The above discussion, which by no means pretends to be an exhaustive treatment, draws attention to the possibility of using ordinary demand and supply analysis in the explanation of changes in the money wage level. This possibility is more fruitful than has been assumed in post-Keynesian theory, which has often taken for granted that money wages and all their changes must be treated as a result of exogenous forces. The ordinary gap analysis of monetary theory is extremely valuable for the analysis of money wage changes, and it is even useful in the case where wage determination is wholly in the hands of great labour market organizations. For the evaluation of different full employment definitions this is important ; for if it is the balance between the partial disequilibria on the submarkets, and not the unemployment in itself which is decisive for the development of money wages, there is no reason why we should not be able to obtain a 100 per cent employment with stable money wages. The crucial point is to handle the problem of the partial disequilibria in the submarkets.

Chapter 6

WAGE POLICY AND FULL EMPLOYMENT[1]

BY

VALENTIN F. WAGNER
University of Basel, Switzerland

A FUNDAMENTAL problem in the theory of employment is whether inflation is inevitable under full employment and whether there is any definite theoretical and practical criterion for judging where the borderline of inflation lies. An associated question is whether wages can be kept stable under full employment and what measures are appropriate in the field of wage policy.

I. THE KEYNESIAN VIEW

The modern view of the relation between full employment and inflation is dominated by Keynes. According to Keynes, there need be no fear of inflation so long as there is underemployment in all branches of the economy and so long as supply is completely elastic. Prices will begin to rise only when the economy approaches full employment and bottlenecks arise. Inflation will become manifest on a broad front as soon as the full employment level is reached. If effective demand continues to be in excess of effective supply (projected investments are greater than voluntary saving), then national income can go on expanding only in nominal terms. The expansion will be absorbed by a mere rise in prices, preceded or followed by a rise in wages.

Faith in this formula has been all too unquestioning. It is true that in underemployment an expansion will cause prices to rise less than when an expansion of the volume of money continues at full employment level. But Keynes's formula must not be expected to be valid in all circumstances. The history of the great majority of business cycles goes against its general validity. Prices begin to rise in all upswings, and it has been observed that 'price inflation may set in long before full employment or the zone of bottlenecks are reached'.[2]

[1] Translated by Elizabeth Henderson.

[2] Gottfried Haberler, 'Bemerkungen zum gegenwärtigen Stand der Konjunkturtheorie', *Wirtschaftstheorie und Wirtschaftspolitik: Festschrift für Alfred Amonn zum 70. Geburtstag* (1953), p. 228.

Keynes's formula replaced the quantity theory, a rigid and mechanistic formula which was the target of justified criticism. But the new theory, too, is mechanistic and cannot be relied upon in all circumstances. It completely neglects the part played by expectations and the business mood. Even the United Nations' report on full employment points out that there are exceptions to the Keynesian formula. Prices would rise even when there is underemployment, 'if the sellers of goods and productive services held out for higher prices in response to an increase in demand'.[1]

The older formula, according to which prices are, in the short run, determined by the existing movements of money and goods, would seem to correspond more closely to reality. Indeed, it corresponds better to Keynes's own doctrine. According to the latter, an expansionary process is possible only so long as there is a disproportion between effective demand and effective supply, or between intended investment and voluntary saving. This clearly implies that, even during the process of expansion, there must be inflationary pressure called forth by the excess of effective demand over effective supply.

There is no need to stress the point that not every general rise in prices is strictly of an inflationary kind. It has become customary to speak of reflation rather than inflation in the case of the general price increase in the early stages of an upswing, because there is re-establishment of a normal price-cost relation. Apart from reflationary processes of adjustment, genuine inflationary movements may occur even when there is underemployment.

In Germany, a highly questionable addition has been made to this formula of Keynes.[2] Not only is it said that prices cannot rise when there is underemployment and supply is elastic ; it is further held that an expansion of investment in a state of underemployment does not require any simultaneous saving, indeed that simultaneous saving on a scale corresponding to the volume of investment would make expansion altogether impossible. With this addition, the formula becomes a plain recommendation for an inflationary full-employment policy. However, this thesis has nothing in common with Keynes's formula, which requires that the additional investment must be matched by an equal volume of voluntary saving. The truth is that even with complete elasticity of supply, an increase in the prices of consumption goods can only be avoided by saving

[1] United Nations, *National and International Measures for Full Employment, Report by a Group of Experts* (1949), p. 22.

[2] Erich Schneider, *Einführung in die Wirtschaftstheorie. III. Teil : Geld, Kredit, Volkseinkommen und Beschäftigung*, pp. 127-129.

to the full extent of new investment. This means that two conditions must be fulfilled in order to safeguard stability of consumer goods prices. Supply must be completely elastic, and saving must match investment. But for the above-mentioned reasons price stability is not assured, even by the fulfilment of those two conditions because prices are also affected by other factors. Nor can we subscribe to Keynes's view that the required saving is made available by the economic process simultaneously and spontaneously.

II. Four Types of Full Employment

The discussion so far shows that Keynes's formula cannot be taken as a guide for a full-employment policy. Indeed, a deliberate and consistent full-employment policy is likely to be accompanied by a particularly marked inflationary pressure.

It is not possible to establish a clear dividing line between full employment and inflation by means of a criterion of universal validity and mechanical mode of operation. The danger of inflation will vary according to the external circumstances in which full employment is realized. The following cases may be distinguished :

(1) Full employment without any full-employment policy.
(2) Full employment as a result of a full-employment policy. The policy measures adopted are not designed to eliminate the price mechanism ; the government does not pursue any planned and comprehensive investment policy, but it tries to influence those economic elements which stimulate private investment. It acts through such measures as cheap-money policy and tax reduction.
(3) Full employment as a result of a full-employment policy, but the government pursues a deliberate and active investment policy, through large-scale public investment or a comprehensive spending policy with a view to increasing consumption.
(4) The government permanently pursues a full-employment policy on the assumption that the cessation of full-employment measures would be followed by an immediate set-back.

These four types of full employment differ in the method by which full employment has been reached. In the first case, full employment is due exclusively to market forces. In the second case, it is the result of a policy essentially designed to stimulate private activity. In the third case, the government actively intervenes in the economy and deliberately engages in public investment, or in a spending policy designed to increase consumption, on the assumption that its full-employment policy can be stopped as soon as full employment has been reached. In the fourth case, full-employment policy becomes a permanent institution, because the government believes that a set-back is inevitable unless the public authorities take part both in the planning of investment or consumption and in actual investment. This kind of policy implicitly or explicitly is based upon the theory of secular stagnation, according to which the immanent stagnation tendencies of mature economies force the government permanently to pursue full-employment policies. The permanent character of such full-employment policies is to some extent conditioned by doubts that a full-employment policy can be followed by a self-sustained boom. We are here faced with a problem of great moment for any full-employment policy, namely what is to follow the full-employment measures, the problem of 'the changing of the guard'.

The danger of inflationary pressure differs greatly in the four cases. It is, from the theoretical point of view, clearly greatest in the fourth case, since full-employment policies continue even after full employment has been reached. In this case systematic inflationary pressure is a necessary part of full-employment policy, bearing out Keynes's view and that of some of his adherents [1] that a permanent slight inflation creates the most auspicious conditions for full employment.

In the third case, however, inflationary pressure will be less. According to Keynes's formula, inflation becomes manifest only when full employment is approached and bottlenecks begin to arise. Since at least theoretically the full-employment measures are to come to an end when full employment is reached, there would then be no reason to expect any permanent inflationary pressure which would have to be counteracted by appropriate measures. However, we have shown that Keynes's formula is not a reliable criterion of the emergence of inflation, since both business cycle experience and theoretical argument admit of the possibility of general price increases at an earlier stage. Indeed, such a contingency is all the more likely with a deliberate and active full-employment policy which, in this third case, is wider in its scope and effect than in the

[1] 'A policy which maintained demand, and thus investment schedules above full employment level, and then controlled actual projects by direct licensing might have superior effects socially. All entrepreneurs would remain eager to venture and those could be eliminated whose contribution is regarded as least essential.' — T. Balogh, 'Comment, Monetary Policy: A Symposium', *Bulletin of the Oxford University Institute of Statistics*, 14 (1952), p. 164.

second case. For the same reasons the psychological mood, too, will be favourable to an inflationary price rise, since price inflation can be set in motion by appropriate expectations.

In the second case, the inflationary pressure is obviously less, and in the first case there is none as a consequence of the full-employment policy. Nevertheless the experience of business cycles shows that there is still a danger of inflationary price rises. Attempts have been made to develop full-employment policy in such a way that it does not have an inflationary effect. This would not be a policy of suppressed inflation, but a policy where unemployment is tackled by measures that affect individual markets which are especially hard hit. A policy of this kind, however, is not the same as Keynes' full-employment policy, which is conceived on a macro-economic scale, influencing effective over-all demand. The policy which operates only in particular markets lacks the very thing which is most characteristic of Keynes' full-employment policy, namely, its macro-economic universality. The question arises, moreover, whether a full-employment policy of this nature could really succeed in preventing an inflationary rise in wages and prices.

The foregoing remarks should certainly not be taken to imply that full employment, and more particularly any and every policy of full employment, leads to an inflationary rise in prices and wages, although there is no doubt that the problem of inflation has always been and still is the central problem of full employment.

The fallibility of Keynes's criterion is illustrated by yet another circumstance. The price level has been known to remain stable at extraordinary high levels of employment, even with a slight increase in employment. Such a situation has been clearly observable in Switzerland since 1951.[1] The cost-of-living index has hardly changed at all and can for all practical purposes be regarded as having been stable since July 1951, when the price inflation due to the Korean war came to an end. The wholesale price index has actually gone down by about 8 per cent since May 1951. At the same time the level of employment has continuously been very high during the last three years. Compared with the unemployment of 3–5 per cent of wage earners which the United Nations report considered compatible with a state of full employment, unemployment in Switzerland during the last three years has been negligible. The maximum was less than 1 per cent of the labour force. There is justice in referring to overemployment rather than to full

[1] In reading this and the immediately following paragraphs the reader is reminded that the paper was presented in September 1954. [Ed.]

employment. The supply of labour was not rigid during this period, as should have been the case under conditions of full employment. The number of non-agricultural workers has increased since 1950 by about 100,000, that is, by practically 6 per cent of the total non-agricultural labour force. Part of this increase is probably accounted for by foreign labour. At present some 175,000 registered foreign workers are permitted to work in Switzerland. Thus, the supply of labour was still elastic during this period.

It can be argued that this stability of the price level was made possible only by the influx of foreign labour. In the period up to 1948, which was characterized by pronounced inflationary pressure, there was also a considerable influx of foreign labour into Switzerland. But this did not prevent prices from rising. A further explanation, such as the increase in productivity, must therefore be found for the stability of prices since 1951. The main reason for citing the example of Switzerland is to show that Keynes's formula cannot serve as a rigid criterion but must be modified in the light of particular circumstances. The assertions which it contains are true only under certain given and constant or static conditions, and they do not apply to the varying circumstances of real life.

The state of full employment in Switzerland has come about without any deliberate full-employment policy. The economy is exhibiting some symptoms, such as extraordinarily low rates of interest, which are usually regarded as the result of deliberate measures. But in Switzerland interest rates are low not because of any planned cheap money policy, but as a result of the operation of market forces. It may be assumed that with a full-employment policy of the third type discussed above, there would, in the same circumstances, have been an inflationary price rise. The fact remains, and deserves to be noted, that it is possible for an economy to have a pronounced boom for several years at a time when prices are slightly falling.

The above considerations demonstrate that no definite and sharp line can be drawn between full employment and inflation. The effects of full employment on the price level, and thus on the level of wages, can differ according to the manner in which full employment comes about: whether it is the spontaneous result of unhampered market forces or the consequence of a deliberate full-employment policy, and whether such a policy takes into account the operation of free market forces or consists of far-reaching and possibly permanent government intervention. Keynes's formula is therefore not a reliable guide in matters of full-employment policy.

III. The Post-War Experience

The question arises to what extent the full-employment policies pursued in many countries during the post-war period have been responsible for the movement of prices and wages since 1945.

Price movements during this period were fundamentally determined by the following factors :

(1) The large backlog of demand in the immediate post-war years.
(2) The loosening of price controls in the various countries.
(3) The Korean boom.

The first two circumstances supported prices and wages mainly from the demand side, independent of full employment or of policies directed to this end. In the course of these processes the price-wage spiral was set in motion, but it can be said that the inflationary movement was mainly induced from the demand side. The excess demand had its origin in the war, but owing to the policy of suppressed inflation it could not become effective until after the war, when the policy of freezing purchasing power and of wage and price controls was relaxed or discontinued. The rise in prices and wages was due not to post-war full-employment policy, but to wartime full employment.

It is interesting to compare the price movements during and after the first World War with those during and after the second World War. During the first World War there was no policy of suppressed inflation, and prices rose quite considerably during the war itself. During the second World War such a policy succeeded in markedly slowing down the price movements. On the other hand, when the policy of suppressed inflation was relaxed or discontinued after the war, prices rose considerably. It could be said with some justification that, while the policy of suppressed inflation during the second World War slowed down the rise in prices, the price increase made up for lost time after the war when backlog demand became effective. The advantage of the method practised during the second World War was not that it prevented inflation, but that it mitigated it and spread it over a longer period.

The price increases up to 1948 were not primarily due to full-employment policies. It is probably true to say, however, that the full-employment policies pursued in many countries must have slightly reinforced the inflationary tendencies. By contrast, the wave of high prices which originated in the second half of 1950 with the Korean boom, did have a connection with full employment, although it was not the result of a deliberate full-employment policy. By the end of 1948 the period of backlog demand had come to an end. From 1949 to the beginning of 1950 an increase in unemployment indicated a falling-off of effective demand. The renewed rise in prices in many countries from the autumn of 1949 to the middle of 1950 was a result of the 1949 devaluations.

So far as the Korean price boom is concerned, we must distinguish between the direct effects of this exogenous event and its indirect effects via rearmament. The direct effects became visible in the speculative rise of prices in the world markets. This had no more than a loose relation with full employment. The high prices were a result of buyers' and sellers' revised price expectations, that is, of speculative buying against future shortages and price increases ; they came to an end as soon as stocks were laid in. The Korean boom also led to a rise in the level of employment as a result of the expansion of rearmament. This effect was more lasting. Apart from the effect of speculative buying on raw material markets, the renewed inflationary movement was, to an overwhelming extent, the result of increased armament expenditure by governments.

It can be said, therefore, that rearmament engendered practically full employment, and full employment was responsible for price inflation. Neither full employment, nor the price and wage increases, were the result of deliberate full-employment policies ; full employment was a by-product of the Korean war. In spite of full employment, the unemployed percentage of the civilian labour force available for hire, at the seasonal peak was comparatively high in the United States, where it did not fall below 3 per cent until 1953. The unemployment figures for Great Britain were considerably lower, ranging between 1·3 per cent and 2·1 per cent during the period 1949–1953. At best, then, it can be said that there was practically full employment ; but we cannot speak of overemployment.

Nominal wages rose in all countries, though in differing degrees. Real wages developed in a most varied way. In the United States real wages rose by about 12 per cent from 1949 to 1953 in spite of rising prices. In Sweden real wages rose by as much as 15 per cent. In these two countries wages were not only quickly adjusted to the price increases, but went considerably beyond them. Although the rise in wages was in the first instance due to a rise in prices, it no doubt accelerated the price inflation. This is reflected in the greater price increases in these countries. In Great Britain, on the other hand, real wages fell a little during the same period. In the

Netherlands, too, they fell, although the decrease was almost entirely made good in 1953. The greater rise in American real wages may be partly a consequence of a greater increase in productivity, but there is no doubt that the American wage rise is responsible for the stronger inflationary pressure, for the rise in the British and Dutch price levels was much smaller.

Post-war experience does not enable us to reach any clear and certain conclusions. It can be said, however, that it was not full-employment policy that was immediately responsible for the inflationary price rise. What was decisive was the backlog demand and the relaxation of price controls, and to some extent the devaluation of currencies. Full-employment policy reinforced these tendencies, but did not create them. On the other hand, there is a direct connection between full employment (though not full-employment policy) and the inflation arising from the Korean crisis. It is noteworthy that the price rise was marked, even though the full-employment level was barely reached.

IV. The Relation between Employment and Inflation

The question is often asked, what level of employment is required to safeguard the stability of wages and prices. Formulated in a different way, we may ask whether it is necessary for some unemployment to exist in order that wage and price stability shall be assured, and what percentage of unemployment is necessary to this end. The question can best be answered in the terms of Alvin Hansen's theory.[1] Hansen considers that in a free market economy, such as the United States, a stable level of prices can be maintained only if there are always several million unemployed. Since the wage level is one of the most important determinants of the price level, stable prices depend upon stable wages. According to Hansen, then, the permanent existence of a reserve labour force of several million would be necessary for the maintenance of a stable wage level. This would mean that in a free market economy price and wage stability is not possible when there is full employment.

Hansen also believes that when prices rise as the full-employment ceiling is approached, the price rise is not the result of a preceding wage inflation. He considers, instead, that the rising prices are a

[1] Alvin H. Hansen, *Monetary Theory and Fiscal Policy* (1949), p. 101. 'The thesis I wish to examine, then, is that under the price system continuing full employment is in the nature of the case not feasible, and that to secure stable prices it is necessary to have several million unemployed'.

result of a deficiency of fixed capital, to undercapacity of the existing capital equipment. If the economy approaches a state of full employment, then prices will rise rapidly, since the intersection point of the steeply rising marginal cost curve and the marginal revenue curve is a point at which profits are very high, prices being far above average costs. Thus the rising prices would be the result, not of higher wages, but of rapidly rising marginal costs due to undercapacity. But price stability is likely to be a necessary condition of wage stability. The price increase is bound to lead to a wage increase. For all practical purposes, it can be said that Hansen's view implies that stability of prices and wages is safeguarded only so long as the economy is not fully employed and there exists a minimum labour reserve.

This thesis clearly has a certain kinship with Keynes's theory. It is obvious that prices must rise when the full-employment level of the productive apparatus is approached. But Hansen's thesis says rather more than that. It says that prices begin to rise because the stock of fixed capital is insufficient. If the stock of fixed capital were large enough and there were no undercapacity, full employment could be reached without any rise in prices. In this context undercapacity would then simply mean that the optimum size of all firms, that is, production at lowest unit cost, would be insufficient fully to employ the economy, and that full employment could not be achieved without a rapid increase in costs. Prices would thus rise while wages remained stable.

Nobody will be inclined to deny that in the real world it will be hard to find an economy suffering from no undercapacity in the sense that all firms are of optimum size and that full employment can be reached at minimum unit costs. It is not possible to establish a general rule indicating the degree of unemployment necessary to ensure wage stability. The establishment of such a criterion would presuppose exact knowledge of the cost structure in the various branches of the economy and such knowledge is most unlikely ever to come within our reach. This theory makes no allowance for the fact that the cost structure is subject to constant change. Prices are also determined by factors other than costs and the number of unemployed, particularly in the short run. The most that can be said is that there is every likelihood that, as the economy draws closer to full employment, the danger of an inflationary rise in prices increases. This does not mean, however, that prices are bound to remain stable when unemployment has reached a certain level. As has already been shown, a general increase in prices is also possible at a time of underemployment.

V. Full-Employment Policy and Controls

Finally, the question arises whether price and wage controls are necessary in order to prevent the inflationary pressure on prices in a state of full employment. This question is still a matter for discussion in those cases in which full employment is a consequence of the operation of the free-market mechanism. The supporters of the policy of full employment, however, are unanimously agreed that prices and wages must be controlled in order to avoid the danger of inflation.

A deliberate and consistent full-employment policy will necessitate price and wage controls, particularly if this policy is marked by a high level of public investment. According to Keynes, such controls are not necessary so long as there is underemployment and some labour remains unemployed, for, provided the supply of goods and labour is elastic, wages and prices need not rise. Changed expectations and dispositions, however, can lead to an increase in prices and wages even before full employment is approached. To prevent such an increase, any systematic full employment policy will have to have recourse to wage and price controls at an early stage.

All this presents something of a dilemma to economists advocating a permanent full-employment policy. The problem of inflation then assumes a really acute character, and price and wage controls become necessary measures of full-employment policy. The basic reason for a permanent full-employment policy is the fear that any discontinuation of such a policy would be followed by a deflationary set-back. The recurrence of unemployment is to be avoided at all costs and the dangers of inflation viewed with less apprehension than are the dangers of deflation. Full-employment policy is to be continued even at the risk of a general price increase. This is the point of view upheld, for instance, by Balogh, by President Truman's economic advisers, and even by the United Nations' report on full employment.

It will readily be appreciated that a great responsibility rests on the parties in collective bargaining. We distinguish, nowadays, two kinds of inflation according to their origin : demand-induced inflation, which is due to an excess of effective demand over supply ; and cost-induced inflation, which is due to wage increases, leading in their turn to inflation of prices if the employers succeed in passing the increase in labour costs on to the consumers. In an inflationary process both forms are usually operative and it is hard to separate one from the other. There can be no doubt, however, that the race between prices and wages is partly the result of the exploitation by the trade unions of a favourable strategic situation on tbe market. It is precisely this circumstance which makes wage control necessary, since it is unlikely that trade unions will refrain from availing themselves of favourable opportunities. Trade unions therefore have a great responsibility. There is general agreement amongst all the proponents of full-employment policy that wages and wage policy occupy a strategic position and a full-employment policy can be pursued only if it is possible to prevent a rise in wages and a cost-induced rise in prices.[1] For this same reason the supporters of such a policy are of the opinion that price and wage controls are an essential part of the policy's practical machinery.

A similar responsibility rests upon the entrepreneurs, of course. If they respond to an expansion of effective demand by an immediate marking up of prices, even when costs have not risen, then a wage increase becomes inevitable. Since it is unlikely that entrepreneurs will voluntarily refrain from exploiting a favourable market position, the introduction of price controls becomes necessary.

These considerations help to prove that a full-employment policy cannot safely rely on the validity of Keynes's formula but must resort to price and wage controls at an early stage. Wage policy is of particular importance because wages occupy a strategic position in the process of inflation. A cautious and restrained wage policy by the entrepreneurs and the trade unions themselves may therefore be able to forestall the necessity for wage controls.

[1] Joan Robinson, *Essays in the Theory of Employment* (1937) ; Alvin H. Hansen, *Monetary Theory and Fiscal Policy* (1949).

Chapter 7

WAGE RATES IN A MODEL OF THE SYSTEM

BY

WILHELM KRELLE
University of Heidelberg, Germany

In the analysis of the general wage level there are two problems which must be distinguished. The first is the determination of the money wage rate. Ordinarily there is a 'world of monopolies' in the labour market — trade unions, trade associations, and big companies — and the average money wage rate finally agreed upon by all parties to a wage dispute is a function of the prevailing aims of the trade unions, their relative financial and cohesive strength, the fixed cost burden of the economic sector in question, public support of either side, government intervention, and many other things. This is the special field of labour economists, and has been analysed by Professor Dunlop in his study of wage determination under trade unions.[1]

Given the money wage rate, the second problem arises: How will prices, production, employment, imports, exports, and therefore the real wage be determined as a function of the money wage rate? This is the problem which we will consider in this chapter.

I. The Model

Only a general interdependent system which shows the monetary flows as well as the real flows (i.e. determines prices and production) can possibly be expected to lead to an answer to this problem. Such a system is in general nonlinear, since the product of prices and production is very likely to appear in the equations. Furthermore, there is no general solution if, after the elimination of the other variables, the equation for the remaining one is higher than the third degree, although in all practical cases solutions for the special set of coefficients may be found. The calculation necessary in this procedure goes beyond the capacities of a single person. Thus we are confined to models with as few nonlinearities and variables as

[1] J. T. Dunlop, *Wage Determination under Trade Unions* (1944).

possible describing the basic economic facts in the simplest possible way. The model here proposed is a static one and contains directly or indirectly the money and commodity flows between firms, wage earners, capitalists, government, bank, and foreign countries. Unknown factors are the total level of activity or total output x and the price level p, which are both simultaneously determined by all the parameters of the functional relations between the different flows and by the money wage rate. This being accomplished, we easily demonstrate the effects of a change of the money wage rate on production, prices, real wage, distribution of income, and other magnitudes. Taken together with the theory of the money wage rate as given by Dunlop and others, this may perhaps constitute a useful wage theory.

Since all the results depend on whether the model is chosen so that all features of importance for our problem are depicted with reasonable accuracy, this section will elaborate on the model itself before we come to the application. The functional relationships assumed to exist between the flows mentioned above are the following: the first relation is the production function. Within a certain neighbourhood of 'normal' capacity $\bar{x}$ (for which plants are built) we may expect a linear approximation remaining within the range of the confidence limits of the function itself. Since we only intend to analyse the relations prevailing in this neighbourhood of $\bar{x}$ and exclude all bottleneck and slump phenomena, we assume the material input and labour input to be proportional to the output. The next relation shows the division of the total material input into imported goods and the home demand as a function of the relative price deviation $p_f \,.\, d - p/p$ at home and abroad, assuming a normal import of $\alpha = 1/3$ of the total derived demand (p means the price level at home, p_f the price level abroad, and d the exchange rate, units of own currency per unit of foreign currency). Whatever the import function, we always find a certain range around the point of exchange rate equilibrium $p_f \,.\, d = p$ where the import price elasticity y_i can be considered to be constant. The same applies to the exports with the export price elasticity y_f. As to the tax structure, we assume three kinds of taxes: constant taxes T_c, taxes dependent on the level of activity or special taxes T_s, and turnover taxes t_t. Total profits are considered as a function of production. Profits are defined in the Ricardian sense comprising all sorts of property income and entrepreneurial windfall profits. Since we are always in the framework of a static system, 'normal' profit gained at the capacity point $\bar{x}$ is equal to the 'normal' interest r on the invested physical capital k evaluated at the going price p. This leads to the term

rkp for the 'normal' profit. Assuming that profits vary proportional to the relative deviation of production from capacity, then $rkp\left(1+\frac{x-\bar{x}}{\bar{x}}\right)$ is the profit function. Monetary consumption of the wage earners is given by $a_2xwc_I(1-t_w)$. From total wage income a_2xw (w = monetary wage rate) there is a deduction for direct taxation (tax rate t_w) which may be considered to be proportional to the income in the neighbourhood of the equilibrium point. From what remains, the proportion c_I will be spent (usually $c_I<1$). As a matter of fact, this proportion depends on the price level, too, but we shall neglect this relationship. In our static context we are not confronted with business cycle phenomena ; consequently this simplification is tolerable.

For the capitalists a similar function applies. We shall call t_p the tax rate on profits and c_2+s_2 the consumption and investment coefficient of the profits. We shall usually assume $c_2+s_2>1$, that is, the entrepreneurs spend some or all or more than the money saved by the wage earners. Since we are in a static system, the effect of investment on the capital stock will be neglected. With given monetary demand, the real demand is simply assumed to be reciprocal to the price.

Now we may write the equation for the total real demand or total production as follows :

$$\text{(2a)}\quad \overbrace{(a_{11}+a_{12}k)\left[1-\alpha\left(1-\eta_i\frac{p_fd-p}{p}\right)\right]}^{\text{Internal material factor demand}}+\overbrace{\frac{c_Ia_2xw(1-t_w)}{p}}^{\text{Consumption demand of wage earners}}+$$

$$+\overbrace{\frac{(c_2+s_2)rkp\left(1+\eta\frac{x-\bar{x}}{\bar{x}}\right)(1-t_p)}{p}}^{\text{Consumption and investment demand of capitalists}}$$

$$+\overbrace{\frac{a_2xwt_w+rkp\left(1+\eta\frac{x-\bar{x}}{\bar{x}}\right)t_p+T_sx+t_tpx+T_c+D_g}{p}}^{\text{Government demand}}$$

$$+\overbrace{E_0\left(1+\eta_f\frac{p_fd-p}{p}\right)}^{\text{Export demand}}\qquad =x.$$

D_g means the monetary budget deficit ; the other notations have been explained earlier.

The equation determining the price level p (or we may say in analogy to the partial equilibrium analysis: the supply equation) becomes:

(3a)

$$\overbrace{(a_{11}+a_{12}k)\left[1-\alpha\left(1-\eta_i\frac{p_fd-p}{p}\right)\right]p}^{\text{Costs of internal material input}}+\overbrace{(a_{11}+a_{12}k)\alpha\left(1-\eta_i\frac{p_fd-p}{p}\right)p_fd}^{\text{Cost of imported material input}}$$

$$+\overbrace{a_2w}^{\text{Costs of labour input}}+\overbrace{t_tp+T_s+\frac{T_c}{x}}^{\text{Indirect taxes}}+\overbrace{\frac{rkp}{x}\left(1-\eta\frac{x-\bar{x}}{\bar{x}}\right)}^{\text{Profit margin}}=p.$$

This means simply that the price level is determined by the costs of production and the profit margin. To facilitate the computational work p is substituted for p_fd at the end of the second term of (3a). That amounts to assuming that the firms always calculate their costs on the basis of the prices of the home-made factor. The error introduced by this procedure is very small since we are only considering points in the neighbourhood of the equilibrium and the second term is absolutely small anyway. Gathering terms, substituting $c_1^*=c_1(1-t_w)+t_w$ and $c_2^*=(c_2+s_2)(1-t_p)+t_p$ and simplifying we get:

(2b)

$$x=\frac{rkc_2^*(1-\eta)+\dfrac{T_c+D_g}{p}+E_0\left(1+\eta_f\dfrac{p_fd-p}{p}\right)}{1-(a_{11}+a_{12}k)\left[1-\alpha\left(1-\eta_i\dfrac{p_fd-p}{p}\right)\right]-\dfrac{a_2wc_1^*}{p}-\dfrac{T_s}{p}-t_t-\eta\dfrac{rkc_2^*}{\bar{x}}}$$

and

(3b)

$$p=\frac{a_2w+T_s+\dfrac{T_c}{x}}{1-(a_{11}+a_{12}k)-t_t-\dfrac{rk}{x}\left(1+\eta\dfrac{x-\bar{x}}{x}\right)}.$$

(2a) or (2b) gives the real demand x as a function of the price level p and the wage level w and other economic parameters. (3a) or (3b) gives the price level as a function of the total production x, the wage level w, and other economic parameters. Considering the inverse function, (3a) or (3b) determines the production as a function of the price level, the wage rate, and other parameters. It therefore may be taken as some sort of supply function.

Thus we have two quadratic equations in the two unknowns x and p. They are represented in Figs. 1 and 2 for stable exchange rates, different values of η and the values of the parameters listed below.[1] Their point of intersection P determines the solution of the system. We see that both 'demand' and 'supply' may rise or fall according to the value of η. For high production elasticities of profits we get both curves rising, for low values of η we get both

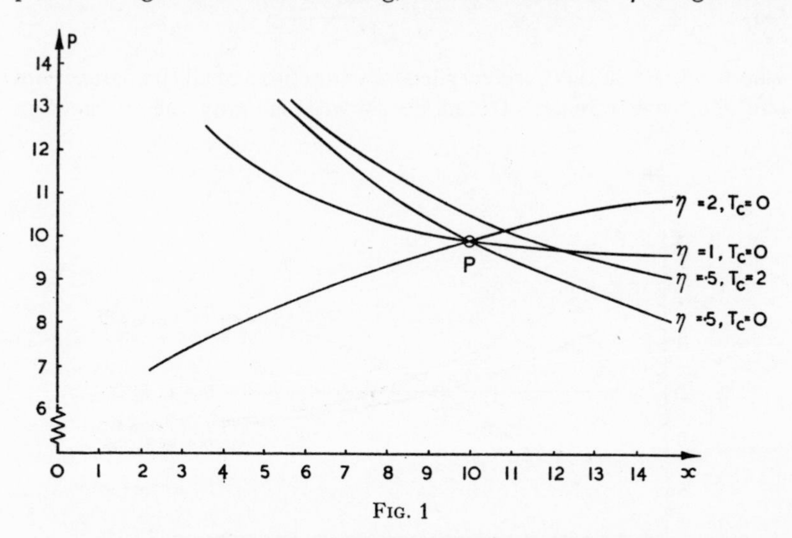

Fig. 1

curves falling. In either case it can be shown that the stability conditions are fulfilled. The shape of these curves, however, is without interest to us. We are only concerned with the equilibrium point P and its shifts for changing money wages w at different sets

[1] Values of the parameters (fitted roughly to a European type of economy):
$\bar{x} = 10$ production capacity (in units of output per year).
$k = 30$ capital stock (in units of output).
$w = 10$ monetary wage rate.
$a_{11} = 0{\cdot}15$ material input coefficient for raw material.
$a_{12} = 0{\cdot}005$ material input coefficient for reinvestment.
$a_2 = 0{\cdot}4$ labour input coefficient.
$r = 0{\cdot}0666$ 'normal' profit rate (if actual production equals capacity).
$t_t = 0{\cdot}05$ turnover tax rate.
$T_s = 0{\cdot}5$ special tax (= production tax per unit of output).
$t_w = 0{\cdot}1$ tax rate on wages.
$t_p = 0{\cdot}2$ tax rate on profits.
$c_1 = 0{\cdot}9$ consumption coefficient of wages.
$c_2 + s_2 = 1{\cdot}225$ consumption and investment coefficient of profits.
$\eta_f = 1{\cdot}111$ price elasticity of exports.
$E_0 = 1$ 'normal' export demand in units of output (if world market prices equal internal prices at the going exchange rate).
$\alpha = 0{\cdot}333$ 'normal' production of material input to be imported (if world market prices equal internal prices at the going exchange rate).
$\eta_i = 0{\cdot}5$ price elasticity of imports.
$p_f . d = 10$ price level of the world market in own currency (at the current exchange rate).

of parameters. Therefore we need the analytical expression for P, i.e. the solution of the system (2a), (3a) respectively (2b), (3b). It is obtained by the general elimination method[1] and leads to an expression for x of the shape.

(4a) $$x = \frac{-B^* \pm \sqrt{B^{*2} - 4A^*C^*}}{2A^*}$$

where A^*, B^*, and C^* are very lengthy functions of all the parameters and the wage rate w. It can be shown that only the minus sign

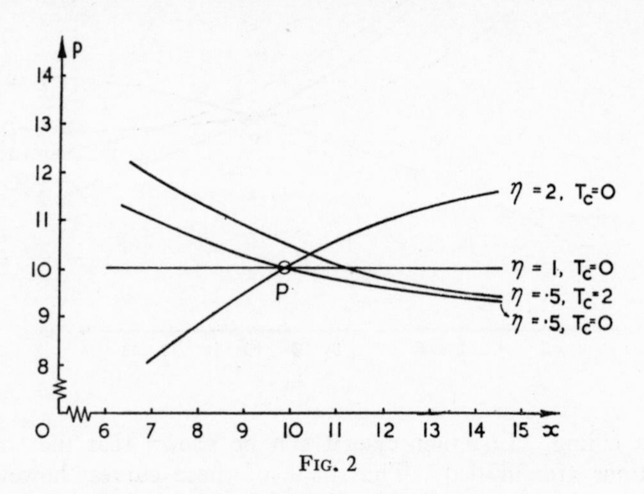

Fig. 2

before the root expression has an economic meaning in the context of our system. We can simplify (4a) substantially by assuming $\eta = 1$ and $T_c = 0$ which gives $C^* = 0$ and further substantial simplifications within the expressions for A^* and B^*, thus rendering (4a) to

(4b) $$x = -\frac{B^*}{A^*} = \frac{AT^{\cdot} - BE_0(\eta_f - 1)}{BC^{\cdot} - AD^{\cdot}},$$

with
$$A = 1 - (a_{11} + a_{12}k) - t_t - \frac{rk}{\bar{x}},$$
$$B = a_2 w + T_s,$$
$$C^{\cdot} = 1 - (a_{11} + a_{12}k)[1 - \alpha(1 + \eta_i)] - t_t - \frac{rk}{\bar{x}} c_2^*,$$
$$D^{\cdot} = (a_{11} + a_{12}k)\alpha\eta_i p_f d + a_2 W C_1^* + T_s,$$
$$T^{\cdot} = \underbrace{T_c}_{=0} + D_g + E_0 \eta_f p_f d,$$

[1] See Van der Waerden, *Modern Algebra* (1931), part 2, ch. i.

(4b) is the solution of the system (2a), (3a) for stable exchange rates. For a flexible exchange rate ($p_f d = p$ always) and for the same assumptions $\eta = 1$ and $T_c = 0$ the solution is

$$x = \frac{AT - BE_0}{BC - AD} \tag{4c}$$

with A and B as above,

$$C = 1 - (a_{11} + a_{12}k)(1 - \alpha) - t_t - \frac{rk}{\bar{x}} c_2^*,$$

$$D = a_2 W C_1^* + T_s,$$

$$T = \underbrace{T_c}_{=0} + D_g,$$

The system behaves differently according to whether we keep the exchange rate constant or not. The solution for p may be obtained by substituting (4c) or (4b) into (3b) with $\eta = 1$ and $T_c = 0$ there. The simplifications which led to the more agreeable terms (4c) and (4b) above render p independent of x. Of course, for $\eta > 1$ prices would rise with $x > \bar{x}$; for $\eta < 1$ prices would fall in the same case. The influence of T_c is not very important if T_c stays within reasonable limits (Fig. 2). So we have to bear in mind that all following propositions are only valid for $\eta = 1$ and must be modified in the sense mentioned above if $\eta \neq 1$. This is the general set-up and we now may proceed to our wage problem.

II. Production and Employment as a Function of the Money Wage Rate

The first question to be considered is how changes in the money wage rate influence production and therefore employment. In a general interdependent system, in contrast to partial equilibrium, it is not at all certain that higher wages reduce employment. We get the exact answer by considering the partial derivatives of (4c) and (4b). In the case of a fixed exchange rate in (4b) the change of production induced by a change in the wage rate is given by:

$$\frac{\partial x}{\partial w} = \frac{1}{N_1^2} a_2 A \{E_0(\eta_f - 1)[T_s(1 - c_1^*) + (a_{11} + a_{12}k)\alpha \eta_i p_f d] + T^{\cdot}[A c_1^* + C^{\cdot}]\} \tag{5a}$$

where N_1 means the denominator of (4b). It is seen at once that $\partial x / \partial w$ may be zero, e.g. for $\eta_f = 1$ and $T^{\cdot} = 0$, but also in several other special combinations of the parameter values, and that $\frac{\partial x}{\partial w}$ may have either sign for other combinations.

In the case of flexible exchange rates, the partial derivative of (4c) with respect to w is :

$$\frac{\partial x}{\partial w} = \frac{1}{N_2^2} a_2 A E_0 T_s (c_1{}^* - 1) \tag{5b}$$

where N_2 means the denominator of (4c).

Now $\partial x/\partial w$ is much more likely to vanish. It becomes zero for $T_s = 0$ (i.e. if there are no taxes proportional to the level of activity) or for $c_1{}^* = 1$ (i.e. when the wage earners consume all their income). According to $c_1{}^* \gtrless 1$ (5b) may have either sign.

Some rules which may be derived by analysing (4b), (4c), (5a), (5b) are :

(1) With fixed exchange rates and in the case of elastic export demand and inelastic import demand (the values of the parameters in footnote 1, p. 95) there is a strong negative relation between the wage rate and employment. Employment is the more sensitive to changes in wages, the higher the consumption coefficients of wage earners and capitalists (see Fig. 3, calculated from (4b) and (4c)). Increases in wages raise the price level (see (3b)), and this reduces the exports and enlarges the imports, a process with repercussions far greater than the change in exports and imports itself. This is well known from the theory of the foreign trade multiplier.

(2) With flexible exchange rates, exports and imports are not touched by changes in the wage level. Employment is far less sensitive to the wage level (see Fig. 3). The smaller the consumption coefficient c_1 of the wage earners, the more employment is reduced by rising wages. For $c_1 > 1$ there is a rising employment wage curve : the higher the wages, the higher the employment. This would render a 'classical' labour market unstable. But this is no argument against extending the analysis into this field since there are no longer classical labour markets. With higher consumption and investment coefficient c_2 of the capitalists, the opposite influence arises : the wage employment function becomes more and more sensitive and negatively inclined to changes in wages.

(3) How will the above result be influenced by changing the assumptions about export and import price elasticities ? An analysis of (4b) and (4c) shows that rising export price elasticities very soon lead to substantial reactions of employment to changes in the wage level. Even in the case of zero export price elasticities, a negative dependence of employment on wages remains (because of the

unchanged import price elasticity). Only the case of flexible exchange rates leads to a negligible but still negative reaction of employment. The same result applies for changes in import price elasticities.

(4) Has the tax structure some bearing on the wage employment function? (4b) and (4c) lead to the conclusion that with stable

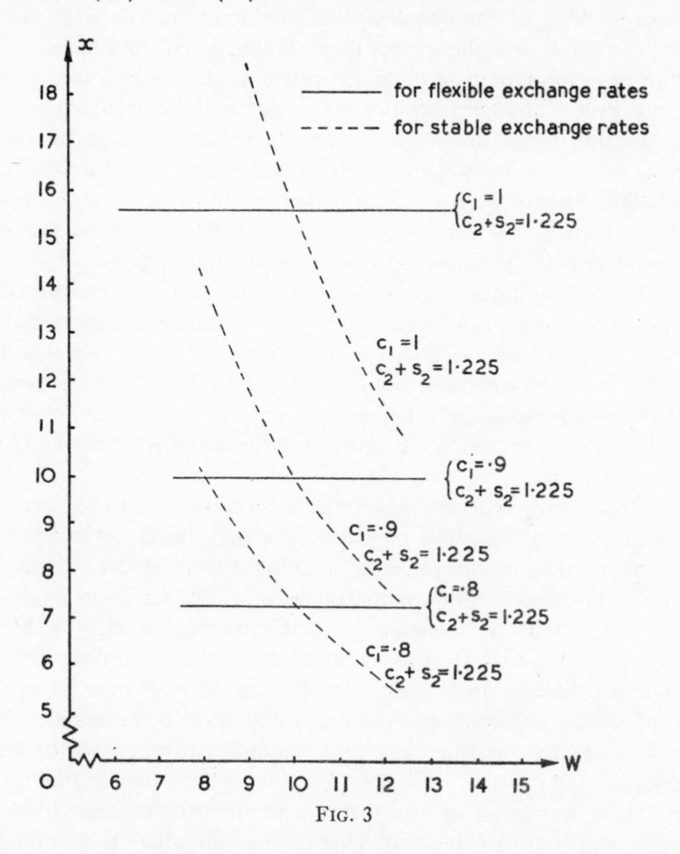

FIG. 3

exchange rates rising, production taxes T_s and rising turnover taxes t_t lead to absolute less employment without changing the sensitiveness of employment to wages in an important way. This conclusion follows from the fact that indirect taxes raise price by the same amount and influence exports and imports adversely.

(5) With flexible exchange rates, both higher production and higher turnover taxes lead to higher employment. But higher production taxes make employment more sensitive to changes in the wage level, and higher turnover taxes make employment less

sensitive. No common-sense explanation for this result is readily apparent. The main difference between the two taxes is that a higher turnover tax leads to higher prices, which in turn raise the tax burden. This is not the case with a tax proportional to the level of activity.

(6) Higher taxes on wage income lead to higher employment in any case, as long as the consumption coefficient of the wage earners is smaller than 1 and the government disburses all its income. The reaction of employment to changes in the wage rate becomes slightly more sensitive. The same applies in the case of flexible exchange rates.

(7) Higher taxes on profit income have just the opposite effect as long as the consumption and investment coefficient of the capitalists is greater than 1. A substitution of a tax on wage income by a tax on profit income to any degree whatsoever must therefore tend to decreased employment under these assumptions.

(8) Increasing budget deficits raise employment in either case. The advantageous employment effect is perhaps exaggerated by (4b) and (4c) because of the assumptions $\eta = 1$ and $c_1 = 0{\cdot}9$. This leads to a high government deficit multiplier dx/dD_g of between 11 and 9 for fixed exchange rates and 15 and 11 for flexible exchange rates, depending on the wage level and the absolute amount of the government deficit.

(9) The 'going' interest rate r which is considered to be necessary to keep the capital invested by capitalists may be changed by trade union actions or governmental or sociological influences. How will this effect the wage employment function ? We see from analysing (4b) and (4c) that in the case of stable exchange rates a higher interest rate leads to less employment and renders employment less sensitive to changes in wages. With flexible exchange rates, the effect of rising interest rates on employment is reversed. The rising sensitiveness to the wage rate remains, although the absolute sensitivity is very small. This is due to the fact that higher profit income leads to higher consumption and investment, and the consumption and investment coefficient of the capitalists is assumed to be greater than 1.

III. Prices as a Function of the Money Wage Rate

Prices as well as production are a function of the wage rate. (3b) gives the relation. We see that for $T_s = T_c = 0$ prices rise by the same proportion as wages; for $T_s > 0$ less than proportional. The influence of the other parameters is easily seen from (3b).

IV. The Real Wage Rate as a Function of the Money Wage Rate

Since prices are a function of the money wage rate, it is possible to compute the real wage as a function of the money wage. A rise in money wages always leads to a rise in real wages as long as there are taxes proportional to the level of activity. For $T_s = 0$ the real wage is independent of the money wage. The real wage goes down absolutely with rising taxes and rising interest rates, of course.

In interpreting this result, one should remember that total production is also influenced by a change in the money wage rate. The real wage does not contain this influence. It only gives the real wage rate of the employed worker and this always rises (with the exception of $T_s = 0$) with higher money wages. Total social product may decline, of course, according to the results in section II.

V. Full Employment Money Wage Rates

As explained in section II, employment is a function of the money wage rate (among others). Now assume that some sort of automatic functioning of the labour market or the deliberate policy of the trade unions or of other agencies influencing the money wage rate tend to equilibrate the wage rate just at the point of full employment. How will this rate change with changing consumption and investment coefficients of wage and profit earners, import and export elasticities, interest rates and the tax structure ? We may answer this question by solving (4b) and (4c) for w. Denoting the production which gives full employment by x_0 and the corresponding wage rate by w_{x_0} we get for fixed exchange rates

(6a)
$$w_{x_0} = \frac{AE^{\cdot} - T_s L^{\cdot}}{a_2 G^{\cdot}}$$

with
$$E^{\cdot} = T^{\cdot} + x_0[T_s + (a_{11} + a_{12}k)\alpha \, . \, \eta_i p_f d],$$
$$L^{\cdot} = C^{\cdot} x_0 + E_0(\eta_f - 1),$$
$$G^{\cdot} = E_0(\eta_f - 1) + x_0(C^{\cdot} - Ac_{\mathrm{I}}^*) = L^{\cdot} - x_0 C_{\mathrm{I}}^* A,$$

and $T^{\cdot}$, A, $C^{\cdot}$ as in formula (4b).

The formula for flexible exchange rates is

(6b)
$$W_{x_0} = \frac{AT + T_s(x_0 A + E_0 - x_0 C)}{-a_2(x_0 c_{\mathrm{I}}^* A + E_0 - x_0 C)}.$$

The abbreviations are used as in formula (4c).

The following propositions are verbal expressions of certain properties of (6a) and (6b).

(1) The full employment or equilibrium wage rate changes with different consumption and investment propensities c_1^* and c_2^*. In the case of fixed exchange rates the equilibrium wage rate rises with rising consumption and investment coefficients of both wage and profit earners, but more by far with rising consumption coefficients of the wage earners. High consumption of the labour force therefore leads to higher equilibrium wages. In the case of flexible exchange rates the sensitivity of the equilibrium wage rate to changes in the consumption and investment coefficients is very much greater. The effect of a rising consumption coefficient of wage earners is also much larger than that of a rising consumption and investment coefficient of capitalists.

(2) What happens to the equilibrium wage rate when the interest rate r changes? That depends mainly on the values of the consumption and investment coefficients and the import and export elasticities, at least in the case of stable exchange rates. *WW* in Fig. 4 represents (6a) for the values of the parameters given in footnote 1, p. 95. The equilibrium wage rate declines with rising interest rate. But this is reversed when the consumption and investment coefficient of the capitalists is higher (curve *W′*W′), and it is also reversed when the price elasticity of exports and imports is lower. Thus, we really have to know the actual values of the parameters in question fairly well before making any propositions in this case. But for flexible exchange rates (W^*W^* in Fig. 4) the case is unambiguous: a higher interest rate leads to a higher equilibrium wage rate. This is the consequence of our making $c_2+s_2>1$ and $c_1<1$: the greater the profit income the more investment demand appears; the higher therefore the wage rate has to be to reduce the labour demand to the equilibrium point. It does not follow now that a higher money wage rate means a higher real wage rate, as in the case of section IV, because now the interest rate is not constant and prices rise more than proportional to the wage rate. It can be shown that in our case the real wage usually falls with rising money wage and rising interest rate. This result is certain in the case of stable exchange rates.

(3) The equilibrium wage rate is also influenced by the tax structure. From (6a) it follows that for a fixed exchange rate the equilibrium wage rate falls with rising turnover tax rates. Higher consumption and investment coefficients lead to somewhat higher sensitivity of the equilibrium wage rate to changes in the turnover tax and, of course, to an absolute higher level of the equilibrium

wage. For a flexible exchange rate, the behaviour is quite the opposite : a higher turnover tax leads to a higher equilibrium wage rate. This curve moves upward for higher consumption and investment coefficients and coincides with the curve of equal real wage so that the real wage rate remains constant. The effect of changing the special tax T_s (proportional to the level of activity) is quali-

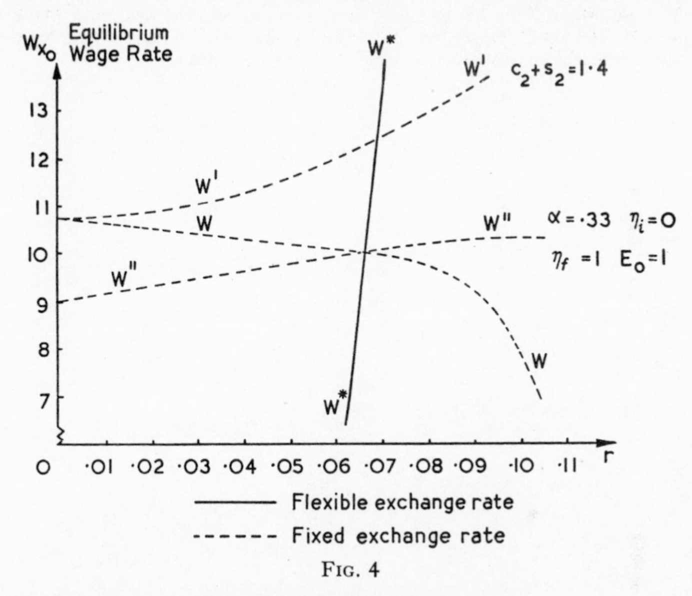

Fig. 4

tatively different at fixed and flexible exchange rates : in the former case the equilibrium wage rate rises with higher T_s; in the latter case it declines.

The model has not been fully explored by the preceding analysis. The calculation of the balance of trade as a function of the money wage rate leads to interesting results ; the conditions for the compatibility of external and internal equilibrium are to be analysed ; or values of the parameters should be calculated which maximize the real income per head of the population (not only the real income of the employed workers). The effects of dropping the assumptions $\eta=1$ and $T_c=0$ have to be studied quantitively. Then one has to go into the difficult business of finding out econometrically the possible range of the relevant parameters for an economy. And, finally, the model has to be made dynamic. But this is a programme for the future. For the time being we may conclude by stating that given the money wage and technology, the real wage, employment or production, exports and imports and prices depend in the way demonstrated above on the 'going' interest rate, the tax structure, the budget deficit, the consumption and investment coefficients, the elasticities, and absolute amounts of imports and exports, and the profit elasticities.[1]

[1] After this paper was written, my attention was drawn to the excellent article of D. B. J. Schouten, 'The Wage Level, Employment, and the Economic Structure', *International Economic Papers*, no. 2 (1952), pp. 221-232. Using a simpler model, he reaches some of the conclusions above in an easier way.

PART III

THE IMPACT OF THE LABOUR UNION

Chapter 8

TRADE UNION BEHAVIOUR AND WAGE DETERMINATION IN GREAT BRITAIN

BY

B. C. ROBERTS

London School of Economics, London, England

ECONOMISTS have sought to fit a trade union into the framework of economic analysis by considering it as a form of institution analogous to the firm. They have assumed it to be a monopolistic seller of labour seeking to maximize the incomes of its total membership. This view of a trade union has been severely assailed by Professor Ross [1] on the grounds that it bears little relation to reality. The central proposition of the Californian School is that a trade union is a political institution dominated by the primary motive of survival and operating in an economic environment. Formally its objectives are to maximize the economic welfare of its members, but the attainment of these objectives will be constantly modified by institutional necessities, so that it cannot be assumed that a union will behave automatically in the same manner as a business enterprise whose primary object is to maximize profit.

Professor Dunlop has countered these criticial views with a firm adherence to the economist's model of the union as an income-maximizing institution. He rejects the 'tendency to see political elements as dominant in wage determination' since that represents a 'preoccupation with the very short run to the exclusion of more persistent factors'.[2] There is no denying, he admits, that wage fixing under collective bargaining is different from wage determination when unions do not exist, but the emphasis on political wage setting has given the impression that there can be no economically rational wage policy under collective bargaining.

The distinction between behaviour that is political and behaviour that is economic is quite often difficult to draw. That is to say almost all political decisions have economic consequences and all economic decisions have political consequences. Therefore, the Ross-Dunlop conflict is to some extent a question of which word is

[1] Arthur M. Ross, *Trade Union Wage Policy* (1948).

[2] John T. Dunlop, *Wage Determination under Trade Unionism* (1944).

placed first. A trade union might be described as a political institution operating in an economic environment, or as an economic institution operating in a political environment. The real problem would seem to be to decide which are the most important factors affecting the behaviour of trade unions. Are they, as Ross is apparently asserting, mainly those which arise out of the institutional requirements of a union, or are they mainly those which arise from a rational economic calculation of what will maximize the income of their members ?

An examination of the objects, organization, and behaviour of British trade unions in the post-war years may throw some light on these questions.

I. Objects and Structure of Unions

The objects of British trade unions are both economic and political. The primary aim of the unions is to improve the wages and working conditions of their members, and to reform society by securing political change. These two objectives are closely connected and cannot easily be separated. Though the unions have supported socialistic policies on ideological grounds, political change has often been sought for the purpose of enabling the unions to protect or advance the vocational interests of their members. On the other hand, the economic policies of the unions have been influenced by their political interests.

A union composed of craftsmen will naturally be concerned in the first instance with the protection and welfare of craftsmen. The sectional interest of a trade unionist, however, extends from that which he has in common with a fellow worker of the same skill, craft, grade, department, and firm to the sectional interest of the working class as a whole. At one end of the scale unions exist in Britain based on a handful of workers in a particular firm. Such is the National Amalgamated Association of Nut and Bolt Makers with a membership of thirty. At the other end of the scale is the giant Transport and General Workers Union with 1,300,000 members in over 200 industries. At least seven different types of union can be distinguished ; single craft, multicraft, diluted-craft, industrial, general, occupational, and professional. Very few unions have a complete organizing jurisdiction over the field of membership which they claim. They differ widely in their constitutional forms ; probably not one of the 704 trade unions which exist in Britain has a constitution precisely the same as that of another. Each union has its own unique characteristics, and its behaviour pattern reflects the traditions, method of organization, and particular type of workers it organizes.

The unions have developed formal and informal functional federations which bind diverse types of unions together for the purpose of collective bargaining which is now conducted on a multi-union, industry-wide basis. At a higher level, about 85 per cent of the total trade union membership is in organizations affiliated to the Trades Union Congress, and nearly 60 per cent is affiliated to the Labour Party. Formally the T.U.C. has only limited powers, but in practice it acts as a union of the unions in relation to government on matters of wider economic, social, and political importance and its policies carry great weight with the unions. The institutional development of the unions has thus been conditioned by the economic and political ends they have sought to achieve.

II. The Power of Leaders and the Rank and File

These developments have tended to strengthen the authority of the national leaders. The actual power of union leaders to take effective decisions, however, varies a good deal. There is, for example, an immense difference in the amount of authority enjoyed by the national officers and executive council of the Amalgamated Engineers and their counterparts in the Iron and Steel Trades Union. In the Engineers the executive authority is relatively weak and is subject to the control of a rank and file national committee which exerts its constitutional authority to the full. In the Steelworkers, on the other hand, the executive council has plenary powers. It may arrive at decisions and agreements with employers which are subject to no further formal check, since this union holds no national conference. Its rules specifically state that any agreement made by the representatives of the union is absolutely binding upon the members.

In general, however, most unions fall between these two extremes, and it would be true to say that, while there is little direct check upon leaders during the course of negotiations, they must be able to carry with them the support of the active lower level leadership ; they must be able to persuade the rank and file delegates at conferences to support their policies ; and they must be able to secure the votes of members in referendums and elections for office. The British trade union leader of today considers himself to be a responsible industrial statesman : his status is assured and he is ready to accept responsibility with pride.

Whichever party is in power, the trade unions are consulted about every measure that affects them. They are represented on no fewer than sixty governmental committees [1] and have access to ministers at almost any time they desire. Although the unions generally have accepted the responsibility which has flowed from the vast increase in their power and influence, these attitudes are not accepted by all trade union leaders. Communists, for example, seem to despise the attitude of responsibility and attempt to destroy it by appealing to the sectional interests within the unions. Differences in political ideology and the struggle for control of the unions, therefore, to some extent enter into policy making. But it is, of course, not only Communists who are critical of the policies of the national leaders. Conflicts exist also between the different functional levels of union leadership: shop stewards and local leaders are naturally primarily concerned with matters which affect their sphere of interest, while national leaders must take into account the interests of the union as a whole, the interests of the trade union movement as a whole, and indeed be concerned with the impact of union policies on the nation as a whole. However, while there is a gulf between the sophisticated arguments that trade union leaders nowadays use when explaining their policy and the opinions of many of the active rank and file, it is not so wide as sometimes appears.

Though the lower level leaders see in general outline the problems to which wage claims may give rise, this does not prevent them from demanding wage increases which exceed what could reasonably be granted without serious economic repercussions. The attitude of trade unionists tends, therefore, to be ambivalent; they think about wage claims at two levels and show an extreme reluctance to relate the general proposition to the specific case in which they are involved. The nature of wage claims made by a union is therefore determined by institutional and economic factors. Quite frequently the hands of the senior officers have been tied by a resolution passed at a delegate conference. In recent years the leaders of the Engineers and other unions have bluntly told their conferences that the amount the delegates were asking was unrealistic, but were unable to persuade the conferences to leave the amount of the claim to be decided upon by the National Executive Committee. In many cases, therefore, the claim made by a union has been the expression of political opposition to the leadership rather than a serious reflection of what might be expected. In the case of the claim made by the Confederation of Shipbuilding and Engineering

[1] Sir Vincent Tewson, *Trades Union Congress Annual Report, 1950*.

Unions for an increase of £2 per week in 1952, it was openly admitted that the object was to make the maximum political capital out of the reluctance of the established leadership and to precipitate industrial conflict if the claim was rejected.

Not all unions pursue the kind of policies characteristic of the Engineers, the Electrical Trades Union, and others in which the Communists exercise a good deal of influence at the shop-steward level, but most of them pitch their claims far in advance of what they expect to achieve. This is done partly for bargaining reasons, but probably mainly because a wage claim expresses all the antagonisms and frustrations felt by the workers about the industrial system of which they are a part. Whatever the level of the claim, it will have the support of the members, but when they know that the amount for which they are asking is ill-founded — as they usually do when claims are excessive — they cannot easily be persuaded to back it by a display of force. The actual settlements, therefore, often bear little relationship to the amounts at first demanded.

A sample of 430 wage claims in 1948 examined by Peacock and Ryan showed that 'in 1948 the workers received on the average about one-half of what they claimed ; in 1949 this had fallen to about 40 per cent. During 1950 and the first nine months of 1951, however, the settlements were on the average 70 per cent of claims. In recent years claims have tended to be larger and settlements lower.' [1]

It is, therefore, necessary to distinguish between the amount that is claimed by a union and the level at which it is prepared to settle. Whilst trade union leaders often have to put forward claims which they know will not succeed, their freedom to settle is in fact considerable, though they cannot entirely ignore the feelings of the active members of the rank and file without facing the danger of a revolt.

Thus the structure of a union, the power of the leaders, the force of opposition, the effectiveness of communication with the rank and file, all play a significant part in determining the attitude of a union towards the wages question.

III. Wage Restraint

The influence of general political and economic factors on the behaviour of the unions was clearly demonstrated between 1948 and 1950. The unions then accepted a policy of wage restraint

[1] Alan T. Peacock and W. J. L. Ryan, 'Wage Claims and the Pace of Inflation', *Economic Journal* (June 1953), pp. 385-392.

because they realized that the nation faced the immediate danger of rapid inflation and a balance of payments crisis. The Labour Government was in office and the unions did not wish to render impossible its task of restoring the nation's economic prosperity. The policy of wage restraint was, however, only accepted on the basis of an undertaking by the government to try to prevent prices and profits from rising. The policy proposed by the government was not a rigid wage freeze — though it was often described as such — but it permitted increases so long as they satisfied certain conditions. The entire policy was voluntary and was not imposed on the unions, nor were there any legal or administrative sections to enforce it.

The General Council of the Trades Union Congress felt unable to accept the government's policy on behalf of the trade union movement on its own authority. It therefore called a meeting of representatives of the executives of all the affiliated unions and recommended to them that the policy should be endorsed by the trade union movement. The General Council emphasized that its policy was designed to maintain real wages ; 'what matters most is not the size of the wage but what the wage will buy'.[1] Not every union was convinced, but the view of the General Council was upheld after a prolonged debate. Its *Report* was approved by 5,421,000 and opposed by 2,032,000 — a majority of 3,389,000. This procedure of the General Council throws light on its powers over the affiliated unions ; these are mainly persuasive and fall a good way short of the power enjoyed by the central bodies of the Scandinavian trade union organizations.

The upward movement of wage rates was slowed down by the policy of restraint, and the pace of price increases was slowed by subsidies and price control until the Korean War and the devaluation of 1949 began to make themselves felt in mid-1950. Although 95 per cent of public companies maintained their dividends at the level they had been at the inception of the government's policy, much was made out of the fact that gross profits, and hence reserves, had increased. The unions by this time were chafing at the check which acceptance of this policy had imposed upon them, and it came as no great surprise when at the meeting of the Trades Union Congress in September 1950 the wage restraint policy was defeated. It might be said that abandonment of wage restraint was the result of the unions' economic interests reasserting themselves over their political interests. However, having voted for the end of wage

[1] Trades Union Congress, *Report of Proceedings* (March 27, 1948), pp. 43-53.

restraint, congress then voted to continue the prohibition on strikes which had existed since 1940, and it was not until the following year that this was abolished.

The immediate result of the abandonment of the wage restraint policy was a considerable increase in both the number and size of wage demands, but the leaders of the General Council of the T.U.C. still continued to stress the need for restraint and responsibility, and the lifting of the prohibition on striking did not lead to any significant increase in the willingness to strike.

IV. Willingness to Strike

The reluctance of the unions to use the strike as a means of enforcing wage demands is a marked feature of the rise in their status. It is not a new development, but stems back to the 1920's when the changes occurred which led to the unions changing their attitude towards the national strike.[1] There has in fact been no national industrial stoppage in Britain since 1932, although there have been threats of a national railway strike on at least two occasions. The unions have not abandoned the strike, but as Sir Walter Citrine said in a remarkably prescient address in 1929, 'The very magnitude of strikes will compel a change in strike policy. A trade union body cannot bring out two million men with the same light heart as it might bring out fifty men.'[2]

If British unions were to use their power to its full extent it would tend to jeopardise, if not destroy, the position which they have attained. When Ernest Bevin set out to create a big union and to build up the power of the T.U.C., he did so because he believed that powerful unionism would make strikes unnecessary. Of course, Bevin was too intelligent to fail to see that power alone would not bring about the results he desired. When he was at the Ministry of Labour he developed an atmosphere of tripartite co-operation between labour, industry, and the government and consolidated the developments which had already been under way for more than a decade.

During the past fifteen years unions have grown used to the idea that, rather than resort to a strike, they should either go to arbitration or accept the intervention of the Ministry of Labour as an impartial conciliator and investigator. All the efforts of the

[1] Hugh Clegg, *Some Consequences of the General Strike* (January 1954).
[2] Sir Walter Citrine, *The Future of Trade Unionism* (1929).

politically inspired opponents of these developments to persuade the unions to readopt a policy of militant strike activity have failed and are to continue to fail so long as there is no significant change in the status of the unions.

The following table shows the number of work people who received net increases in weekly wages, and the net amount of increase in weekly wage rates at the end of each post-war year, and the number of man days lost through strikes beginning in that year.

TABLE 1

WAGE INCREASES AND DAYS LOST IN STRIKES
1945–1953

Year	Number of Individuals (000s)	Estimated Net Weekly Amount of Increase in Wage Rates (£000s)	Aggregate Number of Working Days Lost in Stoppages (000s)
1945	7,303	1806	2827
1946	7,908	2901	2138
1947	4,973	1735	2389
1948	7,757	1898	1935
1949	5,206	1076	1805
1950	7,414	2046	1375
1951	12,262	6570	1687
1952	11,484	4456	1769
1953	8,937	2398	2142

Source : *Ministry of Labour Gazette.*

There is no significant relationship between the number of working days lost and the amount of increase in weekly wage rates during this period. The vast majority of strikes were primarily concerned with 'frictional' issues, and up to 1951 most of them were unofficial, that is to say they were not calculated acts of union policy, but in many cases ran directly counter to it.[1]

V. INFLUENCE OF THE COST OF LIVING

While the rise in the status of the unions and a broader understanding of the general economic problems which faced the nation made it possible for the unions to pursue a policy of wage restraint, there is little doubt that the continuous rise in the cost of living tugged them in the opposite direction and stimulated wage demands.

[1] See K. G. J. C. Knowles, *Strikes : A Study in Industrial Conflict* (1952).

Practically every wage claim that has been made has stressed this factor.[1] Statistics of price and wage movements have been bandied about and there has been a great deal of confused argument about the accuracy of the Interim Retail Price Index. The unions have sought to show that wage earners' real incomes have fallen and that higher profits have meant a redistribution of income in favour of employers. The actual movement of retail prices and wage rates and earnings in money and real terms, since 1938, is given in Table 2.

The principal aim of the unions after 1950 was to restore the fall in real wage rates which they had suffered during the wage

TABLE 2

RETAIL PRICES, WAGE RATES AND EARNINGS
1938–1953

Year	Retail Prices	Wage Rates		Earnings	
		Money	Real	Money	Real
1938	100	100	100	100	100
1947	161	170	106	198	123
1948	175	178	102	217	124
1949	180	183	101	226	125
1950	185	187	101	237	128
1951	202	202	100	260	129
1952	221	219	99	281	127
1953	227	229	101	301	133

Sources: Retail prices — *London and Cambridge Economic Service Bulletin*. Earnings — Bowley, *L.C.E.S. Bulletin Special Memorandum*, No. 50, Table B. *Ministry of Labour Gazette*. Wage Rates — *London and Cambridge Economic Service Bulletin*.

restraint period. It might well be argued that the larger increases in wage rates secured in 1951 contributed to the substantial price increases of that year and the next, and that the unions were, therefore, acting irrationally and would have been wiser to have continued the policy of wage restraint. The reply of the unions to this argument was that prices would not have moved up so sharply had employers been prepared to cut rising profits, and that if employers refused to do this themselves then it was the responsibility of the government to control prices directly. When the government failed to do this, the unions held it responsible for the rise in prices, forgetting the effect of their own wage policies.

Peacock and Ryan were not in fact able to discover any 'significant lagged or unlagged correlation either with the actual changes or with

[1] Peacock and Ryan, 'Wage Claims'.

the rate of change in the Interim Index during previous months'. 'But', as they say, 'this does not sever the nexus between cost-of-living changes and the timing of wage demands, for institutional factors are here of prime importance.'

VI. The Spread between Wage Rates and Earnings

The nationally negotiated straight time wage rates have very little meaning to many workers. A small sample of workers indicated that they often only had a hazy notion of the basic wage rate which had been established by collective bargaining at the national level. What they were very clear about was the amount which they usually had in their pay packets and they had an average level of expectations of what they ought to receive. In order to maintain their labour force, or to increase it, many employers have been willing to pay above the agreed rates, to allow incentive schemes to produce larger earnings than strictly necessary to satisfy agreements, to give merit bonus awards, to work more overtime and week-end shifts than was essential, with the result that actual total earnings in manufacturing industry, docks, mines, and sections of transport are far above the collectively agreed upon basic wage rates. There are, of course, considerable differences between different plants in the same industry and different occupations. At one extreme it is not uncommon to find workers receiving more than 100 per cent above their basic rate, and at the other extreme there are considerable numbers of workers who take home no more than their basic wage rate.

The fact that there are these wide differences has some effect on union demands and union bargaining. The low incomes of some workers and the wide difference in earnings opportunities induce discontent and pressure for higher incomes ; this usually takes the form of a demand by the union for an increase in the basic wage rate, which, if successful, then generates further changes throughout the earnings structure. However, when earnings are high compared with basic wage rates, it is not easy to persuade workers that they should cease work in order to secure an increase. Recent strike ballots in the engineering and building industries, when the membership of the unions rejected proposals that a demand for higher wages should be supported by strikes, were certainly strongly affected by the feeling among the workers that they had more to lose than to gain by a stoppage of work. There is a strong desire on the part of many union leaders to consolidate the earnings differential into the wage rate and thus close the spread, but since neither workers nor employers are prepared to give up the advantages which they enjoy under the present arrangements, the differential between wage rates and actual earnings continues to be wide.

Before the war, the gap between wage rates and earnings was relatively narrow, but war-time economic conditions, post-war inflationary pressures, and high levels of employment opened it wide. Since wage rates are usually determined by national negotiations or by a statutory award covering an entire industry, they are likely to be fixed at about the level which the average firm can pay. There is, therefore, considerable scope for local bargaining and for employers wishing to attract labour to push up the earnings structure. This situation is made possible by the level of profits the economic policy of the government permits. That is to say, if, as a result of the government's pursuit of an inflationary budgetary and financial policy, the level of business earnings is high, employers will be ready to increase wages. It does not follow, however, that because employers will be prepared to push wages up under inflationary conditions they will be willing to do this by a nationally negotiated industry-wide collective agreement. They will, of course, make concessions to trade union pressure, but they prefer to keep national increases to the minimum since these are more difficult to reduce should conditions change.

Thus it may be said that under full employment — that is when unemployment is around 1 to 2 per cent — and when the government is maintaining an inflationary monetary and budgetary policy, employers will take the lead in pushing up earnings whether or not the unions press for higher wage rates. The rise in earnings will in turn induce the unions to demand higher rates, since the increase in earnings will have widened the differentials in take-home pay between those earning only basic rates and those able to make more, but so long as there is excess demand they will not be able to close the gap between wage rates and actual earnings.

Since unions seek to secure the highest level of money wages for their members subject to overriding considerations, they will not be deterred from making general claims even if some firms are hardly in a position to meet them. While under full employment unions are little concerned about the effect of wage increases on the level of employment in industries engaged with supplying goods to the home market, they are conscious of the relationship between wages, costs, and prices and do take some account of it in the export industries. How much influence this factor will have on union wage policies will depend upon the situation in the industry concerned and the assessment the unions make of it in relation to the future welfare of the members and the organization. In an industry like the British railways, the unions have been influenced by the fact that no government is likely to allow it to go out of business. While railway wages have fallen behind because of the poor economic shape of the industry, the unions are able to reckon on their demands, to some extent, being met by government intervention.

The degree to which unions accept the fact that the wages of their members are dependent on the output and costs of industry is illustrated by the support which they have given to efforts to increase productivity. There are those unions which refuse to accept any responsibility for raising productivity, and very often agreements made by national leaders are opposed by the rank and file when attempts are made to implement them. Thus the process of decision-making based on the economic knowledge of the leaders is modified and sometimes frustrated by the attitude of the membership.

VII. Wage Pattern

Since neither the unions nor the employers nor the government want to become involved in strikes, all three parties are concerned to see that reasonable advances in wages are given. For example, in the railway dispute at the end of 1953 it was known that the union was likely to refuse less than a 6s. per week advance. In this event, it was no great surprise when the offer of 4s. made by an arbitration board was rejected and a strike threatened. Four shillings was too low, though 5s. 6d. might have been accepted. In this case, the sympathy of the public was on the side of the railwaymen, as the award was much lower than the general trend of awards at this time, and further, the wages of railwaymen had fallen well behind in the post-war years. Similarly, when the engineers asked for a 15 per cent increase, it was generally reckoned that they would receive about 5 per cent — which was in fact what they were offered and accepted.

It is, therefore, possible to forecast the results of a particular claim with a fair degree of accuracy. It is even possible to forecast the level of wage increases that are likely to be secured in the next few months, since they will normally fall into the established pattern of expectations. Some writers consider that this pattern is established by the engineering unions,[1] and others by the agricultural workers.[2]

[1] E.g. Industrial Correspondent of *The Sunday Times* (July 4, 1954).
[2] *The Economist* (June 19, 1954), p. 955.

Unlike the case of the United States, where collective agreements usually run for a definite time period, the practice in Britain is to make them for an indefinite duration. There has been a tendency in recent years for some unions to make an annual claim for wage increase, but this is by no means general practice and the interval between the presentation of one claim and the next varies widely.

The Industrial Disputes Tribunal, Wage Councils, and other wage-fixing bodies tend to fit their awards into the pattern. These statutory bodies give no reasons why they have decided upon a particular amount, and the only principle they follow in theory is that of considering each claim on its merits. But there is a good

TABLE 3

TOTAL AMOUNT SECURED IN WEEKLY WAGE INCREASES (£000s)

	1945	1946	1947	1948	1949	1950	1951	1952	1953*
	1774	2860	1786	1921	1074	2040	6547	4426	2397
	Percentage of Total by Methods of Settlement								
1. Voluntary negotiations	59	85	56	82	43	65	72	53	25
2. Statutory bodies	10	10	30	9	33	19	17	19	36
3. Arbitration	28	4	13	3	13	8	5	13	20
4. Sliding scales	3	1	1	6	11	8	6	15	19

Source : *Ministry of Labour Gazette.*

* These figures are not adjusted for subsequent corrections and therefore they are slightly different from those in Table 1.

deal of evidence which indicates that they are considerably influenced by the relative movement of wages.[1] During 1953 the pattern of awards made by the Industrial Disputes Tribunal was so consistent that it aroused criticism from trade union leaders who accused it of pursuing a 'wages policy'. Personal conversation with members of these various bodies reinforces the impressions that 'fair relativity' is almost certainly the most important principle on which they act. Since, however, many of the most important unions never have their disputes taken to the Industrial Disputes Tribunal and the proportion of wage increases determined by all the statutory wage-fixing authorities is normally smaller than that determined by

[1] Cf. H. A. Turner, *Arbitration : A Study of Industrial Experience* (Fabian Research Series, 1952), p. 17.

voluntary wage makers, it is unlikely that the trends are established by them. Moreover, a large proportion of the claims which go before the I.D.T. are ones where the union is asking that some previously established rate should be applied to a particular firm or sector of industry which claims to be outside the scope of the rate.

The sharp fall in 1953 was due to the sudden stiffening of the employers' attitude to wage increases following the effects of the tighter monetary policy of the government, the hardening of export markets, and also possibly expectations of an American depression. It is unlikely that these figures mark the beginning of a persistent trend against voluntary wage determination.

While shifts in relative wage rates are less important than changes in the cost of living in the stimulation of wage demands, they clearly exercise a powerful influence over the levels of wages accepted by unions. In spite, however, of the tendency for one union to seek the same amount of wage advance as another and for

TABLE 4

WEEKLY MONEY WAGE RATES

	Printing	Engin-eering	Ship-building	Building	Coal	Textiles	Agri-culture
1938	100	100	100	100	100	100	100
1945	125	151	155	135	179	164	203
1952	215	209	228	221	369	232	319

annual patterns to be established, this has not led to the freezing of interindustrial relativities. There have been considerable changes in comparative industrial wage rates since 1938.

What has brought these changes about ? Can they be attributed to union organization ? This seems hardly likely since the relative advance of the miners and agricultural workers is clearly not due to union organizations, but to the economic position of the industry. Wage advances in both industries have far outstripped the others, yet mining is well organized and agriculture only poorly so. The engineering industry is well organized and has an extremely militant union, but it has not been able to secure increases in wage rates commensurate with its demands. If comparative earnings were examined, the picture would be somewhat different, but this would not affect the point, since earnings are determined to a smaller extent than rates by trade union policy.

If unions do not appear to be the main factor influencing inter-industry wage differentials, they may be much more significant with regard to intra-industry differentials. Mr. Turner has suggested that the structure of wages has been mainly shaped during the last fifty years by the mass organization of workers, the growth of large-scale unions, and multi-union industry-wide collective bargaining.[1] These developments have led increasingly to wage demands of the flat-rate type because the big unions contain a high proportion of unskilled and semi-skilled workers who are, therefore, able to exert a strong pressure for an equal advance in money terms. Turner further asserts that while employers may oppose the claim of a union *in toto*, they rarely oppose the form of the claim. Thus mass unionism and comprehensive negotiations have imposed their own logic on the structure of wages.

There can be little doubt that the developments of trade unionism have influenced the structure of wages, but I think that Mr. Turner has underestimated certain factors. The most significant of these are the general advance in education and altered social status of the lower-paid workers, which together with the change in technical skills has made possible the great increase in the earnings of the non-craftsman. The growth of mass unionism and multi-union bargaining has taken place alongside these other fundamental changes, and it could not have been achieved without these developments.

The behaviour of British trade unions in the post-war years shows clearly that they have been influenced by both political and economic factors. The policies which they have pursued have been affected by the nature of the organization, type of membership, constitutional arrangements, and the power and ideology of its leaders and rank and file. Equally influential has been the economic state of the industry in which the members for whom it has been bargaining were employed, whether it was expanding or declining, whether it was suffering from a shortage or a surplus of labour, whether it was likely to receive a public subsidy, and whether it was sheltered or exposed to competition. The general state of the economy has also exercised a profound influence ; continuous full employment, inflationary pressure, rising prices, balance of payments crises, devaluation, and the development of the welfare services have helped to shape the mould into which trade union wage policy has been cast.

In principle, the problem of building a model of a trade union as an economic institution is no different from that of building a

[1] H. A. Turner, 'Trade Unions, Differentials and the Levelling of Wages', *The Manchester School of Economic and Social Studies* (1952), pp. 227-282.

model of a firm. The modern business firm is also a political institution operating in an economic environment and it too has institutional requirements which often impel it to behave differently from what is assumed of a purely economic agent. The assumption that a business firm will seek to maximize its profits is about as valid as the assumption that a trade union will seek to maximize the money wages of its members, but the behaviour of both is affected by many other factors which require analysis.

Professor Ross and his Californian colleagues would appear to be completely justified in their criticisms of the economists' model of trade union behaviour because it has failed to take account of other factors. On the other hand, they are clearly not correct in their assumption that trade union wage policy is primarily determined by political factors. The survival and growth of the organization, the personal power of the leaders, and other institutional factors clearly enter into the process of determining a union wage policy, but unions cannot escape from the pressures generated by economic forces. The wage claim is often an attempt to escape, but the settlement is usually a recognition of the economic facts of life. The contention of Professor Dunlop that wages are primarily determined by economic facts and not by internal political pressures is amply demonstrated by British experience.

A realistic analysis of trade union behaviour, however, must take into account the political factors as well as the economic, especially in the formulation of generalizations. Trade unions do try to maximize the incomes of their members, they do try to maintain their real wage rates, they do take into account the employment effect, and it is not unreasonable to base analysis on assumptions that they behave in this way, providing that it is recognized that in any given situation other factors may also be decisive.

Chapter 9

INFLATION AND WAGE DIFFERENTIALS IN GREAT BRITAIN

BY

H. A. TURNER

University of Manchester, England

THE relative antiquity of collective bargaining in Britain may give custom and convention a greater influence on the fixing of wages there than is general. What follows is an interpretation of British experience, particularly that of the period of full employment since 1940, but much of it may have an application to other 'high employment' economies of the Western type. There seems to be a dual relation between the inflationary trend characteristic of such economies and the system of wage differentials. Attention has been largely concentrated upon the effects of inflation on relative wages. Wage relationships, however, may also play a more positive rôle in sustaining the inflation and determining its form.

I. WAGE RELATIONSHIP AND THE PRESSURE FOR WAGE INCREASES

A prominent feature of recent British wage trends has been the influence of the 'coercive comparison'. A large part of the strikes currently classified as wage disputes turns out, on nearer investigation, not to consist of actions for wage increases as such, but of attempts to maintain a relationship the workers concerned regard as established by custom : some margin over, or partly with, another group of workers.[1] The current language and practice of British industrial conciliation is full of terms — 'due relativities', 'proper parities', 'customary differentials' — which embody this comparative concept. The very term 'fair wages' is given by the Resolution of Parliament which governs wages under government contracts just the meaning that these wages are to be comparable with those under collective agreements in private industry. The

[1] I refer to a number of instances of such disputes in a paper, 'The Effects of the Present Wage Structure' (British Institute of Management, 1953).

principle is explicitly expressed in the formula regulating the pay of civil servants. It seems to have been the most important guide to arbitration awards.[1]

It might be thought that this insistence on the maintenance of 'established relativities' would lead to stability. And it is true that the extension of collective bargaining has been associated with a certain rigidity in wage relationships. There are important instances of wage differentials that remained unchanged, despite economic upheavals, for thirty, fifty, or even (in the textile industry) for sixty years. This is, generally speaking, since the scope of collective bargains in the trades concerned widened beyond that of individual firms.[2] While in cases where such an 'established relativity' can no longer be maintained, the change usually occurs, not as a gradual modification but as a sharp break, accompanied by obvious conflict. An interesting example of this occurred in 1951, when the government, because of a persistent shortage of policemen, gave them a very large increase in pay. Since 1920 wages in the fire service had been varied with those of the police. The refusal of the 1951 increase to firemen provoked their widespread and prolonged refusal to continue on duty.

The system of 'established relativities' is, however, by no means self-consistent. One major point of friction is between wages of time workers in the same industry or firm. At their initiation, collective agreements usually establish wage rates which will yield comparable earnings for piece-work and time-work. British collective agreements often specify that piece rates shall be arranged to yield earnings a fixed percentage above time rates.

The recurrent gap between piece-workers' and time-workers' earnings is an important factor in the prominence of the mining and engineering industries in British wage demands. The latter industry illustrates both another such friction and the rigidity associated with widely based collective bargaining. In most British industries, 'industry-wide' collective agreements are the rule. In engineering the agreement was first devised in 1917 and provided for two classes of worker: apprenticed craftsmen and labourers. The growth of mass production has produced a great class of 'semi-skilled' workers: the unions and employers' organizations have so far found it impossible to adapt the traditional structure of standard rates to these operatives, so their wages continue to be bargained

[1] See the writer's *Arbitration: A Study of Industrial Experience* (Fabian Research Series, 1952).

[2] Several such cases are analysed in the writer's 'Trade Unions, Differentials, and the Levelling of Wages', *Manchester School of Economic and Social Studies* (September 1952), pp. 244-258.

in individual establishments. Such local bargaining gives speedier results than industry-wide negotiations so that wages of mass production operatives have in some cases risen above those of skilled mechanics.[1]

Another source of friction is the alternative arrangements of wage differentials that are possible. The 'due relativity' between, for instance, the wage of a skilled worker and that of his less skilled assistant may be 'established' in terms of a proportionate difference or an absolute cash sum, and different occupations have contrasting (and long-standing) customs in this respect. Workers of these different occupations may be employed in the same industry, or even in the same establishment. Thus a substantial general increase in wages inevitably produces disparities in pay between workers of comparable skill. Thus smelters in the steel industry have a percentage differential over labourers, while mechanics' differentials have been fixed in cash ; many wage demands have arisen from this anomaly.

A similar consequence may follow from the successful prosecution of a general wage demand by a combination of more and less skilled workers. Such general demands have been, almost invariably, for a common percentage or absolute increase in the different wage rates concerned. If the group secures a percentage advance, its lower-paid members may complain that the skilled workers' cash advantage has been unfairly increased : if the advance is uniform in cash, the skilled workers protest that their differential has been relatively diminished. Either type of demand thus entails a certain aftermath of discontent. The leading rôle of railwaymen in recent British wage demands, for instance, is partly attributable to the reduction of locomotive engineers' wage differentials by a series of standard cash advances.

The industries which have played the leading part in recent British wage movements are those in which such frictions as the above are most acute. Railwaymen, for instance — though their agreed wage rates have moved in step with those of collective agreements generally — have suffered a steady comparative worsening in their earnings, because they enjoy neither the piece-work pay of other 'organized' industries nor the opportunities of local and individual bargaining offered by certain less 'organized' trades.[2]

[1] See 'Earnings in Engineering, 1926-1948', by K. G. J. C. Knowles and D. J. Robertson, *Bulletin, Oxford Institute of Statistics* (June 1951).

[2] Miss G. Evans, of the Economic Research Section of Manchester University, has just completed an analysis of the post-war movement of agreed wage rates industry by industry. Comparing this with the movement of earnings, and allowing for the effect of overtime, the extent to which average wages actually paid exceed

These frictions between the comparative standards of particular groups of workers present themselves to union leaders as a recurring complex of sectional pressures for wage adjustments. But where any substantial group of members is concerned, selective or discriminatory wage demands usually provoke discontent among those who do not profit by them, so that union leaders usually prefer in such cases to seek a general increase in wages. So these sectional frictions commonly express themselves, in a way determined by the necessities of collective action, as general wage demands.

II. Employment Levels and the Pressure for Wage Increases

The preceding argument is that, given a general situation of high employment, the British system and techniques of collective wage regulation permit particular groups of workers to increase their wages faster than the generality. Other workers then demand wage increases to restore 'established relativities'. The unions' tendency is to convert such sectional wage demands into general demands. General wage increases, however, are only palliative, and may themselves — by their effect on differentials — provoke renewed discontent.

This is not, of course, presented as the sole factor in continuing wage inflation. But it seems a persistent one, which may explain why wage demands continue to be pressed by unions when the factors usually put forward to justify them — increases in prices or profits — are not obvious. For instance, it does not seem that either of these factors sufficiently explains the failure of the rigid 'wage stop' imposed (by agreement between the T.U.C. and the government) in January 1950. Between that month and September 1950, when the 'wage stop' began to give way before persistent wage demands, the cost of living increased [1] only 1 per cent and the profits currently declared by industrial companies did not reflect the onset of the Korean boom until near the end of the year.[2] But

the centrally agreed wage rates appears to vary from nil to about 20 per cent. This variation does not appear to be related to the relative profitability or labour shortage of different industries, but seems most pronounced in industries (a) where piece rates are common and physical productivity has increased ; (b) where opportunities for local bargaining are greatest.

[1] A. T. Peacock and W. J. I. Ryan in 'Wages and Inflation : Influences on the Timing of Claims', *Manchester Guardian* (May 15, 1952), suggest a rise of 5 points in the British Index of Retail Prices to be required to generate a wage demand.

[2] Estimated from *Financial Times* monthly analysis, 'Trend of Industrial Profits'.

average earnings rose about 4 per cent, and it is clear (since most centrally agreed wage rates were 'frozen') that considerable 'inequities' must have developed.[1]

Whatever the relative importance in stimulating wage demands of changes in prices, profits, and wage relationships, the effect of the last factor does seem especially precise. First, changes in the relative wages of associated groups of workers seem immediately and acutely perceived (especially if an accustomed 'relativity' has existed between them) by the workers themselves. Second, to any trade union, an increase in the wage rates of an associated union's members is an instant commentary on its own leaders' efficiency. High employment has strengthened the comparative principle in wage fixing for four reasons. First, by strengthening the unions themselves. High employment is accompanied by increasing union membership. Where (as in Britain) the unions' own structure cuts across the boundaries of different occupations and industries, the result is to widen the area of interwage comparisons and to multiply the number of points on which each group of workers rests its particular standard of 'fair wages'. British trade unionism has, of course, a mixed structure of 'horizontal' craft and general labour unions and of 'vertical' industrial unions, so that few unions confine themselves to one industry, and few industries are organized by one union alone.

The second effect of high employment is usually to increase the area and effectiveness of collective bargaining, because employers become more willing to accept its restraints. Since any widely based collective agreement is usually founded on the wage relationships existing at its initiation, the effect is commonly to set, formalize, and make explicit 'relativities' which may before have been merely conventional or even indeterminate.

Thirdly, the government's desire to avoid the disturbance of prosperity by industrial conflicts — and particularly its more recent assumption of the responsibility to maintain full employment — has driven it to encourage the orderly regulation of wage questions. This it does by establishing conciliation services, arbitration tribunals, legal wage boards, and the like. It has been noted that such institutions lean heavily upon interwage comparisons and upon 'established relativities' to form their decisions.

The fourth reason is that, while a departure from 'established relativities' may be resented by workers, when unemployment is widespread, those who do not gain an increase may accept the fact

[1] A more detailed commentary is given in Turner, *Arbitration : A Study of Industrial Experience*.

for fear of losing their jobs. But such departures are often remembered as injustices, and the collective memory which the unions represent is longer than that of individuals. When the fear of unemployment dwindles, not only is insistence upon 'the maintenance of relativities' strengthened, but some groups may try to reassert a former status. A major example of this concerns the increase in wages of London printers which initiated the collapse of the official 'wage stop' of 1950. This was granted after a dispute (involving a major stoppage of work) originating from an event of 1922. In that year's wage conflicts the rates of provincial printers were cut more than those in London, so that a previously established wage differential was widened. The provincial printers accepted the situation until after the second World War. They then tried to re-establish the pre-1922 margin. The London printers reacted to their final success by demanding the restoration of the post-1922 differential.[1]

The history of British collective bargaining suggests in any case certain long-term trends. Once collective bargaining has become established in a particular sector of employment, its scope tends to widen so that the whole of the industry concerned is, in effect, regulated by collective contracts, even if all the employers are not formally party to them. There is a similar tendency for regulation of wages to become established in industries where the trade unions are not strong enough to enforce it themselves. Here, particularly, the aid of the state has been enlisted. The effect of the current British national arbitration system, for instance, is virtually to make legal enforcement of agreed wage rates available to any union that desires it, while the system of legal wage boards (originally designed to ensure minimum standards in certain badly organized trades) has in effect become a widely used device for 'organized' employers and workers to impose the terms of collective contracts upon the unorganized.

There is thus a trend to the centralization of collective bargaining. Industry-wide agreements tend to replace local or occupational contracts. Even where the various employers in an industry are not formally party to a single agreement, the trade generally will follow the lead set (as in the printing, steel, and cotton industries) by a particular sectional agreement, or even (as in chemicals) by the wage contracts of a particular firm.

Associated with these trends is a certain uniformity in the results of collective regulation. This uniformity is first and most prominently

[1] See 'Report of a Court of Inquiry into . . . a Dispute between the London Master Printers' Association and the London Society of Compositors', Ministry of Labour (October 1950).

marked in wage increases, which are added to the diverse existing wage rates. But there then follows a gradual process of standardization, in which general minimum wage rates are established, a number of minor wage differences (like variations in wage rates between localities) are eliminated, and finally the minimum wage rates approximate also to maxima.[1] In Britain, the phenomenon of uniform general wage increases has been recurrent under industry-wide contracts, although outside the public services and monopolistic industries only a few trades have yet reached the last stage of collective bargaining, in which a structure of standard wage rates absolutely determines the earnings of employees.

These trends appear to reflect both the effects of internal solidarity in employers' and workers' organizations and their desire to prevent 'unfair competition' by the unorganized or less disciplined. But this long-term development has been irregular. The London printers' example illustrates how the system of 'established relativities' may break up in the presence of rising unemployment, but tends to reform when employment is high. As it reforms, its diverse internal frictions help to incite a general pressure for wage advances. At the same time its elaboration has ensured that the advances secured in certain leading industries shall be imitated throughout the economy.

At what level does unemployment cease to be a barrier to this tendency? Certainly, at some point considerably short of full employment. Thus in 1952–1953 there was a fall in British industrial employment which was partly concealed by widespread partial employment and by the dismissal of 'marginal' workers who did not register as unemployed, but which probably amounted to some 4 or 5 per cent.[2] Industrial profits fell sharply and the cost-of-living ceased to rise. However, the rhythm of wage demands (and increases) apparently continued without significant abatement. While in the cotton industry, where recorded unemployment alone amounted to some 30 per cent, the unions not only presented to the employers a demand for a general wage increase but persisted to the point of partial success. It seems that the cotton unions were more fearful of their members' wage rates falling behind those of other industries than of the less determinate effect of a wage increase on employment. So long as any important group of workers was in a position to press home wage demands (and any significant unemployment, of course, is likely to be uneven in its incidence), a similar choice would

[1] This conclusion I particularly base on a study (as yet unpublished) of collective bargaining in the United Kingdom cotton industry over the past century.

[2] See H. A. Turner, 'Measuring Unemployment', *Journal of the Royal Statistical Society* (Part I, 1955), pp. 28-50.

confront other unions. One has no means of determining exactly the critical degree or general unemployment at which sectional wage demands would become effective and most other unions induced to follow suit. But if a guess will serve to illustrate the point, one might say that once employment comes within, say, 6 or 7 per cent of 'full', a general and persistent pressure for wage increases will develop. Average wages might, of course, start to rise well before that point.

III. Restraints on Wage Increases

The process of successive wage cycles has, however, the appearance of a steady and controlled march rather than a runaway stampede. One reason for this is that the protracted rituals of contemporary collective bargaining combine with the elaborate system of dependent comparisons it creates to impose certain restraints upon wage movements.

In Britain the presentation of wage demands has assumed a certain annual or biennial rhythm, corresponding to the unions' habit of periodic representative conferences. Their settlement has acquired an equal formality. Most demands are stalled until settlements are reached in the leading industries. These involve lengthy negotiations with the employers (who are aware of their trades' strategic position), and commonly involve arbitration procedure and government intervention. This intervention is compelled by the need to forestall a breach of industrial peace, not that of economic moderation. But its effect is to give an implicit approval to the settlement it secures. The general wage advance follows.

A second restraint is imposed by what seems an extension of the comparative principle into time. In each cycle of wage increases, since their pattern became settled during the second World War, the average weekly wage rate seems to have increased by much the same amount. It seems that unions are not prepared to accept much less — or employers to concede much more — than they did in the previous cycle.

The movement has, nevertheless, an inexorable quality. The official 'wage stop' of 1950, for instance, achieved no more than a temporary halt, and the wage cycle which terminated it was followed so shortly by a second round of wage increases as to cancel its effect. One might say that the trend of collective bargaining's recent development is to give wage earners as a whole what many salaried employees have enjoyed for a long time as individuals — a periodic increase of pay.

It is curious, however, that each successive general increase in wage rates has resembled its predecessors, not in proportionate but in absolute terms, so that the pace of the movement shows a relative diminution. In so far as prices follow wages, this means, of course, that the inflationary effect of wage advances tends also to diminish. The British economy, indeed, seems very near the point at which productivity (increasing at a proportionate rate) will overhaul the advance of wages.

This tendency for the effect of the wage pressure to diminish might be attributed to a reduction of the 'frictions' in wage relationships, following from the gradual standardization and simplification of the wages structure as collective bargaining extends and improves its techniques. However, it seems also probable that the repeated general advances of wage rates have established a certain expectation, among organized workers, upon their leaders' future performance. The arithmetic progression of wage advances may be connected with another phenomenon of the recent period — the tendency of the successive general increases in wage rates to be uniform in terms of cash.

IV. Narrowing of Wage Differentials

A most notable feature of this time has been a diminution of relative differences in wages. This 'narrowing' has been very general : we shall discuss it mainly in relation to differentials for skill and responsibility among manual workers as its most prominent and typical case. This demonstrates also the factors operating upon local and inter-industry differentials. Sex differentials and the differential between wages and salaries (i.e. for non-manual labour) have been subject to the same general force, but in these cases its working has been modified by special circumstances which would involve more detailed discussion than is possible here.

This narrowing has been attributed to the spread of popular education and to technical change. These things have certainly contributed to the reduction of particular differentials. But there is no obvious correlation between the rate of technical and educational progress and the general movement of differentials. Relative skill differentials, for instance, were pretty constant in Britain during the latter nineteenth century and up to the first World War. They then declined sharply, but were partly restored in the inter-war period. The narrowing, however, was resumed with the coming of the second World War and has continued to the present day.[1] There is, therefore, a certain inverse connection between the general level of employment and that of relative differentials. So the narrowing has also been attributed to the greater fluctuation of employment among unskilled workers and the general high employment of recent years. But the relative scarcities of skilled and unskilled labour do not seem greatly affected by general fluctuations in employment. We have had, for instance, many recent cases of local unemployment caused by a shortage of skilled labour.

There are, in any case, certain employments where — although they have been quite as subject to changes in technique and in the general levels of education and employment as others — occupational differentials have suffered very little diminution. Some other explanation than these three factors is therefore required.

In Britain the narrowing of differentials has been associated with periods of rapidly rising wages, and particularly with the growth of mass trades unionism (as opposed to the exclusive 'labour aristocracies' which preceded it). As mentioned above, trade unions prefer to demand equal wage advances for all their members : mass trade unionism has, on the whole, chosen to demand increases which are equal in absolute terms. The general preference for such 'flat-rate' increases has been the first cause of the narrowing.

This preference has been strongest in certain industries (like building and woodworking) where the organization of workers was once confined to exclusive craft unions, and where apprenticeship is still a necessary qualification for entry to skilled jobs. While unskilled labour remained unorganized, these craft unions were able to maintain their members' relative differentials. When the mass unions appeared, however, the craft unions were generally driven to combine with them in bargaining with employers. The choice of flat-rate wage demands by these combinations seems to have been largely dictated by the numerical preponderance of the less skilled workers.

The preference for flat-rate advances has been almost exclusive among certain one-time craft unions that later opened their ranks to unapprenticed workers. These unions have been competing with general labour unions for membership among the unskilled. A union of this type dominates the alliance of British engineering operatives ; every wage demand of this combination from its formation in 1917 until 1952 was for a uniform cash advance.

This form of wage demand has therefore been selected by the

[1] For a statistical analysis see K. G. J. C. Knowles and D. J. Robertson, 'Differences between the Wages of Skilled and Unskilled Workers, 1880–1950', *Bulletin, Oxford Institute of Statistics* (April 1951), pp. 109-127.

major unions because it is most attractive to the mass of less-skilled, lower-paid workers. But certain unions have usually presented percentage wage demands, or (like the steel workers) maintained relative differentials by other devices. These unions have not experienced the general compulsion to canvass the allegiance of the less skilled. They were formed and dominated by the most skilled workers, but did not exclude unskilled labour. On the contrary, the skilled workers sometimes (as in certain of the cotton unions) compelled their assistants to join, thus continuing, in effect, to determine the latter's wages, and excluding general labour unions from their industry. On the other hand, such unions have not interested themselves in expanding into other employments : they are, therefore, not compelled by a need to maintain some parity between members in different industries — as are the great craft and general labour unions. But these exceptional unions have no apprenticeship system, and entry to the better paid jobs is by promotion from the less skilled workers. In these cases it seems that the lower paid have been reconciled (or, at least, divided in their opposition) to the maintenance of abnormal differentials by the chance of ultimately enjoying them.

Some unions have generally preferred the 'percentage' form of wage demand because they wish mainly to recruit higher-paid employees. But the general direction of unionism's advance has been towards the lower-paid mass. The average effect of wage demands has thus been somewhat to increase differentials in cash terms, but far from enough to maintain them relatively. In the last year or two a certain reaction against flat-rate demands has set in. This may be explained by a growing consciousness of their effect, the accumulated resentment of skilled men, and (with the slowing down of the unions' expansion) the diminution of the pressure of interunion competition for the lower-paid workers' allegiance. However, this reaction has so far been mainly expressed by a reversion to percentage demands which halt the narrowing but do not reverse it.

It may be that this policy has not been unacceptable to employers. Skilled labour does not readily change its occupation, and is slow to train. The growth within individual industries of combination among employers (and of private and public monopoly) may have concentrated competition for labour upon unskilled workers who are not yet committed to particular trades. While labour shortage has obliged industry to compete with the home for such workers, it is quite possible that a narrowing of differentials would have occurred without the modern unionization of the less skilled.

But that is speculative. In general, employers have accepted the form of union demands, and confined themselves to bargaining about the amount of the general advances. Thus the industries where relative skill differentials have been abnormally maintained are ones where employers are strongly disciplined and where the unions' insistence on the system of recruiting skilled workers by promotion (as opposed to apprenticeship) absolutely prohibits their movement between firms. This renders competitive bidding for skilled labour not only restricted, but useless. These industries have suffered by the relatively low wage they offer unskilled labour. Nevertheless, the employers have generally preferred to accept the situation rather than provoke disputes about differentials.[1] The main factors, therefore, remain the policy of unions and the attitudes of workers.

The broad argument here has been that the growth of collective organization that has accompanied high employment has imposed on British wage movements a particular pattern of repeated (almost regular) cycles of wage advances, which have also so far involved a reduction in most relative wage differentials. This pattern reflects very largely the working and internal necessities of the institutions now concerned in the fixing of wages, and amounts to an implicit wage policy.

The pattern has not so far shown itself amenable to direct state action : the unsuccessful 'wage stop' of 1950, for instance, represented a governmental attempt to limit wage increases in a selective fashion. The government might disrupt it by monetary policy, but only if it were prepared to accept a politically uncomfortable degree of unemployment.

Such significant modifications to this pattern as have occurred have been of two kinds. First, those arising from the uneven tenure of collective regulation and its imperfect techniques, and from the exceptional institutional arrangements of certain trades. Second, from the few economic changes which have been sufficiently drastic to practise the system of 'established relativities'. Only two major examples of this occur to the writer. On the one hand, the violent 1952 recession in the cotton trade so delayed the cotton workers'

[1] It does not in any case seem that the greater freedom to pay wages above the collectively agreed rates of employers in less disciplined industries has offset the effects of union wage policies. Knowles and Robertson ('Earnings in Engineering, 1926–1948') suggest occupational relative earnings to have followed broadly the trend of relative wage rates. Inter-industry differentials have also been affected by the predominance of flat-rate claims, and here Miss Evans's study suggests that the narrowing in relative wage rates is reflected (though not to the full extent) in relative earnings.

participation in the contemporary wage cycles as, in effect, to reduce their relative wage rates substantially. On the other, the rapid post-war expansion of the vehicle industry made the employers there reluctant to accept the discipline of the engineering employers' association. Wages in the biggest motor-car factories were thus bargained on the spot, producing high relative wages.[1]

Most recent economic developments appear, therefore, to have taken the system of 'established relativities' as given, so that adaptation must otherwise proceed by changes in the employment distribution. The economy's tolerance of the wage pattern may, then, be partly attributable to the fact that, given a generally high level of employment, few economic changes involve such particular shortages or surpluses of labour as to disrupt it. The evidence, in any case, suggests that the distribution of labour between industries is less affected by differences in wages than by employment opportunities.

[1] See Knowles and Robertson, 'Earnings in Engineering, 1926–1948'. It is interesting, however, that the individual motor-car producers have now adopted a system of regulating wage advances by reference to engineering collective agreements that virtually 'freezes' the wage differential.

Chapter 10

AN ANALYSIS OF UNION MODELS AS ILLUSTRATED BY FRENCH EXPERIENCE[1]

BY

HUBERT BROCHIER
University of Grenoble, France

THE incorporation of the extraneous element represented by unionism into wage theory, which has remained characterized by marginal analysis, is bound to give rise to difficulties.[2] To what kind of analytical treatment is union behaviour to be submitted? What assumptions should be formulated about it? To what factors is it to be linked? At the present moment, two currents of thought can be discerned in English and American literature. The first, in its attempt to preserve a certain homogeneity of wage theory, tries to use the analytical apparatus created for the firm and puts forward a purely economic explanation of union behaviour, namely one based on the maximization of a certain monetary value. The other trend of thought considers the trade union as an essentially political body and stresses the irrationality of union behaviour, which is said to derive from the mechanism of arriving at decisions within the union organization.

As is often the case, this dispute between the upholders of economic and of political theories tends to lose sight of the precise questions originally involved and has strayed into abstruse epistemological problems. In our view, both these rest on debatable methodological positions. After a brief summary and critique of both, we therefore propose to put forward a third interpretation of union behaviour, based on a different methodology and illustrated by some examples taken more particularly from trade unionism in France.[3]

[1] Translated by Elizabeth Henderson.

[2] N. Belfer and C. F. Bloom, 'Unionism and Marginal Theory', *Insights into Labor Issues* (1948), p. 239. For earlier attempts, see J. R. Hicks, *The Theory of Wages* (1933), and J. Marchal, 'Les Facteurs qui déterminent le taux des salaires dans le monde moderne. Du prix du travail au revenu du travailleur', *Revue économique* (July 1950), pp. 129-157.

[3] I wish to express my gratitude to Mr. J. Marchal and M. H. Bartoli for their suggestions in connection with this paper.

I. Present Models of Union Action

It was extremely tempting for economists reared in the marginalist tradition to use the analytical apparatus which had been constructed for the theory of the firm. This method offered the advantage of preserving the homogeneity of the economic explanation and of allowing trade unions to be readily integrated into a general wages theory. Besides, this method also left open the seductive possibilities of analogy. It was thus that an 'economic model' of the union was worked out. Dunlop has formulated it most clearly,[1] and according to him it is both possible and useful to consider the union as an enterprise representing the wage earners of whom it is composed and trying to sell its members' labour on the market at the highest price.[2] There exists for the union leaders a relation between the wage level which their action has achieved and the number of workers affiliated to their union ; this relation is, in its logical foundation, analogous to the demand curve for the products of a firm. The membership function, together with the demand curve for labour, makes it possible analytically to determine the rational policy designed to maximize the union 'product'.

The first difficulty encountered by this theory is the precise definition of the product to be maximized. According to circumstances, union practice can vary among different possibilities. It would seem, however, that, according to Dunlop, the assumption closest to reality is that of the pursuit of the highest total wage bill.[3]

Dunlop is under no misapprehension with respect to the complex nature of union reality. However much he formalizes union aims, however much he reduces the union to its economic functions, the union remains for him something specific. He stresses its importance as a unit of decision, which superimposes upon individual preferences collective choices formulated through political channels. Moreover, he recognizes that there are certain elements capable of disturbing the rational nature of the action of organized labour ; the level at which negotiations take place, the degree of organization amongst workers, the limitations of the number of members and the seat of political power inside the unions. Dunlop is thus led to a closer examination of the various wage policies pursued by organized labour and to the recognition of non-income aims, such as better working conditions, paid leave, and control of innovations endangering

[1] J. T. Dunlop, *Wage Determination under Trade Unions* (1944), 2nd edition (1950).

[2] *Ibid.*, p. 32.

[3] *Ibid.*, pp. 44 and 119.

the employment level. He does not attach much importance to the form in which claims are presented. 'What trade unions say about their broad wage policies is much less important than what they do',[1] he says, and he regards the presentation of union policy often as no more than a dramatization of some rational behaviour.

This highly schematized summary does not, perhaps, do full justice to Dunlop's work, which is rich in detailed observation. There remains the fact, however, that the general explanatory principle is that of the maximization of the wage bill (or of some other quantity), the interaction of the membership function, and of the demand for labour. It is this hypothesis which constitutes the fundamental point of discussion.

This model of analogy is certainly intellectually very seductive, but there are such blatant differences between the trade union and the private firm pursuing maximum profit that it is not surprising that another radically different interpretation of union behaviour has been put forward. The authors representative of this second current of thought try to evolve a 'political', and no longer purely economic model of organized labour : 'unions are not profit-making institutions and are as much political as they are economic',[2] writes R. A. Lester. A. M. Ross develops the same idea on several occasions : 'The trade union is a political institution which participates in the establishment of wage rates. To conceive the union as a seller of labor attempting to maximize some measurable object (such as the wage bill) is a highly misleading formulation.'[3] The union is thus a political institution and, as such, is fundamentally different from the private firm.

Moreover, union reaction against a hostile environment and frequently the need to struggle for survival are apt to occasion policies not strictly in accordance with economic rationalism.[4] Finally, the union is a body which encompasses and represents diverse interests, and this heterogeneity has its influence on the organization's policies, which vary according to the predominance of one or the other group.

This, incidentally, is the explanatory principle to which the upholders of the political model have recourse most frequently.

[1] Dunlop, *Wage Determination*, p. 50 *et seq.*

[2] R. A. Lester, 'Labor Monopoly and Business Monopoly : a Faulty Analogy', *Readings in Labor Economics and Industrial Relations* (1951), p. 393.

[3] A. M. Ross, 'The Trade Union as a Wage-fixing Institution', *American Economic Review* (September 1947), p. 587.

[4] Ross, 'Wage Determination under Collective Bargaining', *American Economic Review* (December 1947), p. 822 : 'A sixty-day strike over two cents an hour may be irrational in the economic lexicon, but viewed as political behaviour, it may have all the logic of survival'.

For them the content of union decisions is determined by the political mechanism of the formation of decisions inside the unions. Three kinds of aims must be reconciled : the formal, official aim of the welfare of union members ; the institutional aim of the survival and development of the union ; and, finally, the personal ambition of union leaders.[1]

The accent is thus on the constitution of the union as an autonomous institution possessing its own interests and its own laws of development. This means a complete shift in the central problem, which now becomes one of explaining how union action is related to the decisions of union members. What is needed here is a study of union democracy, of the influence of various factions, of the relative weight of opinions at the base and at the top of the hierarchy. Research so far has yielded most diverse results, seeing that there is great variety in the origin and effect of the pressures to which union leaders may be subject. There is evidence of some uncertainty in the analysis of decisions manifestly designed to exert a direct influence on the level of employment. Certain authors maintain that union leaders are faced with strong pressure from below on the part of the workers who want to safeguard their jobs, and that this pressure determines union policy in many cases.[2] Other authors hold that it is useless for unions to concern themselves with the employment level, since it is impossible, even *a posteriori*, to retrace in any exact manner what effect wage changes have on employment.[3] Finally, the existence of large wage differentials, too, must be attributed to political factors in a wider sense.

II. The Inadequacy of Economic and Political Models

In spite of their opposition, both theories seem to us open to criticism, although from different points of view. First of all, we must hold serious reservations with regard to the 'economic' model of union policy. We must respect the intentions of the authors who have formulated it and remember that they were concerned not with explaining the whole of the union phenomenon, but only its contribution to wage determination. None the less, there remains the question whether this limitation does not arbitrarily curtail

[1] Ross, 'The Trade Union as a Wage-fixing Institution', p. 571. A similar definition is to be found in R. A. Lester, 'Labor Monopoly', p. 393.

[2] Such is the view of G. P. Schultz and C. A. Myers, 'Union Decisions and Employment', *Readings in Labor Economics*, pp. 285-288.

[3] A. M. Ross, *Trade Union Wage Policy* (1948).

reality, whether this abstraction still leaves a valid principle of explanation.

It seems doubtful whether recourse to the principle of maximization was really necessary in the construction of a theory of union action. It is true that this technique of economic analysis, in its application to the firm, has a long history and comparatively impressive theoretical achievements to show. But in our days it seems more and more debatable. The controversy around the marginal theory of price formation, the full cost theory, has brought to light serious doubts about this theory's accordance with reality. On the other hand, numerous studies have underlined its lack of precision. We may recall K. E. Boulding's interesting observations to the effect that the tendency towards equilibrium appears more general than the tendency towards maximization and recall his formulation of a number of alternatives to take account of union behaviour.[1]

Our reservations can but be reinforced when we turn to the possible application of the maximization principle to union action on the occasion of wage negotiations. Our reservations can be formulated as follows: The assumption that union action can be adequately described by the maximization of a certain monetary aim implies the complete subordination of the non-income aims of unionism, as well as economically completely rational behaviour by union leaders.

Neither of these propositions seem to us compatible with the diversity of union experiences. These have shown that in some countries union leaders in making their decisions repeatedly substituted a more long-term political rationality for short-term economic rationality, which, while remaining true to the condition of the workers, refrained from immediate claims in order the better to consolidate a political position which was expected to lead to durable results. Thus the restraint of the Trades Union Congress in Great Britain under the Labour Government made possible a relative, but effective, wage stop in that country.[2] Similarly, it is a fact that during the first few years after the Liberation in France, the Confédération Générale du Travail was led to exercise restraint in its demands for higher wages, and to stress the need for increasing production. In so doing, they sacrificed often justified claims to

[1] According to this author union policy could be based on a comparison with wage levels in other sectors. It might also be assumed that the dissatisfaction of union members leading to strike action could be a function of the period elapsed since the last wage increase. K. E. Boulding, *A Reconstruction of Economics* (New York, 1950).

[2] J. Lhomme, *La Politique sociale de l'Angleterre contemporaine*, Bibliothèque de la Science Économique (1953), pp. 119-122. Cf. also Y. Mainguy, 'L'Inflation contenue en Grande-Bretagne', *Économie appliquée* (April/June 1950), p. 317.

the support of a government with which they found themselves in sympathy to a certain extent.[1] These, then, are two examples of how, in some countries and in some circumstances, economic ends are subordinated to political union aims.

In our view such behaviour can by no means be regarded as an exception to a general behaviour still resting on economic rationalism alone. Unionism has more than one dimension and to suppose *a priori* that one aspect will always prevail over the other is to take an arbitrarily limiting view of unionism.

There is another reason which prevents us from attributing purely economic motives to union action. This is the formation and mentality of union leaders. True, the excellent business knowledge of American labour leaders and their businesslike behaviour has often been stressed.[2] However, such observations merely confirm us in our inclination to take a relative view of the guiding principles of union action, since the mentality and the possibilities of action of union leaders vary greatly from country to country. In France, for instance, union leaders often have no more than elementary knowledge of the situation of the industry in which they operate. How, indeed, could it be otherwise, when the employers carefully refrain from making public any elements of information on the situation of their firms ?

In this respect the behaviour noted by Dunlop seems to be characteristic of American unionism, which, in Hoxie's sense,[3] has essentially remained a business unionism and thus differs profoundly from most European unionism.[4] All this leads us to reject the notion that union behaviour in wage matters can be explained adequately by one general, universal, and invariable principle.

However, let us admit for a moment, as a working hypothesis, that maximization of the total wage bill is a valid explanatory principle. Even if it be valid, there is nothing to say that this principle is really useful as an explanation ; on the contrary, its scope would seem to be very restricted. This leads us to a second reservation : namely, the application of the principle of maximization to union action lacks precision to the point of becoming useless.

[1] Cf. J. L. Guglielmi and M. Perrot, *Salaires et revendications sociales en France, 1944–1952*, C. E. E. Études et Mémoires (1953), p. 63 ff.

[2] Dunlop, *Wage Determination.*

[3] R. F. Hoxie, *Trade Unionism in the United States* (1921).

[4] Cf. A. Sturmthal, 'National Patterns of Union Behaviour', *Journal of Political Economy* (December 1948), pp. 515-527, and P. Waline, *Les Syndicats aux États-Unis*, Cahiers de la Fondation Nationale des Sciences Politiques, No. 22 (1951). The last-named author quotes a declaration made by John Lewis in 1947, before a committee of Congress : 'A union organization is a business organization. It is subject to competition, much like a firm. It must be conducted in the same manner', p. 79.

Any general principle of action and type of behaviour applied to an economic agent or an economic institution can only play its analytical part properly if it allows of the deduction of a precise reaction to given external stimuli. In our field the principle of maximization clearly does not meet these requirements.[1] The first thing to do is exactly to define the quantity to be maximized, and this is not always an easy matter. Secondly, it is necessary to determine the methods to be used by the union ; this is by no means a matter of detail, as might appear, because the choice of the method of action may have a lasting influence on the result, that is on the wage level. A union may, for instance, try the effect of restrictive measures, or it may, on the contrary, co-operate with the employer in raising the price of the product. It is fairly unlikely that these two methods will lead to the same wage level.

These are only two examples of the innumerable options open to organized labour in its effort to maximize wages. J. T. Dunlop has given us a long, though perhaps not exhaustive list of such options. It is then up to the economist to look closer into the many forms of union action possibly compatible with the pursuit of a maximum wage, and the choice between which is determined by factors extraneous to the theory. These different forms of action may lead to different wage levels.

In such circumstances the principle of maximization seems to us no longer to have a great analytical value, since it is unable to shed any light on the forms of union action and leaves the really important content of these decisions to be found elsewhere.

It seems to us that the 'political' theories of union behaviour exhibit more realism, but dissatisfaction with the economic models by no means implies full satisfaction with the political ones. In any case, the two theories could perhaps be reconciled. In fact, their explanations are complementary as much as contradictory. The main concern of the political models is to show the genesis of union decisions ; they try to establish the group responsible for the decisions : thereafter it may well be that union action may be explained by the attempt to maximize the welfare of the dominant group. The maximization principle thus appears limited rather than excluded.

The question remains whether the above-mentioned lines of research used for the 'political' model can by themselves provide a

[1] We might also mention the lack of realism of certain other hypotheses, such as that about the membership function, of which R. Mosse rightly states 'that it rests on no empirical datum, and is in flagrant contradiction to labour psychology'. Cf. R. Mosse, *Les Salaires bilans de la connaissance économique* (1952).

valid explanation of union action in wage matters; whether the avowed aims of unionism are only the ideological mantle donned by the divergent interests existing side by side within the organizations.[1]

The factors of internal politics explain neither the existence nor the over-all behaviour of labour organizations. All that these factors do is to give expression to the compromise by which groups of different interests and judgment adjust these latter to the needs of common action. In this respect we agree with Dunlop, who regards these political elements as a short-term factor only destined to become less important and finally to disappear with a long-term view of the process of wage fixing.[2]

However much we are indebted to the constructors of the 'political' model for having shed light on the important part played by internal union organization, we must not, in matters relating to the choice of wage policies, forget the importance of the ideology and the political objectives of the trade union movement, nor of that which we shall summarize in the terms union structure and economic structure.

III. Integration into a Single Theory of the Various Explanatory Elements of Union Action

Such a multiplicity of factors constitutes a threat to the coherence of the explanation. We must try to reduce them to a simple scheme, as all theory must do. To this end, we must use an appropriate methodological frame.

Economic theory is here faced with a major methodological choice. If it remains timeless and neglects duration, as these models do, it must needs lead either to a single principle of explanation, which seems naïve and indeed almost useless as soon as it is confronted with reality; or else to dilution in the multiplicity of effective behaviours. This would really amount to evading the central problem of any sociological explanation, namely that of the relations between the history of social facts and the equilibrium of a society at a particular moment in its development.[3]

The history of economic thought exhibits two persistently alternating currents:[4] the one stresses equilibrium and the other

[1] Cf. A. M. Ross, 'The Trade Union as a Wage-fixing Institution', p. 568.

[2] Dunlop, *Wage Determination*, Introduction, pp. 3 and 4.

[3] Cf. J. Piaget, *Introduction à l'épistémologie génétique*, vol. iii, 'La Pensée biologique, la pensée psychologique et la pensée sociologique' (1950), p. 210.

[4] Cf. André Marchal, *Méthode scientifique et science économique, le conflit traditionnel des méthodes et son renouvellement* (1952).

evolution — synchronism and diachronism. Present-day economic explanations — even dynamic explanations — remain within the framework of a social equilibrium contained in a narrow slice of time. It must be recalled, of course, that the schools of thought which have tried to integrate historical factors into economic theory have not always covered themselves with glory. There is no occasion to renew the errors of the historical approach.

However, the two types of explanation must be reconciled within the framework of economic theory itself — that is, the genetic or historical explanation, and the functional explanation relating to the forms of equilibrium.[1] Such conciliation appears fraught with difficulties, but not altogether impossible ; it implies, not the complete abandonment, but the relativization of the present theoretical apparatus. To render a valid account of wage determination, we must indeed attribute a certain behaviour, a certain probable course of action, to the unions. But instead of floating in mid-air, this behaviour must be circumscribed within a certain structure and be anchored in certain historical events.[2] As such it can be utilized as a hypothesis valid for a given point in history and a given environment, and is completely different from a behaviour understood as the intrinsic property of a given organization.

A number of arguments in favour of such a presentation could be derived from the writings of the builders of the present models themselves. One of the strongest of such arguments seems to us the existence of a theory of union growth side by side with the study of union politics.[3] That such a theory of the development of unionism is possible and necessary implies that a number of factors neglected in the model now used to explain wage fixing have to be regrouped and taken up in an over-all explanation. We are, indeed, not unaware of the difference between our point of view and that of the authors for whom union growth and wage policies are two entirely different fields, quite alien one to the other. But it seems to us that the coexistence of the two separate fragments of theory bears witness to certain logical incompatibilities ; if, for instance, we have to explain the growth of unionism according to a historical model, what then happens to the membership function which links the

[1] Cf. J. Piaget, *Introduction*, p. 213.

[2] Among the most recent studies on this subject we may cite J. T. Dunlop, 'The Development of Labor Organization : a Theoretical Framework', *Insights into Labor Issues* (1948), pp. 163-193, and J. Shister, 'The Logic of Union Growth', *Journal of Political Economy* (October 1953), pp. 413-434.

[3] J. Åkerman proposes a somewhat similar method for business cycle analysis in his articles 'L'Analyse structurelle des variations économiques', *Bulletin de l'Institut de Recherches Économiques et Sociales de l'Université de Louvain* (December 1948), and 'Cycle et structure', *Revue économique* (January 1952).

number of union members to the wages obtained by the union ?

It is only when the studies on union growth will have been rescued from the wastepaper baskets of economic theory that we shall really be able to make valid statements about union behaviour, because this behaviour is always linked to the structure and the history of the labour movement.

There can be no question of presenting in this report any examples of the application of a method which needs more than hasty synthesis.[1] We can merely throw out some suggestions showing that an analysis which is both structural and historical might render a logical account of certain forms of union action which appear as mere accidents or as negligible imperfections from the point of view of the current models.

If the American unions generally exhibit a behaviour analogous to that of the private firm and thereby lend a certain degree of realism to the economic model of their actions, and if, on the contrary, French unions act according to essentially political criteria (in the sense of long-term objectives aiming at a transformation of the social organization), it may well be that these differences may be found to be due to fairly deep-rooted reasons of economic environment and particularly of the rate of economic progress in the two countries.[2]

A joint study of union concentration and the development of wage policies would also be most useful.[3] This would no doubt reveal a first phase of craft unions, when these organizations which were the heirs of the early labour traditions of craftsmen were above all concerned with defending themselves against the mass of unqualified workers.[4] To that stage corresponds a policy of discrimination reflected in the disparities between traditional wages and factory wages [5] and restrictive practices with regard both to entry into the organization and to the labour market.[6] The unionism of that stage

[1] A good example of this approach may be found in the work of J. L. Guglielmi, *Naissance et formation des trade unions des mineurs en Grande-Bretagne, 1843–1919* (1952).

[2] On the link between the characteristics of French capitalism and those of the trade union movement, see the astute remarks of a philosopher, J.-P. Sartre, 'Le Communisme et la paix', *Les Temps modernes* (April 1954), pp. 1776-1778 *et passim*.

[3] An interpretation based on comparable methodological principles is to be found in Jules Vuillemin, 'Les Syndicats ouvriers et les salaires', *Économie appliquée* (1952), pp. 261-337. It is founded on inequalities in the development of capitalism and the degree of homogeneity of the proletariat.

[4] Cf. Jean Montreuil, *Histoire du mouvement ouvrier en France des origines jusqu'à nos jours* (1946), pp. 111-116.

[5] See Labrousse, *La Crise de l'économie française à la fin de l'Ancien Régime et au début de la Révolution*, cited by J. Vuillemin, *op. cit.* p. 268.

[6] J. Montreuil, *op. cit.* pp. 31-32.

was a factor of wage differentiation ; it retained a local character, and instead of aiming at great numbers, it was out to safeguard the relatively privileged position of skilled workers.[1]

In a second phase mass trade unionism came to replace the unionism of minorities.[2] The trade union movement spread to unskilled workers who, if they had no tradition nor combative spirit to contribute, at least brought in numbers. At the same time there was a process of concentration ; organizations were no longer based on crafts but on industries, and they became fewer. They federated and acquired a certain unity on the national plane. This development was responsible for profound changes in union behaviour. The gap between different wages tended to diminish, since wage claims now applied more and more to the whole of the jobs in an industry. At the same time we witnessed the emergence of a union bureaucracy. This highly important event reinforced the tendency towards centralization.

But this situation was only transitory. It paved the way for a third phase marked by ever greater industrial concentration and government intervention in economic affairs. In its turn, unionism continued on its road of expansion, now directed no longer towards the labouring masses but towards the middle class, the office workers, and government employees.[3]

These circumstances imposed new conditions of action on the unions. Important decisions were now taken on the national plane, where the decisive battles were waged. The national labour organizations were compelled to exercise their action on the same plane. Strikes became more and more general in character ; the elements of success tended to shift from the labour masses of big industry to certain strategic points of the public sector. Now wage claims most often turn around one single figure (or a general percentage increase), the range of the wage hierarchy becomes smaller and smaller. Wages are a rigid mass ; trade unions no longer fear that any increase obtained by an organization may result in loss of employment by its members, since employers are unable to replace them by cheaper labour. In practice the unions thus represent all the workers, whether they are union members or not. On the other hand, the principle of negotiation on the national level introduces a new variable into the economic horizon of union leaders : the

[1] The situation of the American Federation of Labor towards the end of the nineteenth century was a somewhat similar one. See P. Waline, *Les Syndicats*, p. 11, and R. Marjolin, *L'Évolution du syndicalisme aux États-Unis*.

[2] Michel Collinet, *Esprit du syndicalisme*, Les Éditions ouvrières, (1951), chap. i : 'Du métier à l'industrie'.

[3] Cf. André Marchal, *Le Mouvement syndical en France* (1945), pp. 76-78.

general price level.[1] One of the most thorny problems they now have to resolve is to determine the highest possible wage level which is compatible with price stability.[2]

These few schematic notes do not pretend to be even a rough sketch of a general theory of union action. They are merely intended to point out that it is not very fruitful to speak of union behaviour in the absolute, leaving aside all structural and historical considerations.

In summary, the results of this paper may be put briefly in three propositions :

(1) The use of an 'economic' model of union behaviour corresponds to conditions strictly limited in time and space, and cannot be generalized without losing that which in this environment may be valid. Moreover, even in this limited framework, economic models cannot give a valid explanation of all aspects of union action.

(2) The mechanism of the formation of decisions inside union organizations often plays a considerable part and must be taken into account. This is a notable contribution of the 'political' models.

(3) Neither considerations of purely rational economic action, nor political factors, are sufficient for a satisfactory explanation of union wage policies. The latter must be related to economic development as a whole, and union action must be examined in its interactions with the social body of which it is a part.

[1] Union responsibility with respect to the price level is only part of the problems of what has been called 'integrated and constructive' trade unionism. Cf. R. Goetz-Girey, *La Pensée syndicale française, militants et théoriciens* (1948).

[2] It can be shown, too, that union behaviour again undergoes profound changes in the course of an inflationary process. In such a case unions would seem to try to avoid having their members fall victims to inflation either by initiating a general movement of wage increases the moment a certain critical gap appears between wages and prices or by demanding a sliding wage scale. On this point see A. Page, 'La Liaison salaire-coût de la vie', *Revue économique* (January 1953), pp. 31-62, and J. Guglielmi and M. Perrot, *Salaries et revendications sociales*, pp. 102-112.

Chapter 11

WAGE THEORY AND SOCIAL GROUPS[1]

BY

JEAN MARCHAL
University of Paris, France

ECONOMIC reality, unlike physical reality, differs in different parts of the world, and is subject to constant change. If an area enclosed by three straight lines is termed a triangle, this is a proposition which is valid without reference to time or space. By contrast, a proposition such as 'wages are the price of work' has significance only in an economic system where there are prices in the precise sense which economists attach to the word, and where work is considered a merchandise in the sense that it is a marketable thing capable of having a price. The very existence of the definition, with all the mechanisms and correlations it implies, depends upon a set of beliefs, behaviours, and institutions. It is linked to an economic system and changes with it, whether this is a matter of cause or effect.[2]

I. A Change in the Basis of Setting Wages

In these circumstances even research limited to the major western European or American countries has to face the fact that many a circumstance has changed since the beginning of the nineteenth century. A central change is that wage rates are no longer

[1] Translated by Elizabeth Henderson.

[2] J.-B. Say's *Cours d'économie politique* (1850 edition), vol. ii, p. 45 : 'It is the relation of supply and demand which regulates the price of that merchandise we call the labour of a workman, just as it regulates the price of all productive services'.

The author was well aware of the links between his proposition and the basic institutions of the régime : private property, freedom of transactions, and the existence of competitive markets. Indeed, after having formulated the above proposition, he dwells on the relatively small number of employers as against a generally abundant supply of labour, on the disadvantageous position of the workers who must take employment or die, and, finally, on the fact that employers' coalitions are allowed while workers' coalitions are illegal ; he concludes that 'the nature of things as well as the dominant position of the upper classes of society tend to keep salaries down to subsistence level or sometimes even below'. 'Good institutions can mitigate the hardships' resulting from this situation, but to 'oblige anyone to pay more for work than the price at which its execution is offered, would be a violation of property and a blow to the freedom of transactions'.

determined by discussion between a great number of isolated buyers and sellers who do not co-ordinate their actions, nor even by discussion between local unions lacking well-defined, mutual connections. Wage rates are, on the whole, though of course not without exception, determined by discussion involving the great employers' and workers' organizations on a national level, as well as by the official or semi-official intervention of government. This latter, in turn, cannot be considered an entirely independent power, since it has in part become an additional battlefield where the parties engage in their struggle with different means.

The discussion has shifted from the level of the firm, considered in isolation, to the level of the entire nation. It no longer involves individuals but organizations, and it takes place simultaneously in the markets which have profoundly changed and in the government.

How can this fact be explained? Three factors are operative, whose force and combination varies among countries. (1) The technical development of production has tended to assemble the sellers of labour in great industrial centres and to give the workers a uniform way of life and a growing solidarity. Similarly, technical development has, on the side of the buyers of labour, led to an increase in the average size of firms and to the establishment of numerous connections between firms.

(2) Better means of transportation and communication have enabled buyers and sellers of labour to move more readily and have stimulated them to acquire a common outlook and to co-ordinate their actions on the national level.

(3) Ideological factors in Europe, and particularly in France and in Great Britain, have influenced large strata of the population to take the view that wages are not the price of a merchandise, the monetary counterpart which the individual buying labour pays to the individual selling work, but the income which society, through the medium of entrepreneurs, channels towards all those who have fulfilled their social duty by supplying labour of appropriate quality and quantity, in order that they may lead a predefined way of life.[1] In the United States both employers and labour have, instead, more or less rallied to the view that wages, even though they are an element of production cost, also represent purchasing power, and since it is the purchasing power at the disposal of a large part of the population, its level, through the medium of aggregate demand, exercises an

[1] See my articles, 'Les Transformations intervenues dans la notion de salaire à l'époque moderne', *Coopération* (June 1955), p. 12, and 'Contribution à la construction d'une théorie de la distribution du revenu', *Economia internazionale* (1954).

influence on the development of the entire economy. The difference in reaction is characteristic of two mentalities. But in both cases the result is identical. It means that the establishment of average wage rates and the general level of wages is a national affair which is the concern of the whole community and must be discussed on that plane.

The French experience of the last few years is instructive as to the importance of these factors. During the last war the public authorities were led to take the determination of wages into their own hands. After the end of hostilities, the government, 'anxious to free the economy', proposed and obtained the law of February 11, 1950, which restored to employers' and workers' organizations the task of determining wages through collective agreements. The law merely specified that no wage may be below a national guaranteed minimum (*salaire minimum interprofessionnel garanti*, frequently known as SMIG), which the government was to determine after consultations with the employers' and workers' organizations. A subsequent law of July 18, 1952, imposed on the government the obligation to revise this minimum wage whenever the monthly cost-of-living index in Paris changed by more than 5 per cent.

The intention of the government and of parliament was quite clearly discernible in the discussions preceding these laws ; it was to create a system characterized as follows :

(a) At the base there is the national minimum wage, below which no wage may fall. (b) The national minimum wage once fixed, the various unions in different fields enter into negotiations and determine the minimum wage for each category of workers which must be equal to or higher than the national minimum wage. A scale of wages for different work is thus established. (c) In various firms wage scales are then fixed which may not be lower than these minimum wages.

The entire system rested on assumptions quite contrary to reality. It presupposed the existence of numerous employers' and workers' organizations, distinct both on the occupational and geographical level and without any but a very loose co-ordination. It failed to take into account that there are relations among employers and workers which regroup both on the national plane. In practice, the neglected factors, namely the existence of solidarity amongst the workers and of solidarity among employers, and the presence of organizations reflecting this solidarity, were powerful enough to give rise to a significant change in the whole system.

The national minimum wage has changed its meaning. In all the agreements which have been concluded, minimum wages for occupational categories were established as functions of the national minimum wage and linked to it in a formal manner. This does not mean that the employers' and workers' organizations have given up discussing the basic wage rate and are leaving the government to fix it, but simply rather than let their constituent unions negotiate collective agreements, they prefer to enter into mutual contacts within the framework envisaged for the establishment of the national minimum wage. This has the advantage that they discuss on a national level a question which seems to them of national scope.

Negotiations for minima for different occupational categories and various regions have shown that the unions have not adopted a particularist attitude. It soon became apparent that to change a category of labour in one branch meant calling forth immediate wage demands by the corresponding categories in all other branches. When employers' or workers' unions negotiate in one branch or one region, the central organizations stand behind them since every change is susceptible of having general repercussions, and, in fact, it is these organizations themselves which negotiate.

This does not exclude the play of more specific factors on the local or personal plane. Firms may pay one or more categories of workers' wages higher than the established minima. But any change in a minimum as a result of negotiations on the national plane will involve a change in these wages too.

This is not a situation peculiar to France. It is true that studies on national wages policy by English authors such as Worswick and Flanders [1] are more concerned with indicating what should be done than with describing what actually happens. Thus, Flanders surely outlines an ideal, rather than reality, when he states that wages should be increased only in cases when their rise is justified by the exigencies of a national wages policy, and that there are three such cases: improvement in the standard of living of low-paid labour; greater productivity (with certain reservations); and adjustment of inequalities in wages when they stand in the way of a sufficient recruitment of labour. Flanders indicates, none the less, that in Great Britain, as elsewhere, the general factors which we have listed come into play and that discussions on wage rates tend to shift towards the national plane and to involve general organizations. Macro-economic factors are developing to the detriment of micro-economic factors.[2]

[1] G. D. N. Worswick, 'Stability and Flexibility of Full Employment', *The Full Employment* (1944); A. Flanders, 'Wages Policy and Full Employment in Britain', *Bulletin of the Oxford University Institute of Statistics* (April–June 1950).

[2] See Jean Lhomme, 'Le Problème d'une politique nationale des salaires en Grande-Bretagne', *Revue économique* (March 1952), p. 183.

Any wages theory of a truly macro-economic character, in line with the facts of today rather than with those of a former age, has three essential requirements : First, the usual concept of wages must be replaced by a wider concept. Second, the behaviour of the groups involved must be studied. Third, wages theory must be integrated into a general theory of national income distribution.

II. A Wider Concept of Wages

The discussions on a national plane between employers' and workers' organizations do not as a matter of fact concern just direct wages, the sums to be paid out to the workers by firms, but they include the total income which is to accrue to workers in one way or another, and by one mechanism or another.

The Office of Economic Studies of the French Finance Ministry has traced the development of labour income from 1938 to 1951. It has distinguished two parts of labour income : wages directly paid by entrepreneurs to workers and social transfers received by the latter through the intermediary of government or other public agencies. The figures were all expressed also in 1938 francs, so as to eliminate the effects of changes in the value of money. The results are shown [1] in Table 1.

This table shows that while the workers as a group in 1951 received indirect wages in the form of social transfers well above those of 1938, their actual pay packets, expressed in 1938 francs, had shrunk in about the same proportion, so that the purchasing power at the disposal of the labour group barely rose by 4 per cent.

This result is the more remarkable in that aggregate labour income in 1951 was spread over slightly greater numbers, that the average working week increased from 40 hours in 1938 to 45 hours in 1951, and that the average productivity of labour increased. 'For the same working time,' states the report, 'and notwithstanding the improvement in yield, the wage earner now receives less purchasing power than in 1938. It is only by furnishing additional work that the wage earners as a whole have regained their purchasing power.'

This suggests, though strict proof is lacking, that general factors having to do with the power of the labour group in relation to other groups and with the institutional situation condition the size of the total labour income. So long as these factors remain unchanged,

[1] *Rapports du Service des Études Économiques et Financières du Ministère des Finances sur les comptes provisoires de la nation des années 1951 et 1952 et sur le budget économique de l'année 1953* (1953), p. 45.

everything that increases one of the components of this total income, say social transfers, involves a diminution of another component, namely, direct wages.

The obvious conclusion is that we should think in terms of labour income units in a wider sense. It is certainly possible that certain factors affect only direct wage rates. But a true explanation, a really realistic wages theory, must be built upon the foundation of labour's share in the national income and not merely on direct wages as is usually done.

At the beginning of 1954 the French government was faced with a demand for higher wages through an increase in the national

TABLE 1

LABOUR INCOMES IN FRANCE

1938–1951

Year	Wages 1000 Million Current Francs	Social Transfers 1000 Million Current Francs	Labour Incomes : Wages + Transfers 1000 Million		Purchasing Power Index of Labour Incomes 1938 = 100
			Current Francs	1938 Francs	
1938	176	4	180	180	100
1946	1045	80	1125	141	78
1947	1530	150	1680	153	85
1948	2520	280	2800	165	92
1949	2775	525	3300	173	96
1950	3130	600	3730	177	98
1951	3950	750	4700	188	104

minimum wage on the part of the labour groups, who intended in this way to obtain a proportional increase in all wages. The government's response was no less characteristic. By its decree of February 6, 1954, the government raised the national minimum wage, which became 115 francs per hour for the Paris region as against 100 previously. But since it wished to avoid this increase spreading over the whole range of wages, the government qualified this increase, by a device of doubtful legality, as a 'degressive indemnity not applicable to all grades',[1] and thus intervened, as it had no right to do, in the determination of the hierarchy of wage scales.

By a fiscal reform law of April 10, 1954, the public authorities

[1] The word degressive was specially invented by the legislators in their embarrassment. It is supposed to indicate that the wage increase granted by the decree is not a uniform one, but becomes proportionally less for higher wages.

modified the rules for computing the progressive surtax which, together with the proportional tax, constitutes the general income tax in France. In particular, they decided that wages and salaries were to be counted for surtax purposes only at nine-tenths of their value. The surtax being progressive, the gift so presented to wage and salary earners in most cases exceeded 10 per cent of the tax, since it is the most highly taxed portion of income which disappears or shrinks. Moreover, this gift is the higher, the higher the taxpayer's income. For an unmarried taxpayer having no other income than wages or salary, the tax reduction on 300,000 francs per year amounted to 6700 francs, or 2·2 per cent of his income. But if his income is 3 million francs a year, then the tax reduction amounts to 112,000 francs, or 3·7 per cent.

No doubt wishing to prevent a chain reaction among the various social groups and an inflationary price rise, the organizations in the labour market and the government preferred allowing this benefit to the higher wages in the form of a diminution of the tax collector's share rather than through an increase in the pay packet.

We see again that a realistic theory of wages needs to build upon the whole of the income labour receives in one way or another, through social transfers or tax reduction rather than merely by the direct wage.

In these circumstances the value of splitting the study of income distribution into two parts (inquiring first into the primary distribution and then into redistribution) appears highly debatable.[1] The proponents of this distinction are well aware of the fact that if the government uses its authority to shift purchasing power without any counterpart in productive services, it also engages in a whole series of activities which directly or indirectly contribute to the satisfaction of needs and are therefore productive.

> Economists have acknowledged [writes Brochier],[2] that no distinction can be made between the productivity of a private and a public police force. The same holds true of the services of education, justice, and even of the army, and *a fortiori*, also of public services of an economic nature. If these activities were not carried out by the government, they would in one form or another be carried out by private persons and would thus be the source of incomes which nobody would hesitate to consider the incomes of production.

[1] T. Barna, *Redistribution of Incomes through Public Finance in 1937* (1945); H. Brochier, *Finances publiques et redistribution des revenus* (1950).

[2] H. Brochier, *op. cit.*, H. Stern, 'Les Dépenses de l'état dans le revenu national', *Economica* (May 1943).

The proposed method, then, consists in first studying, under the name of primary distribution, the incomes arising out of the contribution of some productive service, it being irrelevant whether these incomes apply to the private or to the public sector of the economy ; as a second step, the method would then take account of the transfers without counterpart which the government can enforce as between various categories of individuals. Primary distribution measures 'incomes such as they arise from production' ; redistribution coincides with the incomes put at the disposal of consumers.

In the economies of England and France in the middle of the nineteenth century the distinction is readily applicable. Isolated individuals buy and sell labour. Their relations in markets which are largely competitive give rise to wage rates which, together with other elements, ultimately contribute to the determination of profit rates. Subsequently, some of these individuals are required to shoulder a tax burden which channels incomes to other individuals. But these taxes are small. In such circumstances it is possible to begin with a study of the mechanism of wage formation and with the various incomes derived directly from production, only later to proceed to governmental actions resulting in a redistribution of these incomes. However, it should be stressed that this approach cannot be dissociated from two circumstances which no longer exist today : the isolation of the buyers and sellers of labour and the modest size of the transfers.

Buyers and sellers of labour today are organized into large groups and their discussions take place on the national plane, in the framework of markets, as they are still called, or of public institutions. Moreover, the taxes and transfers involved have become much larger. The workers now have to balance everything they receive and spend, and to regulate their behaviour accordingly. A worker cares little whether he receives a higher pay packet from the firm where he is employed, or benefits from a reduction in the tax he has to pay the government out of his wages. In either case his purchasing power increases. Similarly, an entrepreneur may complain and try to raise his sales prices when a collective agreement or a public wage award force him to pay higher wage rates ; but he will react in exactly the same way to any increase in the taxes which affect his activities.

The proponents of the distinction between primary distribution and redistribution are well aware of the impossibility of separate study of incomes in the private and the public sector. They are agreed that wage formation in nationalized industries does not come about by any mechanism basically different from that of wage formation in the private sector and that the two processes are interconnected. Indeed, they have taken pains to define redistribution, not as the formation of incomes the source of which is the State, but as the correction, by the mechanism of public finances, of the distribution of productive incomes arising in both the public and the private sector.

In so doing they have misunderstood the new character of income distribution which involves organized groups confronting each other on the national level. The distinction between incomes due to production and incomes due to transfers becomes obscured and is no longer usable. The reactions of the labour group, just as those of the entrepreneur or any other group, are functions of its total income, that is to say, of everything it receives both at the moment of its contribution to a productive service and on any other occasion.

Logical inquiry thus reaches the same result as the practical observations made earlier. What is needed is a theory of the total income of labour, a theory of wages in the widest sense, and not in the narrow sense involved in a theory of social transfers. In order to construct such a theory it is necessary to analyse the general behaviour of the social groups concerned.

III. General Behaviour of Workers and Employers

We have already stressed that the contacts in the labour market from which wage scales result are no longer made by isolated individuals nor even by numerous unco-ordinated unions, but by groups organized on a national plane. In theoretical terms, it can be said that competition has been replaced by bilateral monopoly or by bilateral oligopoly, according to whether the various workers' and employers' organizations are taken to make common cause or still to have divergent interests.

The markets of bilateral monopoly and bilateral oligopoly differ fundamentally from those of perfect or imperfect competition, so much so that it is probably a mistake to use the term market for both cases. In competitive markets an individual's action of changing his own supply or demand has no effect on the price. There is therefore no need to inquire into the special motives which determine the behaviour of any one buyer or seller. The economist merely needs to study the general and rather simple and crude motives which inspire the majority of buyers and sellers.

In markets of bilateral monopoly or bilateral oligopoly everything is different. The market mechanism of price formation is of only minor importance. More precisely, it is closely conditioned by the behaviour and the motives which inspire the parties involved, and these parties are only few in number.

Wages have by no means the same significance for workers who sell labour and for entrepreneurs who buy it. For workers, wages are the means of subsistence and of leading a certain kind of life. For entrepreneurs, wages are an element of production cost. But it must not be forgotten that production cost itself, together with the sales price of the product, is one of the elements determining profit, that is to say the entrepreneurs' income.

The overwhelming majority of those who sell labour services have nothing but their wages to live on. They have always aspired to wages which would permit them and their dependent children to lead a decent life. In competitive markets this aspiration could not find expression. When wage rates were low, as was the case in France during the nineteenth century, this aspiration induced workers to increase the labour supply so as to get a sufficient income. They accepted long working days and sent their wives and children to the factories at an early age. The result was disastrous, for this increase in the labour supply called forth a new fall in the wage rate and the condition of the workers remained wretched.

But once markets are so transformed that the price is no longer imposed on the parties, the labour organizations are quite logically led to a different attitude : they calculate what a worker, an employee, a technician needs to live in the proper manner recognized by public opinion, and they then demand that the wages cover these expenses.

It may be objected that this involves the risk of excessive wage rates which would not permit the employment of all the workers. In such a case the pressure of unemployment would make its weight felt and would force labour organizations to accept a reduction of wage rates, just in the same manner as under a règime of competition.

On the other hand, labour organizations may be prepared to sustain a certain amount of unemployment for quite a long time, by providing assistance schemes for the unemployed, by trying to shift the burden of their maintenance wholly or partly onto the public authorities, or, as was the case in 1936, pressing the government to reduce the legal working time. In addition, labour organizations acting on the national plane deal with the possibility of trying to diminish the income of another social group. In so far as it is possible, a rise in wages need not necessarily become a charge on production cost, since the increase in one element of cost may be compensated for by the decrease in another. Unemployment need not automatically result. By means of a mechanism which we shall later analyse in detail, labour can thus introduce new factors into wage formation.

Firms, for their part, may find themselves under the necessity of agreeing to nominal wage rates which, in view of the sales price of their products, constitute an excessive charge. Profits are curtailed to an extent which appears excessive so that not enough can be set aside for necessary depreciation nor for the distribution of adequate dividends to executives and shareholders. However, by virtue of their larger size, smaller number, and closer relations, these firms now have possibilities which the isolated firms of yesteryear lacked : they can raise the sales price of their products to compensate for the effects of higher wages and to restore former profit levels. It would seem that such a price increase can be carried through all the more readily since the workers, who represent a large part of the population, have higher nominal incomes and the price rise will therefore probably not induce them to diminish the quantity of goods they normally purchase.

So long as incomes, and particularly wages, were established by negotiations involving isolated buyers and sellers in competitive markets, it was possible to construct a two-step theory of distribution. The first step was to determine nominal incomes by confronting the demands of the buyers and sellers of various services while assuming the value of money to remain stable. This was a perfectly admissible assumption, since neither buyers nor sellers, in isolation, could exercise any influence on the prices of goods and since their whole behaviour rested on the notion of the stable purchasing power of money. The second step, which involved the theory of money rather than the theory of distribution proper, was to define the conditions determining the general price level. The comparison between nominal incomes and general price level yielded real income rates.

Everything is different when negotiations between isolated individuals on competitive markets are replaced by discussion between organized groups at a national level. Forced to accept a general wage increase in monetary terms, the entrepreneurs will try to compensate for the effects on their profits by raising the sales prices of their products.

It would seem that the price increase should be of a lesser percentage than the wage increase, since wages constitute only part of the cost of production. In fact, as is well shown by French experience in recent years,[1] the entrepreneurs are out to maintain

[1] V. P. Bauchet, 'Évolution des salaires réels et structure économique', *Revue économique* (May 1952), p. 297 ff.

the real volume of their profits, taking account of the price rise they intend to initiate. What they wish to stabilize is not the monetary amount of their profits, but the ratio between that amount and the general price index which is bound to rise as a result of their action. If the state of demand allows, entrepreneurs may even try to make use of the opportunity to improve that ratio.

In western Europe entrepreneurs are in a very strong position because of the existence of numerous open or secret agreements and because, in the words of an American report,[1] competition is generally regarded as legitimate in the fields of quality of goods and services but must not be allowed to extend to prices. Indeed, the official national accounting statistics in France show that in 1951 there occurred a general price increase allowing the maintenance of previous profits not only in sectors of scarcities but also in sectors where demand fell off and where unsaleable stocks began to accumulate. It would be a mistake, however, to think that no reactions are possible in the United States where, in many important branches, the structure of production is such that a small number of very large firms is surrounded by small satellites.[2] It is axiomatic that, faced with a general increase in wages and in the prices of industrial products, all social groups which make up the population[3] will try by various means, through the markets or political channels, to maintain their income in real terms or even to increase it. This entails a depreciation in the value of money, and such depreciation is bound to lead to new labour action, if labour is determined to improve its standard of life.

The real question from the point of view of the distribution of national income or of wages in their wider sense, is to determine the conditions under which wage earners as a social group can succeed in its attempt and establish a lasting equilibrium more advantageous to itself.

The chain of effects of a general rise in money wages, a rise in industrial prices, a rise in agricultural prices, and a new rise in wages may lead to an increase in the volume of goods produced. This latter rise is the consequence of the pressure of increased demand. The first thing to examine, then, is the manner in which an increase in the purchasing power of the wage earners, and possibly

[1] Clarence B. Randall, *A Creed for Free Enterprise* (1952), p. 149 ; David S. Landes, 'L'Ésprit d'entreprise en France', *Nouvelle Revue de l'Économie contemporaine* (December 1953) ; and Harbison and Burgess, 'Modern Management in Western Europe', *American Journal of Sociology* (July 1954), pp. 15-23.

[2] J. K. Galbraith, *American Capitalism, The Concept of Countervailing Power* (1952), pp. 35 and 98.

[3] The concept of the social group will be discussed below.

of other groups, is distributed among the various demands. Next, we have to inquire into the elasticity of production in the various sectors. But there may also be an increase in the volume of output due to autonomous factors. Particularly as regards agricultural products, which occupy an important place in workers' budgets, there may be increases due to favourable weather or to persistent efforts on the part of the government and agricultural organizations to increase farm yields.

Supply and demand will tend towards equality, but equality may come about by variations in price or in quantity. On that basis it would be impossible to define the conditions of stable equilibrium. From the strictly economic point of view, an equilibrium established by means of a sharp price rise and a small increase in output is neither more nor less stable than an equilibrium obtained by a large increase in output and a small price rise.

Any social group is always greatly attached to the standard of life it has had during the preceding period. If that standard is diminished, either by accidental circumstances leading to a falling off of goods available or by the action of other social groups, then we shall witness the emergence of what we may call social tension within the first group. This group will take action with all the means at its disposal, on the markets or through political channels, to increase its nominal income.

This social tension will subside but very slowly, either through a lowering of the standard of living of the members of the group, who gradually get used to lower consumption, or through a reduction in the size of the group, some of its members leaving and joining other groups, which enables the remaining members to live better. For instance, small shopkeepers may become wage workers or farmers may go into the cities and accept industrial employment.

On the other hand, when the standard of life of a group rises, we can assume that the social tension and its members' desire for improvement subsides, at least for a time. The tension will not arise again until a good deal later, when the members of the group will have become thoroughly used to their new condition or when the group grows by the influx of people from other groups.

All this suggests that we have here the elements for a determination of the conditions of stable equilibrium. Let us suppose an initial situation in which the group of wage earners wants to raise its standard of life. This means that social tension in this group is higher than normal, and that the gap between desired expenditure and actually possible expenditure has become unduly large.[1] An inflationary process results. Three series of effects can occur: an increase in the volume of output in various sectors; increases or decreases in the size of various social groups; and changes in their habits of life and in their view of what is strictly necessary. Stable equilibrium will be attained when these three effects will again have reduced to normal the social tension within the groups concerned.

It is obvious that it will be easier to re-establish equilibrium if production has risen a lot. Then the absolute share and possibly even the relative share of the wage earners in the real national income can be increased without any reduction, or even with a more or less marked increase, in the share of other groups.

We must add, however, that if some other group, let us say retail traders,[2] has benefited by the inflationary process and has either grown in number or got used to a higher standard of living, then it will clearly be more difficult for the workers to increase their aggregate real income. Unless production has grown very considerably, the workers will then be able to obtain satisfaction only if the government takes measures of credit policy, for example, or in the field of monopoly control, to reduce the trade margins which are the shopkeepers' income or else to reduce the number of shopkeepers.

Any study of wages which is to have real explanatory value should, therefore, in our view proceed as follows: study the effects on the demand for various goods of a rise in the total wage bill; the manner in which production reacts to foreseeable changes in demand; and also the effects on the size and requirements of other social groups. If the workers wish to improve their lot then they must look at the consequences of any strategy they might employ from all these points of view. This entails a good deal more than the simple pursuit of higher money wages, and the labour leaders are beginning to realize this. It is true that such a rise in money wages will nearly always be necessary at the beginning. But it must be handled skilfully, adjusted to varying circumstances, in short, integrated into a plan.[3]

As an example, and so as to give a concrete content to what we have said, let us briefly retrace what happened in France since the

[1] See particularly the survey made by the Marseilles Chamber of Commerce, which attempted to measure the 'degree of lacking satisfaction' by products for four occupational groups. (F. A. Dufour, *Une Enquête sur la consommation à Marseille*, Chambre de Commerce de Marseille, 1953.)

[2] In France, as a result of an increase in the number of retail distributors due to inflation, trading profits rose between 1938 and 1949 from 9·7 to 11 per cent of net national income at factor cost.

[3] H. Brochier, 'Le Plan de dix-huit mois', *Reconstruction* (May 1954), p. 16.

end of the last war. In Table 2 we have assembled indices relating to the total wage bill and to the aggregate value of agricultural products reaching the markets.

During 1946 and 1947 the disturbances caused by the war were not restored and there continued to be a lack of manufactured goods on the French market. Some purchasing power was set free in the wage-earning group, and this was directed towards agricultural produce. Will the workers, then, obtain more of the latter ? By

TABLE 2*

WAGE AND AGRICULTURAL INDICES IN FRANCE 1938–1950

1938 = 100

Year	Wage Bill	Volume of Agricultural Products reaching Markets	Agricultural Prices	Value of Agricultural Products reaching Markets	Purchasing Power of Wages in Terms of Agricultural Products
	(1)	(2)	(3)	(4) = (2) × (3)	$(5) = \frac{(1) \times 100}{(4)}$
1938	100	100	100	100	100
1946	630	65	1080	707	89
1947	880	77	1310	1008	87
1948	1500	83	1825	1517	98
1949	1760	96	1890	1814	97
1950	2050	103	1980	2039	100

* The figures of the first three columns are borrowed from Le Bourva, *L'Inflation française d'après-guerre, 1945–1949* (1953), p. 138 ; the figures of the last two columns are calculated on the basis of the former.

no means, for agricultural production, too, was well below the 1938 level. The marketed quantities dropped from 100 in 1938 to 65 in 1946 and 77 in 1947. What the workers did in turning towards agricultural markets the purchasing power that had become disposable, the other social groups did too. The means so shifted by the latter were larger, because in the first place their resources were larger and in the second place they used to apply a greater part of their income to the purchase of manufactured goods. Agricultural prices rose sharply. The purchasing power of wage earners in terms of agricultural products fell from 100 in 1938 to 89 in 1946 and 87 in 1947.

This phenomenon is readily explicable in terms of the allocation of incomes in the various groups as between various expenditures, and in terms of the reactions of production. But if we wish to get to the bottom of things we must add that the equilibrium so obtained is not stable in the long run. Indeed, social tension inside the labour group grew, as is shown by numerous signs. For a number of reasons it is not possible to reduce the size of the group at all. An adjustment to a lower standard of life could only come about very slowly and is, in any case, not desirable. So the inflationary process went on.

In 1949 and 1950 the situation tended to get back to normal. More manufactured goods reached the market. Agricultural production was close to its 1938 level, 96 in 1949 and 103 in 1950. The index of agricultural prices which had got ahead of the index of the wage bill slowed down its advance and both returned to comparable levels : 1890 and 1760 in 1949, 1980 and 2050 in 1950. The purchasing power of the wage bill in terms of agricultural products returns to levels comparable with pre-war ones : 97 in 1949 and 100 in 1950.

After 1953, for autonomous reasons, agricultural production was abundant. On the one hand, the weather was favourable ; on the other hand, the persistent efforts on the part of the government and farmers to raise agricultural productivity bore fruits. Was the social group of farmers able to improve its standard of life significantly ? For lack of certain data we can give no definite reply. But from what we do know it would appear that the improvement was only slight. French agriculture reached a critical point. Certain products were no longer absorbed by the domestic market and part of it had to be exported. But the measures making such exports possible have not yet been taken. The strategic situation of the agricultural group is thus not a very strong one, at least for the time being. Agricultural prices have fallen. This suggests that two other social groups should have been able to improve their standard of life : on the one hand, the workers whose real wage bill has gone up, and, on the other hand, the traders who, according to certain observers, have intercepted part of the price fall.

Indeed, a number of indications show that social tension in the labour group has decreased, and in contrast social tension has increased in the farming group. From the practical point of view, and it coincides with our analysis, it would seem that the French government will either have to take measures to reduce the numerical size of the farming group or else to proceed to a rational organization of the export of farm products. As regards the workers, they could probably improve their over-all situation by associating themselves with the government's efforts to re-establish sufficient competition in the distributing sector, restrict certain undue margins, and reduce the number of shopkeepers. Thereby they would endow with efficacy any further increases in nominal wages, which otherwise might give rise to general price rises and thus fail to be translated into any lasting improvement in real wages.

IV. Integration of the Theory of Wages into a Theory of National Income Distribution

No wage theory can be built upon the two social groups of labour and entrepreneurs alone. The theory of wages has no autonomous existence, or at least only a very limited one. There is only one single general theory of the distribution of national income. A double revision of the existing theory thus suggests itself : revision of the groups concerned, and revision of the factors to be considered as data and variables.

Traditionally a distinction has been made between those who supply labour, who supply capital, who supply raw materials, and finally entrepreneurs, who supply the function of enterprise.[1] But this distinction goes back to the early classical writers, and it is closely linked to the whole set of institutions and behaviour characteristic of the economic system at their time. It rests on the assumption that the entrepreneur is the essential instrument of distribution. To produce goods, this entrepreneur needs factors of production ; he buys them on the free markets and thereby gives rise to the price of services. This price of services is considered as the only constituent element with respect to individual incomes. For the economists of that time, each individual's income is obtained by multiplying the price of the services, determined in the manner described above, by the quantity of productive services the individual can place on the market. But this quantity itself is considered as a datum and is not the object of any research. With such a set of institutions and behaviours, and for that particular conception of research, the above distinction between four types of suppliers may be considered adequate.

Today, however, the determination of the basic rate and of the general wage scale involves organized groups which confront each other in various fashions : in direct or indirect negotiation, in the course of the establishment of collective agreements and notably of the budget on the national plane.

[1] J. Marchal, 'The Construction of a New Theory of Profit', *American Economic Review* (September 1951).

It is these groups which a theory of distribution needs to take into account. Which are they and what, correspondingly, are the types of income to operate with ?

Observation suggests a distinction between what we shall call activity incomes or subjective incomes, and property incomes or objective incomes. Activity incomes have the characteristic feature that they constitute the chief resources of a set of people who employ the same methods, or related methods, in order to maintain those incomes at a satisfactory level. Provisionally we can name three such incomes, clearly distinct from each other. For each of them, however, there arises the question, from our point of view, whether it is truly homogeneous or should not be subdivided into several autonomous types of income.

(1) First we have the income of the workers, or wages, defined as the income of those whose only or at least main asset is their labour power.

Several questions arise on examination of those incomes. Are the salaries and wages earned by those employed in government agencies or in nationalized undertakings to be considered as of the same nature and as obeying the same laws as the salaries and wages of those employed in the private sector ? Are the remunerations received by the higher ranks, both in the private and the public sector, of the same nature and do they obey the same laws as the wages of the lower ranks ? All these remunerations, in spite of their differences, present sufficient common features and, above all, interrelations to allow the category of incomes under consideration to be treated as homogeneous. The effort to maintain these incomes at a satisfactory level is made by the same organizations or by organizations in close mutual relationship. What stands in the foreground of discussions on wage rates is always the same kind of consideration relating to the standard of living of people who have nothing but their labour power to subsist on. Finally, the rates obtained by one of the categories often serve as a point of reference and as a guide for the determination of the other rates.

(2) Secondly, we have the profit of entrepreneurs in industry and trade, defined as the income of those who, as individual entrepreneurs or corporations, risk the money capital at their disposal in the process of production, trying to create a difference between the total receipts received from consumers on sale of the products and the total outlays needed for the purchase of means of production.

It may be asked whether this kind of income should not be considered in two different parts : the profits of individual entrepreneurs and the profit of corporations.[1] In fact, even though the representatives of the two groups are sometimes associated in different organizations, they always join forces in any discussions with other social groups and particularly with wage earners and with the government. Their methods of action are analogous and closely connected.

Others may wonder why we are speaking of the profits of corporations, instead of singling out, amongst those profits, those which belong to the entrepreneurs proper, in the precise sense of the word. But it is a very tricky business to find out who is, or are, the true entrepreneurs in a corporation. Whatever abstract criteria may be applied, their application in practice always remains uncertain. Statistics often distinguish between the incomes of individual enterprises and corporations, but they never give any indications of the incomes of pure entrepreneurs. The concepts of profit of individual entrepreneurs and profit of corporations are thus much more useful.

Moreover, we may add that the managers of corporations in practice act in the name of the whole company. Eventually, no doubt, the profits made are distributed between the managers, true entrepreneurs, and shareholders, who simply supply the money capital engaged in the business. But this is an internal question which is quite distinct from that of distribution on the level of the national community and does not interfere with the latter. There is no common front of shareholders in various companies struggling with a common front of managers. It is the companies themselves which are the economic agents involved on the social plane. And on that plane the only thing that is of interest and susceptible of giving rise to reactions is the total profit made by the corporations. How this total profit is distributed amongst the various categories of participants in the company is another question, just as is the distribution of the family income among the members of the family.

(3) Finally, there is farming profit, which is quite distinct from industrial profit and obeys different laws. Economists clinging to tradition often confuse the two types of profit. However, there are many indications that farming profit is not of the same nature as industrial profit and obeys different laws. Statistics always mention it separately. The organizations of farmers are distinct from those of industrial producers and are often in opposition to the latter.

[1] This question has been treated in the light of American experience in J. Lecaillon, 'Liaisons directes et liaisons inverses entre les revenus dans l'économie américaine contemporaine', *Revue économique* (January 1954), p. 1.

The conditions of life and production are different. Finally, farmers employ their own distinct means of defending their income and establishing it at a satisfactory level. Industrialists readily enter into agreements, but farmers, numerous and dispersed as they are, invoke the intervention of the government and the installation of systems of market regulation and price and income guarantees.

Property incomes are a second type of income, very different from that we have just examined and in many ways much closer to the traditional type. Wages, industrial or commercial profits, and farming profits in effect represent the main, and often sole income of people belonging to a well defined social group. The workers, the entrepreneur, the farmer all consider that what they receive for supplying their labour, running an enterprise, or cultivating the soil should enable them to live, to occupy a certain place in society, perhaps even to save a certain amount and to make certain investments. If the level of their incomes falls below that which, as a whole, they consider a minimum level, they react in one way or another. A tension arises which is such that it can call forth a change in the distribution of incomes. This tension will not disappear until, as a result of changes in the amount of income or of an adjustment in the way of life, equilibrium is once more established between actual income and income considered justified — at least so far as the majority of the group is concerned.

The incomes we are discussing now do not accrue to a well-defined social group but to all those members of one group or another who possess either money capital which they lend to others against a contractual rate of interest, or real estate, the services of which they use themselves or which they rent to others.

In the past it is possible that such incomes could constitute the main or sole income of definable social groups. In the nineteenth century there was, and not in France alone, a group of property owners living on the yield of its monetary and landed property. In practice there is no such group nowadays. To be a property owner is no longer a distinguishing feature. Apart from negligible exceptions, the members of the French community are, today, workers, managers, or farmers. Some members of these groups possess monetary capital or landed property which they do not use in their own enterprises and put at the disposal of others against interest or rent.

Because these incomes do not, for the majority of those who enjoy them, constitute their main income, their recipients have organized themselves only much later and their organizations are much less powerful, owing to the diversity in the condition of their members. Moreover, these incomes have remained factor prices. This means that the price is formed on the markets for the services in question without reference to the circumstances of those who supply the services. The question is not to furnish any social group with means of subsistence, but simply to determine the value of a good, the sum of money which must be paid in order to obtain the good.

Finally, these incomes are highly vulnerable from the social point of view. A worker whose wage is insufficient can try to enforce a raise by striking. The industrial or commercial entrepreneur, the farmer, who consider their profits too low, can in one way or another restrict their production. No such possibility is open to anyone who supplies money or real capital. It is true that the owner of money capital can put his savings on strike, as it were, by spending the whole of his income or hoarding some of it, if he considers the interest rate too low. But nothing is easier, in present circumstances, than to break such a strike. If no savings are available on the capital market, entrepreneurs can have recourse to the method of self-financing and public authorities can raise taxes or create money. If private saving is withheld, it is replaced by any one of the forms of forced saving. As regards owners of real estate, they are in no better position, since these properties are hard to disguise and are therefore easily requisitioned or taxed. It is true that the taxation of rents has its disadvantages, and there is ample evidence of this in France herself. If rents are fixed too low, house owners fail to maintain their houses properly and abstain from building new ones. But the reaction needs a long time and during the period which must elapse before a price rise can come about, the owners received a reduced income.

Property incomes, so defined, seem to be two in number : there is the income from money lent, or interest, and the income from material goods rented, or rent. There are well-known relations between the two.

Without pushing the analysis any further we consider that a realistic theory of income distribution needs to take account of these new income categories, with their characteristic features. It is also necessary to discover the direct or inverse relationships [1] which may exist among them or between them and national income. At least for the purposes of research with which we are here concerned, the traditional categories are out of date and not sufficient.

At the same time we must revise our notions of what is a datum and what variable. It is usual to consider as given everything

[1] Cf. V. Lecaillon, *Revue économique*.

which characterizes the structure of an economy, for instance the organization of its markets and their more or less competitive nature. The structure being assumed to be stable, research is directed towards the factors operating within its framework. These factors are considered the variables of the system. By and large, we have a contrast between structures, which change but slowly and the transformations of which are left for the sociologists to study, and the static or dynamic mechanisms characterizing a given structure, which are the exclusive object of economic research.

However, observation of modern economies suggests that this distinction is no longer applicable, at least at present. The distinction was certainly in line with reality during the nineteenth century, when the essential economic agents were isolated individuals with limited power of action. Structures were indeed stable and developed only slowly under the diffuse pressure of badly organized groups hardly acting consciously. These structures were, on the whole, competitive, which means that within their relatively stable framework there operated chiefly individuals. It was, in such circumstances, fairly easy to distinguish two fields of study : on the one hand the development of institutions and structures, which was left to the sociologists, and on the other hand the play of mechanisms within a set of institutions and structures, with which economists concerned themselves.

Today individuals are of course still capable of exercising an influence, and indeed it would not be desirable that they should be reduced to impotence. But developments have restricted their field of action. Side by side with individuals, indeed above them, the groups which they have created intervene. If these groups do not today represent the only economic agents, they do represent an essentia lone. This has been acknowledged in all countries, and the importance to which the theories of monopoly and oligopoly have risen is proof of it.

Groups act differently from isolated individuals. So far as groups are concerned, it is no longer easy to distinguish between their action on a structure and their action within a structure. So long as the labour market was a competitive one, it was easily possible to distinguish two types of action : on the one hand the action of those individuals in increasing or diminishing the quantities supplied or demanded and giving rise to an increase or a decrease in wage rates, on the other hand the efforts of these same individuals to form unions and thereby reduce competition on the labour market, to obtain intervention on the part of the government, and finally, by these two means, to change the basic structures. As soon as the individuals are replaced by groups the distinction loses much of its meaning. In their negotiations with employers' organizations on a national level, in the presence of public authorities, the labour organizations may just as well propose a change in institutions which obstruct them as a change in wage rates within the framework of these institutions. The two questions are treated in simultaneous and related discussions. The share of labour in the national income can be increased just as well by a reorganization of the commercial apparatus as by a general wage increase. The workers may press for either, as is shown by discussions currently taking place in France. In these circumstances we may well ask whether there is any advantage in economists retaining the traditional distinction between data and variables and, indeed, we may ask whether this distinction is still possible.

It is a result of technical progress that there are much closer relations than before between the members of the national community. There is greater conscious solidarity among the workers, among the entrepreneurs, and among the farmers. Factors acting on the national level are growing in importance, without, of course, wholly eliminating the others. While there are variations among countries, these factors everywhere assert themselves.

If collective factors are growing in importance in all countries, the theory of wages must logically move to the macro-economic plane. We would wish to suggest three points :

(1) A wider concept of the income accruing to those who live by their work must be adopted and therefore the distinction between primary distribution and redistribution loses much of its interest.

(2) Attention must be focused on the behaviour, in a broad sense, of the groups which buy and sell labour. Stable equilibrium can only come about as a result of reactions often affecting the general price level only if there is sufficient compatibility between the desires and the means of each and the structures of the groups and of production.

(3) The autonomous existence of the theory of wages is very limited. The theory of wages must be merged into a general theory of national income distribution. This probably involves a revision of the parties to be considered and of the traditional distinction between data and variables.

PART IV

THE WAGE STRUCTURE

Chapter 12

WAGE RELATIONSHIPS — THE COMPARATIVE IMPACT OF MARKET AND POWER FORCES[1]

BY

CLARK KERR
University of California (Berkeley), U.S.A.

ONE modern version of Adam Smith's famous observation (Book I, Chapter 8) might read: 'Workmen are always in constant and uniform combination to raise the wages of labour above their actual rate'. Now this version would not be so true as Smith's about 'masters' (as Smith himself noted), for their combination is less the 'natural state of things'. Workers, being more numerous and diverse, have less of a community of interest than masters and a greater need for formal bonds. These formal bonds, over the past century, have been supplied by labour unions in many trades and industries in those industrialized nations which are organized into pluralistic systems, and a major purpose of most of these unions has been to modify 'market forces' by group decisions and organized power in setting wages.

A classic question in economics has been the extent to which this organized power has exerted its will over market forces. Some economists in recent times have judged the impact to be substantial[2] and even potentially disastrous;[3] others that it has been minimal or even virtually non-existent.[4] This chapter concludes, on our current state of knowledge, that no categorical answer can be given because unions have had varying degrees of impact on the five

[1] Melvin K. Bers, Graduate Research Economist, Institute of Industrial Relations, University of California (Berkeley), was helpful in the development of this paper.

[2] See, for example, A. M. Ross, *Trade Union Wage Policy* (1948), p. 48.

[3] See, for example, Henry Simons, *Economic Policy for a Free Society* (1948), p. 48 ff. and pp. 121-259; and C. E. Lindblom, *Unions and Capitalism* (1949).

[4] See, for example, J. T. Dunlop, *Wage Determination Under Trade Unions* (Preface to 1950 edition) and his review of Lindblom's *Unions and Capitalism* in *American Economic Review* (June 1950). See also Milton Friedman, 'Some Comments on the Significance of Labor Unions for Economic Policy', in *The Impact of the Union*, D. M. Wright, editor (1951), p. 215; and K. E. Boulding, *The Organizational Revolution* (1953), p. 94.

different types of differentials into which a nation's wage structure can be divided: (1) interpersonal, (2) interfirm, (3) interarea, (4) interoccupational, and (5) interindustry. The impact on the first two, it will be found, has been considerably greater than on the last two. We must then turn to an explanation of why the impact should vary so substantially; why there should be such a shift in the incidence of trade union power from one set of differentials to the other. The answer given is that a sharp downward plunge in motivation and an equally sharp upward surge of the power requisite to effect alterations in differentials occur as we move from the first three (and particularly the first two) to the last two.

The customary dichotomy of 'market' and 'power' forces lacks full precision. 'Power forces' often work through the market as well as on price directly; and 'market forces' themselves contain elements of power to the extent that persons or groups can and do directly influence the demand or supply side of the market. It might be more useful to speak of 'individual responses' on the one hand and 'institutional behaviour' on the other.[1]

'Individual responses' are the expressed preferences of individual workers and unorganized employers in response to the environmental context in which they find themselves. While in totality their actions affect the result, their individual actions taken separately do not succeed in manipulating their environment. 'Institutional behaviour' is comprised of the policies and practices of groups of individuals in the dominant corporation, the employers' association, the trade union, or government.

When a market responds largely to the first type of action, it might be designated as a 'natural' market, however imperfect it may be aside from collusive action itself; and when to the latter, an 'institutional' market. Most actual markets will, of course, have characteristics of both of these types; and then some evaluation is in order of the comparative influence of these two types of forces. Our question is then, to rephrase it, to what extent have wage differentials been affected by the entry of 'institutional behaviour', in addition to 'individual responses', into the supply side of the labour market; and how may the varying extents be explained.

[1] Lester divides the forces at work into 'competitive', 'impeditive', and 'anticompetitive'. The first category includes competitive drives among companies but also among unions. The second includes the standard 'frictions' of lack of knowledge, personal attachments, and so forth. The third includes a miscellany of practices such as pattern following by an employer and restriction of entrance to the trade by the union. R. A. Lester, 'A Range Theory of Wage Differentials', *Industrial and Labor Relations Review* (July 1952).

I. Wage Differentials

Interpersonal Differentials

Institutional policy quite universally regularizes, when it does not eliminate, differentials among persons doing like work in the same plant — with one sometimes quite major exception. The differentials may be regularized by a piece-rate system, or by seniority increments, or by a formal method of merit recognition, if a flat rate for the work is not introduced. The union contract, the company job evaluation system, and government wage regulations all have the effect of banishing the purely personalized rate. Such personalized rates, reflecting the merit of the worker or the prejudices of the individual foreman or employer, are quite normal in the 'natural market'.

'Job selling' by foremen, wage discrimination by supervisors, and the secrecy of individual arrangements have given way to formalized rates for the job. The movement towards centralization of hiring by employers and the experience in several countries with governmental wage controls have aided this change, as well as trade union pressure. While statistical proof of union influence is largely lacking, at least one study in the United States indicates a close association between unionization and formal wage structures.[1] 'Individual rates' are most common in those areas where unionism is not influential. Formalized wage structures were shown, also, to be closely associated with increasing size of the enterprise.

The one important exception is differentials between men and women doing the same work. These have been largely eradicated in the United States, particularly during the 1940's, but they are still customary in some other countries, such as Germany.[2] The degree of elimination may well relate more to the general social status of women in the community than to union influence.

Interfirm Differentials

In the absence of unionism, the labour market normally displays a wide dispersion of wage rates for the same type of work among

[1] Otto Hallberg, 'Wage Formalization in Major Labor Markets, 1951–1952', *Monthly Labor Review* (January 1953). See also comments in R. A. Lester, *Company Wage Policies* (1948). In Denmark, however, some unions permit a system of 'elastic' wages allowing for both individual and collective bargaining. See Walter Galenson, *The Danish System of Labor Relations* (1952), p. 146.

[2] They have, however, been regularized there in the sense of being made subject to contractual arrangements. (See C. Kerr, 'Collective Bargaining in Post-War Germany', *Industrial and Labor Relations Review*, April 1952.) In Germany and some other countries there are also established differentials for youths below the regular rates.

firms operating in the same product and labour markets.[1] Lester, on the basis of data for some sixty-odd cities in the United States, generalized that the high wage plant normally paid 50 per cent more in rates, occupation by occupation, than the low wage plant.[2] The findings of Reynolds in his New Haven survey are consistent with this, although they relate to more than a single industry at a time.[3] The Lester data were taken from a period of turbulent wage movements during the second World War. But numerous wage surveys covering less unusual times demonstrate a normal dispersion, odd stragglers aside, of at least 25 per cent from top to bottom.

While union policy does not always aim at full uniformity,[4] unionization is closely associated with increased uniformity. Two recent studies in the United States have noted this. One found a considerably lower dispersion of rates in the more highly unionized of two metropolitan areas.[5] The other concluded that within a single metropolitan area, namely Los Angeles, unions reduced and even abolished interfirm differentials in the industries they organized.[6]

This phenomenon is not limited to the United States. It occurs wherever unions are able to organize all the firms producing the same product in the same labour market area. In fact, it may be more manifest in other nations where the 'master agreement' has met less employer resistance than in the United States. In some countries, as Germany, the 'master agreement' is even extended by law to cover all employers. The achievement of this uniformity is an essential part of the union programme of 'taking wages out of competition'. It flows also from the activities of employers' associations and the application of government minimum wage regulations.

Interarea Differentials

What are usually called 'geographical differentials' are, in part, interindustry differentials in the sense that the industry mix varies

[1] See L. G. Reynolds, 'Wage Differences in Local Labor Markets', *American Economic Review* (June 1946), for an early emphasis on the significance of these differentials.

[2] R. A. Lester, 'Wage Diversity and its Theoretical Implications', *Review of Economics and Statistics* (August 1946).

[3] L. G. Reynolds, *The Structure of Labor Markets* (1951), chap. 7.

[4] See, for example, George Seltzer, 'Pattern Bargaining and the United Steelworkers', *Journal of Political Economy* (August 1951). The cases to which Seltzer refers, however, are usually in different labour markets and partially differentiated product markets.

[5] J. L. Dana, *Wage and Salary Relationships in Los Angeles and San Francisco Metropolitan Areas — January 1952*, Bureau of Labor Statistics, United States Department of Labor (June 1953).

[6] F. C. Pierson, *Community Wage Patterns* (1953), p. 152.

from one area to another and for this reason alone the general average of wages would be expected to vary ; and, in part, real geographical differentials in the sense that different rates are paid for the same type of work. The term 'interarea differentials' is used here in the second sense of relative rates of pay for the same kind of work in the same industry but in different geographical areas. Here union policy has generally favoured the reduction or elimination of differentials, particularly where there is an interarea product market.

In the United States interarea differentials have been narrowing gradually both over-all and industry by industry.[1] This is probably largely due, as Reynolds notes,[2] to the increased dispersion of manufacturing industry around the nation and the reduced importance in some areas of a large localized supply of agricultural workers. In some industries with nation-wide markets, such as steel, automobiles, and meat packing, union agreements have brought a reduction or elimination of geographical differentials. In other industries with local product markets, like building trades and service trades, no similar result has been attempted or achieved.[3]

Oxnam describes a similar narrowing of differentials among the several states in Australia,[4] but does not relate this to union policy. In Germany, where highly formalized wage structures are subject to well-developed collective arrangements, interarea differentials (including urban-rural differentials) have either been eliminated or substantially narrowed and precisely prescribed.[5]

Evidence about the impact of unionism on interarea differentials is less conclusive than for interpersonal and interfirm differentials. Union pressure generally is directed towards the narrowing and regularization of such differentials, but the over-all effect certainly has been substantially less than in the case of the first two types of differentials.

[1] See J. W. Bloch, 'Trends in Wage Differentials : 1907–1947', *Monthly Labor Review* (April 1948) ; R. A. Lester, 'Southern Wage Differentials', *Southern Economic Journal* (April 1947) ; H. Ober and C. Glasser, 'Regional Wage Differentials', *Monthly Labor Review* (October 1946) ; and Pierson, *Community Wage Patterns*.

[2] L. G. Reynolds, *Labor Economics and Labor Relations* (1949), p. 332.

[3] On a less spectacular level, unions have often raised wage rates for the same type of work in the same industry in labour market areas adjacent to the metropolitan districts where they first establish their organizational strength.

[4] D. W. Oxnam, *Wages in Australia, 1913-14 to 1949-50*, paper given before the Australian and New Zealand Association for the Advancement of Science, Brisbane (May 1951).

[5] See Gerhard Bry, 'Trends and Cycles in German Wages', *Proceedings*, Industrial Relations Research Association (1953) ; also Kerr, 'Collective Bargaining in Post-war Germany'.

Interoccupational Differentials

Occupational wage differentials have undergone a most significant narrowing in recent decades in the United States, Western Europe, Australia, and New Zealand, with one very important exception.[1] In the United States the margin for skilled workers has dropped over the past half-century from over two to under one and one-half times that of unskilled workers.[2] Since 1880, in the United Kingdom, the differential has also been cut in half, although it was not so great to begin with.[3] An almost equal reduction has occurred in Australia over the period since 1914.[4] In more recent periods, reductions have occurred in Austria, France, Germany, Italy, Netherlands, Norway, and Switzerland,[5] and also New Zealand.[6] The great exception, and a most interesting one, is Denmark (another possible one — although the evidence is less complete — is Belgium).[7] In Denmark the differential did not narrow over the period 1938–1948, nor from 1920 to 1949, although it did decrease substantially from 1914 to 1920.

This narrowing of occupational differentials has been an important massive and highly controversial social phenomenon. Turner views trade unions as a substantial causative force, as unions follow the policy of flat increases, as they seek to recruit to their ranks the unskilled, as they endeavour to avoid undue incentives to employers to break down skills and use machines, and as they pursue egalitarian

[1] What has happened to 'compensation' differentials (wages and 'fringe benefits' taken together) is a different and more complex question ; and an increasingly important one with the growth of 'fringe benefits'. The 'compensation structure' is a more meaningful, if less tractable, concept than the 'wage structure'. On the currently available evidence it is almost foolhardy to estimate whether occupational 'compensation' differentials are or are not behaving similarly to occupational wage differentials.

[2] See H. Ober, 'Occupational Wage Differentials, 1907–1947', *Monthly Labor Review* (August 1948) ; and T. Kanninen, 'Occupational Wage Relationships in Manufacturing, 1952–1953', *Monthly Labor Review* (November 1953).

[3] See K. G. J. C. Knowles and D. J. Robertson, 'Differences between the Wages of Skilled and Unskilled Workers, 1880–1950', *Bulletin of the Oxford University Institute of Statistics* (April 1951) ; and J. A. Flexner, 'Great Britain : Wage Trends and Policies, 1938–1947', *Monthly Labor Review* (September 1947).

[4] See D. W. Oxnam, 'The Relation of Unskilled to Skilled Wage Rates in Australia', *Economic Record* (June 1950) ; also Oxnam, 'Some Economic and Social Consequences of the Australian System of Wage Regulation', paper given before the Australian Institute of Political Science, Sydney (July 1952). See also Sir Douglas Copland, 'The Full-Employment Economy with Special Reference to Wages Policy', *Oxford Economic Papers* (October 1953).

[5] Changes in the Structure of Wages in European Countries', *Economic Bulletin for Europe*, Second Quarter (1950). On France, see also H. I. Cowan, 'France : Wage Trends and Wage Policies, 1938–1947', *Monthly Labor Review* (August 1947).

[6] International Labour Office, *Wages — General Report* (1948), p. 95.

[7] See *Wages — General Report*, p. 96 ; and Galenson, *The Danish System*, p. 179, 'Changes in the Structure of Wages in European Countries'.

policies to minimize internal strife.[1] Knowles and Robertson, however, see unions as having a relatively minor and largely unpurposeful effect as they support, for other reasons, flat increases and the simplification of wage structures.[2] Reynolds [3] and Samuels [4] consider the impact of unionism a temporary one as organization first spreads from the ranks of the skilled to the unskilled. Fisher [5] and Clark [6] find the explanation for reduced differentials lying almost entirely outside unionism in the spread of public education and its effect on the relative supply of skilled and unskilled workers. Among other explanatory factors have been listed the impact of full employment in raising the demand for the unskilled,[7] of mass technology which reduces the level of skill, of egalitarian tendencies generally which are expressed in many ways, including state minimum wage regulations.

As to the weight to be given these several factors, there is little incontrovertible evidence. My own view, which will be set forth below, is that the impact of unionism is seldom the major factor involved; and that, in the long run, its influence is generally in the direction of maintaining, not reducing, occupational differentials.

Interindustry Differentials

Clay wrote that there had once been a 'system' of wages in Great Britain.[8] It might almost be said that there is a 'system' of wages which operates in a recognizable form in a number of the industrialized nations — not an entirely uniform and constant system, it is true, but one according to which the several series of interrelationships are roughly similar. It is the variations, not the likenesses, which call for explanation. Lebergott found interindustry rankings, with a few major exceptions, to be much the same in six countries (United States, Canada, United Kingdom, Sweden,

[1] H. A. Turner, 'Trade Unions, Differentials and the Levelling of Wages' *Manchester School of Economic and Social Studies* (September 1952).

[2] Knowles and Robertson, 'Differences between the Wages of Skilled and Unskilled Workers'.

[3] *Labor Economics and Labor Relations*, p. 331.

[4] N. J. Samuels, 'Wage Variations in the United States', *Personnel* (September 1952).

[5] Allen G. B. Fisher, 'Education and Relative Wage Rates', *International Labor Review* (June 1932).

[6] Colin Clark, *Conditions of Economic Progress*, 2nd edition (1951), pp. 458-483.

[7] For a dissent from the customary view that occupational differentials widen significantly in depression, see P. W. Bell, 'Cyclical Variation and Trend in Occupational Wage Differentials in American Industry since 1914', *Review of Economics and Statistics* (November 1951).

[8] H. Clay, *The Problem of Industrial Relations* (1929), p. 74. See comment in J. R. Hicks, *Theory of Wages* (1935), p. 80.

Switzerland, Russia); [1] and the Economic Commission for Europe study shows somewhat the same pattern.

A second general observation about interindustry differentials is that they are narrowing (percentagewise) over time. Oxnam has demonstrated this for Australia,[2] Woytinsky for the United States,[3] and the Economic Commission for Europe study for Western European countries.[4]

Has unionism had an appreciable effect on these differentials? [5] Douglas thought it had not as between unionized and unorganized industries.[6] Ross at first challenged the observation of Douglas, but later agreed that, except in the case of new organizations (a point made also by Douglas), unionism has had little appreciable effect in the United States.[7] Essentially similar results to those of Douglas have been obtained by Garbarino, Rees (for the steel industry only), and Dunlop,[8] all also having analysed American experience. Levinson essentially agrees, except that unions may hold up the level of wages in an organized industry in a depression when wages in unorganized industries are not faring as well.[9]

[1] S. Lebergott, 'Wage Structures', *Review of Economic Statistics* (November 1947).

[2] *Wages in Australia, 1913/14 to 1949/50.* See also Copland, 'The Full Employment Economy'.

[3] W. S. Woytinsky, *Employment and Wages in the United States* (1953), pp. 507-510.

[4] On Great Britain see also Flexner, 'Wage Trends and Policies', and on Germany see also Bry, 'Trends and Cycles'.

[5] Actually there are two questions: (1) Has unionism been a source of comparative advantage to workers in unionized as contrasted with unorganized industries?; and (2) Has unionism changed the pattern of relationships among organized industries? The literature is almost solely concerned with the first of these two questions, partly because it has been the more debated point and partly because statistical evidence is more easily procured.

[6] Paul H. Douglas, *Real Wages in the United States* (1930), pp. 562-564.

[7] A. M. Ross, 'The Influence of Unionism upon Earnings', *Quarterly Journal of Economics* (February 1948); A. M. Ross and W. Goldner, 'Forces Affecting the Interindustry Wage Structure', *Quarterly Journal of Economics* (May 1950); Slichter considers this not yet fully proved. (S. H. Slichter, 'Do the Wage-Fixing Arrangements in the American Labor Market have an Inflationary Bias?' *American Economic Review*, May 1954.)

[8] J. W. Garbarino, 'A Theory of Interindustry Wage Structure Variation', *Quarterly Journal of Economics* (May 1950); A. Rees, 'Wage Determination in the Steel Industry', *American Economic Review* (June 1951); J. T. Dunlop, 'Productivity and Wage Structure', in *Income, Employment and Public Policy* (1948). For a contrary view to that of Dunlop (and Garbarino) that a relationship exists between productivity differentials and interindustry wage differentials see F. Myers and R. L. Bowlby, 'The Interindustry Wage Structure and Productivity', *Industrial and Labor Relations Review* (October 1953). Myers and Bowlby conclude that while such a relationship existed at one time, it has not in more recent periods. (See also reply by Garbarino and rejoinder by Myers and Bowlby in the same journal, June 1954.) See also Slichter, 'Wage-fixing Arrangements'.

[9] H. M. Levinson, *Unionism, Wage Trends and Income Distribution, 1914–1947* (1951). See also D. Creamer, *Behaviour of Wage Rates during Business Cycles* (1950). It should be noted, however, that wages in the construction and bituminous coal industries, once well organized, fell unusually far during the Great

Sobotka, further, reached the judgment, after a study of the building trades, that craft unions may be a source of wage advantage to their members.[1] The three likely exceptions to the general rule that unionism has not been a source of wage advantage to workers in organized industries, then, are (1) new and thus aggressive unions (which may also be offsetting the prior monopsony power of employers); (2) unions in periods of substantial unemployment; and (3) craft unions with their restrictions on entrance to the trade.[2]

It is evident from this review of the literature and the available data (both of which relate more to the United States than to any other country) that the impact of unionism on wage differentials has not been uniform:

(1) Personal differentials have largely been eliminated or brought under formal control in unionized sectors.
(2) Firm differentials within the same product and labour markets have generally either been much reduced or wiped out.
(3) Area differentials have been occasionally eradicated and frequently diminished, particularly where there is interarea product competition.
(4) Occupational differentials have been much reduced, but there is little evidence that this is a result of union policies.
(5) Industrial differentials have also been reduced, but have apparently not been greatly affected to date by unionism.

For the first two types of differentials the impact of unionism has been substantial; for the third (at least in the limited situation of interarea product competition), significant; and for the last two, minor.

The intrusion of unionism into labour markets does not present

Depression in the United States. (See Leo Wolman, 'Wages in the United States since 1914', *Proceedings*, Industrial Relations Research Association, 1953.) The basic forces at work over the course of the cycle are probably what is happening to employment but particularly to prices from one industry to another, with very little reference to unionism. (See Dunlop, *Wage Determination Under Trade Unions*, chap. 7.)

[1] S. P. Sobotka, 'Union Influences on Wages: The Construction Industry', *Journal of Political Economy* (April 1953). The construction industry in the United States, however, may be a special case. It stands somewhat higher in interindustry wage rankings than in several other industrialized countries on which information is available. (See 'Changes in the Structure of Wages in European Countries'.)

[2] This may be a finding largely related to American experience; and the factor in American experience which may most count for the special results of craft unions is their comparatively heavy emphasis on the closed shop and the partially closed union. In Denmark also, where the craft unions have close historical connections with the craft guilds of earlier times and their tight apprenticeship systems, they apparently have also been a source of differential advantage.

a clear-cut case of 'market forces' versus 'power'. For the power of the union is sometimes ranged alongside the market forces and they work in the same direction. Also, the opposition to union power may not be market forces, or market forces alone, but the power of the employers or the government. We turn now to a general explanation of why union power has been more effective in transforming some aspects of the wage structure than others.

II. The Selective Impact of Union Power

Is there any general explanation of why union power has achieved so much rearrangement of some wage differentials and so little of others ? The explanation offered here is that the impact of unionism on wage differentials has varied (1) directly with the strength of the motivation of workers and their organizations to exercise control, and (2) inversely with the amount of power requisite to effect such changes.[1] It would, of course, be surprising if this were not true. What, then, can we say about intensity of motivation and the magnitude of power requirements in each of the five types of differentials which constitute wage structures ?

As we shall see, where motivation is most intense, power requirements tend to be least in magnitude. Were it otherwise, trade unionism would have to endure much greater frustrations ; for what it could best achieve it would least want, and what it most wanted it could least achieve.

The Intensity of Motivation

The idea of the 'just wage' has never died, although the meaning of justice in this regard is perhaps less clear than it once was and there are many more wage rates to be adjusted one to the other. The 'just wage', it is often remarked, is largely an ethical rather than an 'economic' concept. But one purpose of organization, as in the Middle Ages, is to make it both. Now this is not to suggest that this is the only purpose of organization in the labour market, nor that the customary appeals to justice are always sincere, but only that the achievement of justice, however defined, is a real and major goal. This is particularly true in the early days of unionism. The drive to end discrimination, to get 'equal pay for equal work', to

[1] It should be noted that power and motivation are not entirely independent factors. The degree of power required may affect motivation ; and the intensity of motivation may affect the amount of power available.

obtain the 'standard rate', is behind the original organization of many, if not most unions.

This drive for the 'standard rate' is particularly insistent at the level of interpersonal relationships in the same work place. Workers are physically close to each other and comparisons are easy to make. It is less forceful but still quite intense as it relates to interfirm differentials in the same labour and product markets. Here the incentive comes not from one worker eyeing another at the next bench, but from workers in low-wage plants thinking they are worth as much as those in high-wage plants and the workers in high-wage plants feeling uneasy about unfair competition possibly threatening their jobs. Considerations of equity for the one group and security for the other move hand in hand. The motivation is more a result of thought processes and less one of glandular response than in the case of interpersonal differentials for the same jobs in the same plant.

When we move out of the same labour market area, the strength of the inducements to uniformity subsides. Knowledge of the total situation is less personal and less complete, comparisons are made on a less individual basis, similarities are less striking — the cost of living may be different, market conditions diverse, and so forth. Particularly when produce market competition is less intense or even non-existent, the interest in uniformity is much reduced, although the equity of interarea relationships may still be a factor; but the coercion of wage competition is absent.

When we turn to occupational differentials the character of the situation changes quickly. Dissimilarity is now the essence of the problem. Degrees of skill, of responsibility, of unpleasantness must be estimated and weighed, and this takes intimate knowledge and careful judgment. Equal pay for equal work gives way to equivalent pay for equivalent work; and there is little agreement on what is equivalent.[1] While workers may generally agree that there should be the same pay for the same type of work in the same plant, labour market area, or industry, motives become mixed within the work force in regard to appropriate occupational differentials. The unskilled wish equality or some close approximation; the skilled want to be differentiated on the grounds of their skill.

Thus almost no unions in the United States have a general policy on skill differentials, as Bell notes,[2] although nearly all have definite

[1] As skills become more diversified with the progressive division of labour, particularly at the semi-skilled level, comparisons become increasingly difficult to make. See R. L. Raimon, 'The Indeterminativeness of Wages of Semi-skilled Workers', *Industrial and Labor Relations Review* (January 1953).

[2] 'Cyclical Variation', *Review of Economics and Statistics* (November 1951).

policies, however imperfectly enforced, on interpersonal, interfirm, and interarea differentials. It is often said that craft unions favour the skilled workers and industrial unions the unskilled. But this is certainly not universally true. Industrial unions must be sensitive to potential revolts of their skilled members, and skilled workers quite normally are influential in an industrial union beyond their relative numbers. The differential between skilled and unskilled workers in the construction industry (organized on a craft basis) in the United States has narrowed over recent decades much more than in the steel and somewhat more than in the automobile industries (organized on an industrial basis).[1] In the steel industry a formal contractual job evaluation plan sets differentials, and in the automobile industry special adjustments for skilled workers have been made to offset the effect of flat cents-per-hour increases. Industrial unions too, with very few exceptions, are hierarchical organizations.

In Denmark the skilled workers, after a time, resisted further reductions in their differentials, although they had once supported a 'solidaristic' wage policy.[2] In Norway and Sweden the unions have maintained a policy of improving 'the relative position of traditionally low-paid groups of workers';[3] but the statistical evidence does not indicate that this policy has had the effect of narrowing differentials more rapidly than was occurring in other comparable nations. In the Netherlands the Foundation of Labour (a joint employer-union organization) has endeavoured to maintain (not reduce) occupational differentials in the post-war period at their approximate pre-war relationship, but apparently without substantial success, for the wages of the unskilled have in fact risen much faster than those of the skilled.[4]

Unions may, however, unwittingly have had two effects on occupational differentials. First, the organization of the skilled may originally have spread differentials a bit and the subsequent organiza-

[1] H. M. Douty, 'Union Impact on Wage Structures', *Proceedings*, Industrial Relations Research Association (1953). Bronfenbrenner notes: ' Robert E. Strain, "Occupational Wage Differences: Determinants and Recent Trends", unpublished Ph.D. dissertation, Wisconsin, 1953. Strain finds that skill differentials have narrowed as rapidly and to approximately the same extent in industries organized on a craft basis, or largely unorganized, as in industries where industrial or "mass unionism" has been important.' (M. Bronfenbrenner, 'The Incidence of Collective Bargaining', *American Economic Review*, May 1954.)

[2] Galenson, *The Danish System*, pp. 180 and 186. The labourers have a strong and separate union of their own.

[3] 'Changes in the Structure of Wages in European Countries'; on Norway see also J. Inman, 'Post-War Wage Policy in Norway', *Bulletin of the Oxford University Institute of Statistics* (July and August 1950).

[4] See P. S. Pels, 'The Development of Wages Policy in the Netherlands', *Bulletin of the Oxford University Institute of Statistics* (July and August 1950).

tion of the unskilled narrowed them again ; [1] and, second, across-the-board and pattern increases, particularly as applied by industrial unions, may have reduced them somewhat. But neither of these results generally has grown out of deliberate policy on occupational differentials *per se*.

Interindustry differentials confront unions with much the same problems of unclear motivation as do occupational differentials. New elements of dissimilarity enter in — different families of occupations, working conditions, product market arrangements, among many others. Here, also, the workers in the highly paid industries wish normally to maintain their relative superiority, however much those in the low-paid industries might wish to narrow the gap.

Thus, in summary, the unions speak with a distinct although decreasingly loud voice on interpersonal, interfirm, and interarea differentials ; but in halting tones, if at all, on interoccupational and interindustry differentials. A great drop in strong and unambiguous motivation takes place as they move from 'equal work' to 'unequal work' situations. The 'equal work' orbits are generally the most coercive.[2]

The Variation in Power Requirements

Group motivation to be effective must be expressed through the exercise of power, and this power may need to be exercised not only against 'market forces' but also against the opposing power of organized employers or the state, and even against discordant factions internal to the union institution. Thus the power required to effect changes is not just the opposite of the strength of market forces.

At the level of interpersonal differentials the individual employer usually stands alone — and confused. On the one hand, he may like his prerogatives, including the right to reward those who gain his favour or whose work merits it ; but, on the other, a formal wage schedule reduces grumbling, is easier to administer (particularly for the large firm) than a person-by-person rate system, and has some obvious ethical appeal to it. Moreover the employer, who is likely to pay more attention to personal differences in productivity

[1] See Sobotka, 'Union Influences on Wages'.

[2] This is not to suggest that political forces, like rival unionism, may not be of pre-eminent importance in individual situations. For an interesting discussion of such 'orbits of coercive comparison' see A. M. Ross, 'The Dynamics of Wage Determination Under Collective Bargaining', *American Economic Review* (September 1947).

than the union, can make some relatively easy adjustments to adapt to the 'standard rate' by eliminating the poorer workers or by forcing them to raise their output.

Interfirm differentials are more difficult for a union to assault. Now it must organize similar firms in the entire labour market area. But the union is not without aid and comfort from the enemy. High wage firms may accept or even welcome union action to raise the wages of their low-wage competitors; and uniformity of wage levels is often a necessary prerequisite to uniformity of price in the product market — with or without union support. Moreover, uniformity of wage levels can be as essential to the internal harmony of an employers' association as it is to a union; and tactics in bargaining with an aggressive union dictate removal of the 'whipsaw' approach of first raising the low-wage firms in the name of equality and then the high-wage firms in the name of preserving historical positions.

Once uniformity is achieved there is normally little to destroy it, at least at the 'official' level. Effective rates, however, under conditions which favour the 'wage slide' (to be noted below) may depart, even substantially, from the 'official' level. The low-wage firms have either been eliminated or have become efficient enough to survive at the standard rate; and unions do not normally press for wage rates which would force unionized employers to cease operations or break with the union. A standard rate, too, and perhaps one at much the same level, might well be the result of market forces if the labour market were more perfect than it usually is. Unionization, instead of 'distorting' the interfirm wage structure, may act instead as a substitute for greater labour mobility.

The reduction or removal of interarea differentials demands an additional accumulation of power by the union. To be effective the union now must organize beyond a single labour market area, even on a national basis. In a large country, such as the United States, this may be quite difficult, and peculiarly so if there are regions which are especially hard to organize, like the southern states; and, in the absence of complete organization, plants may be able to run away from one area to another. Also the union must either negotiate contracts on an interarea basis, or be able to establish effective policy for its local branches negotiating area by area. Moreover, employers, if product market competition is confined to local labour markets, will normally uniformly oppose, even strenuously, the standardization of wages among different product markets. Also, wage differentials tend to be more widely dispersed over a series of labour markets than in a single market, and thus less tractable to standardization. But the state may enter here and range its power alongside that of the unions through minimum wage laws or laws on the extension of contracts ; and wherever labour mobility is increasing and product markets are widening, 'market forces' are also conducing toward uniformity.

As far as occupational differentials are concerned, something can be done about them quite readily at the plant or industry level, and in totality this can have some effect. This can be done consciously or almost inadvertently, as Knowles and Robertson comment,[1] through policies of the flat increase and simplification of the wage structure which are intended to serve other purposes. But occupational differentials, given the occupational diversity among industries, are, in part, also interindustry differentials. Consequently, in order to control occupational differentials generally, as interpersonal and interplant and sometimes interarea differentials are controlled, would require a national union federation with considerable influence over its constituent elements. What is requisite is a single policy covering the building trades, the textile industry, and many others, all at the same time. Perhaps only in Norway and Sweden do the union federations have this much power, if they wish to use it.

A great social force is at work on occupational differentials. This force is the changing nature of supply and demand in the labour market as industrialization progresses. The absolute demand for skilled workers is certainly larger in an advanced industrial state than in one entering industrialization ; but the need for skilled workers is much more critical in a nation undergoing industrialization, and particularly in one where the process is rapid.[2] Percentagewise, the additional need for skilled men is much reduced as industrial societies mature. In Russia, for example, in 1928, skill differentials about matched those in the United States a quarter of a century earlier, and then widened as the first five-year plan speeded up the process of industrialization.[3] Concurrently with

[1] 'Differences between the Wages of Skilled and Unskilled Workers.'

[2] The general theorem advanced here is : The lesser the degree and the greater the rate of industrialization, the wider will be the occupational differentials and the greater the premium for skill ; and the greater the degree and the lesser the rate of industrialization, the narrower will be the occupational differentials and the greater the premium for distasteful work.

[3] A. Bergson, *The Structure of Soviet Wages* (1946). Bendix also notes a widening of skill differentials in the Russian zone of Germany with the Russian emphasis on industrial expansion there after the second World War. See R. Bendix, *Managerial Ideologies in the Russian Orbit of Germany*, unpublished MS. (1953). Skill differentials are rather greater in the United States than one would normally expect for a country at its stage of development. Large-scale immigration undoubtedly held down the level for unskilled workers for a substantial time and the differentials are particularly wide in the South which is industrially underdeveloped.

the smaller percentage increase in demand for skilled workers, as industrialization becomes well established, the supply of skilled workers greatly increases through the effects of public education,[1] and perhaps also a concomitant reduction of class or social discrimination, while the supply of unskilled workers dries up as agriculture becomes a smaller segment of the economy, as income and the trade and service industries draws also on the ranks of the unskilled.

We may, in fact, be witnessing currently a great social phenomenon of occupational differentials being turned partly on their heads. Already they have been greatly narrowed and in some cases reversed, as, for example, when common labourers come to receive more than skilled office workers.[2] If this is the social process at work, then we should not be surprised that the narrowing of differentials has not caused a shortage of skilled workers, for their comparative plenitude has, in fact, caused the narrowing.[3] Adam Smith's first wage-determining factor (Book I, Chapter 10), 'the agreeableness or disagreeableness of the employments themselves', may come to be a most influential one once the 'difficulty and expense of learning them' have been much more equalized; and, it should be noted, unskilled work is quite frequently more disagreeable than skilled.

Unions have probably not had much effect on the historical narrowing of occupational differentials. These differentials began narrowing in some countries before unions were effective and have narrowed since that time in non-union sectors as well as organized sectors. The movement has not been at a uniform rate but has gone in spurts, particularly during the first and second World Wars. Once having narrowed under the pressure of full or overly-full employment, the differentials have not dropped back to their prior

[1] See Fisher, 'Education and Relative Wage Rates', and Clark, *Conditions of Economic Progress.* See also comment of Tinbergen on relation of educational opportunities to skill differentials. (J. Tinbergen, 'Some Remarks on the Distribution of Labour Incomes', *International Economic Papers*, 1951.)

[2] For a discussion of the narrowing of the white-collar manual worker differential over the past century in the United States see K. M. McCaffree, 'The Earnings Differential between White Collar and Manual Occupations', *Review of Economics and Statistics* (February 1953). This differential has narrowed more rapidly in the United States than in some other countries, like Germany, where a 'closed education' system based on class lines has protected white-collar employees just as the 'closed shop' has craft workers in the United States.

[3] See A. Flanders, 'Wages Policy and Full Employment in Britain', *Bulletin of the Oxford University Institute of Statistics* (July and August 1950). See also comment in Lester, 'A Range Theory of Wage Differentials'. It is sometimes argued that skilled workers must be in relatively shorter supply than unskilled workers because the unskilled in a depression make up a disproportionate number of the unemployed. But this can be explained by a general pushing down of workers and those on the bottom, the unskilled, go out.

relationships in periods of less than full employment.[1] The long-run trend has worked itself out partly gradually and partly in these forward jumps.

In the future, however, unionism may well be an impediment to further narrowing, as it protects the position of skilled workers in particular and as it stands generally for a continuation of established and formalized differentials perpetuated through contractual arrangements and the development of conventional patterns. Already this has happened in Denmark, as noted above, where craft unions are particularly strong,[2] and for a substantial period of time (1920–1950) in Australia, where government wage setting is of pre-eminent importance ;[3] and it has been attempted in the Netherlands.[4]

Interindustry differentials may well follow the same course as occupational differentials. They also are narrowing and a long-run reversal is taking place in interindustry relationships in favour of those industries, like mining, where the work has heavy disutility factors connected with it. Such a parallel development is to be expected because interindustry differentials are, in significant part, skill differentials.[5] This is particularly true at the extremes. The

[1] This long-term trend explains why Bell, 'Cyclical Variation', did not observe a widening of occupational differentials in depression periods. The standard statement is that the differentials narrow in prosperity and widen in depression. Because of the effect of this long-run trend, the former is true, but not the latter.

[2] Galenson, *The Danish System*, also notes that 'nationwide bargaining on the Danish model creates a propensity toward rigidity in wage structure' (p. 186). It is my own view, albeit somewhat heretical, that, in the long run, industrial unions may often grant more protection to skill than craft unions, despite the early cry of industrial unions that they are the special benefactors of the unskilled. This is, first, because industrial unions gather within the same decision-making unit both unskilled and skilled rates and thus can subject them simultaneously to control ; while craft unions usually leave the unskilled on the outside in other decision-making units less subject to control. Industrial unions thus can hold the rates for the skilled and the unskilled apart if they wish and usually they will, since the skilled workers are the long-service workers and the most influential members. Craft unions cannot really hold the rates apart because only one set of rates — those for the skilled — fall within their control. The width of the gap is the distance between two levels, only one of which the craft unions can control. Second, under the craft system, both the unskilled and skilled rates are 'in the market' and the unskilled rate by itself must be high enough to permit adequate recruiting ; while, under the industrial system, the combined rate structure does the recruiting. That is to say, unskilled workers are attracted not only by the unskilled rates but also by the skilled rates to which they may expect to advance through time and the operation of a seniority plan. Just as the unskilled rate can be somewhat lower because of the prospect of higher rates ahead, so also the skilled rates are 'out of competition' in the sense that recruiting is usually from within and not from the open market and it can be 'artificially' high without being very obvious.

[3] However, the differentials were narrowed substantially before 1920 and have been again since 1950. (See Oxnam, 'The Relation of Wages of Unskilled and Skilled Workers in Australia'.)

[4] See Pels, 'The Development of Wages Policy'.

[5] See Lebergott, 'Wage Structures', on the association between skilled and unskilled rates, industry by industry ; also Slichter, 'Notes on the Structure of

high-ranking industries historically have been industries with many skilled workers ; the low-ranking industries have been industries with many semi-skilled and unskilled workers (and usually also a high proportion of women). The contribution of the skill mix to the wage levels of the several industries is also indicated by the similarity in interindustry wage differentials among countries where other potentially influential factors, like the organization of workers or the structures of product markets, are quite diverse. Additionally, the narrowing and reversal of rank order of interindustry differentials can best be explained by the narrowing and reversal of rank order of occupational differentials.

The skill mix, while it is probably the basic underlying force in determining interindustry differentials, is not the only important factor. Ability to pay, influenced by many factors, including the concentration of production, is of very substantial importance.[1] So also is the secular expansion or contraction of employment for particular industries at particular times, the geographical location of different industries and their cyclical price sensitivity,[2] among other factors. Factors other than occupational differentials are probably particularly important for the series of industries between the extremes of those with a high skill mix and those with a low. Thus, just as occupational differentials affect interindustry differentials, so also changes in interindustry differentials (for reasons other than changes in occupational differentials) will, in turn, affect occupational differentials.

If the narrowing (and scrambling) of occupational differentials is to continue to cause a narrowing (and scrambling) of interindustry differentials,[3] what effect is unionism likely to have on this process ? Probably the major effect is in the direction of preserving differentials, once established, because of the penchant for pattern following. Organizational pride and leadership survival are often intimately linked to the preservation of established wage relationships. But the pattern is seldom followed exactly ; the economic situations

Wages', *Review of Economics and Statistics* (January 1950), also Deneffe, 'The Wage Structure of the Federal Republic', *Wirtschaft und Statistik* (July 1953) — for example, the high rates of cleaning-women in the coal mines. Similarly a big and high wage industry (like automobiles in Detroit or shipbuilding in Hamburg) may pull up low-wage industries in its area, and vice versa.

[1] See, for example, Garbarino, 'A Theory of Interindustry Wage Structure Variation', and Slichter, 'Notes on the Structure of Wages'. It appears likely that control of entrance into the labour market and reduction of competition in the product market raise wage rates more effectively above the 'natural' level than does direct bargaining pressure ; restriction and collusion open more doors for gain than the strike.

[2] See Dunlop, *Wage Determination Under Trade Unions*, chap. 7.

[3] The reduction of regional variations has also served to narrow interindustry differentials in the United States.

of industries do change over time ; and so do interindustry wage differentials, whether through changes in negotiated wage levels or through the process of individual employers bidding for labour, particularly during high peaks or low troughs of the business cycle, despite union inclinations to formalize them.[1] What other effects may unions have on interindustry differentials ? They cannot assure an advantage to organized industries over unorganized, because, among other reasons, non-union employers can follow right along. Nor can they control differentials among organized industries except through very substantial centralized power over their member elements, and then only if they can also impose their will on the employers.

The amount of power requisite to control or even to influence differentials increases precipitately as we pass from the simple case of interpersonal differentials on through to the complex one of interindustry differentials. The purpose of the application of power changes also from highly consciously attempted elimination of interpersonal, interfirm, and interarea differentials to less consciously attempted stabilization of interoccupational and interindustry differentials, and, thus, from egalitarian reform to caste-conscious rigidity. The slogans associated with the former sometimes obscure the contribution to the latter. Appearance and reality go their separate ways.

As a union movement adds to its power it would be expected to penetrate effectively first into the control of interpersonal differentials (where the motivation is also the strongest) and last into interindustry differentials (where the motivation is also much reduced). The degree of effective penetration into control of wage differentials is, also, one measure of the true power of unions.

We remarked earlier that what the unions and their members most wanted they could best secure. Also, where the unions are consequential, they are also largely beneficial (in that they help achieve results which would flow from full employment and more perfect labour and product markets) ; and where they are less beneficial (impeding the rearrangement of differentials encouraged by the equalization of opportunity which tends to accompany industrialization), they are also less consequential.

What effect, then, does unionism have on the over-all distribution

[1] In Denmark, however, the unions have had remarkable success in maintaining almost unchanged for a substantial period of time intercraft (which in Denmark are also in large part interindustry) wage differentials. See Galenson, *The Danish System*, p. 181.

of wage and salary earnings among persons? The pattern of earnings distribution must change greatly as industrialization progresses, although statistics are largely lacking to demonstrate this. In Stage One there must be (assuming a substantial number of agricultural labourers) a heavy concentration of persons at the low end of the distribution. In Stage Two a second 'hump' appears at the high end of the scale as skilled 'aristocrats of labour' are recruited. In Stage Three a third 'hump' appears in the middle representing the semi-skilled; and this 'hump' grows and grows. In Stage Four only one 'hump' is left — in the centre — as the unskilled have their rates raised and the skilled their rates relatively reduced; and inside this 'hump' some skilled jobs shift to the left of the distribution (like white-collar occupations) and some less skilled jobs (like coal mining) shift to the right. The effects of unions on this historical process are probably as follows: (1) to pull up the very low rates a bit (by eliminating the low-paying firms and areas or forcing them to pay more); and (2) to hold up the high rates a bit against the pressures for narrowing; and (3), within the 'hump', to stand as an element of rigidity against the transposition of rates from one side to the other. But, in totality, they lack the influence to effect, through collective bargaining, a major redistribution of income among persons.

Böhm-Bawerk, forty years ago, as many had before and even more have since, discussed this same problem.[1] He set in opposition to each other 'power' and 'natural economic laws' and posed the issue: 'The great problem, not adequately settled so far, is to determine the exact extent and nature of the influence of both factors, to show how much one factor may accomplish apart from, and perhaps in opposition to, the other'. His main illustration was from the labour market and his conclusion was that, with a few exceptions,[2] 'there is, in my opinion, not a single instance where the influence of control could be lasting as against the gently and slowly, but incessantly and therefore successfully, working influence of a "purely economic order"'.

The problem is still not adequately settled and may never be, for we are working with a very tangled web of forces. The answer offered here is that neither market forces (or what we have called 'individual responses') have basically governed in fact nor is power,

[1] Eugen von Böhm-Bawerk, *Control or Economic Law* (1914), translated by J. R. Mez (Eugene, Oregon, 1931). See also discussion in E. Preiser, 'Property and Power in the Theory of Distribution', *International Economic Papers* (1952).

[2] The main exception was where union power offset the pre-existing monopsony power of employers.

or perhaps more accurately 'institutional behaviour', the compelling force which has determined wage differentials.

The problem is too complex for a single reply. Union policies have often brought major, and presumably permanent changes in two of the differentials we have examined — personal and firm ; and have had some, and presumably also permanent effects on area differentials. They have not evidently, however, been a dominant factor affecting the other two — occupational and industrial. The general explanation given here is that the degree of penetration of trade union influence into the establishment and maintenance of wage differentials is related directly to the intensity and clarity of the motivations of the workers and their organizations, and inversely to the amount of power requisite to the task.

Chapter 13

THE IMPACT OF COLLECTIVE BARGAINING ON THE WAGE STRUCTURE IN THE UNITED STATES

BY

LLOYD G. REYNOLDS
Yale University, U.S.A.

THE impact of trade unionism on relative wage rates and on the allocation of resources has been a standard subject of theoretical economic discussion for decades. Trade unions were presumed to be analogous to business monopolies in intent and general strategy and their behaviour deducible from first principles, whereby the economic consequences could be predicted from the established body of value theory.

Alongside this theoretical tradition there has been developing a body of empirical evidence on union activities and on the behaviour of relative wage rates. The data rarely tally with the hypotheses we would like to test — a standard complaint in economic research. They are sufficient, however, to provide some check on the reliability of deductive reasoning about union behaviour. The purpose of this chapter is to reduce somewhat the present gap between theoretical analysis and the growing abundance of information about wage determination and wage behaviour.

I. The Impact of Unionism and the Problem of Verification

Instead of the impact of unionism we should more properly speak of the impact of collective bargaining on wage structure. Employer objectives and employer resistance to union demands are always present, and although the nature of collective bargaining places the union in the rôle of aggressor, this does not necessarily mean that the union has a preponderant influence on the outcome.

How has the evolution of the wage structure over the past twenty years differed from its probable evolution in the absence of collective bargaining? In the absence of collective bargaining, a wage increase in a firm is attributed to 'market forces' or to a managerial decision more or less strongly influenced by market forces. Under collective bargaining the same increase is announced as a union victory, with an implication that the union was wholly responsible for it. It is clear, however, that much of what happens under collective bargaining would have happened in any event. In a particular situation there may be an incremental effect of trade union pressure, and it is the presence and size of this incremental effect which we would like to discover. One can be sure, however, that the incremental effect of trade unionism will typically be much less than the total change in the wage level, and much less than the union alleges it to have been. One has constantly to beware of this 'optical illusion', this tendency to overstate the impact of unionism by falling into simple *post hoc* reasoning.

Another danger besetting work on this problem is the reification of hypothetical models of trade union behaviour. A trade union, it is argued, is a monopoly, since it attempts to fix the price of labour. By analogy with the behaviour of business organizations possessing monopoly power, we can theoretically deduce the policies which an intelligent and informed union monopolist would adopt, and explore the economic consequences of these policies. This is a perfectly legitimate prelude to empirical study, but in the hands of some economists hypothetical models of union behaviour tend to become a substitute for empirical study and has led, at least in the United States, to a considerable muddying of the genuine issues.

There is also a tendency to regard the advent of collective bargaining as a drastic shift from a régime of perfect competition in the labour market to a very different monopolistic market structure. Empirical investigations, however, are gradually revealing the complexity and imperfection of labour market processes and the dangers of reasoning by analogy from commodity markets. Competitive forces are certainly present ; but one has to reason also with ignorance, immobilities of various sorts, non-pecuniary motives on the part of both buyers and sellers of labour, the pressure of unemployed workers at most times, a poorly developed marketing mechanism for labour, and other factors which warp the wage structure away from the hypothetical competitive pattern. It is neither useful nor necessary, then, to assume the existence of a perfect labour market under non-union conditions. Rather is it possible to construct more realistic models of wage determination under non-union conditions, models which admit many of the characteristics of actual labour markets.

The most fruitful approach might be, first, to develop hypotheses about how trade unions — not 'pure monopolies', but unions as we actually know them — are likely to behave in wage bargaining, and how this behaviour may affect each of the significant dimensions of wage structure. Second, to test these hypotheses against existing statistical materials on wages. This should lead to the development of a body of valid generalizations about the wage consequences of collective bargaining. Third, to contrast the wage structure as it develops under collective bargaining, not with the hypothetical wage structure which would exist under perfect competition, but with the actual wage structure which exists in non-union labour markets. It may quite possibly turn out that the bargained wage structure lies closer to the competitive pattern than does the non-union structure. In any event, the investigation should not be biased by taking a position on this point before the evidence has been examined.

Since the evidence is by no means as good as might be wished, this paper will deal more with hypotheses than with settled conclusions. It should be emphasized also that we shall be working at a low level of generality. The discussion which follows is focused solely on the experience of the United States over approximately the past twenty years. There should be no presumption that the conclusions will be valid for any other country, or even for the United States in subsequent decades.

II. Union Wage Policy

We must first make a few remarks about the theory of union behaviour in regard to wages. The trade union is an economic organization which does not behave economically in the sense of following a maximization principle. It is reasonable to take profit maximization as a first approximation to business behaviour, because some attention to profit is a condition of survival for the firm, and because the maximization concept provides a useful clue in analysing specific decisions on prices, output level, and other matters. The trade union, however, is not engaged in buying and selling. It does not make a profit if wages are set high, nor does it become bankrupt if wages are set low. It is a regulatory body engaged in determining the minimum standards under which production may continue, and is perhaps more nearly comparable to a government agency than to a business concern. The ingenuity which some economists have devoted to the question 'What does a union try to maximize?' thus seems largely wasted, for the indications are that unions do not try to maximize anything.

Wage decisions are typically taken by the elected leaders of the union, and the members play a passive or ratifying rôle. Stability of leadership and long tenure in office are characteristic of American unions. There are, to be sure, situations in which the officers of a union are hard pressed by a rival union competing for the same clientele, or by a rival faction within their own union. In these cases the officers may have to weigh every action, including wage decisions, in terms of their short-run political consequences. As a general rule, however, union officers act within rather wide limits of tolerance. There is some minimum which they must achieve in order to keep the members content with the union and its leadership ; but they need not go beyond this to strive for the maximum which the union's strength would make possible.

Union leaders will accept a wage reduction only under great pressure of economic circumstances. Less powerful, but still influential, is the notion that increases in the retail price level should be matched by at least equal increases in money wage rates, so that real wages do not decline. During periods of rapid inflation this notion finds expression in cost-of-living 'escalator clauses'. Even where formal escalator clauses are absent there is pressure for maintenance of real wages.

In addition, union leaders give weight to the movement of certain other wage rates in the economy, which, for one reason or another, are regarded as neighbouring or strategic rates. This is the phenomenon which has been variously termed 'wage constellations' (Harbison), 'orbits of coercive comparison' (Ross), and 'wage contours' (Dunlop). These comparisons involve both the absolute level of wages and the rate of change in a particular year. The contours are marked out by the scope of competition in product markets, local competition in the labour market, and the demarcation lines of union organization.

Union leaders are also influenced by the strength of employer resistance to their wage demands. They appraise this partly by observing the employer's behaviour in bargaining negotiations, and partly by direct information on the economic situation of the company or industry — sales, new orders, profits, and other key variables in the immediate past, and the estimated movement of these variables in the near future, which is particularly important in cycle-sensitive industries. Putting all these things together, the union must try to judge the employer's 'sticking point'.

To what extent does this constitute an 'economic', to what extent a 'non-economic' pattern of behaviour on the part of union leaders ? There is a natural temptation to take extreme positions on this matter. Those who consider economic factors very important tend to assert that unions must be maximizing something, whether they know it or not. It is argued that unions behave as if they were conscious of a sloped demand curve for their labour. Indeed, some would argue that unless unions are implicitly using demand analysis and unless they are implicitly maximizing some monetary quantity, the economist must take their behaviour as an unexplained datum.

This position tends to beget an opposite sort of extremism. Those who cannot stomach the assertion that unions are really maximizing some quantity under a labour demand curve tend to swing over to a 'political' or 'sociological' model of union behaviour which minimizes the rôle of economic data. These models, however, are at least as ineffective as 'pure' economic models in explaining concrete union behaviour, and some synthesis of economic and non-economic models is obviously required.[1]

The clue to such a synthesis lies partly in the fact that economic data affect union policy at second remove, as it were, by shaping the reactions of employers and union members. The day-to-day manœuvring of the actors on the stage may be explainable in political terms, but as one attempts to penetrate more deeply into the determinants of behaviour, however, one encounters economic data as a major factor. The behaviour of an employer in collective bargaining will be heavily influenced by his economic situation, in transmitting pressures from the product market and from other factor markets, and in bringing these to bear on wage determination. Union leaders need not directly perceive marginal value productivity curves and the like, but they must be accurate judges of employer reactions. They must also be constrained by attitudes of their members which are heavily influenced by economic events — changes in the retail price level, the level and rate of change of employment, the movement of wages in neighbouring companies and industries. This is not exactly a labour supply function, but it serves some of the purposes which the labour supply function serves in competitive wage theory.

Another clue to reconciliation of the 'economic' and 'non-economic' approaches lies in a recognition that economic forces are more compelling in some situations than in others. Economic forces are likely to constrain the wage bargain more narrowly during depression than during full employment or inflation; and they are likely to be more powerful in industries where vigorous competition

[1] See M. W. Reder, 'The Theory of Union Wage Policy', *Review of Economics and Statistics* (February 1952), pp. 34-45, and Albert Rees, 'Union Wage Policies', Industrial Relations Research Association, *Interpreting the Labor Movement*, December 1952, pp. 130-148.

exists in the product market than in quasi-monopolistic industries.

Sufficient research would probably reveal that, in a vague and general way, unions react as they 'ought' to react on economic grounds, depending upon the elasticity or inelasticity of demand for union labour. While the general direction of reaction may be predictable on this basis, however, its precise magnitude is not. One needs a more complicated apparatus and, above all, more empirical content for our theoretical boxes.

III. Occupational Differentials

Hypotheses

Occupational differentials mean the relative wage levels of the range of different occupational groups in the same establishment, or at most in the same industry. This restriction is necessary because otherwise occupational differentials become confused with other things, notably interindustry differentials. The skill composition of different industries varies considerably. Some, such as building and printing, are manned largely by skilled craftsmen. Others, such as textiles and clothing, include mainly semi-skilled and unskilled workers. If wage-raising conditions are most favourable in the high-skilled industries, and if unions in those industries take advantage of this fact, the gap between the highest and lowest jobs in the economy may be widened through a shift in interindustry differentials. (See section V below.) When we speak of 'differential' we mean the percentage relationship between the wage rates in question rather than the absolute or cents-per-hour differences.

It seems reasonable that the effect of collective bargaining on occupational differentials will depend on the extent and method of union organization. If manual workers in a company are unionized but white-collar employees are not — a very common situation in the United States — one might expect that the manual group would gradually improve its relative position. As among different levels of manual worker, one can visualize at least three possibilities :

(a) If the highly skilled employees are organized in one or more craft unions, while the low-skilled employees remain unorganized, one might expect that the skilled group would improve its relative position over the course of time, and that occupational differentials would widen.

(b) If both the highly skilled and low skilled are organized, but in different unions, the outcome is difficult to predict. The highly skilled, who are usually more difficult to replace and form a small part of payroll cost, will presumably be in the stronger bargaining position. If they bargain separately, and if they follow self-interest exclusively, they may quite possibly widen their differential over the low-skilled workers. On the other hand, if all unions in the company bargain together, and if the skilled men contribute their strength to the advancement of the unskilled, occupational differentials may remain fairly stable and perhaps may even narrow.

(c) A third possibility is that all manual employees may be organized in a single industrial union. In this case low-skilled workers will usually form the bulk of the membership, and union policy, if not dictated by them, must at least seem reasonable in their eyes. They may be expected to favour a narrowing of occupational differentials, and the most plausible assumption is that such a narrowing will occur.

Evidence [1]

It is reasonably clear that manual workers have improved their position relative to white-collar workers over the past twenty years. It is even clearer that, within the manual group, unskilled and semi-skilled workers have improved their position relative to the skilled craftsmen. Besides the unprecedented growth in American trade unions in the past twenty years, there are several other reasons why occupational differentials might have narrowed even in the absence of collective bargaining.[2]

(1) In the background lies the cutting off of mass immigration to the United States in the early 1920's. This cut more heavily into the supply of unskilled labour than the supply of craftsmen. (2) Extension of public education and the high percentage of young people who complete a full twelve years of schooling has reduced the willingness of young people to take unskilled jobs, while at the same time swelling the potential supply of skilled and clerical workers. (3) Many types of 'unskilled' work are acquiring some elements of skill, labourers are working with ever-increasing assistance from mechanical equipment, with a consequent increase in their productivity. (4) The federal minimum wage law passed in the late 'thirties tended to force up the bottom of the wage structure ;

[1] See W. S. Woytinsky, *Employment and Wages in the United States* (1953), ch. 40 ; Harry Ober, 'Occupational Wage Differentials, 1907–1947', *Monthly Labor Review* (August 1948) ; H. M. Douty, 'Union Impact on Wage Structures', *Industrial Relations Research Association, Proceedings* (December 28–30, 1953), pp. 61-76.

[2] The discussion which follows draws heavily on H. M. Douty, 'Union Impact on Wage Structures', one of the most penetrating discussions of this matter which has appeared in recent years.

the result was a compression of occupational differentials. (5) Perhaps most important has been the almost continuous rise in wages and prices from 1941 to 1953. A simple way of adjusting to price inflation is uniform cents-per-hour increases to all employees. Since inflation bears most heavily on the lowest-income groups, this policy (which amounts to a larger percentage increase for the unskilled than for the skilled) can readily be defended as equitable. In any event, it was widely adopted during these years and was encouraged by government wage policies.[1]

When account has been taken of these factors, how much remains which can be attributed specifically to union policies and strength? At a minimum, the trade unions made little effort to counter the trend toward narrower differentials. From the mid-'thirties through the early 'fifties a large number of unions continued to demand and secure equal cents-per-hour increases for all employees, with the necessary result of reducing occupational differentials on a percentage basis. The reasons for this have not been fully explored, but one may surmise that they include such things as: the preponderance of low-skilled workers in the new industrial unions, the willingness of even the skilled workers to assist in bettering the position of the unskilled, preoccupation of union leaders with union recognition and other problems more urgent than that of skill differentials, responsiveness to government policies which favoured raising the incomes of the poorest groups at the most rapid rate, and the apparent equity of equal cents-per-hour increases as a way of meeting rising living costs during an inflationary period.

There are indications that many employers would have preferred to make uniform percentage increases in wage rates and would have shown more concern for the relative position of the skilled worker.[2] It is almost certain that a large proportion of non-union employers have used a percentage basis in making wage adjustments. One can thus conclude that unionism has been an independent factor of some strength making for uniform cents-per-hour increases, and thereby for a narrowing of occupational differentials.

Within the last few years a number of unions which had pursued equal cents-per-hour increases for ten to fifteen years have begun to show concern for the position of the most skilled employees, and have recently sought either percentage increases or graduated cents-per-hour increases giving larger absolute amounts to the higher-paid

[1] See the *Termination Report of the National War Labor Board* (1948), vol. i, p. 209.

[2] For evidence on this point from one city see L. G. Reynolds, *The Structure of Labor Markets* (1951), chap. vi.

workers. In 1949 and 1950 only about 20 per cent of the wage settlements reported to the Bureau of Labor Statistics provided larger increases for the skilled workers. By 1953 about 40 per cent of the settlements contained such provisions.[1] The United Automobile Workers have sought several special increases for the highly skilled tool and die makers. The United Steel Workers have made a particular effort to maintain occupational differentials from 1947 through 1953. In 1953, for the first time, skilled workers in the machinery industry actually increased their percentage differential over the unskilled.[2] Despite this recent movement, however, the net effect in the past twenty years has been towards a narrowing of occupational differentials.

If the hypothesis advanced earlier were correct, this effect should have been most marked where all employees are organized in a single industrial union, and less marked where the skilled men are organized separately in craft groups. There has been no thoroughgoing attempt to test this hypothesis, but on the basis of casual observation, it does not fare very well. In the printing industry, organized on a craft basis, differentials have been fairly well maintained. In 1938 the average union scale for hand compositors exceeded the average rate for bindery women by 127 per cent; by 1952 this differential had fallen only to 101 per cent. One can find other cases, however, in which differentials have been drastically reduced, despite the prevalence of craft organization. In the railroad industry, as in the building construction industry, uniform cents-per-hour increases for everyone have been the general rule since the mid-'thirties, despite the powerful organizations of the engineers, firemen, and other skilled groups.[3]

Turning to the industrial unions one finds a similar diversity of experience. In several major industries, including the automobile industry, occupational differentials have been sharply compressed. In the basic steel industry, however, there has been very little reduction. In 1938 blowers earned about 85 per cent more than labourers in blast furnace departments. By 1951 this percentage had declined to 80 and is probably a little below 80 at present. In

[1] Data secured from U.S. Bureau of Labor Statistics: *Monthly Report on Current Wage Developments*.

[2] Data reported in *Monthly Labor Review* (June 1954).

[3] This industry, to be sure, is a special case. Its labour relations are governed by a separate statute, and few of the wage adjustments since 1936 have been made without the intervention of an emergency board or arbitration board. It is these boards which have typically recommended equal cents-per-hour increases. While these increases have in the end been accepted by the skilled unions, this has occurred under pressure and one cannot conclude that the unions preferred this type of increase.

the woollen and worsted textile industry, and possibly in certain other branches of textile manufacture, the percentage differential of loom-fixers over labourers has actually increased since the mid-'thirties.

It does not appear, then, that there is any marked correlation between type of union organization and the rate of decline in occupational differentials. A more detailed analysis would be necessary, of course, to confirm this observation. If correct, it raises interesting questions. Are the skilled members of an industrial union much more influential than one might suppose from their small numbers alone ? Are the skilled craft unions less aggressive and self-interested than one might expect on economic grounds ? Are they restrained by regard for public opinion or by other considerations from advancing their already high wage scales at a disproportionate rate ? Are they interested in raising the rates of the unskilled, possibly as an underpinning to their own position and a platform for future wage demands ?

Appraisal

There now remains the question whether recent developments have brought the occupational wage structure closer to, or farther away from the structure which would exist in a perfectly competitive labour market. In the absence of precise demonstration one might assert that occupational differentials in the United States before 1930 were considerably wider than was necessary on competitive grounds, that is, wider than necessary to maintain an adequate supply of labour to the higher-paid occupations. There are several reasons for this view. First, one may judge the ordinary criteria for occupational differentials : the craftsman's work is more pleasant, more secure, and carries greater prestige than that of the labourer ; while there is a certain learning period, this is not sufficient to justify so large a premium in earnings, nor can high earnings for craftsmen be explained very satisfactorily as a rent for scarce talents, which can scarcely be a factor in many manual occupations. Second, one may note that occupational differentials in most European countries have long been narrower than in the United States, yet it has apparently been possible to man the skilled occupations. Third, the narrowing of differentials in the United States during the past twenty years does not seem to have destroyed the incentive to seek skilled employment. One does not hear of any shortage of applicants for white-collar jobs, despite the relative decline in their wage level ; nor is there a serious shortage of people willing to train for the skilled crafts. This is the nearest one can come to an empirical test of whether present occupational differentials are 'correct' from a competitive standpoint.

This evidence would imply, then, that the events of the past twenty years have brought the occupational wage structure closer to the competitive pattern. To the extent that collective bargaining has been a factor in the situation, the influence of collective bargaining has been in a competitive direction. I think this is true both as regards the general increase in manual wage rates relative to clerical rates, and as regards the increase of unskilled manual labour relative to skilled labour. In both respects collective bargaining has helped to speed up an equalization of earnings which might eventually have resulted from competitive forces alone.

If present tendencies continue, however, they may eventually lead to differentials which are too narrow from a competitive standpoint. Over any extended period, on the other hand, there is a natural check to the undue narrowing of differentials, a check which does not exist in the case of needlessly wide differentials. If differentials should become so small as to create shortages of skilled and specialized workers, employers would clearly have an incentive to widen them again ; and it is doubtful whether many unions would oppose wage increases which employers were willing to concede. Another reaction would doubtless be to economize skilled labour, in part by a deliberate de-skilling of more and more occupations. To some extent job content can be adjusted to the width of occupational differentials rather than vice versa.

IV. Interplant Differentials

Hypotheses

The accepted hypothesis regarding interplant differentials is that trade unions try to impose approximately the same wage level on rival producers of the same product. The maxims of 'equal pay for equal work' and 'the standard rate' have a long tradition, according to which union members in low-wage companies press for wages to be brought up to the higher level which members in other companies are receiving for the same work. High-wage companies are also likely to favour industry-wide standardization on competitive grounds.

The really decisive factor making for wage uniformity is the pressure of competition in the product market. A firm which is allowed to pay less than the prevailing rates may, by undercutting the prices of its competitors, become a threat to the entire wage and price structure of the industry. A standard wage scale thus comes to be viewed by union and employers alike as a method of 'stabilizing' the industry, of 'putting a floor under competition'. It follows that the area over which a union attempts to impose a standard rate will be related to the area of competition in the product market. In retail trade, service, building construction, and other local industries the union may be expected to establish a standard scale for each locality, but it will not be essential to bring different localities to a common level. In manufacturing industries, on the other hand, where transportation is a minor factor and competition is national in scope, the union will be under pressure to develop a standard scale for all employers, regardless of location. There are serious difficulties in the very concept of wage uniformity or wage equalization among firms. Precisely what is to be equalized? [1] The possibilities include:

(1) Hourly rates for workers actually paid on a time basis. This means the equalization of workers' hourly earnings, except for possible payment above the scale during periods of labour shortage. Average direct labour cost per unit of output (referred to hereafter as unit labour cost) will not be equalized because of non-uniformity in both plant efficiency and quality of labour.

(2) Hourly minimum rates for workers paid on a piece-rate or other incentive basis. This will not equalize the average hourly earnings of workers on the same job in different companies, unless the companies follow identical standards of piece-rate determination.

(3) Piece-rates per unit of output. This will not equalize workers' earnings because of variations in both plant and workers' efficiency. It will equalize unit labour cost, but is compatible with wider variations in average total unit cost.

(4) Earnings per unit of skill and effort required (Marshall's 'efficiency earnings'). [2] On this basis, piece-rates in different plants would be so adjusted as precisely to offset variations in the quality of tools, materials, supervision, and other factors outside the worker's control. A worker putting forth a given amount of skill and effort would then earn the same amount, regardless of the plant in which he was employed. Earnings of workers on the same job would not necessarily be equalized, but differences would reflect only

[1] See Richard A. Lester and Edward A. Robie, *Wages under National and Regional Collective Bargaining* (1946).

[2] Alfred Marshall, *Principles of Economics*, 8th edition (1938), pp. 548-549.

differences in skill and effort among the workers themselves. Unit labour cost would of course not be equalized. Unit total costs would be more unequal than under (3), because the least efficient firms would be obliged to pay the highest piece-rates. Marginal firms would receive an added penalty and efficient firms a bonus under this arrangement.

Looking at equalization from the worker's standpoint, only (4) will equalize earnings for workers of equal efficiency. From the employer's standpoint, only (3) provides assurance of equal unit labour costs, with its presumed effect of stabilization on competition. In general, the methods which will ensure uniformity of earnings will destroy uniformity of labour costs, and vice versa. Faced with this dilemma, both employers and unions seem to give greatest weight to uniformity of labour costs. An effort is sometimes made to protect workers against abnormally poor plant conditions by prescribing higher piece-rates, extra payments, and so on; but beyond this earnings are left to fall where they may.

Evidence

The actual impact of collective bargaining on interplant differentials is difficult to determine. There are good indications, however, that collective bargaining does tend to reduce wage dispersion among competing firms.

The evidence is clearest in the case of local industries — building construction, newspaper and job printing, retail trade, hotel and restaurant service, laundries, and so on. Here the standard union scale, applied uniformly to all unionized employers, is the general rule. Wage agreements are usually negotiated between the union and an association of employers in the locality; but even where negotiations are conducted separately with each employer, the union typically requires identical terms. The formulation of union wage policies is rather decentralized. Local unions go their own way with general advice and assistance from national headquarters, and the wage levels established in different localities show considerable variation.

Where employers compete on a regional or national basis, as they do in most branches of manufacturing, wage policy is more highly centralized in the national organization, and local unions are less free to deviate from national standards. In its most thoroughgoing form the national union undertakes systematic classification of all jobs in the industry, evaluation of their relative worth, development of a standard scale, and application of this scale to all firms in the industry through a master agreement between the union and an employer federation. But such industry-wide agreements, quite common in some countries, are still rather rare in the United States. The typical situation is rather one in which a national union bargains separately with each employer in the industry, but in the course of successive annual negotiations attempts to 'herd' them in the general direction of a common wage level.

One device used for achieving this purpose is for each union to establish a certain wage 'target' for a particular year, which is first tested out in negotiations with one or more employers. It is then proclaimed as a 'pattern' which should be enforced on all other employers in the industry. To the extent that the union succeeds in this policy, and to the extent that demands are couched in cents-per-hour terms, the necessary result is a reduction in percentage differentials among different employers.

If there are large interfirm differentials at the outset, however, it would take many years to approach a common industry wage level by this method alone. Unions tend to accelerate the process by pulling up low-wage companies at an even faster pace, and occasionally by retarding the rate of increase in the top companies. When this process is far enough along, it may become feasible to make a single jump to the goal of a standard wage scale for the industry.

The American industries in which the process, if not completed, is at least far advanced, includes pressed and blown glassware, pottery, fully fashioned hosiery, flat glass, Pacific Coast pulp and paper mills, basic steel, cotton textiles, and men's clothing.[1] One might perhaps add coal mining, railroad transportation, and a number of other industries. The various specific techniques have included efforts in some industries to equalize actual hourly earnings, in others basic hourly rates, in others piece-rates, in still others labour cost per unit of output. A piece-rate basis of payment seems more conducive than time rates to development of industry-wide wage agreements. The piece-rate basis facilitates adjustment to differences in worker efficiency, plant efficiency, and plant location.

Even where wage standardization is far advanced, the policy is rarely enforced rigidly on every firm in the industry. There are frequently marginal firms which might be put out of operation by a standard wage, particularly a standard scale of hourly rates. In these cases local union leaders and members will often be willing to make wage concessions in order to protect their jobs. National union leaders are typically reluctant to permit payment below the

[1] See Thomas Kennedy, *The Significance of Wage Uniformity* (1949).

standard scale. Where concessions are made, they are regarded as temporary ; and they are frequently accompanied by a requirement that the employer take steps to improve plant efficiency. In a number of industries — clothing, hosiery, steel — the union itself has an engineering department which provides free consulting service to marginal employers who must improve their efficiency in order to survive.

Appraisal

The chief causes for inequality of wages among firms in the same industry may be listed as follows:[1] (a) Differences in the quality of the labour employed by different firms. In this case, however, there would be uniformity of efficiency earnings and of unit labour costs. (b) Workers may be of uniform quality, but the imperfection of the labour market may permit employers to pay differing wage levels and still attract an adequate labour supply. (c) The efficiency of equipment, supervision, and other non-labour facts may differ among firms, and wage rates may have to be adjusted in such a way as to offset these variations. This might produce a rough uniformity of total unit costs and permit all firms to remain in competition. This case, of course, requires an imperfect labour market and should perhaps be regarded as one possibility under (b).

The interfirm wage differences in any actual industry probably reflect some combination of these elements, the proportions varying from one case to the next. If, however, one asked what would be the effect of eliminating each element separately, the answers to each question could then be recombined to provide a general appraisal of wage levelling through collective bargaining.

(1) Suppose, first, the variation in workers' hourly earnings is due entirely and exactly proportionate to differences in ability and effort. If the industry operates under piece-rates, equality of piece-rates in all firms would be a condition of full equilibrium, since this would enable earnings to vary in precise relation to output. A standard scale of piece-rates laid down through collective bargaining would thus have no disturbing effect.

If the industry operates under time rates differences in labour efficiency would be reflected in different levels of hourly rates in the various firms. If an effort is made to raise the wage levels of the lowest firms and impose a standard scale on the industry, this clearly would have a disturbing effect by imposing higher unit labour costs on the firms with an inferior labour force. These firms

[1] We omit discussion of differences in geographical location until section VI.

will begin to suffer losses and will face elimination unless they can raise the quality of their labour force *pari passu* with the rise in their wage level. If the process of wage levelling is sufficiently gradual, if employers are reasonably free to alter their labour force by discharges and new hirings, and if the industry in question is a small factor in the total labour market, it may be quite possible for firms to make the necessary adjustments. The outcome may be a new equilibrium with a uniform quality of labour in all firms corresponding to the uniform level of hourly wage rates. This implies that many workers will have been forced out of this industry into others whose wage structure is either not standardized at all or standardized at a lower level. There is no insuperable difficulty in imposing uniform quality requirements within a single (relatively small) industry, provided there remains sufficient room for quality variation among other industries.

The effect of imposing a uniform scale of minimum hourly rates, while earnings are computed on a piece-rate basis, will be intermediate between the two previous effects. It will impose considerable pressure on the firms with the poorest labour force. The pressure will not be so serious as that of uniform time rates, however, because there remains an escape valve in the gap between the hourly minimum and actual hourly earnings. The firms with an inferior labour force may survive partly by holding this gap considerably below that which exists in the superior firms. If the union will not permit this and insists on a uniform gap throughout, the effect becomes identical with that of uniform time rates.

(2) Suppose now that quality of labour, and of all other hired factors, is identical throughout the industry. Some employers, however, more aggressive or self-interested than the others, take advantage of the imperfection of the labour market to pay lower wages than their competitors.

There can be little doubt that this is a real possibility. It arises partly from worker attitudes, employer hiring practices, and union rules which interfere with free interfirm movement of labour. Equally important are frequent periods of underemployment, and the continued influx of young people into the labour market which provide a pool of particularly malleable and exploitable labour. Most employers at most times are not really operating on a rising labour supply curve.[1] They are able to expand employment considerably at their existing wage level simply by posting a 'help wanted' sign or by telephoning the employment service.

[1] See L. G. Reynolds, *The Structure of Labor Markets* (1951), chaps. ix–x ; and The Supply of Labor to the Firm', *Quarterly Journal of Economics* (May 1946).

This combination of circumstances makes it possible for an employer to offer lower wage rates than his competitors to workers of identical quality and still attract an adequate labour supply ; and the large differences in the wage levels of employers in the same labour market suggest that this actually happens. Part of the observed wage differences undoubtedly reflects variation in labour quality, but the differences seem too large to be explained entirely on this ground. There are strong indications that monopsonistic exploitation exists on a significant scale.

In this situation the effect of imposing a uniform wage scale throughout an industry is quite simple. There will be a transfer of income from owners to workers in the firms which have been paying substandard wage rates. If the low-wage firms have expanded in order to maximize profits they may now have to contract, and there may be some re-allocation of labour resources in the industry. The end result, however, is to establish that uniformity of efficiency earnings which would have existed from the beginning in a perfectly competitive labour market.

(3) A third possibility is that the efficiency of non-labour factors may vary from firm to firm, these differences not being fully offset by variations in factor prices. Some firms may have newer and more efficient equipment, or a superior plant layout. In any industry where technological advance is rapid the newer plants will tend to have a cost advantage over older plants. There is reason to think that managerial efficiency varies greatly, and that this is by no means fully compensated by salary differences. The market for business executives, about which very little is known, may be even more imperfect than the market for manual workers, and there may well be considerable exploitation of the best managers.

In any event, the existence of substantial differences in average total unit cost among competing producers is a well-documented fact. Marshall and other economists remarked on this phenomenon even before detailed accounting comparisons were available. The cost investigations incidental to price control in two world wars, the industry studies of the Federal Trade Commission and the Tariff Commission, and other work has produced a mass of evidence confirming these early observations.

One way in which competing firms can adjust to differences in their non-labour costs is by paying different rates of wages. This possibility would not exist in a perfectly competitive labour market, but it does exist in actual labour markets for the reasons already noted a moment ago. High-cost firms which are hard pressed for survival will react by paying a wage level below the industry average.

Surprisingly, however, there seems to be some tendency for low-cost firms to share the fruits of their efficiency with their employees by paying better-than-average wages.[1] This may be partly a method of recruiting a superior labour force, but it is probably also influenced by altruistic and prestige motives.

What happens if a union enters an industry with wide variation in wages, efficiency, costs, and profits, and tries to enforce a uniform level of wages ? A uniform scale of time rates will put heaviest pressure on the low-wage firms. Uniform minimum hourly rates for piece-workers will exert somewhat less pressure. Uniform piece-rates will exert even less pressure, but will still exert some. In order fully to offset their lower level of output and consequent higher level of unit overhead costs, it will have been necessary for the less efficient firms to pay, not merely less per hour, but also less per piece. An attempt to equalize efficiency earnings of piece-workers, by setting higher piece-rates where production conditions are unfavourable, will of course bear still harder on the marginal firms.

When wage standardization threatens the survival of marginal firms, their first reaction will doubtless be to re-examine their costs and endeavour to reduce them. This is the 'shock effect' which has frequently been observed as an aftermath of minimum wage legislation. After everything possible has been done in removing inefficiency, continued pressure for wage equalization can result only in eventual elimination of the highest cost firms and a corresponding expansion of the more efficient producers.

Where both low-cost and high-cost producers are located in the same labour market area, and where the workers left unemployed by the disappearing firms are absorbed by the expanding firms, it seems clear that resource allocation has been improved. Workers have been moved to positions in which their value productivity is higher than before. Even where the firms are located in different areas and direct transfer of labour is not possible, it can still be argued that there is a gain through concentration of production in the most efficient firms.

We have now considered three possible sources of interfirm differentials, and explored the consequences of wage equalization in each case. Where does this leave us as regards general conclusions ? It is not possible to say exactly how much of the interfirm variation in wage levels which we observe is due to each of these three factors, though we can be sure that each is of considerable importance.

[1] Sumner H. Slichter, 'Notes on the Structure of Wages', *Review of Economics and Statistics* (February 1950), pp. 80-91.

Fortunately the exact mixture of forces does not affect our conclusion, since the effect of wage standardization turns out in any event to be favourable or at worst neutral.

V. Interindustry Differentials

Hypotheses

If all industries were unionized, and if all unions followed 'monopolistic' policies, one would expect wages for a particular kind of labour to be highest in industries where the demand for labour is most inelastic. Wages would be higher, in other words, in proportion as the demand for the product is inelastic, labour forms a small proportion of total cost, other factors are imperfectly substitutable for labour, and the supply curves of other factors are inelastic.

The degree of competition in the product market may also be expected to have some effect. Other things equal, wages will probably be higher where there are few producers and where prices are under firm control than in industries of many producers where price agreement is absent or ineffective. Firms which are organized to translate wage increases into price increases may well oppose wage increases less strongly than firms which see in them a real threat to their survival.

Over the course of time one would expect wages to rise most rapidly where the demand curve for labour is rising most rapidly, whether because of rising demand for the product or a rapid increase in labour productivity. There would, indeed, be some tendency in this direction even in the absence of union organization. Expanding industries will tend to bid up wage rates somewhat to attract an adequate labour force. Static or declining industries will take advantage of the imperfection of the labour market to lag behind the general pace of wage advance. Under trade unionism, however, a larger part of any increase in labour demand will be translated into wage increases, and a smaller part into employment increases than is the case without collective bargaining.

To the extent that some industries are only partially unionized, union strength becomes an additional independent variable, but lack of a precise measurement of union strength makes it difficult to give a clear meaning to this hypothesis. The percentage of employees in an industry who are union members has been the indication most frequently referred to, but its usefulness decreases as more and more industries approach 100 per cent unionization.

Evidence

The possibility that collective bargaining may distort the relative wage levels and price levels of different industries away from the competitive pattern has always been one of the most serious charges advanced by critics of trade unionism. What evidence is there that collective bargaining is disruptive in this way ? In the absence of a highly competitive labour market we cannot judge what inter-industry differentials would exist under perfect competition. Inspection of wage statistics, combined with some knowledge of production methods and job duties in each industry, helps to form an impression that the existing wage levels of certain industries are 'too high' and that those of certain other industries are 'too low', but there seems no way by which this impression can be submitted to an objective test. One might perhaps try to apply the technique of job evaluation in appraising the relative worth of jobs across industry lines.

Another approach would be to examine the wages paid by different industries for a homogeneous occupation which is widely distributed throughout the economy. The leading candidate would probably be 'common labour', which is found in almost every industry and for which statistical records have been collected for many years. A major difficulty, however, is that common labour is not really common. It is light labour in some industries and heavy labour in others, working conditions vary from pleasant to extremely unpleasant, elements of skill are usually present but vary from industry to industry, and the nature of the work done changes over the course of time. Further, the relation between common labour rates and higher job rates varies considerably from industry to industry, and an industry which ranks low in terms of labour rates may stand a good deal higher on an over-all basis.

These difficulties in making cross-sectional comparisons of wage levels have led many students to concentrate on comparisons of rates of change in wages over a selected period of time, usually measured by the change in average hourly earnings for all workers. An attempt is then made to determine whether, after taking account of other factors, one can detect any net effect of union organization.

This kind of study is complicated by the reasons other than union influence which may also account for changes in interindustry differentials. The kind of work to be done, the mixture of skilled and unskilled occupations, the proportion of male and female employees, will change in each industry over the course of time. One would expect a relative increase in the wage levels of industries whose work was becoming relatively more skilled, more arduous, or more largely performed by males. Shifts in the geographical location of industry will distort interindustry comparisons, though this difficulty can be reduced by confining the comparisons to a single region. The rate of increase in product demand and the rate of technical progress in each industry will also influence interindustry differentials for reasons already noted. An attempt to single out the influence of unionism thus leads one into a multiple-correlation analysis, in which some of the independent variables are not readily measurable.

It is not feasible here to review in detail the numerous contributions to this subject which have appeared in recent years.[1] Ross concludes that there was some relationship between unionism and increases in earnings over the period 1933–1946, though he seems to have been mainly concerned with the rate of unionization rather than degree of unionization. Garbarino, working with data for 1923–1940, finds that 'the relationship between unionism and earnings for this period seems to be rather vague. This result may well be due to the fact that the influence of unionism entered the picture so late in the time period'. Dunlop expresses a judgment that economic variables have dominated the changes in interindustry differentials and that unionism has played a minor rôle. Rees, in a study of the fully unionized basic steel and bituminous coal industries during the post-second World War inflation, concludes that their wage levels probably rose somewhat less rapidly than they would have under non-union conditions. Sobotka, on the other hand, concludes that unionism in the building construction industry has raised the wage level of the unionized workers by something in the range of 10 to 20 per cent.[2] Lester and Robie conclude that wages set by regional and national collective agreements do not seem to have risen more rapidly over the last several decades than manufacturing wages in general.

If it turns out that the influence of unionism on interindustry

[1] See Arthur M. Ross, 'The Influence of Unionism upon Earnings', *Quarterly Journal of Economics* (February 1948), pp. 263-286 ; Arthur M. Ross and William Goldner, 'Forces affecting the Inter-industry Wage Structure', *Quarterly Journal of Economics* (May 1950), pp. 254-281 ; John T. Dunlop, 'Productivity and the Wage Structure', in *Income, Employment, and Public Policy*, Essays in honour of Alvin H. Hansen (1948) ; Joseph Garbarino, 'A Theory of Inter-industry Wage Structure Variation', *Quarterly Journal of Economics* (May 1950), pp. 283-305 ; Sumner H. Slichter, 'Notes on the Structure of Wages', *Review of Economics and Statistics* (November 1947), pp. 274-285 ; and Stephen P. Sobotka, 'Union Influence on Wages : the Construction Industry', *Journal of Political Economy* (April 1953), pp. 127-143.

[2] The methodology of this study is interesting, and it is one of the few which have attempted a cross-sectional approach at a single point of time.

differentials is weaker than our original hypotheses suggested, where should we look for an explanation of this fact? The answer may lie partly in the realities of union behaviour and partly in the structure of labour markets. Wage bargaining is only one aspect of union activity, and in the case of old and secure unions it is by no means the most important aspect. Most union leaders, in fact, tend to avoid aggressive wage maximization.

When unions do work actively to force up the top strata of the wage structure, however, there are also other forces working to push up the lower layers, such as the advance of legal minimum wage levels and of benefit rates under social insurance programmes. More important, however, is the normal market effect of a wage increase in some industries on the supply price of labour to other industries. The writer has argued elsewhere that there is at any time a maximum feasible 'gap' between the highest and lowest wages offered for comparable labour in the same labour market.[1] As the top of the wage structure rises, the minimum expectation of workers in the market also rises, and the lowest wage employers are forced to raise wages in order to attract labour. Beyond a certain point, therefore, an effort by the more highly organized and strategically situated workers to increase their advantage over the low-paid must become a futile attempt to rise by pulling at their own boot straps.

This competitive pressure, to be sure, operates most strongly during periods of high employment and may be largely suspended during severe under-employment. What may happen, therefore, is a cyclical alternation of low employment periods during which the well organized widen their advantage over the ill organized, and of high employment periods during which the ill organized narrow the gap once more.

Appraisal

Despite the limitations on union influence, it is scarcely credible that unionism has no effect whatever on interindustry differentials. To the extent that unionism is influential, it must almost certainly tend to bring about a wider departure from competitive norms than would exist otherwise.

In a static and perfectly competitive labour market different industries would tend to pay the same wage rate for workers of equal efficiency employed in the same occupation. Under dynamic conditions, with different rates of expansion in different industries,

[1] Reynolds, *The Structure of Labor Markets*, chap. x.

there would be departures from this standard, but these would be moderate in amount and would tend to be eroded over the long run.

In an imperfect but non-union labour market interindustry differences appear to be considerably larger than this. Profitable and expanding industries seem to pay higher wage rates than they need pay on recruitment grounds alone, while unprogressive or declining industries wallow along in their wake. Differences in industrial structure are fundamental to an understanding of inter-industry wage differentials, and it requires a singular myopia to focus on trade unionism as the prime mover, although its initial impact is probably to produce some further widening of these differentials. Unionism seems to establish itself first and most strongly in those industries which are already towards the top of the wage structure, and in which conditions for further wage increases are most favourable. Taking off from this advantageous position, unions may propel the high-wage industries forward at a more rapid pace than they would have maintained otherwise.

Is this merely a transitional situation which exists in an economy in process of unionization? What is likely to happen if and when all industries are highly unionized? Unionization in the United States is still too fragmentary to provide much evidence on this point, and one could learn more from experience in the more highly unionized countries of Western Europe. It seems possible that when unionism reaches the lowest-wage industries these unions may press forward with sufficient vigour to narrow interindustry differentials once more. In this case, the wage distortion produced by collective bargaining might reach a maximum at some point during the period of partial unionization, and then begin to diminish. The eventual outcome might be a narrower range of interindustry differentials than exists in an imperfect non-union labour market.

VI. Geographical Differentials

Hypotheses

How might one expect the growth of trade unionism to affect geographical differentials? In manufacturing and other industries where there is effective interregional competition, as was pointed out in section IV, the effort of the union to place different plants and firms on an equal competitive basis will work towards a narrowing of geographical differentials.

The problem of a purely local industry is more difficult. If unionism entrenches itself first in the high-wage regions and communities, it may for the time being widen the geographical differentials in the industry. If and when unionism spreads evenly throughout the industry, there may be some tendency towards a narrowing of differentials. Local unions in the low-wage regions and communities may adopt the scales of higher-paid locals as a target and standard of comparison, but one would not expect this tendency to be so strong as in industries where national competition exists.

Evidence

In the case of national industries little need be added to what was said in section IV. The general tendency of union policy has been to reduce interfirm differentials between regions as well as within regions. It is also clear that unions have been flexible and by no means doctrinaire in this matter. In some industries, such as hosiery, the existence of long-standing geographical differences has been recognized by establishing two or more levels of rates, which narrow the previous differentials, but do not eliminate them. In other industries, such as blown glassware, jobs paid on a time basis have been excluded from the master agreement and each local union has been free to adjust these to the prevailing local level. Where a locational disadvantage can be shown, as in the case of textile finishing operations and women's clothing manufacture outside the New York metropolitan area, the outlying firms have been allowed a differential sufficient to keep them in competition.

Where geographical differentials have been eliminated entirely, as in flat glass and basic steel, there has typically been a combination of favourable circumstances : a high degree of unionization, a high degree of industrial concentration, and a situation in which the southern plants were merely branch plants or subsidiaries of northern companies. It is clearly easier in such a situation for the union to force acceptance of wage equalization, and for the industry to adjust to it. In textiles, hosiery, clothing, and light industry generally, union progress in the South has been slow and this has limited what could be done in narrowing regional differentials.

The narrowing of geographical differentials which has occurred in numerous industries is due also to labour and capital migration, which may be presumed to be working in this direction over the long run. The high employment and the increase in price levels over the past fifteen years have also helped to narrow geographical wage differentials, and federal minimum wage legislation and other federal wage policies have had the same effect. Unionism has at most speeded up or intensified a process which was already well under way.

Appraisal

In a competitive economy in full equilibrium, geographical differences in wages could remain only as an offset to :

(a) Differences in living costs in different locations. To the extent that earnings are a factor in migration decisions, it is real earnings rather than money earnings which should tend towards equality. Differences in living costs among regions of the United States are quite small, however, advantages in one item tending to be offset by disadvantages on others.

(b) Differences in the quality of labour in different areas. It has often been argued that labour in the South is markedly less efficient than in the North, and that this justifies a permanent differential in wages. Studies by Lester and others suggest, however, that this factor has been considerably exaggerated. Experienced workers performing under similar conditions seem to produce just as much, or very nearly as much in the South as in the North.

(c) Costs and uncertainties of movement. It can be argued that it will require some potential gain in real earnings to induce a worker to move himself and his household to a new location. On this basis we might expect that areas of labour surplus would never reach full equality in real earnings with areas of labour deficit. A continuing gap may be necessary to keep the migration stream going. This line of argument should not be over-emphasized, however, for there are indications that geographical movement is mainly job-oriented rather than wage-oriented, and migration sometimes occurs even in the face of adverse wage differentials.

It is impossible to make a quantitative evaluation of the combined effect of these three factors in the United States, and it is consequently impossible to say what a competitive structure of geographical differentials would look like. At a very rough guess, there may be a basis for a permanent wage differential of something like 10 per cent between the highest and lowest regions of the country, and an additional 10 per cent between large cities and small towns in the same region.

The set of differentials which would exist in competitive equilibrium, however, is not necessarily the correct objective of public policy under dynamic conditions. It may be desirable to maintain differentials wider than this in order to encourage location of new industrial investment in the southern states and in small towns rather than metropolitan centres. This policy of 'bringing the job to the man rather than the man to the job' could be justified as a way of reducing the volume and costs of migration. One could also support it in terms of the social, political, and other advantages of decentralizing the population from crowded metropolitan centres.

Taking all these considerations into account, one can try to estimate what would be an optimum system of geographical differentials, and how the geographical wage structure of the United States compares with this norm. It may be reasonable to say that both interregional and intercommunity differentials have in the past been considerably greater than optimum, and that they are still above optimum in spite of such narrowing as has occurred in recent decades. A judicious further narrowing of differentials, stopping considerably short of full wage equalization, would probably be in the greatest public interest.

Up to the present time, then, collective bargaining has probably helped to reduce differentials which were needlessly wide and to produce a closer approach to the optimum, though in a few cases unions may have overshot the mark and to narrow differentials unduly. It seems clear that equalization of money wage levels in all communities would have undesirable results. There is no indication, however, that unions in local industries will attempt to go this far ; and one may hope that even unions in national industries will halt at a reasonable distance from this point.

One's attitude toward the eventual effect of unionism turns partly on one's attachment to industrial decentralization as an ideal objective. Those who attach great importance to this objective will naturally be critical of the possible development of a wage structure which would retard the spread of industry to agricultural areas, while those who are more concerned with equity in income distribution will view reduction of geographical differentials with greater equanimity.

This chapter has been concerned with the impact of collective bargaining on relative rates of wages in different localities, occupations, firms, and industries. We have seen that the effects of trade unionism cannot be deduced from first principles and that, on the contrary, simple economic models of union behaviour are likely to be quite misleading. The empirical data examined in this paper are drawn entirely from the United States, but it would be possible to make a similar analysis of any other economy for which adequate wage statistics exist. Until this has been done, one cannot generalize about the effects of unionism on either a comparative or an international basis.

In evaluating the results of collective bargaining one must distinguish : (1) the wage structure which would exist in a perfectly competitive labour market under full employment ; (2) the wage structure which exists in actual labour markets under non-union conditions ; (3) the wage structure which develops in actual labour markets under collective bargaining. There has been some tendency in theoretical writing to compare situation (3) with situation (1) and to conclude that, since collective bargaining does not reproduce the results of perfect competition, it must have an adverse effect on the wage structure. Such a conclusion is clearly illegitimate. The actual effect of collective bargaining must be judged by comparing (3) with (2). If one takes the competitive structure (1) as a welfare norm, it is entirely possible that the wage structure under collective bargaining may lie closer to this norm than to the non-union structure.

In a partially unionized economy, such as that of the United States, one must also distinguish between the observed effects of partial unionization up to the present time, and the potential effects of full unionization at some time in the future.

As regards the effect of collective bargaining in the United States to date, we have found considerable support for the following hypotheses :

(1) Collective bargaining has reduced occupational differentials within particular industries, and has probably brought them closer to what they would have been under perfect competition.
(2) Collective bargaining has reduced interplant differentials, on a national scale in industries characterized by regional or national competition, and on a local basis in local industries. In this respect, also, collective bargaining has probably produced a closer approximation to a competitive wage structure.
(3) Collective bargaining has probably widened interindustry differentials, and in an anti-competitive fashion. Unionism has penetrated most effectively into the relatively high-wage industries, and has tended to 'make the rich richer'.
(4) Collective bargaining has probably reduced geographical differentials, but this effect has been weaker than the first three effects, and largely incidental to the reduction of interplant differentials. The reduction of geographical differentials has probably brought the wage structure closer to competitive standards, though unions in a few industries may have overshot the mark.

It must also be emphasized that, with respect to each of the four tendencies noted above, collective bargaining has been only one of several forces working in the same general direction. It would be a serious error to ascribe more than a minor part of what has happened to union influence. Unionism has perhaps had the greatest incremental effect on interplant differentials (hypothesis 2), with items (3), (1), and (4) following in that order.

It is tempting, but necessarily inconclusive, to speculate about the potential effects of stronger union organization at some later time. We would suggest that tendencies (1), (2), and (4) would operate somewhat more strongly under full unionization than they do at the present time. The tendency toward reduction of geographical differentials, in particular, might well go farther than is socially desirable. On the other hand, tendency (3) — widening of interindustry differentials in a 'monopolistic' direction — might quite possibly be reversed. The development of strong unions in the lowest-paid industries might enable these industries to pull up closer to those which now stand at the top of the wage structure.

Two general impressions remain as one emerges from the literature on this subject. First, there has been a widespread tendency to overstate the net effect of trade unionism on wage structure. Curiously enough, this error has been committed in equal measure by the friends of trade unionism and by its critics. Union leaders and supporters have tended to take full credit for wage advances in unionized industries, while critics of trade unionism have tended to give it full blame for all wage distortions existing in the economy. Neither point of view can stand up under critical scrutiny.

Second, from the standpoint of conformity to competitive norms of wage structure, collective bargaining has clearly had a mixed effect — 'improving' the wage structure in some respects and 'worsening' it in others. The doctrinaire view that trade unions, being 'monopolies', must by definition have an adverse effect on the wage structure, does not stand up well in the light of empirical studies, for one can make at least as good a case for the contrary opinion. It would seem quite unwise at this stage to be dogmatic in either direction.

Chapter 14

UNIONISM AND THE WAGE STRUCTURE IN SWEDEN

BY

GÖSTA REHN

Research Department, Swedish Confederation of Trade Unions, Stockholm, Sweden

USING the background of empirical evidence at hand, we shall now analyse the basic trends of unionism and examine the question whether the rigidity and equalization which unions tend to introduce in the wage structure should be looked upon as distorting influences, in the sense that they hamper the adaptation of the economy towards the best allocation of productive resources.

I. SECULAR LEVELLING OF DIFFERENTIALS

Studies of the influence of unionism upon earnings have to allow for a secular decrease of most types of differentials : namely, between industries, areas, occupations, sexes, and plants. Otherwise the fact that unions have been easier to build among high-wage workers, whose relative advantage was bound to decrease with the lapse of time, would create the impression that unions tend to reduce the relative wages of their members. This impression would be true for manual workers. If we take white-collar workers into consideration, the long-term levelling trend may give an exaggerated impression that the unions have given manual workers a large wage advantage over the non-unionized white-collar groups. But no such correlations can be taken at their face value.

The interplay of unionism and the secular levelling trend has to be more fully analysed. This secular trend is a product of the inter-relation between an increasing level of mass education and an increasing level of national income. In the United States the melting together of heterogeneous social and ethnical groups has also had its effects.[1] One important element behind this process is

[1] See W. S. Woytinsky and Associates, *Employment and Wages in the United States* (1953). On the influence of unions upon equalization, see Arthur M. Ross, *Trade Union Wage Policy* (1948).

non-reversible and independent of the size of the wage differential. This factor is the drive for social status which constantly increases the supply of labour for high-rank jobs. The desire for social advancement is very little affected by any decline in the economic differential between jobs of different status. Quite to the contrary : the higher the level of income of unskilled groups, the greater their possibilities to help their children — now fewer per family — to acquire the qualifications for entrance to higher status groups.

The levelling trend of the whole income structure moves in a complicated manner. It is influenced by changes in the content of jobs and the occupational structure and technical framework of all industries. It does not only mean a narrowing of different job rates ; often it takes the form of wholesale transfer of large masses from low-wage industries to higher-wage industries. The flow of labour from agriculture to manufacturing is a central factor, but the reorganization of many industries, involving the disappearance of outmoded shops and the expansion of rationalized plants, is also important. With the concurrent decline of skilled handicraft and primitive farming, and the expansion of large industries demanding semi-skilled, medium wage work, there would be a reduction of the wage dispersion, defined as mean deviation about the mean, even with an absolutely rigid structure of relative wages.

For all these and many other reasons, attempts to explain a certain development of relative wages through observing its correlation with a single specific phenomenon like the growth and degree of unionism in different industries becomes extremely difficult. We would need a complicated map of the relative wage movements which would occur in the absence of unions, and then we would have to compare it with the actual development to see what changes the unions have been responsible for. We should find many a union created to protect a relative wage position which was bound to deteriorate, not necessarily because of any high level *per se* but because it was high in relation to the new content of the industry's work, or in relation to a decreasing demand for the old type of labour. Furthermore, we should find cases where the incentive behind the labour organization had been the favoured position of an industry to augment wages from the market level to a level more in conformity with the employers' ability to pay. In addition, there are obviously the unions which have been formed in order to enable workers to protect the interests of labour against capital. It is difficult to assess the success or failure or distorting influence of these unions with their various backgrounds on the increase in wages simply by comparing the wage increase in non-unionized industries. The whole situation has to be analysed more carefully.

The old wage structure, through the power of tradition, exercises a considerable resistance to change. During periods of slack business, when the wage level as a whole does not change much, there are no large possibilities of altering the wage structure. In periods of slump and depression unions are able to take a strong defensive stand on their members' wages while other wages fall, thus creating a 'distorted' structure from a long-term point of view. In the course of time, therefore, strong latent forces pressing for a change might develop. In a period of boom and inflation when all wages are moving upwards, these latent forces suddenly can break through and direct the relative outcome of the wage changes. Therefore one cannot draw too simple a conclusion from the levelling tendency during war periods ; the levelling of relative wages is not necessarily the 'natural' result of high or overemployment. It is not necessarily true that full employment as such or alone is the cause of the wholesale equalization of wages.

II. Empirical Evidence

A short account of the Swedish experience since the first World War may serve to illustrate this discussion. Market influences which happened to be parallel with differences in the degree of unionization created large wage differentials in the depression periods, especially the early 'twenties. Farm and forest wages were not protected by unions and decreased 50 per cent in 1920, while wages in manufacturing (already unionized to a great extent) were stable for one depression year, and then fell 30-40 per cent, relatively more in unsheltered (export and competition-exposed) industries, and relatively less in sheltered industries (the internal market : consumption, building). The resulting demand for a more solidaristic wage policy could not become effective in the trade union movement until the late 'thirties. With the lapse of time the lagging industries could make up for their lag, but apparently — judging from later happenings — there were strong elements of rather unquestionable 'inequity' in the pre-war wage structure. During the war years the efforts of the unions, aided by the natural war-time boom in farming and forestry, showed substantial progress in eliminating differentials. A wage stop was adopted with explicit exemptions for inequitably low wages which were successively extended to larger and larger parts of the labour market. (This is apart from the general cost-of-living escalator system, which had a slight levelling impact too.) The reduction in both the inter- and intra-industry wage differentials was rapidly achieved thanks to the absence of external price competition and because of the absence of any strong inflationary wage drift.[1]

The post-war period has been characterized by periods of wage stops, during which the wage drift has tended to distort the union wage pattern, and periods of collective bargaining, where the unions have endeavoured to maintain their own goals in wage policy. The interindustry wage dispersion was at a minimum during the years 1946–1948, just after some rounds of large wage adjustments. Since then the wage drift and the disturbances of the Korean inflation have increased the differentials again in a way which tends to create some unrest in the labour market. The conclusion of a Swedish trade union committee[2] seems justified that unions have the best chances to establish an equitable wage structure in a state of well-balanced full employment: unemployment as well as overemployment reduces their possibilities of carrying on a rational wage policy.

In general, the changes in the interindustry wage structure, resulting in a narrowing of differentials during the full employment period since 1939 imply progress in the direction of 'equity' or towards some job evaluation concept of equal net advantages. Such equity is difficult to judge because of the rather divergent content of jobs. The situation of female labour in different industries, however, may be used to test the inference. Whereas the interindustry wage dispersion of male workers shows many exceptions from the general rule of narrowing towards the mean, the development of the

[1] The 'wage drift' is defined as the rate of increase of actual money earnings per hour above any increase of earnings resulting from changes in the collective agreements or from escalator clauses in such agreements. In Sweden since the war, hourly earnings have risen each year about 2–6 per cent more than pre-calculated on the basis of agreements. This wage drift is sometimes translated 'wage slide' or 'wage gliding'; these expressions are all synonyms. In part, the wage drift is a market phenomenon (a function of supply and demand and increasing intensity of work under incentive schemes). In part, it is a technical phenomenon giving more advantages to workers under certain types of wage systems (minimum wage agreements, flexible piece-rate systems) than to others (fixed wages, time-rate wage systems). The varying rates of technical progress has an influence too. Even those parts of the wage drift which are of the 'technicality' types are influenced by the degree of inflationary pressure. Apparently the wage drift upsets any attempts to keep the wage structure in regulated order because it goes on at different rates for different groups. The wage structure receives an inflationary impact by giving the lagging groups a cause to ask for wage increases through bargaining and by showing the leading groups that 'the employers can pay'.

[2] Swedish Confederation of Trade Unions, *Trade Unions and Full Employment*, English edition (1953). This report gives a comprehensive account of the Swedish war and post-war wage developments together with an analysis of the problems of avoiding inflation in full employment.

interindustry structure of female wages shows that levelling is general. Apparently the explanation is the high degree of uniformity of job content for female workers in different industries. Wages were distorted earlier, but the high fluidity of the labour market, plus the conscious efforts of the union movement under the guidance of the central secretariat based on the demands for equality put forth by low-wage groups, have been creating a more equitable wage structure.

The mean deviation about the mean for female wages in 37 manufacturing industries decreased from 5·6 per cent in 1939 to 2·5 per cent in 1950, the minimum being 2·0 per cent in 1948. For male workers in 52 manufacturing industries (including mining) the same figures were 7·3 per cent and 6·1 per cent; the minimum in 1947 was 4·9 per cent. Since 1950 the dispersion has probably increased about 1 per cent in both cases, because of the slump in textiles and the wage drift in engineering. But in spite of the general narrowing between 1939 and 1950 there were 18 exceptions among the 52 male groups, where the deviation of the specific industry's wage level from the general average wage level increased, in many cases substantially. Also, several high-wage groups went to the low side and vice versa. Among the 37 female groups there were 9 exceptions, mostly of minor importance.[1]

The effect of general unionization and full employment is even more spectacular on the intra-industry, interplant wage structure. In the decades before the war, the Swedish unions and employers' associations made strong efforts to establish nation-wide agreements for each industry. Local agreements with companies paying higher or lower wages were systematically brought under the standard rates. However, a rather flexible system of cost-of-living zones,[2] together with the inherent flexibilities of minimum wage and piece-rate systems, made the agreements adaptable to varying market conditions. During and after the war the ambitions of the unions were to bring the geographical wage structure to conform with the official cost-of-living geography, that is, a reduction of these interzone differences. The interzone equalization was stimulated by the

[1] The influence of geographical cost-of-living differences are eliminated in these figures; they are based on wage figures for each industry recalculated to show their deviations from the average of all industries in each separate cost-of-living zone. However, this elimination of any cost-of-living difference bias from the figures somewhat conceals the actual development of the interindustry dispersion. The reduction of wage differences between zones has meant a real reduction of the interindustry dispersion too; the differences between wages in low and high zones were more reduced than the differences between prices.

[2] The word 'zones' is somewhat misleading. Actually the communities and townships belonging to each 'zone' were mixed and scattered all over the country until the recent reforms of the official zone system.

increase of wages in agriculture and the generally high incomes of farmers; the 'zone dispersion' has been reduced from 30–40 per cent to 15–25 per cent in most industries. At the same time the interplant differences in each zone and each industry have been systematically hunted by the unions in those cases where levelling was not brought about by high employment, competition for workers, and the resulting wage drift.

The following preliminary figures give evidence of a substantial decrease of the dispersion in the differentials between plants of varying size.

	No. of Workers per Plant				
	500	201–500	51–200	11–50	1–10
Engineering					
1939	100	95	94	88	85
1950	100	97	95	93	87
Woodworking					
1939	..	100	92	88	85
1950	..	100	97	95	92

Most of the remaining wage differences, at least in engineering, are a result of the different extent of piece-work in big and small firms. For other industries we have less complete material, but the general trend is clear in most of the important cases: differences are reduced to about half the pre-war size.

The question of union influence upon the occupational wage structure (skill differentials) has not been much studied in Sweden. There is a levelling tendency, and the unions perhaps have had some influence in this direction, but the statistical material does not give much evidence. In the case of Great Britain this question has been studied by Turner.[1] The following points are based on his conclusions: in labour market situations where the general position of labour is weak, the conservative interests among union members dominate, old differentials are upheld. To a great extent this is due to the high percentage of job-conscious craft unions in England. (In Sweden industrial unions dominate, and the degree of this type of conservatism has been less.) In many situations, even during high employment periods, this is the case, but even strong craft groups cannot increase the occupational differentials; they can only put a brake on the levelling trend. The low-wage groups have the

[1] H. A. Turner, 'Trade Unions, Differentials and the Levelling of Wages', *The Manchester School* (September 1952), pp. 227-282.

basic valuations of unionism on their side: it is a good thing to 'level up' a minority group; to increase a differential demands very substantial arguments.

III. The Growing Demand for Equity

We have seen that unionism implies a basic tendency towards the establishing of comparatively rigid but equitable wage structures, thus diminishing the impact of changing market forces and permanent employer aspirations with regard to relative wages. A few additional arguments [1] will show why the principle of equity or 'fair relativity' is likely to gain influence with the increasing predominance of unionism and collective bargaining. (It should be noted, unless otherwise stated, that when we speak of equalization as a synonym for equity we are thinking of wages for equal work.)

The equalization tendency with regard to skill and area differentials (the long-term market phenomenon) makes other differentials less acceptable. If the skill differential is 100 per cent, it is possible that the market, changing product demand, company profit, or mere inertia and tradition create or uphold a 50 per cent differential between two labour groups or industries belonging to classes of similar skill. But if the differential between skilled and unskilled workers within most industries is 50 or 25 per cent, such differences between industries become intolerable. Unions will feel compelled to take considerable trouble to eliminate them, even at the cost of strikes or employment difficulties. At the same time, the improvement of the economic standard of the lowest strata of the population make these less apt to submit to 'natural' market forces with regard to wage levels. Their improved conditions make them more union-minded as well; this is a cumulative process.

Unions, general education, and mass communication bring about an improved level of knowledge among workers and employers regarding wages outside their neighbourhood area; and, consequently, deviations from the general pattern become psychologically less acceptable to them. Job evaluation, with its connotation of some intrinsic value for each job, has a similar psychological impact on a broad scale.

The enlargement of unions make them weaker against internal pressures for equity at the same time as they become stronger against employers; by referring to its own weakness, a union with

[1] See Arthur M. Ross, *Trade Union Wage Policy*.

limited coverage could more easily defend a policy of maximizing total income of union membership through charging what the traffic could bear, that is, adapt wages to the wage-paying capacity of various companies or to employers' greater willingness to pay higher wages for some workers than for others.[1] This might seem to be a paradoxical result of unionization, but it seems to be a fact.

The spread of unionism to all sectors of the economy has similar effects over a broader area. Unions covering a minor sector of the economy could safely pursue an efficient policy of 'group egotism'. When two-thirds of the industries are unionized, the risk of inflation resulting from such a policy becomes apparent. In an inflation the most institutionalized wages are the most rigid : the more the educated employers stick to the agreement instead of paying arbitrary wages, the more this discipline works in the direction of keeping their wages down. This has repercussions on the will of unions to co-operate — and with more highly institutionalized conditions of co-operation some interindustry job evaluation openly or informally tends to become the yardstick for policy, as in New Zealand, Australia, and Holland. It should be noted in this context, however, that in areas like England and Scandinavia even the most centrally minded unionists have avoided too high degrees of centralization ; they have felt it rational to leave room for compromises between equity and market. They know the paradox involved in the weakness of a strong organization in regard to its members' equity demands, which hamper its possibilities of maximizing the members' income in the short run through wage differentiation. At the same time they know that too rigid a wage structure can become obsolete when it runs into sharp conflicts with the market.

In deflationary periods the basic principle of 'no reduction' predominates over the demand for equity in all cases where a union can uphold that principle. In unionist psychology a high wage group always can reckon on much more sympathy and support, when it defends its members' wage level against a downward pressure (to which other unions or non-unionized workers might have to submit) than when it tries to enforce a wage rise in which the other groups cannot follow ; this is so even if the impact of this union behaviour on the relative wage structure were the same in the two cases. And this state of mind is not quite irrational, even if we disregard the well-known arguments of Keynes on this matter. In periods of low activity a relative wage decrease might be the only

[1] See Dunlop's basic assumption with regard to union behaviour : maximization of members' total income with allowance for the membership function, *Wage Determination under Trade Unions* (1944).

temporary way of adaptation to the difficult market position of a group of workers, the alternative being unemployment; wage differentiation (discrimination) in accordance with the momentary market conditions of different industries may be a method of avoiding unemployment in the short run. But in a situation of full employment the necessity for wages to function as an instrument for adaptations is much less. Wage earners form the habit of expecting other adaptations and other means than flexibility of wages. Therefore, the generally increased priority of full employment as a goal for economic policy has strengthened the 'solidaristic', equity-demanding side of union psychology. This changed or changing ideology can be expected to prevail in the future, even in periods of less-than-full employment.

It is suggested here that the demand for 'equity' or 'fair relativity' is the most important long-term implication of 100 per cent unionization. We will not attempt to define the meaning of equity exactly; in principle, this is of course impossible. One might describe it tentatively as remuneration according to average disutility of work instead of marginal productivity or employer arbitrariness. It is apparent, in any case, that the unions are part of the 'revolt against the Market', often deplored by pure theory economists. The important thing is that this revolt does not so much mean the establishment of some sort of monopolies — pursuing a policy of price discrimination in the supply of labour — as the broadening of the equity concept of a common rule to the labour market of the whole country.

IV. Is Equity Distorting?

If the union pattern of an equitable wage structure forced itself upon an economy which functioned on the basis of rational allocation of the labour force and smooth adaptation between labour efficiency and wage levels, it could be claimed that unions distort the economy. Several research results of recent years have, however, made it clear that the 'spontaneous' degree of distortion is much higher than economists probably have been ready to believe, even if, at times, they have been prepared to make large allowances for the frictions and imperfections of the market.

The interfirm dispersion in wages for largely comparable types of work shows enormous differences under non-unionized or incompletely unionized conditions. American investigations indicate a range of roughly 50 per cent down from highest to lowest paying firms with comparable labour requirements. Exact comparisons of job requirements are of course difficult. Reynolds [1] reports about ten large and medium-size firms in one local labour market area using the same job evaluation system. The rate range for one common labour grade was 40 per cent from highest to lowest (inter-quartile range 15 per cent). The result conformed to the general impression of the conditions in the whole area. This was in 1948, after several years of high employment which should have made equalization possible. One could find a certain degree of correlation between the wage level and the quality of workers, but Reynolds concludes that the low-paying firms get a 'better buy' in spite of this. Lester [2] arrives at similar conclusions from his broader studies of the interfirm, interarea, and interindustry wage structures. Myers and Schultz [3] found differentials of 45 per cent (from highest to lowest) for minimum rates in each one of the unionized and non-unionized groups of firms in one city in 1949. These authors stress, however, that these differentials were to a great extent motivated by different requirements. As to intercity differentials, David and Ober [4] have estimated the average level of earnings of average factory workers in 22 large cities, and they found a range of more than 35 per cent practically uncorrelated with cost-of-living differences.

The general results of these and other studies is that wage levels neither get equalized in accordance with pure theory (in spite of the general equalization trend referred to above) nor are they fixed, even by non-union firms, according to any need for attracting labour under the assumption of a sloping labour supply curve. Furthermore, the concept of marginal productivity of labour as a guide for the mutual adjustment of wage levels and volume of production appears not to be readily applicable to the actual wage policies of employers. Wages are much more a function of dynamic, historical, and psychological factors, and employer deliberations take place in quite other terms than those of the marginal productivity theory. High profits and high productivity create high relative wages even where they are not needed to attract labour. A relative reduction of wages, which are unnecessarily high, is often avoided because it would create internal trouble, a decreasing supply of the volume and quality of labour in the existing labour force. On the other hand, the low-wage firms can keep vegetating at their low wage costs without too

[1] L. G. Reynolds, *The Structure of Labor Markets* (1951).

[2] R. A. Lester, 'Results and Implications of Some Recent Wage Studies', *Insights into Labor Issues*, ed. Lester and Shister (1948).

[3] Charles A. Myers and George P. Schultz, *The Dynamics of a Labor Market* (1951).

[4] L. M. David and H. Ober, 'Intercity Differences, 1945–1946', *Monthly Labor Review* (April 1948).

strong a risk that fluctuations in labour will compel them to adjust their wage rates to a higher level. It might be added, that even in the overfull employment situation in Sweden during most of the post-war years it seems to have been possible for low-wage firms to keep going, although with an extra amount of labour turnover. The old workers held on, to a great extent, and casual labour, which always exists, filled vacancies for a short time in any firm which carried on recruiting on a large enough scale. Apparently what these firms lose at the margin through this policy, they regain by the exploitation of their old labour force. This goes largely for big firms in industries with agreements that provide for fixed-rate time wages, which feel compelled by this type of agreement to stick to a policy of no 'wage drift'.

Our studies of the wage-drift phenomenon in Sweden show that there is often a strong direct effect on wages from changes in the productivity of the work; piece-rates cannot easily be adjusted fully to counteract the wage-increasing effects of the introduction of more efficient machinery, and this has its repercussions on the wage level, even for time workers working together with the piece-wage earners. Garbarino's comparisons of wage and efficiency development of different industries revealed a high correlation between the two. The resulting positive correlation between expansion and wages, however, does not show that the relative wage developments were instrumental in relative rates of expansion.

Even the demonstration of a considerable correlation between relative wages and the direction of the flow of labour (increasing wages in expanding industries and areas) cannot be used to show that the wage changes and differences were necessary to direct the movements of labour. Instead, one should to a great extent regard the expansion of employment and the increase of wages as depending upon one common origin: the general good economic position of a firm, a geographical area, or an industry.[1]

There is one simple and fundamental factor that overrides differences between wage rates as a propelling force behind the supply of labour: namely, the availability of job opportunities.[2] These are not decided by the wage earners. If job opportunities decrease in a high-wage area and increase in a low-wage area (or firm, or industry), the natural desire of workers to get work where

[1] John T. Dunlop, 'Productivity and the Wage Structure' in *Income, Employment and Public Policy* (1948), pp. 341-362.

[2] 'The view that workers can be redistributed only by changes in wage differentials seems to be mistaken. They are distributed much more directly and forcefully by differentials in the availability of jobs' (Reynolds, *The Structure of Labor Markets*, p. 245).

it is best paid has a very low influence on the net result of movements in the labour market. One could bring into the picture such things as different degrees of elasticity of labour supply under different circumstances, but the labour market research results already referred to seems to demonstrate that such refinements of the analysis lead to rather unimportant modifications of the conclusions. If jobs are available they are filled if there exists any supply of labour on the market. This is the fundamental thing. And they get filled even if the employer in question pays rates of wages much below the average of the relevant market. Wage differences between firms employing workers of a very similar quality in very similar jobs can persist through decades.

Recent research on the Swedish post-war labour market [1] showed that the flow of labour during one year (1949) certainly had some net effect on the raising of wages (including the migration from agriculture), but that the gross flow was so large that most of the movements must have been very haphazard with regard to the accompanying wage change. It should be conceded, however, that the high mobility of labour during the war and post-war period have contributed considerably to the interindustry and interfirm levelling of wages in Sweden. But the unions had to help the market to a great extent : to 'hunt' the low-wage firms and areas, and thereby to force, mostly involuntarily we must admit, the high-wage firms to abstain from setting inflationary precedents.

If we consider the aberrations of the 'natural' labour market from marginalist theory, it is difficult to maintain that the rigidities and uniformities in the wage structure, which unions progressively bring about, should be regarded as mainly a source of distortion and lack of adaptation. As an approximation to the criterion of pure theory (equal efficiency wages modified only by a need for flexibility caused by temporary frictions during periods of structural change of the production pattern) a union-induced equitable wage structure seems rather more acceptable.

However, the ideology of most economists and employers and their organizations (which often differs from their policy, as is often the case with the unions) seem mostly to regard 'wage flexibility' as a condition of smooth adaptation of the economy to changing conditions. For example :

> Wage differentials, based upon individual company or industry bargaining as opposed to national wage patterns, cushion the

[1] R. Meidner, *Svensk arbetsmarknad vid full sysselsättning* (1954). (*The Swedish Labour Market at Full Employment*, with a summary in English.)

> shock of technological changes and shifts in consumer demand. The growth of differentials contributes toward the flow of labor and capital from marginal industries and companies to areas where they are in greater demand. They have enabled marginal companies to remain in business and satisfy consumer desires, have provided jobs for many workers for whom the alternative might be long periods of unemployment, and have prevented the complete loss of savings embodied in the physical plant and equipment of high-cost companies or industries.[1]

The same authors also quote Slichter's statement that

> requiring concerns with plants in several regions (say both North and South or larger cities and small towns) to pay the same rates for the same work in all plants tends to limit the national product. [Such] wage differentials are needed to stimulate labor to move. . . .[2]

A similar attitude in favour of wage diversity and flexibility according to varying wage-paying capacity is exhibited in statements by officials of the Swedish Employers' Association.

This is a rather paradoxical situation : because of a liberalistic free enterprise ideology employers advocate wage differentiation and flexibility, and because of a solidaristic or socialist ideology unions advocate equity wages implying a rather rigid wage structure ; all this in spite of the apparent fact that wage rigidity and uniformity decreases labour's share while wage differentiation would reduce the share of profits, at least at given levels of employment. Thus both parties have theories running counter at least to their short-term interests. Consequently, neither of them always acts in accordance with his theory. The Swedish Employers' Association actually has co-operated considerably towards an equalization. They seem to recognize that under high employment the labour demand for equity has strong support from the conditions of the labour market. When employer organizations see that any attempts to give relief to low-efficiency companies or industries through wage differentiation would fail, they try instead to introduce 'order and stability' into the wage structure, thereby to the greatest extent disciplining both their members and the workers with regard to wages. This is the best way to dampen the whipsaw mechanisms whereby 'flexible wages' get an inflationary impact during periods

[1] Backman and Gainsbrugh, *The Behavior of Wages* (1948), p. 71.

[2] S. H. Slichter, 'Wage Policies', *Proceedings of the Academy of Political Science* (May 1946), p. 12. See also the writings of the 'Chicago school' (Simons, Friedman), and some contributions in *The Impact of the Union*, McCord Wright, ed. (1951).

when money wage reductions cannot be contemplated anywhere.[1]

In contrast with the conventional theories just mentioned, the conclusions of post-war research concerning labour market behaviour seems to be that the economy needs a wage structure which is fairly rigid and differentiated in accordance with some rough compromise between the theoretical principle of equal efficiency wages and the union principle of equity. On such a basis the 'structure of job availability' can steer the flow of labour much better than incessant fluctuations in the wage structure. Fluctuating wage differentials mainly serve the function of a brake on economically desirable adaptations of industry, while the other side of the coin, the stimulus to desirable movements of labour, has a lesser importance. The fact that high-efficiency firms pay relatively high wages, while low-efficiency firms pay relatively low wages if undisturbed by unions, means that substandard firms can be kept alive for long periods, thanks to their low wage costs.

One might object that the low degree of interdependence between wage differentials and output of labour holds true only in a state of considerably less than full employment; in full employment relative wage movements should be necessary as stimuli to proper re-allocations of labour. But even this is a doubtful proposition. In a state of less than full employment the supply of labour of a firm has a high elasticity because of the abundance of free labour in spite of its low mobility.[2] There is little probability that the unemployment type of mobility, where the unemployed workers rush to job openings, whatever the wage, is the type of mobility leading to the most productive allocation of labour. In a state of full employment, on the other hand, this type of supply and mobility is replaced by the over-all increase of labour mobility through the mobilization of a great part of the workers already employed, which were earlier immobilized by the fear of losing security by quitting their old jobs.

At first sight this situation — the great scarcity of labour making itself felt in the individual firm through a high rate of labour turnover — might seem to make it necessary to play on the keyboard of wage differentials in order to adapt labour supply to labour demand. In one specific respect this conclusion is valid: full employment enforces a reorganization of the wage structure because the freer

[1] In *Trade Unions and Full Employment*, p. 67, we have related a notable case where the Swedish Employers' Association demanded a much higher rigidity and uniformity under one central agreement than the Confederation of Trade Unions contemplated.

[2] Reasoning in terms of elasticities of labour supply is somewhat misleading; it gives the impression that this supply is a function mainly of the price of labour. What we wish to stress is that it is a function of the price of labour only to a very small extent.

mobility of labour reveals the greatest flaws in the old wage structure. But this does not mean that the need for diversity of wages as between different types of labour in all respects of the word, except in regard to quality, has increased. Nor does it mean that a union-enforced uniformity and rigidity has become even more dangerous to 'the effective functioning of our economy' to any higher degree than when unemployment seemingly secures the painless supply of labour to anyone who wants it.

In other words, in full employment the market functions more smoothly. The flow of labour moves more easily than in less-than-full employment. The fact that some employers in such a situation are often tempted to bid up wages does not mean that the resulting provocative wage increases are a good instrument for the proper allocation of labour resources. This allocation cannot be made optimal by luring workers to move into the most inflationary sections of the economy. That would be distorting. A more stable, rigid wage structure is much more apt to promote the proper allocation of labour and other resources, provided the relative wage levels have a good long-run connection with the content of the work in each case, that is, with the theoretical equilibrium wages based on the old Marshallian concept of equal net advantages. If the degree of full employment is so balanced that the unions really have an influence upon wages, their adherence to a non-economic criterion — 'equity' — has a stabilizing impact, which improves the possibilities of the most productive allocation.

In a state of low employment unionism can be one among many causes of distortion in the pattern of wages ; especially sectionalist unions with only partial coverage can have a considerably distorting influence upon the interindustry structure of wages. Fears based on the experience during periods of minority unionism that an expanding unionism would create a wage structure distorted to reflect the different degrees of bargaining power based on organizational strength or aggressiveness and the employers' possibilities of throwing increasing wage costs on the consumers, do not seem to be justified from the empirical evidence. Rather, if unions get both large and strong, it is probable that their direct and indirect influence through collective bargaining and 'sympathetic pressure' over widening 'orbits of coercive comparisons' under the growing pressure of workers' demand for equity tends to create a rather rigid wage structure according to a concept of 'fair relativity'. The moral forces, which they have fostered themselves, prevent the unions from charging as much as the traffic can bear in individual cases ; 'labour monopolies' are a transient phenomenon. Because the spontaneous fluctuations and differentials of wages in a non-union labour force have a very low influence in the positive direction — to steer the streams of labour supply towards the most productive uses — and because they often have a tendency not to level out easily in accordance with the prescriptions of economic textbooks, they can be better characterized as taxing the efficient and subsidizing the inefficient parts of the economy. And in full employment such fluctuations and differentials provoke inflation more than they promote adaptation. In spite of existing differences (which are not very large) between any union concept of equity or fair relativity and the pure theory concept of equal efficiency wages or equal net advantages, we can therefore conclude that full unionization tends to imply more adjustment than distortion in relation to the productivity criteria of economic theory.

Chapter 15

THE EVOLUTION OF WAGE DIFFERENTIALS: A STUDY OF BRITISH DATA

BY

G. ROTTIER

Director, London Office, Institut de Science Économique Appliquée

WAGE differentials in the British economy varied widely in pre-war years while the general level of wages remained fairly stable ; since 1944, however, wage differentials generally narrowed while the general level of wages was constantly rising. The latter period is also characterized by the appearance of a wage slide, that is, of a considerable divergence between the behaviour of negotiated wage rates and of effective earnings.

This paper briefly surveys the evolution of wage differentials in the two periods and notes some theoretical problems suggested by the study of empirical data.[1] We shall not attempt to solve these problems ; the data considered in the paper are sufficient to indicate a possible list of questions which might interest wage theorists, but they are utterly inadequate for providing the answers.

We shall only deal with wages considered as unit cost of labour to the employer, and we shall not study the social wage which is the redistributive element in the income of the wage earner. We shall distinguish between wage rates and average earnings : wage rates are generally determined by collective bargaining, and, in the United Kingdom, usually refer to a week of normal length. (The normal length of the working week is also negotiated.) Negotiated rates may

[1] This survey is based on *Les Salaires en Grande-Bretagne*, Cahiers de l'Institut de Science Économique Appliquée, série B, no. 5 and 6 (1953). This study was prepared at the London Office of I.S.É.A. while the author was Director ; the main research work was done by Mr. E. Lisle. We must acknowledge with gratitude the help we derived from the painstaking comments of several of our British colleagues, particularly Professor E. H. Phelps Brown, Mr. J. Jefferys, Mr. T. McKitterick, and Mr. G. D. N. Worswick. We must also express our gratitude to officials of the T.U.C., the National Coal Board, and the British Ministry of Labour, who allowed us to make use of unpublished data.

be either standard or minimum rates, although there is a progressive tendency for standard rates to be established. Average earnings are obtained by dividing the total wage bill of a given group of workers (generally in an industry) by the number of workers.

I. The Flexibility of Relative Wages and Earnings in Pre-war Years

The general level of wages remained fairly constant in the face of wide fluctuations in the level of employment in pre-war years. The stability of the general level of wages, however, concealed numerous changes in the relative levels of wage rates and of average earnings in different industries. The stability of the general indices of wage rates resulted from movements in opposite directions, wages decreasing in the depressed staple industries, while they were increasing in the new industries located in the southern part of the country and in the building industry. In the first case, both wages and the number of insured employees went down, and the percentage of unemployment increased (Table 1). Weekly earnings did not appear to decrease as significantly as wage rates, but this mainly reflects the strong influence of short-time working on the level of average earnings in the wool and cotton industries in 1924.

In order to study more comprehensively the evolution of earnings differentials between industries, we drew frequency distributions, putting the average level of earnings in each industry on the *x* axis and the insured manpower on the *y* axis, and we studied the variations of some parameters of these distributions and of subdistributions obtained in considering certain groups of industries. In this way we distinguished between the staple industries (coalmining, wool and cotton spinning and weaving, general engineering, shipbuilding, and so on), the new industries (chemicals, automobile, non-ferrous metals, electrical engineering, building), and a less homogeneous group of other industries (mainly consumer goods' industries and public utilities). In some cases we distinguished also between male and female earnings.

In the staple industries average earnings were markedly lower than in other industries in the worst years of the depression and their fluctuations through time were sharper (Table 2).

The structure of relative rates and earnings was modified, therefore, in a way corresponding to changes in the structure of the economy. At the same time, one may notice short- or medium-term variations in earnings differentials. They were significantly wider in 1931 than in 1924, and somewhat narrower in 1938 than in 1931 (Table 3).

TABLE 1

EMPLOYMENT, UNEMPLOYMENT, WEEKLY WAGE RATES AND AVERAGE WEEKLY EARNINGS IN SELECTED STAPLE INDUSTRIES 1924–1938

	1924	1931	1935	1938
Coal:				
Insured employees (1924 = 100)	100	87	78	71
% Unemployment	6	28	25	15
Wage Rates (1924 = 100)	100	86	87	(112) *
Weekly Earnings (1924 = 100)	100	87	85	109
Cotton:				
Insured employees (1924 = 100)	100	98	80	70
% Unemployment	14	39	21	26
Wage rates (1924 = 100)	100	94	86	(92) *
Weekly earnings (1924 = 100)				
Males:	100	96	104	106
Females:	100	97	100	110
Wool:				
Insured employees (1924 = 100)	100	92	86	83
% Unemployment	7	29	13	19
Wage Rates (1924 = 100)	100	86	80	(85) *
Weekly earnings (1924 = 100)				
Males:	100	94	106	109
Females:	100	90	103	103
Shipbuilding:				
Insured employees (1924 = 100)	100	75	60	67
% Unemployment	28	53	39	18
Wage rates (1924 = 100)	100	100	92	(114) *
Weekly earnings (1924 = 100)	100	98	119	137

* = 1939 instead of 1938.

Furthermore, the dispersion of earnings was wider in the group of staple industries than in the other two groups (Table 4).

The study of the distributions of average earnings by industry shows a definite flexibility of wage differentials. The same conclusion appears from a study of the ranking of industries in order of increasing average earnings or of increasing wage rates. Both rankings varied

TABLE 2

MEDIAN OF THE DISTRIBUTIONS OF AVERAGE WEEKLY EARNINGS FOR MALE WORKERS IN THREE GROUPS OF INDUSTRIES, 1924–1938
(Shillings)

	(1) Staple Industries	(2) New Industries	(3) Other Industries
1924	52·3	58·2	58·2
1931	45·3	57·4	58·3
1935	47·7	61·5	61·5
1938	57·9	61·3	63·2

TABLE 3

MEDIAN DISPERSION OF THE DISTRIBUTIONS OF AVERAGE WEEKLY EARNINGS BY INDUSTRY FOR MALE AND FEMALE WORKERS, 1924–1938
(Shillings)

		1924	1931	1935	1938
Male Weekly Earnings	Median	52·9	52·5	61·5	61·2
	Interquartile range	6·0	13·0	14·6	15·0
Female Weekly Earnings	Median	28·2	27·3	31·3	31·8
	Interquartile range	2·0	3·2	4·6	3·2

TABLE 4

INTERQUARTILE RANGE OF THE DISTRIBUTIONS OF AVERAGE WEEKLY EARNINGS FOR MALE WORKERS IN THREE GROUPS OF INDUSTRIES, 1924–1938

(Shillings)

	1924	1931	1935	1938
Staple industries	3·2	4·6	21·2	14·4
New industries	1·2	3·8	8·2	8·8
Other industries	5·4	3·4	7·0	13·4

widely in time, the only constant result being the 'no-bridge' between industries employing mainly men and industries employing mainly women. The ranking according to wage rates was consistently different from the ranking according to average weekly earnings, but an interesting result is that they tended to be closer when unemployment was severe. This is shown by the variations of the rank correlation coefficient (Kendall's ϵ) between the two rankings:

1931	1935	1938
0·71	0·62	0·69

It is a well-known fact that the dispersion of earnings varies more widely with the level of employment than the dispersion of wage rates. The variation of the rank correlation coefficient indicates that the behaviour of the ratio of earnings to wage rates varied also markedly from industry to industry, the effect of the differences being more noticeable when employment was high than when it was low. Furthermore, this applied over a period when the ratio of average earnings to the general wage level did not vary significantly for the economy as a whole. The main problem is whether the flexibility of wage differentials during the interwar years was merely an accident, and, if not, how it can be explained.

Two remarks are significant here. The narrowing of wage differentials has been a long-term process, arising from a wide variety of causes, but it has everywhere been greatly intensified in times of inflation. It seems possible to generalize this remark, and to suggest that, in addition to a secular tendency to narrow, there is a tendency for wage differentials (mainly interindustry differentials) to fluctuate with the level of employment and to be generally narrower when employment is high than when it is low. This is no more than a hypothesis which needs to be tested for different countries and different periods.

The second remark is that the impact of the great depression in the United Kingdom was attended by important changes in the structure of British industry; new industries located in the southern half of the country expanded at the expense of the depressed staple industries. The flexibility of wage differentials may reflect this factor as well as the foregoing one. A plausible assumption would be the existence of some connection between the behaviour of unit labour costs and phenomena of long-term growth.[1] Wages would tend to

[1] This factor was suggested by Lloyd G. Reynolds, 'Wages in the Business Cycle', *American Economic Review, Proceedings* (May 1952), pp. 84-99.

decrease in declining industries and to rise (or, at least, remain stable) in new and expanding industries. There is no general agreement on the rôle of wage differentials to induce movements of manpower between existing industries. There could be a wider agreement on the proposition that new industries, starting from scratch, attract the necessary labour force by paying relatively higher wages than old established industries. This was undoubtedly the case with the motor-car and the electrical-engineering industries in Britain in the 'thirties.

Whatever may be the value of these two assumptions, and whether or not the flexibility of British wages in the inter-war period was an accident, it is clear that one must be exceedingly careful in drawing any conclusion from the behaviour of a general index of wage rates or of earnings. The structure of relative wage rates can be highly flexible in the short or medium run, and it is probably not valid to build a theory on the assumption that the level and the structure of wages are two independent factors.

II. The Wage Structure in the Post-war Inflation

The first result of inflation has been a general narrowing of wage differentials, affecting interindustry, regional, skill, and, to a lesser extent, sex differentials.

For the economy as a whole, a clear convergence of the evolution in time of average earnings can be observed [1] (Table 5). The same is true within particular industries.

TABLE 5

DISTRIBUTION OF AVERAGE EARNINGS BY INDUSTRY:

COEFFICIENT OF DISPERSION $\frac{\text{(Interquartile Range)}}{\text{Median}}$

1943–1951

	July 1943	July 1945	Oct. 1946	Oct. 1947	Oct. 1948	Oct. 1949	Oct. 1950	Oct. 1951
Male: weekly earnings	27·0	21·0	26·5	24·5	17·5	19·0	17·0	13·5
Female: weekly earnings	27·0	30·0	20·0	15·0	12·5	13·0	12·0	11·0
Male: hourly earnings	30·5	29·0	22·0	28·0	21·0	19·0	18·5	16·5
Female: hourly earnings	26·0	21·5	16·5	15·0	14·0	12·5	12·5	11·0

[1] This applies to all manufacturing industries. The behaviour of earnings in some industries exceptionally short of manpower (mainly coalmining and the docks) was an exception. See *Les Salaires en Grande-Bretagne*, vol. i, pp. 139-140.

Table 6 summarizes the evolution of skill and regional differentials in the building industry. London and Liverpool are at the top of the scale of regional rates laid down by collective agreement, and (A3) is the code number of districts where negotiated rates are the lowest.

TABLE 6

SKILL AND REGIONAL DIFFERENTIALS IN THE BUILDING INDUSTRY 1947–1952 *

	1947	1949	1950	1951	1952
London and Liverpool :					
Skilled	100	100	100	100	100
Unskilled	81	80½	84½	86	86½
(A3) :					
Skilled	91½	91¾	91¾	92¼	93
Unskilled	72	73½	76	78	79¾

* Standard hourly rates in London and in (A3) districts expressed as percentage of the skilled rate in London.

In engineering, skill differentials narrowed in a way shown by Table 7 :

TABLE 7

SKILL DIFFERENTIALS IN THE ENGINEERING INDUSTRY *

$$\left(\text{Ratio } \frac{\text{labourer}}{\text{fitter}} \times 100\right)$$

	1931	1938	1942	1948
Wage rates	71	73¾	80½	86
Weekly earnings	67½	69	67½	79
Hourly earnings	67	67½	64½	75

* Knowles and Robertson, 'Earnings in Engineering, 1926–1948', *Bulletin of the Oxford University Institute of Statistics* (June 1951).

Over the same period there was a reduction of the difference between average earnings in different branches of engineering. This is explained partly by the ironing out of regional differences in the cost of living which resulted from rationing, partly by the fact that earnings in different sections of the engineering industry are closely linked to the economic situation of the industries for which they cater. Before the war, earnings were, for instance, particularly low in textile machinery and high in electrical engineering. Table 8 gives the main results.

At the same time regional differentials decreased, but this result is not independent of the former, as most sections of the engineering industry are located near their normal markets.

A second important aspect of the wage structure in the post-war years is the increasing divergence between wage rates and actual earnings. The ratio between earnings and rates rose for the economy

TABLE 8

DIFFERENCES IN AVERAGE EARNINGS FOR ADULT MALE WORKERS BETWEEN SECTIONS OF THE ENGINEERING INDUSTRY

	1931	1938	1943	1944	1945	1946	1947
$\frac{\text{Lowest hourly earnings}}{\text{Highest hourly earnings}} \times 100$	72·5	77·5	78·5	76·5	81	83	85
$\frac{\text{Lowest weekly earnings}}{\text{Highest weekly earnings}} \times 100$	65·5	86·5	78·5	78·0	87	85	90

as a whole. This was irregular, however, for earnings rose much more quickly than rates in some periods when wage rates were relatively stable, and wage rates caught up with the rise in earnings in subsequent periods.

This phenomenon may be conveniently analysed if one separates two sets of factors. The first set includes factors which make for a difference between rates and earnings in the case of an individual worker. The second set includes factors which are only apparent when one considers a group of workers.

In the case of a given individual worker, five main causes can change the ratio of earnings to rates :

(1) Changes in the length of the working week. Negotiated rates (whether hourly or weekly) only apply to work done during the 'normal' period of work defined by the agreement. Weekly earnings will differ from weekly wage rates in case of short time or overtime. Hourly earnings will only differ from hourly rates in case of overtime, due to the influence of overtime bonuses.

(2) The rates paid to a given worker may exceed negotiated rates. This is a recognized procedure when collective agreements fix minimum rates. It is an infringement of the agreement, albeit a common one in time of inflation, when negotiated rates are standard rates.

(3) When it is impossible to pay more than standard rates, the same result can be achieved through the upgrading of workers, without changing the actual content of their job.

(4) Modifications in the incidence of payment by results can also change the ratio of rates to earnings. There may be a change in the efficiency of the worker or a change in the way efficiency bonuses are assessed.

(5) Workers may be entitled to a variety of other bonuses: seniority bonuses, profit sharing, and the like. The incidence of these bonuses may vary from time to time for a given worker, even though the wage rate does not change.

TABLE 9

ANALYSIS OF THE RATIO OF EARNINGS TO RATES IN ALL INDUSTRIES, 1948–1951 *

	Oct. 1948	Oct. 1949	Oct. 1950	Oct. 1951
Wage index	100	102·0	103·0	113·0
Average weekly earnings (constant manpower structure)	100	103·3	108·7	119·5
Ratio earnings/rates	100	101·0	105·3	105·7
Ratio earnings/rates if overtime alone is considered	100	100·3	102·0	102·0
Ratio earnings/rates if payments by results (and residual factors) alone are considered	100	101·0	103·0	103·5

* We start from October 1948, as important changes introduced in British employment statistics in June 1948 make it impossible to give a continuous series for the post-war years.

In a group of workers all these factors operate. But the ratio of earnings to rates can also be affected by a variation in the relative number of workers in each job. This is due to the fact that wage indices are weighted with reference to the structure of the working population in a base year, whereas average earnings are weighted with reference to the existing structure of the working population.

The earnings rates ratio is therefore sensitive to: changes in the (6) industrial, (7) sex, (8) age, and (9) skill structure of the working population.

For the purpose of the study of changes in the structure of unit labour costs, the effect of factors (6) and (8) should be eliminated. Factor (9), however, may be considered as roughly identical with factor (3). There is no reason in the short run to expect wide variations in the actual skill structure of the working population, once factors (6) and (7) are eliminated. Apparent changes in the skill structure therefore largely reflect upgrading within each industry.

It is unfortunately not possible in practice to isolate the effect of all nine factors. British statistics only allow the elimination of factors (6) and (7) — this is done in all the figures we use — and to separate the effect of (1) (overtime) and of factors (2) to (5) and (9) taken together. One may assume that the effect of changes in the age structure were not very important in the period considered. It is unfortunately not possible to make any guess as to the relative importance of factors (2), (3), and (4).

Tables 9 and 10 show the main results for the economy as a whole and for the engineering industry. It is significant that the

TABLE 10

ANALYSIS OF THE RATIO OF WAGES TO EARNINGS IN THE ENGINEERING INDUSTRY

	Oct. 1948	Oct. 1949	Oct. 1950	Oct. 1951
Rates	100	103	106	119·0
Average hourly earnings (constant manpower structure)	100	104	107	117·0
Ratio earnings/rates	100	101	101	98·5
Effect of overtime	100	101	102	101·0
Effect of payment by results and residual factors	100	100	99	97·5

ratio of earnings to wage rates increased sharply between October 1949 and October 1950, when the rise of wage rates was still slowed down by the 'voluntary wage restraint' agreed upon by the T.U.C. and the Labour Government.[1]

Another significant result is that, for the economy as a whole, the effect of payment by results (and residual factors) is only slightly more important than the effect of overtime. We shall see in section III that payment by results may play a much more important part in framing the distribution of earnings within a given plant. The result for the whole economy must therefore be explained by the fact that overtime is fairly generalized in all industries in a period of overemployment, whereas payment by results only exists in particular industries, where its importance is definitely greater than global figures would suggest. The ratio of earnings to rates varies, therefore, a good deal from industry to industry.

The effect of the general narrowing of differentials probably

[1] This factor was also pointed out by E. H. Phelps Brown, *London and Cambridge Economic Service* (May 1951), pp. 42-43.

reduces the ability of wages to play their normal functional part of directing manpower towards the occupations where it is most wanted. The flexibility of the earnings/wages ratio may to some extent attenuate the consequences of this narrowing by permitting some adaptation of the cost structure according to the efficiency of different firms and the prosperity of different industries.

III. Wage Differentials Within a Plant

All the data presented so far have the same limitation : they are averages, covering a more or less wide group of workers. This does not matter in the case of wage rates, which by nature refer to groups. This would not matter either in the case of earnings, if we could obtain a sufficiently detailed analysis of average earnings for homogeneous groups of workers. But the data available in the British case are inadequate in many respects ; particularly, they do not permit a study of the relative influence of overtime and of payment by results for workers of different grades of skill. We tried to obtain some information on these points by making a complete survey of the distribution of the earnings of workers in a few industrial plants of the London region. We cannot claim any general significance for the results obtained, but they might be suggestive for further study.

The results are drawn from two medium-sized plants (300 to 500 workers) specializing in the transformation of non-ferrous metals. The dates chosen for the surveys are the same as those of the half-yearly earnings' inquiries of the British Ministry of Labour. In both cases we give average weekly earnings, average gross hourly earnings, and average net hourly earnings (overtime payments excluded) for each group of workers. The comparison of gross and net hourly earnings indicates the influence of overtime payments on the structure of unit labour costs. For each group we measure the dispersions by the value of the upper quartiles of the distributions of earnings expressed as a percentage of the lower quartiles. All figures refer to adult male workers.

The first result is the extent of the dispersion of earnings for workers of the same group. In Plant II this is almost entirely due to the effect of payment by results. In Plant I, however, the extent of the dispersion of the earnings of semi-skilled workers is largely explained by the fact that they do not form a homogeneous group. A closer analysis [1] revealed the fact that the dispersion of semi-

[1] See *Les Salaires en Grande-Bretagne*, vol. ii, pp. 148-149.

skilled earnings and the ratio of the average earnings of skilled workers to those of unskilled workers varied widely between the six workshops of the plant.

TABLE 11

PLANT I : DISTRIBUTION OF EARNINGS FOR THREE GROUPS OF WORKERS IN THE LAST PAY WEEK OF APRIL 1951

	Gross Hourly Earnings	Net Hourly Earnings	Weekly Earnings
Skilled (279 workers) :			
Average earnings (shillings)	4·7	4·5	224
Dispersion	124	125	134
Semi-skilled (100 workers) :			
Average earnings (shillings)	4·0	3·7	194
Dispersion	138	138	138
Unskilled (136 workers) :			
Average earnings (shillings)	2·9	2·7	152
Dispersion	112	110	138

A second result is the relatively insignificant effect of overtime payments in the two plants considered. On an average, they do not amount to more than 5 per cent of total labour costs. For each group of workers they do not markedly alter the shape of the distribution of earnings.

TABLE 12

PLANT II : DISTRIBUTION OF EARNINGS FOR THREE GROUPS OF WORKERS IN THE LAST PAY WEEK OF OCTOBER 1951

	Basic Wage Rates	Gross Hourly Earnings	Net Hourly Earnings	Weekly Earnings
Semi-skilled workers, 1st workshop (127 workers) :				
Average	2·7	3·7	3·5	187
Dispersion	100	119	115	122
Semi-skilled workers, 2nd workshop (114 workers) :				
Average	2·7	3·7	3·5	178
Dispersion	100	121	118	130
Maintenance workers, skilled and unskilled (69 workers) :				
Average	2·9	3·9	3·6	175
Dispersion	122	121	122	125

The figures confirm the impression that the effect of payment by results is much sharper than the effect of overtime. But since overtime is much more common throughout industry, the total effect of overtime payments has a greater weight than other bonuses, when one considers the whole economy.

Overtime payments have, however, some effect on the relative position of different groups of workers. They go far to explain the fact that the dispersion of weekly earnings is greater than the dispersion of hourly earnings for unskilled and skilled workers. The workers of these groups, mainly engaged in maintenance, have less regular hours of work than semi-skilled workers.

The influence of payment by results and of other bonuses confirms to some extent the assumption that, although the structure of wage rates is becoming increasingly standardized, there remains a definite adaptability of actual unit labour costs, which may respond to the impact of market forces.

It may be assumed that purely economic considerations must still play an important part in explaining the behaviour of wages. The socio-political elements implicit in collective bargaining, especially on a national scale, may be important in determining the general level of wages. But they cannot be enough, and there is still room for a theory of wages based on economic considerations. This theory would explain in particular the behaviour, both in the short and in the long run, of interindustry differentials and of differences in the unit cost of labour between plants.

Chapter 16

STRUCTURAL INFLATION AND THE ECONOMIC FUNCTION OF WAGES: THE FRENCH EXAMPLE[1]

BY

FRANÇOIS PERROUX

Director, Institut de Science Économique Appliquée, Paris, France

ASSISTED BY

EDMOND A. LISLE

Research Assistant, Institut de Science Économique Appliquée

THE share of wages in the French national income is approximately constant and very considerable. Moreover, the structure of wages is highly rigid. We propose to analyse the causes of this rigidity and to show how it contributes to making the economy inherently inflationary. Finally, we shall inquire whether the rigidity of wages does not denote a fundamental misconception of the economic function of wages under any economic system, and we shall suggest a reconsideration of distribution theory.

I. THE SHARE AND THE RIGIDITY OF WAGES IN THE FRENCH NATIONAL INCOME

Table 1 shows the share of wages and salaries in net national product. The very high level of social insurance benefits,[2] compared

[1] We particularly wish to thank M. J. F. Albert, who collected the data used in the empirical study, and Mlle Petit, M. A. Philbert, and M. Vacher of the Ministère du Travail et de la Sécurité Sociale, and Mme Terrat and M. E. Malinvaud, of the Institut National de la Statistique et des Études Économiques, whose help in providing information was invaluable. They cannot of course be held responsible for any errors or for the views expressed in this paper. This study is a continuation of the very extensive research carried on in the field of wages by the Institut de Science Économique Appliquée since 1945 and published in the series: Cahiers de l'I.S.É.A., série B, *La Rémunération du travail et la politique des salaires* (13 studies).

[2] They include payments made under the various social insurance schemes ('general' scheme, agricultural workers' scheme, mine workers' scheme, railway workers' scheme, and so on), family allowances, and civil servants' pensions. Payments under the 'general' and agricultural workers' schemes and family allowances do not benefit wage and salary earners exclusively. On the other hand,

to wages and salaries, deserves to be noted. Wages, salaries, and benefits amount together to nearly 50 per cent of the net national product. In view of the high proportion of the very young and the very old in the French economy, it is likely that social insurance benefits will increase in absolute terms over the next few years.

TABLE 1

NET NATIONAL PRODUCT, WAGES AND SALARIES, SOCIAL INSURANCE BENEFITS 1938–1953

	1938	1947	1948	1949	1950	1951	1952	1953
Net national product, milliard francs	380	3,700	6,010	7,450	8,530	10,480	12,160	12,400
Wages and salaries, milliard francs *	165	1,420	2,370	2,710	3,010	3,830	4,440	4,500
$\frac{2}{1}$ %	43	38	39	38	35	37	36	36
Social insurance benefits, milliard francs †	12	340	550	750	950	1,200	1,450	1,500
$\frac{4}{2}$ %	7	24	23	28	32	31	33	33

Source : I.N.S.É.É., *L'Annuaire statistique*, 1953.

* Income from work transferred from abroad is not included.

† See note 2, p. 251.

This steady increase goes some way towards explaining the downward pressure on the wage level in France. It is impossible both to have one's cake in the form of higher social benefits and eat it in the shape of higher wages. But despite the steadily increasing pressure of social, or redistributive charges on the French economy, it is remarkable that the share of wages and salaries in the net national product is roughly constant. Too much importance should not be attached to one- or two-point variations since the end of the war in view of the margin of error attached to such figures.

some workers' pensions ('allocations aux vieux travailleurs'), state subsidies to hospitals, and public assistance payments are excluded. It is thus not possible precisely to distinguish the social insurance benefits of wage and salary earners only. The probable upward bias of the figures in Table 1, line 4 is unlikely, however, substantially to modify our argument. For an analysis of the redistributive effects of French social security schemes see G. Rottier and J. F. Albert, *Économie appliquée, Archives de l'I.S.É.A.*, no. 2-3 (1953), *La Redistribution des revenus entre groupes sociaux en 1949* and 'The Social Services and Income Redistribution in France' in *Income Redistribution and Social Policy*, edited by A. T. Peacock (1954), pp. 90-138.

We propose to show that besides this constancy of the relative size of the flow of wages and salaries there is also a definite rigidity in the structure of this flow. We shall henceforth deal only with wages, that is, with the incomes of manual workers since they represent the largest and most rigid element of the aggregate flow of wages and salaries. In this context, what do we mean by rigidity? We shall define 'rigidity' in terms of elasticities and flexibilities.

Let $W = mhw$, where W is the aggregate wage flow per period (week, year); m, the total number of workers;[1] h, the average hours worked per worker; and w, the average hourly earnings per worker.

Then, to say that W is rigid in terms of its size[2] is to say that the supply of labour (mh) is inelastic with respect to the price of labour (w) and with respect to income (net national product), and that the price of labour (w) is inflexible with respect to the level of employment, the prices of wage goods and the national product, when those variables decrease, and flexible when they increase.

W and its elements may be subdivided into sectoral wage flows, or wage flows by industry. Each of these sectoral components of W has a rigidity in terms of size which may be analysed in the same way as the rigidity of W has just been analysed. The supply of labour may be less inelastic in the case of a sectoral component of W than in the case of W itself, provided there is some elasticity of substitution between the labour inputs, or the outputs, of the sectors. The difference in rigidity of W and its sectoral components is, however, likely to be merely one of degree. But if the sectoral components of W are rigid in terms of their size then W is also rigid in terms of its structure. And corresponding structural rigidities may be found within the sectoral components of W when they are themselves subdivided into, for example, skill components.

We shall now show how closely the French situation corresponds to this theoretical model. We have assumed the employed labour force to be equivalent to the employable labour force. The following table, indicating the approximate percentage of unemployed in the working population, shows that this assumption is justified.

Changes in the supply of labour, the labour force remaining constant, may be brought about by changes in the hours worked. This does not appear to have been the case in France: average

[1] We assume the total number of workers to be approximately equal to the number of employable people in the economy. In the post-war French situation of full or overfull employment this assumption is legitimate.

[2] This means that it does not increase less than proportionately to the national income.

hours seem to have been around 45 hours during most of the post-war period. There does appear to be a positive correlation between the length of the working week and the level of wages in particular sectors, but in view of the immobility of the labour force, due largely to the housing problem, one cannot conclude that the inelasticity of the labour supply with respect to wages is significantly diminished.

TABLE 2

PER CENT OF FRENCH WORKING POPULATION UNEMPLOYED IN FOURTH QUARTERS 1938–1953 *

1938	1946	1947	1948	1949	1950	1951	1952	1953
10·3	0·25	0·15	0·65	1·10	1·20	0·80	1·30	1·50

* French statistics only give data for the unemployed in receipt of unemployment insurance. This figure is generally considered to be about five times lower than the total number of unemployed. We have therefore multiplied the published figures by five. We must, however, warn against the highly unsatisfactory nature of the figures, which should only be considered as indicative, for only a small economic significance can be attached in France to such figures.

We shall therefore confine our study to the structural rigidity of relative wages (average hourly rates or earnings per worker) and the arbitrary nature of their determination. We shall say that the structure of relative wages is rigid when wage differentials are either constant or decreasing. This extension of the term rigid is justified in view of the fact that diminishing wage differentials make a redeployment of the labour force more difficult and hence tend to perpetuate and even aggravate the existing maldistribution of labour.

Rates and Earnings

We shall confine our study to wage rates for two reasons. First, they are the predominant item in the level and structure of wages and by far the most important object of discussion by the state or by employers' and workers' unions. Second, data on earnings are lacking in respect of sex, age, and skill differentials ; the earnings' structure, in respect of these differentials, may, therefore, be less rigid than the wage-rate structure. Industry differentials seem, however, to be the same whether one studies average wage rates or average earnings : hourly rates and earnings by industry have increased in roughly the same proportion.

Table 3 shows the relative differences between rates and earnings in various industries in October 1953. It is important to note that these differences, which are important in some industries and negligible in others, have remained approximately constant for some years.[1]

TABLE 3

RELATIVE DIFFERENCES BETWEEN AVERAGE RATES AND EARNINGS ON 1ST OCTOBER 1953

	%
Metal production	+22·4
Electrical and mechanical engineering	+15·3
Glass	+16·1
Building materials and pottery	+16·7
Building and civil engineering	+11·0
Chemicals and rubber	+32·5
Food and agricultural industries	+12·9
Textiles	+9·2
Clothing	+0·3
Leather and hides	+6·1
Wood and furniture	+7·5
Paper and cardboard	+19·7
Printing	+13·7
All manufacturing industries (including building)	+12·7
All industries	+12·8

Source: I.N.S.É.É., 'L'Évolution récente des revenus salariaux modestes en France', *Études et Conjoncture* (August 1954), p. 768.

The Determination of Rates and the National Minimum Wage

Wage rates are the most important object of collective bargaining or government intervention. Between 1939 and 1950 they were entirely determined by the state. Inflation prevailed during most of the period and was at its worst between 1945 and 1949. The whole period saw a considerable reduction of all differentials.

In February 1950 free collective bargaining was re-established. State intervention in wages disappeared, except that the government was empowered to fix a national minimum wage (*Salaire minimum interprofessionnel garanti* commonly known as the S.M.I.G.) after consulting the Commission Supérieure des Conventions Collectives[2] and taking due account of prevailing economic conditions. The S.M.I.G. was intended to be no more than a sort of subsistence

[1] Cf. I.N.S.É.É., 'L'Évolution récente des revenus salariaux modestes en France', *Études et Conjoncture* (August 1954), p. 769.

[2] A quadripartite board composed of representatives of the employers' and workers' unions, of the government, and of the social security organizations.

wage, and to have no appreciable influence upon other wages. In fact, it has come to be regarded by everyone as the pivot of the whole French wage structure. Every increase in the S.M.I.G. (except the latest) has almost immediately been followed by a general wage increase. The rise in the over-all index of wage rates has in fact been proportional to the rise in the S.M.I.G. Employers' Associations frequently refuse to negotiate a wage revision until the government has increased the S.M.I.G. The trade unions demand a revision of the whole wage structure every time the S.M.I.G. is raised. Many collective agreements now provide for automatic and proportional increases of all rates should the S.M.I.G. rise. And the government, which sought in 1950 entirely to refrain thenceforth from intervening in wage matters, had, in February 1954,[1] specifically to forbid that the increase in the national minimum wage should entail any corresponding upward movement of the whole wage structure. That this intervention has been successful may be judged by the fact that there has been a further decrease in skill, sex, and regional differentials since the beginning of the year, after three years in which differentials were constant or even slightly increased.

The S.M.I.G., therefore, except when the government has specifically intervened, has in fact proved to be the pivot of the whole wage structure. It is, moreover, the reference price of some other prices, rents in particular. It is thus a leader, or key variable in the French economy. The methods by which it is determined and revised deserve, therefore, some attention.

The Determination of the S.M.I.G. and Sliding-scale Arrangements

The Commission Supérieure des Conventions Collectives must first establish a 'typical' budget to justify the S.M.I.G. it proposes. This budget is defined in the following terms : 'The typical budget, which serves to determine the S.M.I.G., must be understood to mean a budget such that at the very least it shall cover the individual and social needs of the human being that are considered incompressible'.[2]

A majority of the committee (excluding the employers' representatives, those of the government abstaining) decided both in

[1] Since this paper was written a further increase has taken place (October 1954) comparable to the previous one in that the government has once again sought to prevent a wholesale increase of the wage structure. The February and October increases consist of a bonus payable only to the lowest-paid grades of worker.

[2] The notion of incompressibility in the case of human needs is a difficult one to render precisely. See the detailed studies carried out on this subject in France by the I.S.É.A., particularly: Yves Mainguy, 'La Consommation incompressible', *Économie appliquée* (1948), p. 68.

1950 and in 1953 to take as an example of this 'typical budget' the budget of the Parisian unskilled worker. This budget was established in 1950 and revised in 1953.[1] Some doubt may thus be entertained as to whether the 'typical' budget reflects the way a certain low income was in fact spent or whether it reflects the minimum needs that should be satisfied. There is an ambiguity here that has not been resolved.[2]

In view of the lengthy procedure required to revise this budget, which may thus lose all significance when prices are rising fast, it was decided in July 1952 to relate the S.M.I.G. to the index of retail prices in Paris: the S.M.I.G. is to increase in proportion to the index whenever the index rises by 5 per cent or more. The adjustment only takes place upwards. Thus the S.M.I.G. may be raised upon the motivated advice of the Commission Supérieure des Conventions Collectives and must be increased whenever the retail price index rises by more than 5 per cent.[3]

The index of retail prices is based on an inquiry into the expenditure of a working-class family of four in Paris in 1949. The S.M.I.G. is therefore related to two distinct budgets which are quite unlikely to coincide.[4] It is therefore necessary to compare and analyse the 'typical' and the index budgets which together determine the key variable in the French wage structure.

Budget Comparisons and the Determination of Budget Prices

The table on page 258 gives the structure of the 'typical' budget for 1953, the index budget, and, for the sake of comparison, a budget of lower working-class expenditure based on an inquiry carried out by the I.N.S.É.É. in 1951.

The very considerable difference in the 'food' item between the three budgets suffices to suggest the arbitrariness of the references which determine the S.M.I.G. But what is even more important is the way in which the prices of the budget goods are fixed.

[1] It is amusing to hear of the passionate discussions in the committee on the question of deciding how many baths, razor blades, or tubes of tooth-paste the Parisian labourer was entitled to in one year. It may interest readers to note that 50 (not 52!) baths are allowed per year to the labourer, and one shaving-brush every five years.

[2] See André Philbert, *Budget type et salaire minimum garanti. I. Le Budget type de 1953* (March 1954), p. 149.

[3] It is not clear whether, in the event of a 5 per cent rise in the index, the increases in the S.M.I.G. that have taken place since July 1952 would be included in the upward adjustment of the minimum wage or not. There is here an obvious source of conflict. Cf. Philbert.

[4] Here, too, is a possible source of conflict, and of discredit for the index if the Commission argues that it is rising less fast than the 'true' working-class cost of living.

In the case of the index budget, the government directly fixes the prices of goods and services whose weights add up to 34·4 per cent of the total weight of the index. Among such goods and services, or charges, are rents and rates, fuel, light and transport, postal services, tobacco, newspapers, haircuts, and the most important

	'Typical' 1953 Budget	Index Budget	Inquiry Budget
	%	%	%
Food	38·2	58·0	65·3
Clothing	15·6	12·0	6·6
Household	14·9	12·1	12·2
Personal services	10·3	5·7	4·3
Other	21·0	12·2	11·6

foodstuffs: bread, milk, sugar. The government is, moreover, able significantly to influence the prices of many other goods (whose weights add up to another 31 per cent) either because it fixes maximum retail margins (meat) or because it controls the wholesale prices of goods that enter into the index (some manufactured goods). In the case of the 'typical' budget, the weight of the goods and services whose price is fixed by the government amount to 33·5 per cent of the total, and the weight of those whose price is influenced amount to 21·2 per cent.

The government is therefore able to manipulate the prices of most of the goods which compose the retail price index and of about half the goods which enter the 'typical' budget. Since the latter proportion can only be lessened by revising the budget, a lengthy procedure, the weight of the government's influence on the determinants of the S.M.I.G. is considerable.[1]

It should be added that the price fixing is itself highly arbitrary: it is illuminating to read how the price of wheat is fixed (it serves to determine the price of bread, noodles, semolina, and serves as reference price for other foodstuffs). A basic price, originally established on an average cost basis, is multiplied every year by the arithmetic average of the price index of agricultural inputs and the Parisian retail price index of manufactured goods. A certain percentage is then subtracted from the result to correct for the modernization of agriculture during the previous year, and a further percentage is added or subtracted to correct for the size of the harvest. The final

[1] It is, however, worth noting that the government is much more able to influence the prices of the index than those of the 'typical' budget: 20 per cent of the foodstuffs prices of the 'typical' budget are fixed by the government, compared to 33 per cent in the index budget.

result is subject to a tax that varies in proportion to each producer's wheat output, and which helps to subsidize wheat exports. It thus appears that what has become the key, or dominant French wage, the S.M.I.G., is arbitrarily determined with reference to a system of prices that are themselves both artificial and subject to government manipulation.

II. Structural Inflation

The study of empirical data has shown what precisely we mean by the inflexibility of prices and the rigidity of flows and of the wage structure in France today. An analytical classification of the components of structural inflation may be attempted on the basis of these empirical data. To do this we must distinguish the two fundamental aspects of inflation: (1) excess demand and (2) the schedules of relative prices and costs.

In dynamics every economic unit has inflationary potentialities in so far as its share of the total monetary demand exceeds its share of the total supply of products when due account is taken of all the other units. These units are not micro-units but complex units characterized [1] by the fact that the plans of their elementary units (workers) are influenced by the plans of larger units (trade unions, federations, and confederations) outside the context of market relationships. In this sense, which may be determined in terms not of sociology but of economic analysis, these complex units may be said to be structured. From this point of view they stand in contrast to groups of producers that are not structured but fluid, and are merely defined by a coefficient of differentiation or a coefficient of external interdependence. These complex structured economic units have specific inflationary potentialities, by reason of their very structure (defined in economic terms). Since this inflationary potentiality derives from a structure that is economically defined, the inflation it creates may be termed structural.[2]

In the present French situation the prices of agricultural products

[1] F. Perroux, 'Les Macrodécisions', *Économie appliquée* (April–June 1949), p. 9.

[2] In France there are other long-run structurally inflationary pressures, in a different economic sense, which are due to:

(a) The demographic structure — an aged population has a relatively weak propensity to work, to risk, and to create. It has, moreover, a relatively small margin of fresh labour upon which to call in order to adapt the labour force to economic change. Finally, it sometimes happens that an aged population has a high propensity to hoard, to practise fiscal evasion, and to export capital. The result is less new investment and possibly an accumulated stock of purchasing power liable to be used in a way that is not easily predictable.

(b) The political structure — when the conflicts between complex structurated units are such that neither the monetary authorities nor the government can any longer arbitrate, the whole economy becomes incoherent.

bear no relation to the relative scarcity of those products; the structure of relative wages bears no relation to the relative productivity of different types of labour; and the present value of stocks of capital goods is capitalized at market rates of interest, according to anticipated rates of profit that are based on profit margins totally unrelated to the economic efficiency of the entrepreneurs.

These inveterate practices have entered the habits and have modified the mental attitudes of all producers. The terms 'minimum — interprofessionnel — garanti' have become the motto of the whole French economy. The three points that we mention above are confirmed by institutions and legislative or administrative regulations, and cannot therefore be eliminated otherwise than by altering these institutions and regulations.

As a result of the characteristics of the pressures that give rise to excess demand (a), as a result of the characteristics of the schedules of relative costs and prices (b), and as a result of the lasting interactions between these two frozen entities, the French economic system is structurally inflationary. In practice this means: that the contraction or the expansion of aggregate or intermediate monetary flows does not suffice to bring about the necessary corrections; and that the so-called selective measures of intervention (selective credit allocation) are carried out without any valid economic references.

Structural inflation, as it has just been defined, stands in sharp contrast to the inflations that arise from the working of a supple economic system and to the accidental inflations due to exogenous causes under any system. A correct interpretation of wages and a correct wage policy are impossible in France unless structural inflation is rigorously analysed. Structural inflation may be regarded as having three consequences.

(1) A permanent maldistribution of the labour force. When a policy of expansion is applied in the short run, or a policy of growth is applied in the long run, any economic system is liable to meet two distinct limits: the full employment of the labour force, the full employment of installed capacity. It is well known that in practice the two limits are never necessarily spontaneously concomitant, nor even compatible after governmental interventions. But in the French case both limits are devoid of economic meaning; it is only after prices and flows have been unfrozen that a rough idea might be obtained of what the full employment of labour and of installed capacity would be. Both limits change from period to period in a mutually unco-ordinated way. Investment and amortization, which determine installed capacity, change under the influence

of private investments which are distorted by price and income structures, and of public investments which are modified according to changes of political majorities or of political anticipations. Wages, prices of wage goods, prices of other products vary on their own account since the supply and demand of labour or of goods are subject neither to the rules of the market nor to the discipline of an all-embracing plan. In these circumstances the incompatibility of the two limits becomes practically unavoidable. The attempt to set up, in the medium and long run, a quickly growing volume of installed capacity, implying changes in sectoral prices and flows, is paradoxically combined with the attempt to realize the full employment of labour in the short run with existing sectoral prices and flows.

(2) The theoretical and practical isolation of 'a wage inflation' is impossible if the economy is neither in a régime of general micro-economic interdependences, nor in a régime of macro-economic interdependences consisting of aggregate and sectoral flows which remain alterable and supple. The rigidities of all the flows must be considered together if the rigidity of a single flow is to be understood. And all the rigidities must be attacked together if the rigidity of a single flow is to be eliminated or reduced.

In order to arouse a salutary reaction two lessons must be borne in mind which no macro-economic analysis can avoid if it seeks to be rigorous. (a) The product in a modern economy is a function not only of expenditure but of the incentives implied by the different forms and levels of incomes ; and (b) it is not economically justifiable to reason in terms of aggregate flows if the elementary and sectoral flows which make up the aggregate flows are not additive. All that has been said about the French economy shows that the condition of additivity is totally unfulfilled and that incentives are literally submerged in the ocean of countervailing powers. In order to use a macro-economic analysis which is reasonably rigorous, it is therefore imperative that we first escape from the chaos of internal and external protections and interventions which are incorporated in the structure of the productive mechanism. They have also penetrated the mind by means of an illegitimate adulteration of fundamental notions.

(3) The adulteration of the very notion of wages. Incomes may fulfil their economic functions under institutions which differ in form according to economic systems or countries. But there are limits to this institutional indetermination. Institutions and the way in which they are currently interpreted may occasionally obliterate the very economic function of an income.

This seems to be the case in France today. We have too frequently insisted upon the need to cover social costs[1] as a condition of a dynamic optimum in the use of material and human resources, for it to be imagined that we have today forgotten this condition. We only want to point out that, if it is to be fulfilled, the fundamental economic distinction between wages and social benefits must be clearly made and translated into the institutions. The block of distinct ideas and distinct economic functions that is conjured up by the expression 'workers' remunerations' does harm to the cause that was to be served when it was coined and used.[2]

It is not unimportant to know how workers do, in fact, 'interpret' their remuneration : it is certainly indispensable to know the effects of their attitude towards their income, upon the fulfilment of economic functions. Under whatever system of organization is the economic function of wages to obtain a socially usable product ? In this sense a remuneration is not a wage when it is entirely divorced from the productivity of the labour supplied (however rough the imputation). A wage is not a social benefit ; to be able to pay social benefits, it is first necessary to avoid assimilating them to wages ; they have not the same economic functions analysed from the point of view of incentives and of expenditure.

In the present state of social accounting in France we are not in a position to determine intersectoral flows precisely enough to enable a government, assumed to be a perfect economist and obeyed guide, to pursue a coherent policy of incentives and a coherent programme of expenditure by sectors. What value can therefore be attached to a policy of incentives and of expenditure for 'aggregate' flows ?

The French economy, which is structurally inflationary, is attempting to find internal and external equilibria in short-run expansion and medium and long-run growth. The unfreezing of prices and flows and the rediscovery of the economic function of wages are the preconditions of the re-establishment of two propensities which do not appear in Lord Keynes's list of propensities : the first is the propensity to work, defined by the ratio between the increment of output due to an additional effort expressed in real terms, and the increment of wages expressed in real terms.[3] The

[1] F. Perroux, 'Note sur les coûts de l'homme', *Économie appliquée* (1952).

[2] A similar reaction is necessary in the case of profit and the economic functions of profit. The scientific progress, registered until the present time in profit theory, appears to have been linked to an analysis of the economic functions of this income, especially in regard to its ability, under whatever system of organization, to reduce costs, in dynamics.

[3] In terms of elasticity : the ratio between the relative increment of the first term and the relative increment of the second.

second is the propensity to innovate,[1] defined by the ratio between an increment of output occasioned by an economic change sanctioned by the market, and expressed in real terms, and the increment of economic advantage, expressed in real terms, whatever the economic advantage. As able analysts, like Carl Shoup, have shown, the fiscal system may influence the value of these propensities. In a dynamic economy which is tendentially disinflationary (not deflationary) the value of the propensities must be greater than 1. Although empirical verification is impossible, precise and concordant evidence suggests that in an economy which is structurally inflationary, the value of these propensities is less than 1.

We shall limit our conclusion, like our analysis, to contemporary France. In France at the present time the crisis which has befallen the analysis of wages is of a similar nature to that which has beset distribution theory. Structural inflation has adulterated the very notions of our science ; that is to say, it has warped or broken the modern instruments which are necessary not only for the diagnosis, but also for the treatment or operations which are indispensable to its cure.

[1] We are not assimilating the term innovation to the Schumpeterian 'innovation'.

Chapter 17

THE EFFECTS OF INFLATION ON THE WAGE STRUCTURE OF FRANCE[1]

BY

FRANÇOIS SELLIER

University of Aix-en-Provence et Marseille, France

THE post-war period is characterized in France by important changes in the distribution of aggregate wages. The generalized use of the social wage is a manifestation of this upheaval, remuneration being henceforth dependent not only on output or working time but on family circumstances. The necessity of meeting essential requirements in periods of manifest penury leads to equalizing legislation. During that same period the scarcity of manpower, particularly of skilled labour, arising from reconversion and the development of the occupied countries, has led to the practice among employers of raising the wages of skilled workers by means of special output bonuses. An economy of rationing, on the one hand, and the scarcity of skilled labour on the other, makes the formulation of *a priori* ideas on the evolution of the wage structure during inflation a hazardous undertaking. It is therefore fitting to refer to facts and consider how they may be interpreted.

The case of France can be examined from 1936 to 1939, a period when the cost-of-living index rose from 99·2 (1928 = 100) to 143·1 in Paris and from 97·9 to 138 in the provinces. It may also be examined from 1945 till the present day, a period during which inflation has been much more violent and where the retail price index for 34 articles rose, assuming that 1938 = 100, to 1632 in Paris and to 1812 in the provinces in 1948.

In 1952 the index, assuming that 1938 = 100, rose to an annual average of 2464 in Paris and to 2724 in the provinces. From 1949 to 1952 the index for 213 articles (the over-all price index for family consumption) rose to 145·4, assuming that 1949 = 100. One can say that in 1949–1952 France witnessed a rise in the cost of living of the same order of magnitude as in 1936–1939.

But the inflation of the period 1936–1939 is not as significant as that during the post-war period, in the course of which wages,

[1] Translated by Hélène Heroys.

instead of doubling, as happened in certain cases between 1936 and 1939, were multiplied eight or ten times between 1944 and 1953. The effect of these absolute variations on the relative wage structure may be fully examined.

I. Skill Differentials in the Metal Industry of the Paris Region

Wage data for the metal industry of the Paris region are one of the most valuable sources for tracing the evolution of wage differences according to skills because the series shows average hourly wages for the three categories, skilled, semi-skilled, unskilled, at quarterly intervals since the pre-war period.

Table 1

Quarterly Average Wages, Francs per Hour *

	1945	1947	1949	1951	1952
Skilled	34·40	67·91	109	177	189
Semi-skilled	30·84	56·06	91	144	153
Unskilled	23·10	44·30	71	117	122

Source : Bulletin of I.N.S.É.É., Supplement (April–June), p. 57, table xii.

* Family allowances are not included.

On the basis of these data we get the following results if we represent the wages of the semi-skilled as a percentage of the wages of the skilled workers.

1945	1947	1949	1951(4)	1952(4)
89	82	83	81	80

The computation of the percentage of the wage of the unskilled compared with that of semi-skilled workers yields the following results :

1945	1946	1947	1949	1951	1952
74	75	79	77	80	80

In the period 1945–1952 the percentage of the wage of the unskilled compared with the wage of the skilled fell from 67 per cent to 64 per cent. Between 1945 and 1952 the skilled worker consolidated his advantage over the unskilled and reinforced his position even more compared to the semi-skilled.

During that same period the semi-skilled lost ground compared with both the unskilled and the skilled worker. The effects of post-war inflation were therefore such as to crush the semi-skilled between the skilled and the unskilled.

Let us try to interpret these results. In the metal industry of the Paris region the title of skilled worker is won after a lengthy apprenticeship. The moulder personifies that skilled worker. The making of sand casts for casting demands a skill which takes a long time to acquire. All foundries, irrespective of their size, from the big enterprise of the Creusot-Schneider type to the little business which specializes in regional manufactures (foundries of oil presses in the Provence), have this kind of worker. Since the skill is of the non-substitutionary order, supply is highly inelastic. Despite the efforts made by the industry to train apprentices, they are still in short supply. The great relative scarcity of this type of worker was felt in a period of acute development (1945–1948), and thus allowed him to maintain his position, as much *vis-à-vis* the semi-skilled as the unskilled. The case is the more interesting since in the majority of the other cases to which we shall refer, the relative differential between skilled and non-skilled diminished. It is apparent here that certain kinds of skills characterized by a long apprenticeship [1] are able to stand a general rise in wages and in cost of living without a deterioration in their status. Indeed, on the contrary, their relative position improved.

But the semi-skilled whose skill is characterized by a high degree of exchangeability (and a length of apprenticeship which varies from a few days to a few weeks) loses on all fronts. The unfavourable position of the semi-skilled seems to be shared by all non-skilled workers in this industry. Let us look at the chart for wages in this industry done by M. Chabert in his study *Les Salaires dans l'industrie française* (p. 93) with reference to the unskilled, the semi-skilled, the fitter, and the pattern-maker for the years 1920–1952. Confining ourselves to the period with which we are dealing, 1945–1952, we see that as compared with the wage of the unskilled, the wage of the semi-skilled tends downwards, the wage of the fitter is by and large horizontal, that of the pattern-maker tends upwards.

To express a synthesized conclusion: during an inflationary period and in an industry characterized by a relative scarcity of skill, the tendency to compression in the occupational wage structure

[1] An entrepreneur of the Provence whom the author asked how long it took to 'make' a good pattern-maker replied, 'A whole lifetime'.

grows weaker as the wages of the more highly skilled workers are considered.

But thanks to the same series of diagrams, we can usefully round off the observation by examining the variations during an inflationary period very different in character from that which we have just considered, namely, the period 1935–1940. The 1945–1952 inflation (interrupted in 1949 and thrown once more into gear by events in Korea) featured, at least up to 1948, great activity in the metal industry of the Paris region, whereas between 1936 and 1938 economic activity was reduced (the motive power of inflation being then mainly in the field of international finance).

A comparison of the trends of the relative wages of the pattern-maker, fitter, and semi-skilled worker with the wage of the unskilled shows that the downward general trend is more accentuated for the fitter than for the semi-skilled ; it is, however, less accentuated for the pattern-maker than for the fitter. It seems, therefore, that here again, despite the different tendencies noted during the inflation of 1945–1952, the pattern-maker enjoys a privileged position. Even in an inflationary period without activity, his wage stands up better to the tendency of compression than that of other skilled workers (fitters) or semi-skilled workers. But the semi-skilled are subjected to occupational compression compared with the unskilled. During the period 1935–1938, the factor of 'demand for skill' no longer comes into play (except, for rather exceptional reasons, in regard to the pattern-maker) ; the inflationary tendency to compress the occupational structure operates alone, and the degree of that compression is by and large proportionate to the level of money wages.

II. Differences among Average Wages, 1946–1954

Since 1946 the Ministère du Travail has published a quarterly survey of wages in enterprises which employ more than 10 workers, classified according to type of work, professional category, zone, and sex. Each survey gives a table of the average wage rates' indices (1946 : 100) according to industry.

There follow three tables showing average wage rates by industries for four classifications of skill [1] on a 1946 base, for April 1947 (Table 2A), January 1949 (Table 2B), and April 1954 (Table 2C).

[1] The official classification shows three groups :

(a) Unskilled (manœuvres) with two grades (manœuvres ordinaires : I ; manœuvres spécialisées : II) ;
(b) Semi-skilled (ouvriers spécialisés) with two grades ;
(c) Skilled and highly skilled (qualifiés et hautement qualifiés).

Table 2a

Average Wage Rates Observed (1946 = 100)

April 1947 *

Industries	Men				Women			
	Un-skilled	Semi-skilled	Skilled	Highly Skilled	Ordinary Labour	Special Labour	Special Workers	Qualified Workers
	I	II	III	IV	I	II	III	IV
1. Food	145	147	143	146	158	156	151	151
2. Chemical	140	142	140	141	154	153	148	145
3. Rubber	150	150	139	148	159	160	157	157
4. Paper and cardboard	143	141	138	143	156	151	146	148
5. Printing	164	158	151	153	166	161	150	163
6. Textile	154	152	151	151	160	164	156	156
7. Textile manufacture	144	146	142	146	157	157	147	158
8. Leather	144	143	140	144	154	151	150	154
9. Timber	145	147	143	143	152	152	149	147
10. Metallurgic	139	138	138	144	155	159	151	152
11. Metal production	146	148	143	147	160	159	151	155
12. Nonferrous metals	..	151	136	150	..	..	146	153
13. Stone	150	148	143	143	..	..	..	..
14. Building	159	142	135	137	..	..	..	..
15. Ceramic	143	139	139	142	160	155	147	149
16. Transports (railways excepted)	148	149	144	142	..	..	..	..
17. Trade	143	145	140	135	155	155	148	152
Average	144	145	142	145	158	157	152	156

* *Revue française du Travail* (August 1947), p. 716.

TABLE 2B

JANUARY 1949 *

Activities	Men				Women			
	Ordinary Labour	Special Labour	Special Workers	Qualified Workers	Ordinary Labour	Special Labour	Special Workers	Qualified Workers
	I	II	III	IV	I	II	III	IV
1. Metal production	311	300	298	313	324	322	311	..
2. Mechanic industries	316	307	290	288	335	328	310	316
3. Glass industries	295	282	284	281	335	318	311	300
4. Ceramic industries	306	291	272	260	331	317	303	291
5. Building industries	289	279	262	256	..	..	..	..
6. Chemical industries	300	289	282	275	330	317	306	291
7. Food industries	301	294	280	271	332	308	304	297
8. Textile industries	328	313	302	294	345	335	319	317
9. Textile manufacture	309	299	292	286	337	327	302	295
10. Leather industries	311	290	273	265	332	317	291	285
11. Timber industries	286	290	267	245	317	303	289	270
12. Paper and cardboard	297	295	275	270	341	332	293	284
13. Printing industries	312	323	294	290	336	338	295	302
14. Transports	307	293	289	266	..	..	..	..
15. Food trade	318	295	291	274	351	327	304	292
16. Other trade	302	291	282	277	332	323	309	301

* *Revue française du Travail* (January 1950), p. 107.

TABLE 2C

APRIL 1954 *

Activities	Men				Women			
	Ordinary Labour	Special Labour	Special Workers	Qualified Workers	Ordinary Labour	Special Labour	Special Workers	Qualified Workers
	I	II	III	IV	I	II	III	IV
1. Metal production	525	492	470	493	585	527	514	..
2. Mechanic industries	576	547	508	502	609	585	534	560
3. Glass industries	538	520	497	506	630	561	552	552
4. Ceramic industries	554	503	465	435	615	562	510	475
5. Building industries	524	492	457	447	..	..	..	..
6. Chemical industries	549	524	510	500	605	575	546	529
7. Food industries	550	532	502	486	617	573	550	532
8. Textile industries	590	550	519	506	638	597	546	531
9. Textile manufacture	547	518	505	480	625	584	520	491
10. Leather industries	554	508	465	446	607	564	497	472
11. Timber industries	533	511	482	434	601	552	518	471
12. Paper and cardboard	550	538	499	492	642	602	530	513
13. Printing industries	560	553	521	516	601	584	512	534
14. Transports	551	516	493	468	..	..	..	..
15. Food trade	577	536	516	499	643	606	563	521
16. Other trade	540	518	501	492	608	570	525	503

* Three-monthly inquiry mimeographed, p. 20.

These tables permit comparisons during the two phases of post-war inflation. The first phase came to an end in 1949 ; events in Korea in 1950 heralded a second phase which may be considered to have ended in 1954.

Differences according to Skill

Let us first examine these tables, comparing the indices according to skills for industry. The conclusion is clear : indices decrease steadily for men and women in all grades from unskilled to skilled workers. In 1954 the comparison of the indices of the ordinary labourers, the special labourers, and the semi-skilled worker shows no exception. There is one exception in 1949, in the timber industry.[1] The comparison of the indices of the wages of semi-skilled workers and skilled workers reveals one exception in 1954, none in 1949.

These observations are valid for the close of inflationary periods. The question as to what happens in the middle of such a period is worth exploring. The answer is given by the table of weighted averages of hourly wages on April 1, 1947, on the basis of 1946 = 100. The comparison between unskilled and semi-skilled workers leads to the same conclusion. On the other hand, the comparison of the indices of semi-skilled workers with skilled workers yields a contrary conclusion : in all industries the index of the variation of hourly wages of skilled workers is higher than that of the semi-skilled, and in seven out of sixteen industries higher than that of unskilled. The year 1947 is the last one in which inflation in France coincides with a high level of economic activity. In such circumstances manpower scarcity tends to balance the forces of occupational compression. The factor operates in particular in the most highly skilled occupational categories.

When economic activity falls off, as measured by a decline in the hours of work, the premium of scarcity vanishes and only the factors of compression operate. In fact, after July 1947 the index of duration of work ceases to rise.

Differences by Industry and Differences between Male and Female Wages

The above tables of average wage rates by industry and skill show quite considerable differences among various industries. But no single cause seems to explain these differences adequately. In

[1] The tables exclude these groups : 'Various industries, health services, banks, and insurance'.

April 1947 the highest increases in average wages over 1946, aside from the factor of skill, are shown in the textile, publishing, and clothing industries ; the lowest average increases occur in the chemical, metal, and building industries. In October 1949 the highest average indices relate to textiles, clothing, publishing, food, and the metal industry ; the lowest to building. In April 1954 the highest indices are to be found in the food trade and the food industry, in textiles, clothing, publishing ; the lowest index figure is that of the building industry.

Two regular features are thus evident. (1) There are a series of 'privileged' industries, namely, those which employ female labour (textile, clothing, food industry and food trade) ; and publishing, an industry where trade unionism is very strong and wages traditionally very high. (2) The building industry is consistently at a disadvantage. The explanation as regards the average wage is probably related to the fact that labourers in the building industry have since 1945–1946 been increasingly recruited from immigrants from North Africa.

The only elements of conclusion about wage differentiation in times of inflation which these comments yield relate to the industries which employ female labour and to publishing. Whereas the latter is an industry where high wages prevail, the former have low wages.

The case of the publishing industry is particularly interesting : increases in printing have been made from a high starting-point. In 1947 the commentators of the *Revue française du Travail* wrote :

> In this privileged sector the free play of individual initiative has followed the regulations in force only very approximately. The wholesale increases over and above official rates are the highest in existence and wages are markedly higher than anywhere else. The movement towards uniformity which tends to equalize the remuneration of all professional groups has not made itself felt, the existing advantages which were already considerable have been maintained and even greatly increased.[1]

The manpower structure of this particular industry is highly rigid ; skills are departmentalized, trade unions are very strong and ruled by the most highly skilled and highly paid workers.

Wage developments have been entirely different in the textile, clothing, and food industries, where relative increases are due to the fact that the wages of female workers have on an average increased relative to those of males.

The differentiation between the wages of males and females deserves special examination. From 1946 (January) until April

[1] (August 1947), p. 714.

1947 (*R.f.T.*, August 1947, p. 713) the index of wages for males rose from 100 to 144, that for females from 100 to 154. During the whole period 1947–1954, the general index of the average hourly wage for females has throughout registered a marked advance. In April 1954 the index for the wage of the male was 501, for the female 553.

But the average percentage difference between the wages of males and females has remained stable round the figure of an 8 per cent advantage to males. (*Survey* of April 1954, p. 8.) At the beginning of 1946 the difference was 15 per cent. From January 1947, after the adoption of measures intended to secure the application of the principle of 'equal pay for equal work', the difference remained around 8 per cent. That average difference does not, however, represent the relative differences between the wages of males and females according to skill. In 1947 the average difference in females' wages as compared with males were 4·2 per cent for unskilled I, 9·3 per cent for unskilled II, 8·8 per cent for semi-skilled, 11·8 per cent for skilled workers.

The chief beneficiaries of the new policy are undoubtedly the labourers : 'the skilled female labour force is always at a disadvantage' (*R.f.T.* (August 1947), p. 713).

TABLE 3

AVERAGE DIFFERENTIAL OF FEMALE WORKERS' WAGES AS COMPARED WITH MALE WORKERS

	Unskilled I	Unskilled II	Semi-skilled	Skilled	Highly Skilled
	%	%	%	%	%
1947	4·2	9·3	8·8	11·8	. .
1954	6·6	7·6	10·0	12·0	18·0

Source : *R.f.T.* (April 1947), p. 713, and *Enquête trimestrielle* (April 1954)

The average wages of female workers have been revalued in relation to the average wages of males, according to the general rule of the adjustment of differences in an inflationary period whereby those wages increase most whose real money value is lowest. Within the female category, the rule operates in such a way as to put the highly skilled at a disadvantage *vis-à-vis* the unskilled.

Regional Differences

The 1946 legislation on wages created, together with a hierarchical grading by skills, a series of wage zones, the main feature of which was a decreasing scale, the 'Paris Region' serving as basis. The scheduled deductions according to zones had the following values : 5 — 10 — 15 — 20 — 25. Subsequently, they were further reduced and became 3·75 — 7·50 — 11·25 — 13·50. From April 1947 the indices actually followed were, on an average, below the value they should have had if they had been computed on the basis of the wages really paid in the Paris region.

TABLE 4

GEOGRAPHICAL DIFFERENTIALS

1947	1954	1947		1954
Legal Differences		Male	Female	Average
5	3·5	9·7	12·4	12·7
10	7·5	14·7	18·1	17·4
15	11·25	20·0	21·8	20·9
20	13·50	24·1	24·7	23·6
25	..	26·5	28·9	..

Source : *R.f.T.* (April 1947), p. 712, and *Enquête trimestrielle* (April 1954)..

We must note that the zones which legislation favours most are those where the actual difference is greatest as compared with the statutory difference. *Per contra*, the zones least favoured by the law have a relative advantage.

In all cases, where no factor of scarcity or monopoly intervenes, inflation has the effect of compression, whether the differences are due to skills, to sex, to occupation, or to region.

III. MECHANISM OF THE NARROWING OF DIFFERENCES

Wage policy in France between 1945 and 1954 falls into two periods : between 1945 and 1950 wages were in theory governed by legal provisions and the principle of 'pegging down' was accepted up to 1947 after wages had been 'freed'. As from 1950 'free bargaining' superseded regulation. In point of fact, even during the period when wages were pegged down, the principle was constantly overridden, to such an extent indeed that at certain times it was possible to speak of a black market in manpower. The three means generally used to bypass the legal provisions were : the payment of flat rate or output bonuses, upgrading, and the guaranteed wage.

Certain bonuses are reserved to workers on shifts : (namely, workers who normally work eight hours consecutively, apart from a snack break, in two or three consecutive shifts) ; others apply to every worker in certain conditions but represent flat rate compensation (bonuses for heavy work). The output bonus is paid on a flat rate to factory workers on the basis of the volume of weekly production. Output bonuses raise the rates of wages calculated in terms of time, sometimes as much as 30 per cent.

Upgrading consists of putting the worker (especially the ordinary or specialized labourer) in a category higher than that in which he should normally be classified. The guaranteed wage practice consists of making a distinction between the figure which serves as the basis for the hierarchic scale and the figure which corresponds to the guaranteed wage. For instance, the labourer's basic wage being

TABLE 5

AVERAGE MONTHLY WAGES (francs)

	Wages in 1938	After the Increase of 24.3.51	After the Increase of 28.4.51	Average Increase in Relation to 1938
Single man :				
Surface	1·087	23·247	24·642	22·67
Underground	1·283	32·060	33·983	26·48
Father of 2 children :				
Surface	1·129	30·737	32·492	28·77
Underground	1·390	40·550	41·833	30·13
Father of 4 children :				
Surface	1·337	40·717	42·892	32·03
Underground	1·598	49·530	52·233	32·68

74 francs per hour, his guaranteed wage is fixed at 83 francs (wage agreement in the metal industry of Meurthe and Moselle, April 1, 1951).

Those three methods lead to hierarchic compression :

(1) Flat-rate bonuses are to everyone's advantage ;
(2) Upgrading is intended in particular for labourers ;
(3) The guaranteed wage raises the floor of the hierarchic structure, without raising the basic number.

With these practices go legislative measures which tend to distribute transferable income evenly (family allowances ; single wage if the woman is not working).

The management of the Charbonnages de France calculated in April 1951 the evolution of the average of the monthly wages of underground and surface workers between 1938 and 1951, together with the coefficient of increase between those two dates according to family circumstances.

It follows from Table 5 that:

(1) In the case of the single man, the difference between the wage of the surface and the underground worker rose considerably from 1938 to 1951 (going from 15 per cent to 27 per cent of the highest wage).
(2) In the case of the father of 4 children, the difference is far smaller: only 17 per cent.

But here again between 1938 and 1951 we find an instance where the discrepancy remains, owing to the shortage of the most highly paid workers (underground).

Although the problem lies outside the aims of this study, it is important to note that the rule of hierarchic compression affects not only employees in private industry but state employees also. As the methods applied to the former were not easily applicable here, the principle of narrowing decrease had perforce to be openly proclaimed.

That is what occurred on several occasions, of which we will quote two examples: in May 1951 the salaries of personnel whose hierarchic indices were equal to or below 250 were raised by 5 per cent, other salaries by 4 per cent. But the changes are more complex than that. In fact, the increase in salaries including the indemnity for residence, varies between 5 and 6 per cent on the higher rungs of the ladder and amounts to approximately 10 per cent on the lower. Secondly, the decree of September 17, 1953, grants a 'special decreasing indemnity' to low-income state employees (whose index in the hierarchy lies between 100 and 162).

The narrowing of the variation in workers' wages is noticeable in the majority of cases and operates to the advantage of all low incomes: labourers, female workers, or incomes classified according to geographic distribution. Similarly, industries which pay low wages enjoy a relative advantage, they are mostly industries which employ female labour. But there are exceptions to the rule: attention has been drawn to the case of the 'pattern-maker' in a foundry, as well as to the maintenance of the differences in the publishing industry and in the mining industry.

The factors which influence the wage structure in an inflationary period may be classified as follows:

(1) Relative monetary effects. Wage claims are fundamentally justified by the influence of a rise in the cost of living on those

money wages which are closest to subsistence level. There the relationship between money wage and wage goods fully comes into play. The hierarchic argument leads to a good deal of protest, but the monetary illusion arises immediately as increases — even flat rate ones — are granted to relatively high incomes. The real losses are felt increasingly less on higher money wages. That factor explains in part the rôle played by fixed indemnities and the technique of the flat rate.

(2) The relative influence, within an occupation, of highly differentiated skills. M. Chabert notes that the structure of the chart mentioned on page 266 prevails in occupations where trade unions are dominated by the most highly skilled workers. We have seen this factor operative in the publishing industry. Those are very special cases. In general, wage differentiation tends to diminish, on the one hand because of the policy of the trade unions which take in all unskilled workers, on the other hand because of the tendency to increase the numbers of semi-skilled workers, which results in greater interchangeability between the various types of manpower. In so far as an individual exercises a rare skill, he can resist that tendency ; it is easier to do so in the liberal professions.

PART V

THE NATURE OF BARGAINING

Chapter 18

APPROACHES TO THE THEORY OF BARGAINING

BY

K. W. ROTHSCHILD
Oesterreichisches Institut für Wirtschaftsforschung
Vienna, Austria

FOR a long time wage bargaining, like unemployment, was relegated to a modest back seat in the main body of academic economic doctrine. While all great realistic writers from Adam Smith onwards did realize their importance and paid attention to them in special chapters and in appendices, it was mainly 'outsiders' like Marx, Hobson, the Webbs, and a few business cycle and duopoly specialists, who found room in the centre of their theories for a realization that unemployment may be more than merely a consequence of adjustment difficulties or outside interference, and that bargaining can play a major rôle in wage determination. The main stream of economic theory remained comparatively untouched by these important economic phenomena. While unemployed families were suffering severe hardships and trade unionists were risking their lives to secure collective bargaining rights, unemployment was regarded by many writers as practically non-existent and bargaining itself as an empty illusion.

It is not difficult to find the reasons for this astounding one-sidedness, if not to say blindness in many post-Ricardian economic treatises. Two strong motives (not necessarily conscious) combined to produce this result : the desire to preserve a neat theoretical structure, unblurred by such disequilibrating forces as unemployment and bargaining, and the wish to defend the capitalist system — at least in its pure, theoretical form — against criticisms from the growing socialist movement.[1]

[1] In many cases the treatment of these questions reminds one of the satiric lines written by Christian Morgenstern :

> Und er kommt zu dem Ergebnis :
> Nur ein Traum war das Erlebnis.
> Weil, so schliesst er messerscharf,
> nicht sein *kann*, was nicht sein *darf*.

(From 'Die unmögliche Tatsache' in *Alte Galgenlieder*).

It was comparatively easy to exclude bargaining from the leading nineteenth-century wage theories, or at least to show that it must be a futile undertaking. For all these theories relied on rigidly determined supply or demand conditions from which there was no escape. The Iron Law of Wages, by postulating a perfectly elastic supply of labour (in the long run) at the subsistence wage, could easily show that every wage advantage gained would soon be translated into more labourers competing for work and reducing wages to their old level. The wage fund theory in its various forms could dispose with equal ease all claims that bargaining could lead to an all-round improvement in labour's income: with a fixed stock of capital available for wage payments every improvement in one direction would be fully compensated by a deterioration in another direction. Finally, the marginal productivity theory, by taking perfect competition and the supply of the various factors of production as given, could construct an employers' demand curve and determine an 'equilibrium wage', any diversion from which would lead to unemployment or labour shortages, which in turn would press the wage back to its equilibrium level.

In all these theories, then, there was no room for bargaining. And this heritage was carried right into the twentieth century,[1] even though many theorists had expressed their qualms as to the correctness of this view,[2] and growing significance was accorded to bargaining as they descended from the level of pure theory.

It was not until the 'thirties that bargaining broke in on a broader front into the framework of current economic theory itself. The realization that perfect competition was only one of many actual market forms, and a very exceptional one at that, led to a reconsideration of the whole field of price economics and wage theory, considerably widening the scope for bargaining within the field of supply-demand analysis. About the same time the legislation and discussions stimulated by the New Deal favoured the growth of institutional studies and the blossoming of theories in which trade unions and collective bargaining do not enter by the back door but take a central place right from the beginning. The same is true for those theories which, though not taking specific institutional studies as their starting point, discard the traditional tools of analysis in

[1] Thus, in 1928, Mr. Rowe could still claim that 'all existing wage theories appear to ignore the phenomenon which has completely changed the whole condition of the labour market . . . namely, the rise to power of trade unionism', *Wages in Practice and Theory* (1928).

[2] A famous case is John Stuart Mill's statement: 'The doctrine hitherto taught by most economists (including myself) which denied it to be possible that trade combinations can raise wages . . . is deprived of its scientific foundation, and must be thrown aside.'

order to approach the subject of duopoly (and related questions) from a new angle. There remains the wider question with regard to bargaining and the total and relative share of labour. This question, which was foremost in Ricardo's and Marx's mind, is still comparatively neglected in current economic literature.

It can no longer be maintained that the theory of bargaining is neglected. It will also be seen that bargaining theory has received its impulses from different sources so that we cannot speak today of a bargaining theory of wages or even of different, competing bargaining theories, but rather of various elements of a bargaining approach which in many cases supplement each other. I now propose to give a short appraisal of bargaining theory on the three different levels noted in the paragraph above. It should, however, be stressed that nothing like a complete catalogue is attempted, that the classification of a theory into one of the three categories will in some cases necessarily depend on a somewhat arbitrary decision, and that the authors named are given as examples of a certain type of approach and not necessarily as its only or principal representatives.

I. Bargaining and Imperfect Competition Theory

First, then, we have an approach which points out the scope for bargaining within the framework of marginal productivity theory. This is done by dropping some of the simplifying assumptions which had been part and parcel of the early stages of that theory. This approach has a long history, even though many of the contributors were not specifically concerned with the question of bargaining. With the development of imperfect competition and monopsony and oligopoly analysis, this approach was considerably broadened.

As an early example of a type of reformulation falling into this group we can name Edgeworth's distinction between the 'internal' and 'external' margin, once we drop the assumption of infinite divisibility of the labour factor. In many cases these two margins will lie so close together that they will leave little or no room for bargaining,[1] and for this reason the whole principle has been dismissed by some writers as a mathematical refinement with very little practical significance. But this principle may not be without significance for certain skilled jobs, particularly in the salaried range,

[1] In this context, an opportunity for bargaining means that bargaining is possible without affecting employment. That bargaining can be effective via changes in the employment level has, of course, been recognized by all marginal productivity theorists.

and for personal services, where very often the employment of only one or a few persons will be considered. The range between the marginal productivity of an nth and an $(n+1)^{st}$ man may then be wide enough to allow room for bargaining.

But whatever importance one may attach to this point, it remains on the whole a point of nicety. Of far greater significance were a number of objections which, like the slogan for an 'economy of high wages', were all directed against the static assumptions of marginal productivity theory. While the marginal productivity curve is accepted as the employers' demand curve, it is maintained that it is not so much the movements along this curve as the shifting of this curve (and of the labour supply curve, and possibly also the capital supply curve) that has to be watched when the effects of a wage bargain are considered. The imposition of a higher wage may lead initially to some unemployment, but may then produce such a change in the determinants of the wage-employment situation that the unemployment disappears and the higher wage becomes an 'equilibrium' wage.[1] There are different paths by which this new equilibrium may be reached: the higher wage may increase the productivity of the workers, it may force the capitalists to improve the efficiency of the production process (in these two cases the marginal productivity curve moves upward), or it may reduce the supply of labour, because women can now stay at home and children can be kept at school.

The technical refinement of the marginal analysis and the greater realism with regard to market forms brought about by imperfect and monopolistic competition theory opened up new vistas for the combination of marginal productivity analysis and bargaining opportunity. The most striking case was probably that of monopsony. For here it could be shown that where the supply of labour to a firm is not infinitely elastic — a not unrealistic assumption, under classical full employment conditions — the successful bargaining for a higher standard wage may actually lead to increased employment at the new, higher wage level.

But also the closer analysis of the commodity markets yielded results which had a bearing on the bargaining question. Particularly in the case of the kinked oligopoly demand curve it could be seen that the marginal revenue curve can be discontinuous (or vertical) over a considerable range and that within this range changes in costs will not affect the scale of output so that wage bargaining can

[1] For the sake of brevity the argument will always be restricted to the question of a wage increase enforced through bargaining. But the case of downward pressure is, of course, of equal importance and can be treated in an analogous manner.

be successful.[1] In other words, if the oligopolistic market situation imposes a certain output and price policy on the employer, he will be forced to swallow the whole increase in the wage bill consequent on a moderate advance of the wage level.

Finally, we may properly include in this section the related cases of oligopsonistic labour markets and of collusion among employers (open or tacit) not to raise wages. In the first case we have a kinked labour supply curve to the firm [2] and consequently a discontinuity in the marginal cost curve of labour which allows for a certain change in wage levels without affecting the demand for labour. In the second case, that of collusion, the employer, faced with a rising labour supply curve, does not push employment to the most profitable individual level (where marginal productivity equals marginal cost) because he realizes that his own action may induce others to do the same so that in the end wages have been raised throughout the industry and his higher bid remains without effect. In this case bargaining can raise the wage beyond the 'conventional' level without affecting the demand for labour. It is amazing that this rather simple case has received so little attention in wage theory, although it seems to correspond rather closely to the conditions observed in labour markets from Adam Smith's time till the present day.[3]

All the various facets of the bargaining problem advanced in this group do not add up to a bargaining theory. They do not show whether bargaining takes place or how it is done. They rather represent an attempt to rid the marginal productivity approach of some of its assumptions which made it incompatible with the idea

[1] Even with an unchanged output, unemployment can result, if capital can be easily substituted for labour.

[2] This is assuming that a lowering of the wages would not be followed by the other firms for fear that workers would be quickly lost, while a rise in wages would be adopted by others in order to retain their workers. The increased wage offer would then only attract few new workers.

[3] Adam Smith observed that 'masters are always and everywhere in a sort of tacit, but constant and uniform, combination not to raise the wages of labour above their actual rate. To violate this combination is everywhere a most unpopular action, and a sort of reproach to a master among his neighbours and equals.'

And as to present-day conditions we have the following results from a field study in an industrial New England town : 'Aggressive "pirating" of workers employed in another plant is definitely against the code of employers in the area. If the personnel manager of company A learns that someone from company B has approached an A worker and tried to hire him, he will immediately telephone the personnel manager of company B and ask him to let the worker alone. This request is usually sufficient ; for each personnel manager knows that, if he steals a worker today, someone else will steal from him tomorrow, and all have an interest in playing by the rules.' 'Even if the worker takes the initiative and applies for work at another plant, he will usually not be considered for employment unless his present employer is willing to relinquish him.' — Lloyd G. Reynolds, *The Structure of Labor Markets* (1951), pp. 51, 216.

of successful bargaining. This in itself has been an important step. But it remains to be seen whether a conclusive theory of modern wage determination and wage bargaining can be constructed along these in the last resort traditional lines, or whether a different approach would be more fruitful.

II. 'Psychological' and 'Institutional' Theories

We turn now to several different approaches to the bargaining problem. There has been in recent years a remarkable growth of relevant literature. It would far surpass the limits of this chapter to give even a superficial account of these theories. All that can be done here is an attempt at a rough classification and appraisal, so as to set off this group against the theorems enumerated under the preceding section.

The diverse theories falling into this group have in common that they are all more or less dissatisfied with the assumptions of the classical perfect competition or wage theories, and they aim not so much at a reformulation of the old structure as at a bold attempt to build on more realistic foundations. But here the similarity between the different theories ends and we can distinguish two very different origins from which stem these new approaches to bargaining. On the one hand we have the interest in the theory of duopoly, bilateral monopoly, oligopoly, coupled with a recognition that questions of strategy, uncertainty, bluff, and so on, cannot be regarded as exogenous forces, but must on the contrary be treated as decisive causal factors. While most of this literature does not deal explicitly with wages (Neumann and Morgenstern, Brems, Shackle) [1] or deals with wages only as a special aspect of a wider problem (Zeuthen, Fellner),[2] there can be no doubt that its findings are highly pertinent to the bargaining processes in the labour market. We may call this group of theories, which try to throw light on the bargaining process as such in its most general form, 'psychological' theories.

From rather a different angle comes the other group of theories — predominantly American — which also accord to bargaining a central place in their theory, but are concerned specifically with the labour field and with the institutions observed there. These theories,

[1] John von Neumann and Oskar Morgenstern, *Theory of Games and Economic Behaviour* (1944) ; Hans Brems, *Product Equilibrium under Monopolistic Competition* (1951) ; G. L. S. Shackle, *Expectation in Economics* (1949).

[2] F. Zeuthen, *Problems of Monopoly and Economic Warfare* (1930) ; William Fellner, *Competition among the Few* (1949).

in all their variety (as examples we may quote the work of Bronfenbrenner, Slichter, Shister, Dunlop, Ross, Lester, Reynolds),[1] we may call 'institutional' theories, in contrast to the 'psychological' theories mentioned before.

Now, both these groups of theories show in one respect definite progress as compared with the theorems grouped under section I above. They take bargaining as their starting-point, or at least introduce it at an early stage, rather than 'explain it' into a theoretical structure hostile to bargaining. From this it follows that these theories aim in principle at determinate solutions in bargaining situations, whereas the older theories were usually content (and had to be content, because of the nature of the determinant forces in their basic structure) with pointing out indeterminate ranges within which bargaining could take place. The theories in this group are, therefore, true bargaining theories, and thus may be grouped together, in spite of their considerable differences.

But in spite of the ambitious endeavours incorporated in these theories, it is too early to say that a completely satisfactory basis has been found for the analysis and explanation of the process of wage determination under bargaining conditions. The very number of different theoretical models suggests that one is still groping for a powerful and relevant model. The whole subject is at present in a state of flux and it is obvious that it will take time until shortcomings are eliminated and syntheses found. It seems that progress must lie in finding some bridge between the 'psychological' and the 'institutional' theories, both of which are not completely satisfactory, but could probably supplement each other.

The 'psychological' theories have developed impressive models on a high level of abstraction, covering all processes of bargaining. To some extent this result could, however, only be achieved by cutting out many important elements and by concentrating the investigation on some very simple situations. More research will be needed in order to see how far the assumptions about human behaviour and 'rationality' underlying these theories are compatible with conditions in labour markets, and what additional assumptions and complications have to be introduced in order to make them serve more directly the needs of wage theory.

[1] M. Bronfenbrenner, 'The Economics of Collective Bargaining', *Quarterly Journal of Economics* (August 1939) ; S. H. Slichter, *Union Policies and Industrial Management* (1941) ; R. Lester and J. Shister, eds., *Insights into Labor Issues* (1947) ; John T. Dunlop, *Wage Determination under Trade Unions* (1944) ; Arthur M. Ross, 'The Dynamics of Wage Determination under Collective Bargaining', *American Economic Review* (December 1947) ; L. G. Reynolds, *The Structure of Labor Markets*.

The 'institutional' theories have of course the advantage of dealing explicitly with the labour market and its peculiarities. They are more 'cut to measure', can take into account special factors and less 'rational' attitudes. But this greater vicinity to the fullness of real life carries its own dangers. The step from description to theory (although description involves, of course, some rudimentary theory) becomes difficult and there may be undue hesitation to march on to higher levels of abstraction. One cannot help feeling that some of the work done in this field is still unnecessarily complicated and hampered by the use of inadequate theoretical tools and concepts. It will also be necessary to find out how far the results of these 'institutional' theories are conditioned by the special structure of the American labour and commodity markets, and how far they are applicable to all industrialized capitalist countries. (For underdeveloped and colonial countries a special theory would in any case be indicated.)

As has been said before, it is not at all unlikely that in the search for a realistic theory of wage bargaining the 'psychological' and 'institutional' theories can aid each other. As they develop, a closer relation may also be established to the imperfect competition doctrines of section I which could then become mainly a theory of the immediate framework for bargaining situations.[1]

III. Bargaining and the Share of Labour

When the theories mentioned in sections I and II have done everything in their power to elucidate local and industry-wide bargaining processes, a big question remains, namely, the macro-economic question as to the scope and limits of bargaining in relation to labour income as a whole and its share in the national income. This important question which greatly occupied the minds of the classical economists has not benefited much from the recent upsurge of interest in bargaining. In most textbooks on wages and labour it receives only scant attention.[2]

Treatment of this question can be carried out at different levels. And since it touches the most fundamental class interests, it is not

[1] If, as has been suggested (Charles E. Lindblom, 'Bargaining Power in Price and Wage Determination', *Quarterly Journal of Economics*, May 1948), bargaining power should be defined as the outcome of three sources, viz. (a) tastes and motives, (b) skill in persuasion and coercion, and (c) competition from other buyers and sellers, then the necessity of combining the theories from sections I and II becomes quite obvious.

[2] There are, of course, exceptions, as, for instance, Maurice Dobb, *Wages* (1946).

surprising that we shall find that we are quickly pushed into the sphere of sociology when we try to do justice to the problem.

One approach to this problem, the one which is already prominent in the writings of the classics and of Marx, starts from the 'real' side. How far can real wages *in toto* be expanded (or depressed)? The absolute upper and lower limits are easily enough established. For the continued existence of a stationary society they cannot permanently be pressed below the subsistence minimum (however defined) or above the net national product. But in a society which contains a capitalist class the upper limit will be lower. For a reduction in historically established capitalist incomes may lead to a reduction in their investment expenditure rather than in their consumption expenditure (assuming for the moment an uninterrupted circular flow). The lower the capitalists' marginal propensity to consume, the smaller will be the opportunity for pushing wages upward without causing a reduction in the stock of capital and thus undermining the basis for the higher wage bill. This case can be further developed by taking into account the possibility of a temporary reduction of investment expenditure by deliberate non-spending (causing unemployment), or the possibility of increasing the share of labour without making inroads into traditional capitalist consumption when we deal with an expanding rather than a stationary economy.[1] The upper limit for bargaining, minimum wage legislation, and the like, in a capitalist society will, therefore, be necessarily lower than the absolute limit, even if there is no unemployment. Unemployment will tend to reduce that limit still further.

With the widespread interest in full employment and in the stability conditions for full employment in an unplanned economy, more attention has been recently given to the macroscopic bargaining problem from a monetary angle. With the abolition of unemployment, a major check on the upward revision of the wage bill disappears. But if the monetary system is sufficiently elastic, does such a revision not simply lead to proportionate price rises so that all bargaining is necessarily self-defeating and leads to inflation? We cannot go here into the problems of costing, price and wage flexibilities, expectations and timing, which will determine when and to what extent bargaining can succeed under such circumstances. But a very important point arises here. Since higher wages are

[1] This discussion of bargaining possibilities is not contradictory to Kalecki's theory of the share of wages in the national income, which is shown to depend on raw material prices and the degree of monopoly. Every successful wage bargain, by reducing the gap between price and marginal cost, will lower the degree of monopoly and thus increase labour's share. See Michael Kalecki, *Essays in the Theory of Economic Fluctuations* (1939), pp. 13-41.

often passed on in higher prices under full employment conditions, trade unions have begun to realize that it may not be sufficient to press for higher wages, but that it may be necessary to supplement this demand by asking for price control measures, workers' control, and so on. That is, in order to achieve success in bargaining, the parties will not necessarily restrict themselves to the wage bargain proper but will demand such institutional changes as to make a success possible.

Now, if it is granted, as I think it should be, that such demands for price control have also to be regarded as part of the bargaining process and must not be left out of account when the scope or limits of bargaining under full employment are discussed, then there is no reason why we should not go further and view all the institutions and finally the economic system itself as variables in the bargaining process. If we do so, we shall see that many events which are usually regarded as completely outside the field of wage theory or even economics are of vital importance for an understanding of the basic positions from which the adversaries start that finer process of adjustment which is the subject of the theories mentioned in sections I and II.[1] Arguments for and against the sacred nature of private property, racial ideologies ('the negro has to be kept in his place'), fascist endeavours to undermine trade unions and the fight against these tendencies, the position of women in society, all this and many other social, political, and cultural phenomena, no matter in what disguise they may be presented, will have to be evaluated in any historical situation as class attempts to secure or change their bargaining position. If such an extension of bargaining theory seems fantastic to some traditional wage theorists, let them be reminded that it is not by chance that, in Europe at least, the growth of trade unionism has been very closely interlinked with the growth of the political labour movement and of cultural and educational institutions, not least because workers and trade unionists realize that they have to advance on the political and ideological field (universal voting, women's rights, socialism) if they are to be more successful at the bargaining table. Similarly we see in many countries that employers' associations extend, for identical reasons, their activities into the political and ideological sphere.[2] Once we are prepared to proceed from the analysis of isolated workers and employers to trade

[1] For an excellent juxtaposition of the limited explanative value of marginal productivity theory and the wider, sociological background against which it must be viewed, see E. Preiser, 'Erkenntniswert und Grenzen der Grenzproduktivitätslehre', *Schweizerische Zeitschrift für Volkswirtschaft und Statistik* (February 1953).

[2] See R. A. Brady, *Business as a System of Power* (1943).

unions and employers' associations, because these have proved to be of importance in the real world, then there is no reason why we should not go on and investigate the position and the actions of workers and employers, trade unions and employers' associations, outside the personnel office and the conference room, in so far as this has a bearing on the bargaining situation. This may make the theory still more complicated and less amenable to short-cut methods like geometry and algebra, but it will prevent us from looking merely for an explanation of the last five cents that were granted to some group without asking the very decisive question about the general starting-points.

This has been a very summary and incomplete review of bargaining theory, or rather of some of the theory relevant to the bargaining problem. The division of the theories into three groups has been somewhat arbitrary, and no doubt other more useful classifications can be devised. But it is hoped that the above remarks convey (1) that bargaining is at last receiving adequate attention in economic and wage theory, (2) that the concept and the process of wage bargaining are of a complex nature and can be fruitfully attacked from different angles, and (3) that it is now time for an advance on all fronts and a judicious combination of the results achieved.

Chapter 19

THE NATURE OF THE BARGAINING PROCESS

BY

G. L. S. SHACKLE
University of Liverpool, England

I. The Phenomena of Bargaining, a Hypothesis and Some Deductions

The observer of a bargaining process sees two parties who in turn suggests the details of a plan of action in which each is to have a part. The central type of such plans is the exchange of goods or services for money. The process ends when a plan is found to which each party will commit itself on condition that the other is also committed. To such an observer the following questions would inevitably arise :

(1) Why does each party repeatedly reject the plans suggested by the other ?
(2) On what principles does each party decide what kind and size of differences to make between one member and the next of its own series of plans ?
(3) What governs the length of time which elapses between a bid by one party and the next bid by the other ?
(4) Does each party determine the whole series of its own suggestions in advance or does it decide each step in the light of both parties' previous steps ?
(5) On what grounds does each party decide what kind of plan shall begin and what kind shall end its own series ?
(6) Why is the bargaining process sometimes abandoned without agreement ?
(7) Why does not each party reveal to the other the whole series of its plans from the start ?

These questions are framed from a deliberately naïve viewpoint in the hope that our description of the bargaining process may be based on assumptions about human nature and the human situation and not on preconceptions about the bargaining process itself.

If Brown deems a suggestion made by Smith less advantageous than something else that Smith could perhaps be brought to accept,

Brown will reject Smith's proposal. (The essential bargainer is of course both Brown and Smith by turns: our propositions must always be applied in both directions.) This possible answer to question (1) would require us to suppose:

(a) That Brown's purpose in bargaining is to bring the point at which the two parties ultimately shake hands as near to Brown's and as far from Smith's starting-point as he can, to make Smith exchange as much for as little as possible.

(b) Either that no bargainer considers it possible to know the unique plan which will ultimately be agreed on; or else, if he does consider this possible, he believes that actual agreement can only be secured by a step-by-step approach. (Smith would otherwise have made the 'right' suggestion at the outset.)

(c) That neither party takes it for granted that the other has disclosed the only plan to which he would agree.

This answer to question (1) implies that bargaining involves both uncertainty and attempts to deceive. Neither party knows at the outset what undertaking he can secure from the other in exchange for what promise of his own, but Smith is willing to try to mislead Brown about what Smith will in the last resort concede, if necessary, in exchange for specific gains. Deception is only possible because there is uncertainty, and thus these two characteristics of bargaining, uncertainty and the will to deceive, are bound together in the sense that we cannot have the latter without the former (the converse does not seem to be true). If we once grant that deception is a part of bargaining, we thereby grant that uncertainty is a part of it. These inferences further suggest part of the answers to questions (2) and (5). If the purpose of a step-by-step approach is to determine in both meanings of the word, that is, to select or create as well as to discover, the point of agreement, and if each party seeks to 'select' in accordance with his own interests by means of deception, each party will decide the size of each step in his series, and largely also perhaps the starting-point of his series, according to his view of what will best serve this purpose of influencing the other party's beliefs.

This assumed purpose would also in part explain delays by each party in responding to the other party's bids, referred to in question (3), and wholly answers question (7). The remaining questions (4), (5), and (6) are concerned with the ending of the bargaining process. This can evidently occur either by agreement or abandonment. Agreement is easily understandable. There can be a wide variety of plans, any one of which would make both parties better off than if they acted independently of each other ; the exchange, for example, which permits specialization is one of the central themes of economics. Does abandonment occur only when some interchange of bids has convinced both parties that no such range of plans can benefit both ? So long as Brown can see a series of possible plans each representing a further small concession to Smith combined with an advantage to Brown over what his situation will be in case no agreement is reached, why does not Brown continue to move along this series, and why does not Smith, having a similar incentive, move to meet him ? If in such circumstances either party ceases to move, the reason must be some *arrière-pensée* whose nature it is very important for us to investigate. In the nature of the case, the idea of such a mental reservation rests on a distinction between some limited context of a particular instance of bargaining, and a wider context of the general prospects of the bargainer in question. Might not the relevant prospects consist simply of anticipated future occasions of bargaining ?

We have thus made suggestions about questions (5) and (6). If each bargainer, as we have inferred, is uncertain how the other will respond to given suggestions, and these suggestions are intended by, say, Brown to influence the beliefs of Smith to Brown's greatest possible advantage, it seems evident that Brown will base each suggested plan on as much relevant knowledge as he can get, and this surely includes all Smith's suggestions up to date.

In answer to question (4) we must say that the bargainers do not predetermine the whole series of their bids. But it is still possible that a bargainer may predetermine his ultimate degree of worthwhile concession. He will not do so if he is interested only in the particular instance of bargaining, unless this is what we may call 'single-track' bargaining, concerned only with the selection of an agreed value of a single variable. For in single-track bargaining continuing steps of concession by Brown will ultimately carry the value of the single variable to a point beyond which Brown's situation would be worse than if no agreement was reached ; and there is by assumption no second track along which Smith's concessions in regard to a second variable could compensate a disadvantage accepted by Brown in regard to the first variable. Even in many-track bargaining the ultimate degree of concession, the 'end of the tether', may be decided in advance by a bargainer. For his mental reservations may concern the possible combined effect of his concessions of all kinds. If what he wishes to avoid is the very appearance of being one who easily gives concessions, then along every track he may perhaps place an ultimate stop.

Let me now try to summarize the picture of the bargaining process which our unprejudiced observer might build up from these observations, the questions which they prompt, and his inferences from a suggested answer to the first of these questions. For each bargainer the results of any instance (particular specimen) [1] of a bargaining process fall under two heads: those whose determination is the ostensible purpose of the bargaining and those which are unavoidable by-products. We can compare these two kinds of result to the momentum given to a bullet and the recoil of the gun. In conducting a process of bargaining the bargainer must plainly have regard to his total net advantage or disadvantage and this comprises all results of both kinds.

The task of a bargaining process is twofold: to secure some one of the various bundles of improvements in the combined situation of both bargainers, which are to be had by their taking agreed combined action instead of acting, not perhaps in disregard of each other, but without mutual engagement; and to determine the sharing-out between them of whatever bundle of improvements is selected. The bargaining process will either determine both parts of the matter simultaneously or will be abandoned. Each bargainer feels himself ignorant of the outcome until it is actually reached, but each believes that the outcome will be different according as he himself follows this or that detailed course of bargaining action.

Thus his problem is a particular type of the very general problem of choosing amongst courses of action, in uncertainty as to their respective outcomes. The distinctive features which specialize this type of the general problem are, first, that if one of the bargainers sought roughly to characterize or analyse the uncertainties facing him by means of a list of questions, these questions would be concerned largely with the other bargainer's feelings and knowledge: the subject-matter, so to speak, of the first bargainer's uncertainty would be rather concentrated, in contrast with the more various and comprehensive questions that might confront, for example, an investor, and this subject-matter would be the shape or contents of the other party's mind; secondly, the kind of action involved seeks the objective of maximum net advantage for one party largely by striving to limit and distort the other party's relevant knowledge; and thirdly, the by-products are relatively important and arise not simply from what is agreed upon by the two parties, but from the detailed character of the course of bargaining itself.

It follows that such by-products can accrue even in those cases

[1] In the language of John von Neumann and Oskar Morgenstern's *Theory of Games and Economic Behavior* (1944), any 'play'.

where the bargaining is ultimately abandoned without agreement. And it seems plain that each party's course of bargaining will be selected with an eye on these by-products. Through the first of these features, its dependence on deception, bargaining has one thing in common with war, games, crime, and judicial procedure. To classify it thus may be illuminating, for there is a great range of human activities where the desire to deceive plays no essential part. Such are all forms of artistic composition, literary, musical, or visual ; all forms of teaching ; all kinds of scientific investigation and geographical or geological exploration ; all engineering design ; all construction of abstract deductive systems. If, therefore, the question should arise whether bargaining is a desirable or permissible activity, one way of answering would be to point to the company it keeps, and if this condemns it, we should have to ask whether it may not nevertheless be indispensable, or at least the best way, all things considered, of arriving at some kinds of decision.

II. Questions to be Answered by a Theory of Bargaining

In constructing a theory or surveying the theories of others, a set of questions is needed to define the objective of such theories and provide a test of their adequacy. The following list of questions seems to express the purpose of a theory of bargaining :

1. (a) Is the outcome of a bargaining process in any sense determinate, and if so, in what sense ?
   (b) Is it sometimes determinate and sometimes not, and if so, in what circumstances is it determinate, what are the necessary and sufficient conditions of determinacy ?
   (c) Is the determinate solution ascertainable in principle otherwise than by the actual carrying through of the bargaining process, for example, by confidential questioning of both parties by a trusted third party ?
   (d) Are the conditions of determinacy likely to be realized in practice ? Or is there something in the nature of bargaining which implies that functions expressing the preferences and intentions of bargainers cannot be treated as stable and invariant throughout the bargaining process and under bargaining pressures ? Can the changes of such functions be predicted in advance of the bargaining so as to attain determinacy ?
2. In what circumstances will a bargaining process be terminated without agreement ? Are the consequences of such a breakdown likely to involve social costs or public injury beyond the private

injury or costs entailed to the bargaining parties ? If so, what are the remedies ?

3. (a) By what means can each party seek to give the ultimately agreed solution the character he desires ? Do these means consist in changing the other party's tastes or his beliefs ?
   (b) If bargaining involves attempts to change the other party's beliefs, does it for that reason involve deception ? If so, is bargaining condemned as a civilized and desirable method of reaching agreed decisions ?
   (c) What sorts of thing does each bargaining party try to conceal from the other, or what are the matters about which each party tries to influence the other's beliefs ?
   (d) What means does each party use in trying to alter or weaken, or to anchor more firmly, particular beliefs held by the other party ?
   (e) Is it useful to each bargaining party to render the other party's mental picture 'more uncertain' ? If Brown cannot confirm Smith in a particular belief which it would be in Brown's interest for Smith to hold, can Brown effect somewhat the same purpose by shaking Smith's faith in all sharply defined relevant beliefs ? (In other words, by widening the range of relevant hypotheses to which he attaches low potential surprise.)
4. In the case of 'many-track' bargaining (bargaining concerning many variables simultaneously) is it sometimes to the advantage of one bargainer to pretend to attach chief importance to one variable while really attaching more importance to another ?
5. In cases where the public is much affected by the outcome of the bargaining or suffers severely from its protraction, can it be made more likely that agreement will be reached or quickly reached either by confining the bargaining to one or few tracks, or by increasing the number of tracks ?
6. Where many variables are involved in an essentially unified context of bargaining, can the bargaining be usefully broken down into a series of separate processes each dealing with one variable ?
7. In many-track bargaining what aspect or factor is named by the word 'procedure', and what part does this play ?
8. Is there in bargaining any asymmetry, such that an advantage is enjoyed by the party to whom law, custom, or some inherent feature of the situation assigns the first move ? Or is such an advantage enjoyed by the 'seller' or by the 'buyer' ?

The weakness of a list of verbal questions for defining the task of a theory consists in its giving a series of discreet prods in one direction or another instead of a continuous push along the path of a resultant force. The questions unavoidably overlap each other and are partial substitutes ; the list can hardly in the nature of things be self-contained in any fundamental sense, for any question or any answer to it may suggest other questions, and there is no guarantee that these will eventually lead back into the nexus and provide us with a closed system where, given a few initial unproven propositions which seem realistic, all that we want to know can be deduced? Another person would produce a different set of questions and even these might be extended and modified. We will now see briefly how economists have tried to answer these questions.

III. The Bargaining Outcome: Indeterminate or Determinate?

'Contract without competition is indeterminate.'[1] Thus in 1881 Edgeworth absolved economists from trying to explain how in bilateral monopoly a price is ever fixed. The set of data which for Edgeworth, and for all those after him who discussed the problem in the following fifty years, left the price indeterminate consisted in the interests of the two bargainers, those interests which were directly, intimately, and unmistakably involved in some particular occasion of bargaining. A knowledge of these interests, however exact, would not enable a third party to deduce the price which would be finally agreed on, but would only enable him to name limits between which it must lie, one of these limits being a price which would leave Brown indifferent whether an agreement at that price were made or no agreement made, and the other being a price which would similarly affect Smith. In his brilliant article, 'A General Theory of Bargaining',[2] J. Pen gives the names of Böhm-Bawerk, Sir Arthur Bowley, A. M. Henderson, Marshall, Nichol, Pigou, Stackelberg, Stigler, and Tintner as having agreed that economic theory appeared to have nothing further to say. The interests of any economic agent depend, of course, upon his tastes and the precise inventory of his resources, and it is these which, from about 1870 onwards, economists have looked upon as the dominant influences on price. The prices of all goods could be deduced if we knew with sufficient detail, for each person in the market, the answers to the questions 'What does he like?' and 'What does he possess?' It did not occur to most of those who built the beautiful neoclassical structure of static value theory to put upon the same footing as those two questions a third kind of question: 'What does he know?' or 'What does he believe?' At

[1] F. Y. Edgeworth, *Mathematical Psychics*, original edition (1881), p. 20.
[2] *American Economic Review* (March 1952), p. 24.

first sight it is an astonishing paradox of the theory of bilateral monopoly that determinacy should be attainable only by assuming uncertainty in the minds of the bargainers and paying attention to its consequences.

The neoclassics had some intimations of this. Edgeworth quotes [1] from Jevons's *Theory of Political Economy* :

> Such a transaction [viz. in bilateral monopoly] must be settled upon other than strictly economical grounds. . . . The art of bargaining consists in the buyer ascertaining the lowest price at which the seller is willing to part with his object, without disclosing, if possible, the highest price which he, the buyer, is willing to give.

If Brown hopes to conceal something from Smith, he must be conscious of the possibility that Smith is perhaps concealing something from him, and if Brown has indeed this thought in mind, he is in a state of uncertainty. Would it not have been worth while for the neoclassics to follow up this clue ? In their view it would have meant arguing on 'other than strictly economical grounds'. This choice of location of the boundary of economics was evidently approved by Edgeworth, and in our own day Mr. Sraffa has expressed the view that the arts of bargaining and diplomacy are not subject-matter for economics. Plainly this is a matter of taste or of expediency. Yet how can it be expedient to draw the line where it cuts us off from determinate solutions of our problems ?

IV. Hicks's Theory of Bargaining Determinacy

Half a century went by before economists attempted any radical improvement on Edgeworth. Professor Zeuthen's *Problems of Monopoly and Economic Warfare* appeared in 1930 and Hicks's *The Theory of Wages* in 1932. Hicks argued thus : [2]

> We can construct a schedule of wages and lengths of strike, setting opposite to each period of stoppage the highest wage an employer will be willing to pay rather than endure a stoppage of that period. At this wage, the expected cost of the stoppage and the expected cost of concession (accumulated at the current rate of interest) just balance. At any lower wage, the employer would prefer to give in ; at any higher wage, he would prefer that a stoppage should take place. This we may call the 'employer's concession schedule.' . . . Now just as the expected period of

[1] F. Y. Edgeworth, *Mathematical Psychics*, p. 30.
[2] J. R. Hicks, *The Theory of Wages* (1932), pp. 141-144.

stoppage will govern the wage an employer is prepared to pay to avoid a strike, so the wage offered will govern the length of time the men are prepared to stand out. . . . So in their case, too, we can draw up a schedule, a 'resistance schedule', giving the

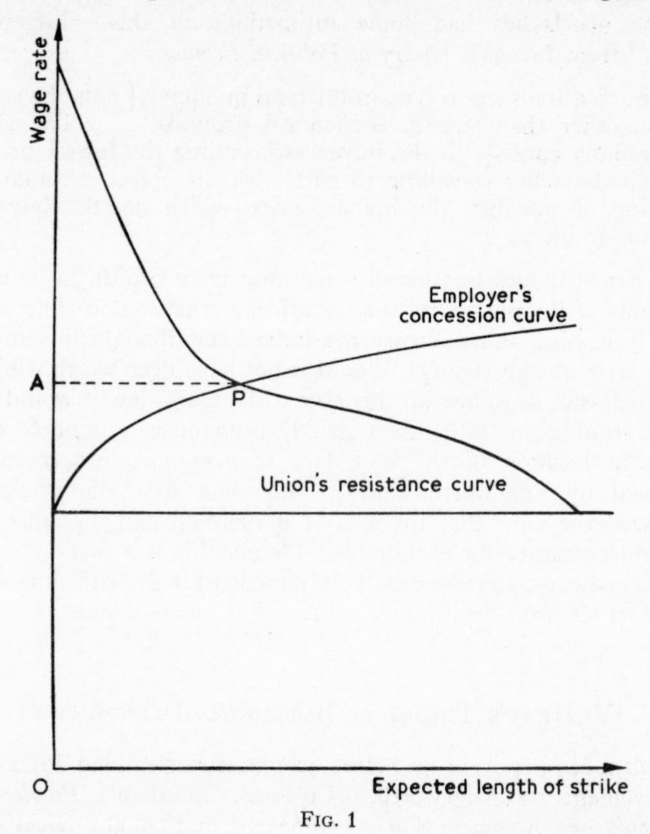

FIG. 1

length of time they would be willing to stand out rather than allow their remuneration to fall below the corresponding wage.

Hicks graphs these two schedules as in Fig. 1 and proceeds: 'The employer's concession curve and the Union's resistance curve will cut at a point P, and the wage OA corresponding to this point is the highest wage which skilful negotiation can extract from the employer'.

It is a question whether Professor Hicks would wish us to interpret this, as Pen does, as a claim that the outcome of the wage bargaining will be determinate at the rate OA. Pen says: [1]

[1] J. Pen, 'A General Theory of Bargaining', p. 25.

> [I] fail to see why the intersection determines anything. Hicks's reasoning is all about the limits of the contract zone, and explains nothing of what happens between these limits. At the intersection of the curves the contract zone is a single point, so there is no problem at all ; but this situation will only be realised by the merest chance. There are no forces compelling the bargainers to the Hicksian point.

We feel that this criticism is just. But the whole meaning of Professor Hicks's construction is very elusive. Part of the difficulty can perhaps be indirectly expressed by proposing a different construction. In Hicks's diagram the employer's concession curve has a positive slope because the wage rate the employer would agree to rather than suffer a strike of any given length is naturally an increasing function of that length, and the gradient decreases because there is some wage rate beyond which it would not pay the employer to continue in business at all. Can we not similarly argue that the longer the strike the trade union members are asked to contemplate, the higher must be the wage rate they hope to gain by it ? In that case what we can call the union's inducement curve will also have a positive slope. But this slope will surely increase in steepness from left to right, because the marginal disutility of the length of a strike will be increasing while the marginal utility of the wage will be decreasing. Thus we might arrive at a diagram like Fig. 2. Now if the union knew that the employer would refuse a wage rate greater than $y(x)$ even if he were certain that the result of refusal would be a strike of length x (if, that is to say, it knew the shape of the employer's concession curve) it would refrain from demanding any wage rate lying on that segment of its inducement curve $u = u(x)$ where $u(x) > y(x)$. Likewise, if the employer knew that the union would face a strike of length x for the sake of a wage rate of u, he would concede any u which was less than the corresponding y. Thus for any $u(x) < y(x)$ the employer would give way, for any $u(x) > y(x)$ he would refuse. If, then, the forms of the u and y functions were known to both parties and each party knew that the other knew them, agreement would presumably be reached at $y = u$, where $x = x_A$.

But an indispensable and indefensible assumption which underlies this result is, of course, the complete knowledge possessed by both parties. The main object of the employer would plainly be to conceal from the union the fact that the convincing threat of a strike of length x_A could exact from him an agreement to a wage rate y_A. On the contrary, he would try to make the union believe that the sure threat of a strike of any given length x would only induce him to concede a wage $y(x)$ less than the union's minimum inducement $u(x)$ for a strike of that length. For if he could succeed in that purpose he would suffer neither strike nor wage increase, and if he did not know this because he was ignorant or uncertain of the form of $u = u(x)$, nevertheless he might well conjecture something of the sort. The union, for its part, would seek to conceal from the

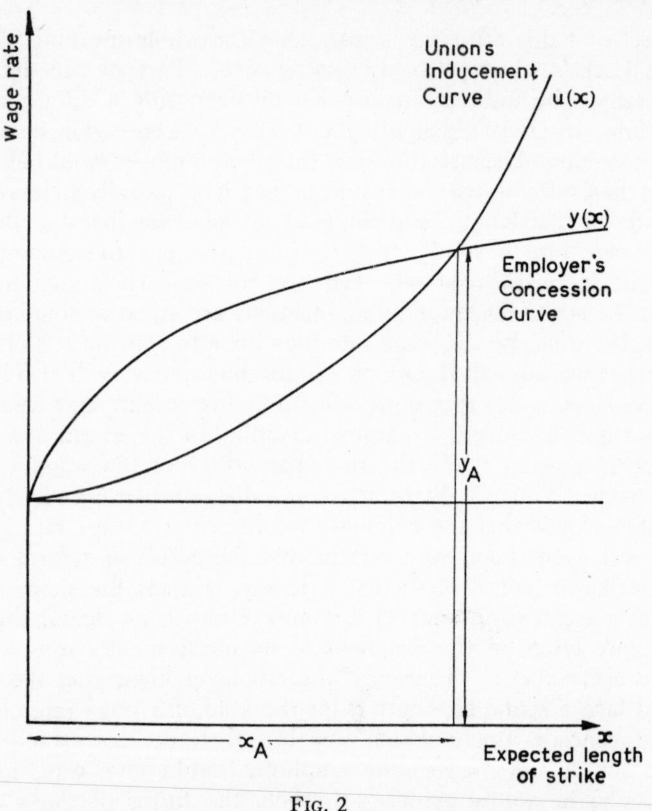

FIG. 2

employer the form of $u = u(x)$ and try to make him believe that, for example, a strike of length $x_B > x_A$ could be faced even in order to secure a wage y_A. For this might persuade him to concede a somewhat larger wage lying on his concession curve to the right of x_A. We must conclude, I think, that in Hicks's theory or in the alternative construction which I have just put forward, suggested by his and obtained from it by substituting my 'inducement curve' for his 'resistance curve', determinacy of the price is only secured at the sacrifice of the essence of bargaining, namely the interplay of threat, bluff, and deception, the endeavour to trade upon the adversary's uncertainty.

It may now well be asked whether we are justified in criticizing Professor Hicks on the basis of a greatly modified version of his theory. The truth is that it is difficult to proceed upon the basis of his own formulation, for there seems to be something very odd about his 'union's resistance curve'. It is hard to avoid the suspicion that Professor Hicks started out, in his quest for bargaining determinacy, with the idea at the back of his mind that he needed a Marshallian scissors diagram and that since the employer's concession curve must evidently have a positive slope it would be desirable for the other curve to have a negative slope. Having gone thus far it would be natural to seek a meaning for the other curve which would make it slope downwards to the right, as required for a guaranteed 'scissors' intersection. But why is a high wage claim associated with a long strike in the employer's mind and with a short strike in the union's mind ? The words 'concession' and 'resistance' convey a suggestion of some fundamental asymmetry, but they are a red herring. The employer and the union are engaged in a tug-of-war, each is resisting the other, either may be forced to 'concede'. The sham dynamic aura thrown out by these words must not be allowed to distract us.

Let us simply ask whether the union will be willing to contemplate a long strike in view or hope of a big wage concession or a small one, and the answer seems plain, a big concession. What, then, has gone wrong ? Briefly we suggest that with Professor Hicks's 'union's resistance curve' (but not with his employer's concession curve) length of strike should be represented, not by the abscissae but by the integrals of that curve in the vertical direction, starting from the horizontal line whose level (at y_0 in Fig. 3) stands for the existing wage. Treating this line in Fig. 3 as the horizontal axis, let us cut up the area enclosed by the curve and the two axes into narrow horizontal strips of uniform vertical width. Of these strips, the lowest, whose lower edge is the line at y_0, represents by its area the degree of resistance which the union would put up against a proposal to limit the wage increase to the small amount represented by the (vertical) width of this strip. The next strip, somewhat shorter and thus of smaller area, represents the extra effort the union would exert to have the concession pushed up to the amount represented by the combined (vertical) width of the two lowest strips ; and so on. Professor Hicks's 'union's resistance curve' is a marginal resistance curve, and its point of intersection with the employer's concession curve has no relevant meaning. Taking

y, the vertical variable measured from y_0, as the independent variable and renaming the horizontal variable as s let us write Hicks's 'union's resistance curve' as $s = s(y)$ and put $z = \int s(y)dy$ for its

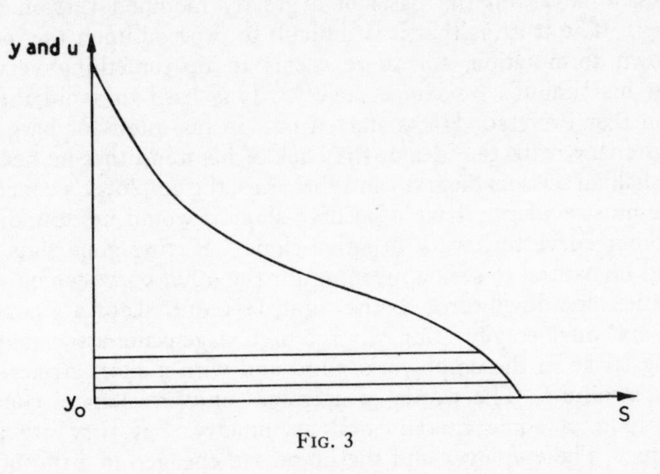

FIG. 3

integral. Then z will be another name for the 'length of strike' variable x and the function, say $y = f(z)$, connecting y and z will be the same, except for the constant $y = y_0$, as the union's inducement curve $u = u(x)$. If we assume the inverse of $s = s(y)$, say $y = F(s)$, to

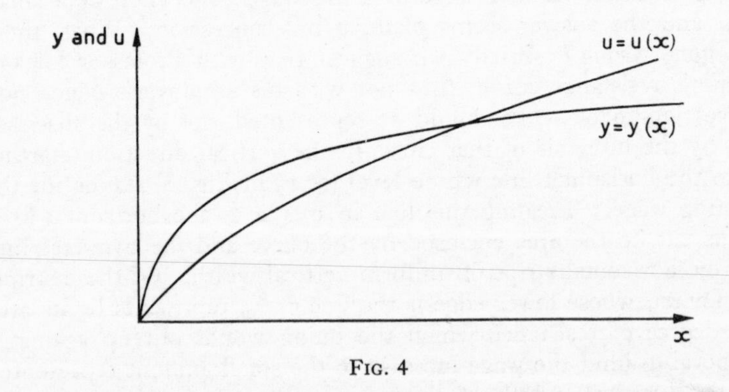

FIG. 4

have the sort of shape given by Professor Hicks in his diagram (our Fig. 1) to his union's resistance curve, then its integral curve $u = u(x)$ will have a slope very steep near $x = 0$ but rapidly decreasing and then becoming fairly uniform. Such a curve is shown in Fig. 4. This shape for the union's inducement curve differs from what we would suggest, and with this sort of slope the curve might or might not have a point of intersection, other than $x=0$, $y=y_0$, with the employer's concession curve. But if Professor Hicks had interpreted his union's resistance curve as a 'marginal' curve he might not have given it the shape he has. With the sort of shape given to the union's inducement curve $u=u(x)$ in Fig. 2 a satisfactory intersection with the employer's concession curve $y=y(x)$ is almost guaranteed.

V. Zeuthen's Theory of Bargaining Determinacy

Professor Hicks's theory, or our alternative version of it, stands in a sort of no-man's-land marking the boundary, both logical and chronological, between the territory of orthodox theories which declare the price in bilateral monopoly to be indeterminate, and that of theories which make the price determinate by invoking the consequences of uncertainty. The Hicks type of theory can maintain determinacy only by assuming away any elbow-room for bargaining. It stands in the sharpest contrast with 'uncertainty' theories, for it assumes that the two bargainers know each other's thoughts and preferences precisely. We pass now to the uncertainty theories, and when we cross the frontier on to this ground the first name is that of Professor Zeuthen.[1]

In the article cited above, Pen summarizes as follows the argument put forward by Professor Zeuthen in 1930 : [2]

> At each step in the bargaining process the bargainer must compare the possible advantages and disadvantages. The advantages consist in the attainment of a more favourable price. The disadvantages consist in the possibilities of a conflict. The decisive factors in a bargainer's choice are not only the magnitude

[1] My first acquaintance with the work of Professor F. Zeuthen on the subject of bargaining and bilateral monopoly was obtained through reading the article here cited by J. Pen, and until I had completed my paper as it stands I had never read any of Professor Zeuthen's own words on this subject, and, in particular, I had never seen his book on *Problems of Monopoly and Economic Warfare*, published in 1930 and now out of print. Professor Zeuthen himself was not able to supply me with a copy of his book (and this disturbed me the more because I have heard it spoken of in terms of the highest praise) but he has now very kindly lent me the manuscript of chapter 57 of his *Economic Theory and Method* (1955), and from this it is even more evident than from Mr. Pen's article that Professor Zeuthen has the distinction of having emphasized as early as 1930 that uncertainty is an essential element of bargaining and that, when we recognize this and analyse its consequences as part of the problem, the bargaining outcome becomes determinate. When writing my chapter on this subject in 1948 (*Expectation in Economics*, 1949), I knew nothing of Professor Zeuthen's long priority in pointing these things out, and hence my omission there of any reference to his work.

[2] F. Zeuthen, *Problems of Monopoly and Economic Warfare* (1930), chapter on 'Economic Warfare'.

> of these advantages and disadvantages, but also the bargainer's estimation of their possibility. The latter expectation, designated as the risk of a conflict, is the central factor in Zeuthen's theory.

Professor Zeuthen [1] considers a trade union whose only object is to make the total wage bill of its members as large as possible and which assumes that the elasticity of demand for labour is zero. At each stage of the negotiation the trade union leaders ask themselves whether it is better to agree on a wage p or to press for a somewhat higher wage p_n at a risk r of precipitating a conflict, that is, a breakdown of the negotiation wherein the N employed members of the union would have a total income of only S_c instead of the income of pN which could be secured by agreeing to a wage p. Then by insisting on p_n the trade union stands to gain $N(p_n - p)$, while it stands to lose $pN - S_c$. The trade union will insist on the higher wage p_n so long as

$$(1 - r)(Np_n - Np) > r(Np - S_c).$$

The greatest value of r at which the trade union would still consider it just worth while to press forward is that value, written by Zeuthen r_{max}, which would make the two sides of the formula equal, and we have

$$r_{max} = \frac{Np_n - Np}{Np_n - S_c}.$$

Zeuthen considers that for the trade union r_{max} will be a decreasing function of p, while for the employer, for whom an exactly parallel formula can be written, it will be an increasing function. There will therefore be some p at which r_{max} is the same value of r for both parties, and Zeuthen believes that at this level of p agreement will be reached. Pen sums the conclusion up as follows: 'The outcome of the bargaining is, according to Zeuthen, determined by the equality of the mutual risk of a conflict that the parties dare to accept, and the maximum risk of a conflict that a bargainer will accept equals the quotient of his possible gain and his possible loss'. Pen points out, however, that there appears to be no reason why 'a bargainer should submit at the moment his adversary accepts the same maximum risk as he does', and accordingly declares that Professor Zeuthen's solution is unacceptable as it stands. However, Pen believes that a real solution is to be found along the path on which Professor Zeuthen has taken the first steps, and he accordingly builds a theory of his own on the basis thus suggested.

[1] In what follows I have slightly reformulated Professor Zeuthen's argument with an altered notation.

VI. Pen's Theory of Bargaining Determinacy

Pen assumes that any specified price p which might be agreed on between a buyer and a seller would give to the seller a certain ophelimity $S(p)$ and to the buyer a certain ophelimity $B(p)$, and that for each party all the factors or influences which affect the degree of his own satisfaction that he associates with each price are subsumed in the shape of his ophelimity function. In particular, the seller Smith will estimate what quantity the buyer Brown will buy at each price p and Smith will consequently have in mind some particular level of p up to which Smith's profit is an increasing function of p and beyond which, because of Brown's decreasing demand, Smith's profit will be a decreasing function of p. Similarly Brown will estimate the quantities that Smith will supply at each p and will have in mind some p below which these will decrease so rapidly with decrease of p as to outweigh the advantage to Brown of cheapness. Thus Pen argues that the seller's ophelimity function $S(p)$, though no doubt affected by other considerations besides profit, will have a unique maximum at some price p_s and that the buyer's ophelimity function $B(p)$ will have a unique maximum at some other price p_b.

Besides the degree of ophelimity $S(p_s)$ which is the greatest the bargaining process can afford him even if he is wholly successful in it, the seller will have in mind another degree of ophelimity specially important to him, namely that degree, positive, zero, or negative, which he would experience in case of 'conflict', that is, a breakdown or abandonment of the negotiation without agreement. This degree Mr. Pen calls the seller's 'conflict ophelimity' S_c. The buyer will similarly have his own conflict ophelimity B_c. Now Pen supposes (so we interpret him although he does not say so explicitly) that at any moment of the negotiation some particular price p is, as it were, the immediate, temporary basis or focus of discussion. At any such moment, then, the seller has the choice between agreeing to this price p and thus securing an ophelimity $S(p)$ instead of the inferior ophelimity S_c, thus avoiding a loss of ophelimity $S(p) - S_c$ which he would suffer in case of a conflict, or of holding out for the price p_s which will give him his greatest possible ophelimity $S(p_s)$. If he takes this second course he risks a conflict for the sake of a possible improvement $S(p_s) - S(p)$ as compared with the ophelimity he could make certain of by immediate agreement on the price p. Further, the seller will have in mind some number r such that $0 \leq r \leq 1$, which will express his estimate of the risk or probability of a conflict in case he rejects any particular price p. If the seller has 'neutral risk valuation' he will then decide to reject any p such that

$$(1-r)[S(p_s)-S(p)]>r[S(p)-S_c].$$

As p increases from a level below p_s, $S(p)$ will increase and r will increase, so that eventually p will reach a level where

$$(1-r)[S(p_s)-S(p)]=r[S(p)-S_c],$$

so that

$$\frac{1-r}{r}=\frac{S(p)-S_c}{S(p_s)-S(p)},$$

or

$$\frac{1}{r}=\frac{S(p)-S_c+S(p_s)-S(p)}{S(p_s)-S(p)}$$

$$=\frac{S(p_s)-S_c}{S(p_s)-S(p)}$$

and

$$r=\frac{S(p_s)-S(p)}{S(p_s)-S_c}.$$

If p reaches this level, the seller will be willing to agree upon it rather than seek to push it higher still. This conclusion is of course only a stage in the complete theory of how the price will be determined, for we have still to consider the buyer. But first Pen seeks to indicate how the seller assigns some particular numerical value to r, and here his argument is a little less clear and illuminating than elsewhere. He writes r, to which of course the seller can only give a numerical value by his own process of thought and estimation on the basis of such knowledge as he can gather, as a function (called, following Schumpeter, the correspection function) $r_s=F_s[B(p)-B_c]$ of the buyer's net contract ophelimity $B(p)-B_c$, that is, the amount by which the buyer's ophelimity in case the price p is agreed on would exceed the ophelimity he would have if the negotiation were abandoned.

Now from one point of view this seems to me to make a true suggestion : for the meaning which Pen has given to the ophelimity functions implies that the buyer will not in fact permit, if he can help it, a conflict (abandonment of negotiation) to occur at any price less than that which makes $B(p)-B_c=0$, and so it is this price, the limit of the contract zone, which the seller really wants to know. If the seller does feel that he knows for certain the exact limits of the contract zone, he will put $r=0$ for any price within this zone.

But from another point of view it seems misleading to write the seller's estimate of r as a function of a price which it is the buyer's chief concern to conceal from him. Pen should have introduced a new symbol to stand for the seller's conjecture of the price which makes $B(p) - B_c = 0$. Introducing the seller's risk valuation coefficient, say Y_s, Pen finally writes, as the condition for the seller to agree to a price p, the equation

$$Y_s \frac{S(p_s) - S(p)}{S(p_s) - S_c} - F_s[B(p) - B_c] = 0.$$

For agreement to be actually reached, an exactly parallel equation for the buyer,

$$Y_b \frac{B(p_b) - B(p)}{B(p_b) - B_c} - F_b[S(p) - S_c] = 0$$

must simultaneously be satisfied. The bargaining process consists in the efforts made by either party to shift one or several of the four elements, namely, the risk valuation function, the ophelimity function, the conflict ophelimity, and the correspection function, which make up the other party's position, and Mr. Pen's argument implies that, provided the price which reduces to zero the buyer's net contract ophelimity $B(p) - B_c$ is greater than that which reduces to zero the seller's net contract ophelimity $S(p) - S_c$, those efforts will continue until agreement is reached at some price within the contract zone thus defined. This price will be determinate in the sense that it will have to satisfy a pair of equations of the kind described above.

This is evidently a different sort of determinacy from that which economists from Edgeworth onwards who have discussed the problem of bilateral monopoly have had in mind when they asserted that the price would in such circumstances be indeterminate. For the essence of Mr. Pen's theory is that the whole nature of the bargaining process consists in an endeavour of each party to change the form of the functions, or the critical values of variables, which compose the other party's position. Can we meaningfully say that a variable is determinate whose value depends on functions which, as part of the very essence of the matter, are changed as the process of determination goes on ?

Pen's theory is one of the most brilliant and most beautiful pieces of theoretical analysis that has been produced in many years past. He makes generous acknowledgments, in particular to Professor Zeuthen ; but those who have influenced his construction in any special and important way are very few indeed. As a result of his masterly forward stride we now have a theory of bilateral monopoly which can stand comparison with those of perfect or of monopolistic competition.

VII. A Criticism of Pen's Theory

There is only one respect in which we do not feel that Pen's theory is satisfactory beyond all reasonable cavil. He concludes that provided the price at which the buyer's net contract ophelimity vanishes is greater than that which annihilates the seller's net contract ophelimity, agreement at some price within the contract zone thus delimited is sure to be attained. In this matter his results, and those of the writer's own attempt at a theory of the bargaining process,[1] are in collision. I expressed the motive which might lead a bargainer to break off a negotiation even within the contract zone as fear of 'loss of face' through retreating a long way from his initial claim, and the consequent injury to his bargaining power in future. In Pen's theory such a consideration is supposed to influence the shape of the ophelimity functions and be taken account of thus, leaving a 'pure' contract zone free, by definition, from the possibility of breakdown. Pen says:[2] 'Apart from the sober profit figures there may, even in the case of bargaining business men, be psychological factors behind the ophelimity functions. . . . Sometimes [such a factor] becomes apparent . . . when the bargainer is forced away from a price he has heavily insisted upon, and he fears to "lose face". In this case the ophelimity function may show a sharp peak at the price that was claimed before.' Here I think there are three points to be made. The first is the minor one that considerations of profit, that is, profit in future negotiations, is surely a large part of the reason for caring about 'loss of face'. But the main question concerns the meaning of the ophelimity functions. Pen would argue that the shapes of these, and in particular the location of their respective maxima, will be such that there is no room for such a large total concession, by one party or the other, as to cause him 'loss of face'. Now we have to remember that it is an essential feature of Pen's theory that the shapes of the ophelimity functions are altered in the course of the bargaining process, and the question arises whether it is at the beginning, when the bargainers make their intitial claims or take up their initial attitudes, that the contract zone is supposed to be already narrow enough to guard against loss of face to either party, or is it after the shapes have undergone some

[1] *Expectation in Economics* (1949), ch. vi.
[2] J. Pen, 'A General Theory of Bargaining', p. 28.

modification in the course of bargaining? If the former, we must ask how each bargainer can have any idea, especially in advance of hearing the other bargainer's initial 'bid', how wide the contract zone is. Does avoidance of breakdown depend on the bargainer who has 'second move' and hears the very first bid of all made by the other before he says anything himself, so that he can set his own aim near enough to the other's to avoid any 'loss of face' of his own?

There are two things to be said about this suggestion. First, we must notice that it assumes an asymmetry in the bargaining process. The whole contract zone might on this hypothesis be shifted, at the very outset, in favour of the bargainer who first announces a price. Such an asymmetry, I think, may well be a realistic feature but it has been ignored by all writers except those who have approached from the viewpoint of the theory of games. To assume such an asymmetry would introduce a new source of indeterminacy unless we suggest some principle by which one bargainer, say the seller, is always selected as the first announcer of a price. Second, there seems to me a more fundamental objection. What reason have we to suppose that the profit to be gained by either party by securing agreement in this particular instance of bargaining must necessarily be sufficient to outweigh considerations of loss of bargaining power, 'loss of face', in future negotiations?

Let us turn to the other possibility, that the contract zone is gradually narrowed down by the process of bargaining itself so that the danger of breakdown is avoided. If this is the explanation, then it must be pointed out that when either bargainer allows himself to be persuaded to alter the price at which his own ophelimity function has a maximum, he is in effect making a concession, which if he has already announced a price based on the earlier position of his maximum, he will be known by the other party to have made, so that such a shifting of his ophelimity maximum will involve 'loss of face' and may therefore be impossible. We think, therefore, that unless we consider each particular instance of a bargaining process to be conducted without thought of future instances, we cannot give to the ophelimity functions all the meaning which Pen gives to them.

VIII. Bargaining Analysed in Terms of Focus Values

In my own attempt at a theory of bargaining, I supposed the seller to be concerned with the following prices:

m his absolute minimum price to accept which would leave him neither better nor worse off than to abandon the negotiation.

g his initial asking price.
j his effective minimum price, the least price permitted by some chosen policy.
v the price, unknown to either party until the completion of bargaining, which may ultimately be agreed on.

Three policies are open to him. The 'possible breakdown' policy consists in such a choice of g and j that even if he concedes the whole difference between them he will not 'lose face' and be handicapped on subsequent occasions of bargaining. The 'possible loss of face' policy consists in resolving to descend from some chosen g whatever distance $g - v$, not greater than $g - m$, may be necessary to secure agreement. The 'combined' policy involves accepting the possibility of some loss of face but also in setting some $j > m$ as the limit of his descent.

A bargaining plan consists in a pair of values of g and j chosen together as an entity. The respective outcomes of various bargaining plans are unknown, and the bargainer will determine for each plan that he has in mind a focus gain and a focus loss. For any plan under the 'possible breakdown' policy the primary focus gain will be that hypothetical value of $x = v - m$ whose combination of numerical size and of associated potential surprise makes it the most stimulating of the whole range of such hypotheses for which potential surprise is less than the absolute maximum. The primary focus loss of any plan under the 'possible breakdown' policy will be the sacrifice of the best hope he could have entertained under the 'possible loss of face' policy. For any plan under the 'possible loss of face' policy the relevant hypotheses will not be those concerning the gross gain $s = v - m$ but those concerning the net gain $x = s - z$, where z stands for the bargainer's estimate of the time-discounted cash value of the injury he will suffer in future bargaining through the loss of face entailed by his present plan. Since x can thus be either positive or negative, any plan under the 'possible loss of face' policy will have one value of x standing for the primary focus gain of this plan and another value of x standing for its primary focus loss. As the final step in choosing amongst bargaining plans, the bargainer may be supposed to go through a mental process which can be represented by his plotting on a 'gambler indifference map', for each plan, a point whose co-ordinates are the standardized focus gain and the standardized focus loss of the plan, and adopting the one which lies on the higher indifference curve.

The buyer can be supposed, *mutatis mutandis*, to choose his initial bargaining plan in the same way as the seller. The bargaining process consists in a confrontation of the two initial plans, and the following out of his plan by, say, Smith, until some bid by Brown adds to or alters Smith's conception of what was in Brown's mind. Smith will then make a revised plan ; and so on. In my book I concluded the analysis, of which the foregoing is a brief sketch, with the following passage :

> By taking account of the bargainer's attitude to uncertainty, that is, by assuming him to have a given preference system for various gambling situations as these are assessed in his own mind in terms of focus-values, we find, first, that it is by no means certain that agreement will be reached even when the seller's absolute minimum price is below the buyer's absolute maximum price ; and secondly, that if exchange does take place, the price, in an important sense, is determinate : it is conceptually knowable in advance, if we are fully informed about the gambler-preference system of each bargainer, and the functions according to which he will draw inferences from a given sequence of 'asking prices' or 'offered prices' announced by the other bargainer.

Let us turn back briefly to our list of questions. In answer to questions 1 (a) and (b) there is no real disagreement between the pre-Zeuthenites and the post-Zeuthenites,[1] except that Professor Hicks stands somewhat apart from both. If our data are restricted to the bargainer's interests in the one particular instance of bargaining, considered in isolation, the price in bilateral monopoly is indeterminate. If we have full knowledge of the parties' expectations and the working rules or functions by which they revise their expectations in the light of fresh data, and of their gambler preferences, the outcome of a bargaining process is in principle determinate. In practice determinacy surely cannot mean that the outcome, except in special cases, could be predicted by a third party, however well informed, in advance of the bargaining, as in question 1 (c). Question 1 (d) can now be seen as requiring a distinction between a special meaning of 'determinacy', or that which calls for stable functions expressing the preferences and intentions of bargainers, and the more general meaning of 'predictable in principle'. Pen's theory implies that in the former sense the bargaining outcome is indeterminate, in the latter sense determinate. On question 2 my own analysis suggests that it is where the negotiation is seen as one of a long or endless series of similar negotiations which will be carried on in the future, that fear of future disadvantage through present 'loss of face' is most likely to lead to breakdown. In the context of wage disputes this may indeed mean much public injury through

[1] This is a doctrinal rather than a chronological classification : a pre-Zeuthenite attitude is still taken by some writers.

prolonged strikes, and a remedy is a pressing need. Pen compresses both tastes and beliefs into the bargainer's ophelimity function, and in answer to question 3 (a) he would say that each bargainer seeks to influence or control both the tastes and the beliefs of the other. To try to influence a person's beliefs does not in the abstract or in general imply deception, but in bargaining it plainly may do so. If deception is bad, bargaining is bad.

It is impossible without further extending this chapter to endeavour to link the foregoing survey with the remaining, more specialized questions in our list. The character of that list as a whole seems to suggest why economic theory has been so slow in coming to grips with the problem of bargaining. Perhaps this discussion has served to indicate that an adequate theory of bargaining requires us to study psychological questions which many economists even today regard as outside the proper scope of economics.

PART VI

LABOUR MARKET AND LABOUR SUPPLY

Chapter 20

LABOUR MARKET THEORY AND EMPIRICAL RESEARCH

BY

CHARLES A. MYERS
Massachusetts Institute of Technology, U.S.A.

I. The Theoretical Model

Economic theory provides a model of the operation of the labour market which helps to explain wage differentials and the allocation of labour between employers, occupations, industries, and regions as the market tends to move toward equilibrium. Marshall, for example, pointed to the 'tendency' of competition to result in 'equality of efficiency-earnings in the same district', and he added : [1]

> This tendency will be the stronger, the greater is the mobility of labour, the less strictly specialized it is, the more keenly parents are on the look-out for the most advantageous occupations for their children, the more rapidly they are able to adapt themselves to changes in economic conditions, and lastly the slower and the less violent these changes are.

The supply price of labour in any occupation is not money earnings alone, but 'net advantages', for 'We must take into account of the facts that one trade is healthier or cleanlier than another, that it is carried on in a more wholesome or pleasant locality, or that it involves a better social position. . . .' (p. 557). Marshall, however, did not assume that competition in the labour market was perfect, and he chided 'the older economists', who must have known better, for seeming to imply this assumption (p. 540). Cairnes, with his 'non-competing groups', was perhaps an exception.[2]

Later, Hicks in *The Theory of Wages* (1932) analysed with great insight [3] the operation of labour markets, as distinct from product markets. 'When the economists of the late nineteenth century wished to concentrate their attention on the imperfections of the labour market caused by costs of movement,' he said, 'they usually contented themselves with the analysis of one special case, where

[1] Alfred Marshall, *Principles of Economics*, 8th ed. (1930), p. 549.
[2] J. E. Cairnes, *Some Leading Principles of Political Economy* (1874), p. 72.
[3] See ch. iv, 'The Working of Competition'.

costs of movement are sufficient to shut out competition over a considerable range' (pp. 60-61). But there are also imperfections in the 'regular labour market'. If there is an increase in the demand for a particular class of labour, this need not force up wages if there are unemployed workers. He added :

> Probably the normal process is for an expanding firm to seek labour through the usual channels, telling foremen to tell their friends, and such haphazard methods, by advertisement, or (nowadays) through Labour Exchanges. At first it will not be difficult to get men of reasonably good quality, but after a time the supply at the old rates will dry up. At this point the expanding firm may take the initiative in offering higher rates, but more probably applicants for work, realizing the market is now getting tight, will demand higher rates. Indeed, the applicants may very well prove to be men who already have a job, but are willing to move if it is made worth their while. In one or other of these ways the wages paid by an expanding firm must ultimately rise (pp. 72-73).

The transmission of the increase throughout the industry is a slow process, however, and 'there can be little question that this slowness is largely responsible for those local differences in wages which present a picture of such bewildering complexity in many trades' (p. 74).

But Hicks concludes :

> The movement of labour from place to place is insufficient to iron out local differences in wages. But the movement does occur, and recent researches are indicating more and more clearly that differences in net economic advantages, chiefly differences in wages, are the main causes of migration. The labour market is not a perfect market ; the equalizing forces do not act quickly and easily, but they nevertheless do act [p. 76]. . . . Potential mobility is the ultimate sanction for the interrelation of wage-rates' [p. 79].

Despite the imperfections, therefore, the link between labour mobility and wage determination was reaffirmed.

II. Empirical Studies in the United States

As sometimes happens in economics, the qualifications made by Marshall, Hicks, and others in the concept of the labour market tended to be forgotten (or assumed and then forgotten) in subsequent refinements of the models and expecially in their textbook presentations. While it is difficult to cite chapter and verse to support this view, the impression was fairly widespread among labour economists in the United States a decade or so ago that economic theory made assumptions about the operation of the labour market which were not realistic. This led to a burst of empirical studies of labour mobility, particularly in various local labour markets, during the period roughly from 1936 to 1950.[1]

Among the university research groups active in these studies were the University of Pennsylvania, the University of Minnesota, Yale University, and the Massachusetts Institute of Technology. The research objectives of these studies differed somewhat, although the Yale and M.I.T. projects were more closely related so that findings could be additive. Some co-ordination was also achieved through the Committee on Labor Market Research of the Social Science Research Council, which was later responsible for initiating a large-scale survey of labour mobility in six cities for the period 1940–1950, with the co-operation of many of the university research centres which had conducted the earlier local labour market studies. Dr. Gladys L. Palmer of the University of Pennsylvania gave general direction to the six-city study, and her summary report of the entire project will be drawn upon heavily in this chapter.[2]

[1] Gladys L. Palmer and Ada M. Stoflet, *The Labor Force of the Philadelphia Radio Industry in 1936*; Helen Herrmann, *Ten Years of Work Experience of Philadelphia Weavers and Loomfixers* (all WPA National Research Project reports done in co-operation with the Industrial Research Department, University of Pennsylvania, Philadelphia, 1938); Herbert G. Heneman, Jr., 'Differential Short-Run Labor Mobilities' (1941–1942), in *Minnesota Manpower Mobilities* (October 1950); Lloyd G. Reynolds, *The Structure of Labor Markets* (1951); Charles A. Myers and W. Rupert Maclaurin, *The Movement of Factory Workers* (1943); and Charles A. Myers and George P. Shultz, *The Dynamics of a Labor Market* (1951); Richard A. Lester, *Hiring Practices and Labor Competition* (1954).

Other empirical studies of labour markets are continuing at Princeton University (under the direction of Professor Richard A. Lester) on the Trenton, New Jersey, labour market; and at the University of California (Berkeley), where Professor F. T. Malm is completing reports on employer policies in the Oakland labour market.

[2] Gladys L. Palmer, *Labor Mobility in Six Cities: A Report on the Survey of Patterns and Factors in Labor Mobility, 1940–1950* (June 1954).

The six cities and the university centres making the analyses were: Philadelphia (University of Pennsylvania); New Haven (Yale University); Chicago (University of Chicago); St. Paul (University of Minnesota); Los Angeles and San Francisco (University of California at Los Angeles and Berkeley). A separate study of patterns of mobility among skilled workers in the six cities was made by the Industrial Relations Section at the Massachusetts Institute of Technology. All initial reports from the seven university centres were mimeographed, and were prepared during the latter part of 1951 and early 1952.

The work history samples were developed as follows: approximately 1900 households were selected in each city, and all workers in these households who were 25 years of age or over in 1951 and had worked one month or more in 1950 were interviewed by trained interviewers under the direction of the United States Bureau of the Census. The exclusion of workers under 25 in 1951 was made to secure a sample which had the same potential exposure to the labour market during the preceding decade. The final sample was considered to represent approximately 3,483,000 workers who met these specifications in the six cities.

The earlier local labour market studies were essentially interested in the following questions : (1) How do workers find their first and subsequent jobs ? (2) How large is the mobile group which voluntarily shifts from job to job ? (3) What do these workers know about alternative job opportunities ? (4) What are the characteristics of the workers who move voluntarily as compared with those forced to move by lay-off or discharge ? (5) Are there patterns of labour mobility between certain occupations, or industries, or sections within the local labour market ? and (6) Does movement tend to reduce or eliminate differentials in earnings for comparable jobs ?

While it is difficult to summarize briefly all these studies,[1] a pattern of labour market behaviour did emerge from the interviews with samples of employed and unemployed workers, and from the study of their wage and employment histories :

(1) Young people seeking their first job and workers looking for new jobs seldom make a systematic search of available job opportunities. They usually take the first job offered. They hear of jobs most frequently through friends and relatives employed in the plant, or through random and haphazard visits to plant employment offices. The public employment service is frequently a last resort for workers unable to find jobs in other ways and for employers with jobs remaining unfilled through other recruitment channels.

(2) Between two-thirds and three-fourths of employed workers remain with their employer throughout a year or even a longer period. Thus, the majority of employed workers are not really in the labour market in the sense that they are looking for better opportunities elsewhere. In periods of unemployment the proportion changing jobs voluntarily is considerably less than one-fourth or one-third.

(3) Workers who leave one job voluntarily for another do not usually have another job offer in mind. They may leave in the expectation that they can find a better job, but their knowledge of available alternatives is apt to be sketchy and their search haphazard. If there is any 'shopping around' for jobs, it comes through this sort of job shifting early in the

[1] For an interpretative summary, see George P. Shultz, 'Recent Research on Labor Mobility', *Proceedings of the Fourth Annual Meeting of the Industrial Relations Research Association* (December 28–29, 1951), pp. 110-118. A longer analysis of mobility studies will be found in the report by Herbert S. Parnes, *Research on Labor Mobility: An Appraisal of Research Findings in the United States*, Bulletin 65, Social Science Research Council (September 1954). Essays on the significance of some of the local labour market studies, written by members of the Committee on Labor Market Research, are found in *Labor Mobility and Economic Opportunity* (1954).

worker's career, rather than through the careful weighing of alternatives available at the moment.

(4) Workers who move voluntarily for other jobs tend to be young, unmarried, short-service workers, frequently women, as compared to those who stay on the job or are forced to move by lay-offs.

(5) When workers do move, they tend to make industrial shifts more frequently than occupational shifts, although this varies with the character and diversification of the local labour market. In a textile city, for example, employer shifts without change in industry or occupation may predominate. In other communities there may be relatively more movement within submarkets of comparable firms, or between geographically adjacent firms in dissimilar industries.

(6) The voluntary movement which occurs does not seem to equalize the 'net advantages' of different jobs. The well-paying jobs are frequently also in firms where other job conditions are also superior, and the ability of workers to move from poorer jobs to better jobs is often limited by employer agreements not to 'pirate' labour, union seniority rules, promotion from within policies, and restrictive employer hiring policies. These limitations tend to weaken, however, during periods of extreme labour shortage.

The over-all impression of local labour markets which emerges from these studies, then, is one of considerable haphazard and apparently purposeless movement, many imperfections, and a weak link between mobility and the equalization of net advantages in different jobs. Most movement appears to be induced by the decline in job opportunities in one plant (or occupation, industry, or region) and the availability or expansion of job opportunities in another, rather than by wage differentials as such.[1]

The worker's view of the labour market, emerging from the open-end interviews, is largely one of limited job opportunities. If he is already employed, the average worker does not consider himself in the labour market at all; he is not constantly looking for a better alternative, even though he may not be entirely satisfied with his present job. If he is a short-service worker, young and unmarried,

[1] Reynolds put this neatly when he concluded from his study of the New Haven labour market: 'The most important thing to be said about *interplant movement* is that most of it is not really interplant movement at all. It does not typically involve a comparison of two opportunities to which the worker has simultaneous access and between which he makes a deliberate choice. The worker is normally propelled out of one company by lay-off, discharge, or dissatisfaction which leads him to quit the job. He then looks about for a new job; but the significant comparison which he makes is between a specific job offer and continued unemployment, rather than between the new job and the old.' — *The Structure of Labor Markets*, p. 241.

he is more likely to move around, getting tips through friends and relatives employed elsewhere, or applying at other plants after quitting his present job. But even this worker is likely to take the first 'good' job he finds, rather than to make a canvass of the market. If he likes the new job, he stays and piles up seniority, and the more he gets the less likely he is to leave. Nevertheless, good wages and a steady job (job security) loom large in his view of what constitutes a 'good' job.

Many of these local labour market studies were made during periods of considerable unemployment (1936–1941 and 1948–1949) in the particular communities, and some covered fairly short periods of two or three years. Would the same conclusions apply to a longer period of more rapid changes in job opportunities? The six-city study covering the period 1940–1950, mentioned above, provided a broader view of patterns of mobility in the United States than emerged from the local labour market studies, although it was not designed to answer all the research questions to which the earlier studies had been directed.

The decade of the 'forties in the United States was, of course, one of major shifts in occupational and industrial employment, resulting first from the conversion to a war economy (1941–1945), and then demobilization and reconversion to a peace-time economic structure after 1945. Three-fifths of the workers in the six-city samples worked for more than one employer during 1949–1950, and only 30 per cent of the men and 17 per cent of the women were employed continuously by one employer during the decade.[1]

Only about one-fourth of the job shifts in the six cities during the decade were initiated by the employer through lay-offs. Voluntary shifts for a better job or for personal reasons predominated among the other reasons, accounting for perhaps 70 per cent of all job shifts.[2] Among the skilled workers who moved, about half changed

[1] An additional 7 per cent of the men and 17 per cent of the women had been employed part of the period by only one employer, and were either unemployed or out of the labour force during the remainder of the decade (Palmer, appendix, table 1). Mobility rates were understated to the extent that workers who may have worked in these cities during 1940–1950 but moved out before 1950 were not included in the samples; and occupational movement within a particular firm (employer) was not counted as a 'job shift'. The term applied only to movement between two employers, and these shifts were then also tabulated according to whether they also involved shifts in occupation, industry, or city. Occupational shifts were measured in terms of the 269 occupations listed in the 1950 United States Census code, and industry shifts by the 146 items in the industry code. Tabulations by occupation and industry, however, were according to major groups — eight occupational and six industrial. As large as the six-city samples were, a more detailed tabulation by occupation and industry would have lacked statistical validity.

[2] Data computed from separate city reports. The only distinction made in the six-city study was between shifts for 'economic reasons' (lay-offs) and 'all

jobs voluntarily for a variety of reasons, principally 'wages' and 'chance for advancement', a third changed jobs because of lay-offs, and the remainder of the job separations were for personal or health reasons, and for military service.[1]

More than half of the job shifts during the decade were 'complex', that is, they involved changes in employer, occupation, and industry. But industrial shifts were more frequent than occupational shifts, since three-fourths of all employer shifts also involved shifts between industries, while only three-fifths involved occupational shifts. Geographical shifts in the six-city sample were indicated by the fact that 40 per cent of the men and 45 per cent of the women who made job shifts during 1940–1950 had lived less than twelve years in the metropolitan area in which they were employed in 1950.[2]

The patterns of occupational mobility in the six cities reflect the changes in labour demand during the decade. During the period of war mobilization (1940–1945), three major occupational groups (craftsmen and foremen, clerical, and professional and technical workers) expanded at the expense of four other groups (labourers, sales workers, service workers, and managers, officials and proprietors, in that order). Then, in the post-war period (1945–1950), almost exactly the reverse occupational movement occurred. Four groups (operative, clerical, labourers, and craftsmen and foremen) declined as managers, officials and proprietors, sales workers, and service workers increased.[3]

Interindustry shifts, which were more frequent than occupational

other' reasons. The latter included discharge and military separations, as well as purely voluntary shifts initiated by the employee. However, a special study of voluntary movement by St. Paul workers showed that discharges and military separations accounted for only 1 and 6 per cent, respectively, of all shifts. University of Minnesota Industrial Relations Center, *Voluntary Shifts of St. Paul Workers, 1940–1944 and 1945–1950.*

[1] *Patterns of Mobility of Skilled Workers and Factors Affecting their Occupational Choice, Six Cities, 1940–1951*, Industrial Relations Section, Massachusetts Institute of Technology (February 1952), mimeographed, table VII, p. 50.

[2] This compares with more than half of the 2100 workers employed in war industries in 1945 who had worked in at least two separate geographical areas during 1941–1945. *Worker Mobility and Skill Utilization in World War II*, United States Department of Labor, Bureau of Labor Statistics (1952), mimeographed, table 26, p. 84.

[3] Palmer, *Labor Mobility*, appendix, tables 15 and 18. A special study in San Francisco showed that the professional and technical group was relatively 'closed', i.e. there was not much movement into or out of the group during the decade. This was also borne out in a study of the lifetime work histories of 935 male heads of families in Oakland, California. Professionals had been in their present occupational group 80 per cent of their working lives. In contrast, more than a third of the persons who owned their own businesses (included in the managers, officials, and proprietors group) came from manual occupations. Seymour M. Lipset and Reinhard Bendix, 'Social Mobility and Occupational Career Patterns', *American Journal of Sociology* (January–March 1952), pp. 369-370 and 496-497.

shifts, followed a similar pattern. During the first half of the decade 1940–1950, the expanding war industries (durable goods manufacturing, transportation, communication and utilities) drew workers from construction, wholesale and retail trade, non-durable goods manufacturing and 'all other' (principally service and industries).[1] Reynolds's observation on an interindustry movement in the New Haven labour market applies equally to the broader six-city study: 'Such barriers to interindustry movement as may have existed before the war apparently crumbled before the intense demand for labour and the special rewards offered to workers in war industry'.[2]

During the second half of the decade, the pattern was again reversed. Construction, non-durable goods manufacturing, wholesale and retail trade, and 'all other' gained at the expense of durable goods manufacturing, and transportation, communication and utilities. Again, the push of contracting industries in the post-war period, combined with the pull of expanding industries, reversed the direction of interindustry movement. More than half of these interindustry shifts made by men, furthermore, involved also changes in occupation, with the exception of the construction industry.[3]

Finally, geographical movement was an important source of labour for expanding industries and occupations in the six cities during the decade, as we have seen. Migrants shifted jobs more frequently than non-migrants during the decade, and also made relatively more complex job shifts involving changes in employer, occupation, and industry. There were significant differentials in migration between the six cities. For example, approximately half of the 1950 male work force in Los Angeles and 35 per cent in San Francisco were migrants, as compared to 16 per cent in New Haven and 13 per cent in Philadelphia.[4]

About one-fourth of the skilled workers in the six cities made geographical shifts during the decade. Long moves, over 500 miles, were frequently made into Los Angeles and San Francisco. There

[1] Palmer, appendix, tables 14 and 17, showing 'net change' in industry groups for persons employed in January 1940, and in December 1944. The major industry groups were: (1) construction, (2) durable goods manufacturing, (3) non-durable goods manufacturing, (4) transportation, communication, and utilities, (5) wholesale and retail trade, (6) all other — including agriculture, finance, business and repair services, personal services, entertainment, professional services, public administration, and persons not reporting industry.

[2] *The Structure of Labor Markets*, p. 35.

[3] In this industry, shifts involving changes in employers only, at the same occupational level, were relatively more important than in any other industry group, although it is noteworthy that they accounted for only 29 per cent of the job shifts as compared to the complex job shift in 46 per cent of the cases. Palmer, appendix, table 31.

[4] Based on individual city reports (mimeographed).

were few significant industry differentials, except that skilled construction workers made relatively more geographical shifts than did other skilled workers. Professional workers were also relatively mobile geographically during the decade.[1]

III. A Flexible and Expanding Work Force

This outline of the patterns of mobility between occupations, industries, and regions during the decade 1940–1950 reveals an internal flexibility in the American labour force which corresponds roughly with the theoretical model of a labour market within which workers move in response to differences in 'net advantage'. While the six-city study does not provide specific reasons why workers moved, or whether movement served to equalize net advantages, we do have some basis for believing that movement was from lower paying to higher paying jobs. As we have seen earlier, probably as much as 70 per cent of all the job shifts were voluntary, and the bulk of these were for higher wages or a chance for advancement.[2] We do not know, of course, whether movement tended to equalize wage differentials ; for various other influences on wages, such as war-time wage controls and collective bargaining, were also operative. But wage differences, as between war industries and so-called less essential industries, certainly operated to channel the allocation of labour during the decade.

The striking fact is that despite the barriers to voluntary movement, both personal and institutional, there was considerable movement when the economy provided opportunities to move to more attractive jobs in expanding industries and occupations during the decade 1940–1950. The fact that more than half of all the job shifts during the decade involved changes in employer, occupation, and industry deserves re-emphasis in assessing the internal flexibility of the American labour force.

Not only was the labour force flexible internally, but it expanded during the 'forties in response to changes in the demand for labour. The expansion during the decade was principally in three groups :

[1] *Patterns of Mobility of Skilled Workers and Factors Affecting their Occupational Choice, Six Cities, 1940–1951*, pp. 47-48.

[2] *Supra*, p. 450. Supporting evidence is found in the special study of skilled workers in the six cities, and also in a study of the tool- and die-makers by the United States Department of Labor. More than half of the tool- and die-makers did not change jobs during the period 1940–1951, but two-thirds of the others made voluntary shifts and over half of these were for 'more pay, promotional opportunities, etc.' *The Mobility of Tool and Die Makers, 1940–1951*, Bulletin No. 1120, United States Department of Labor (1952), pp. 6-8.

(1) women between the ages of 35 and 65 ; (2) young people between the ages of 14 and 20 ; and (3) men and women over 65. After the war, the latter two groups declined relatively, as the peak war-time employment opportunities declined, but it is significant that as late as 1952 'the proportion of married women in the labor force in each age group over 20 was actually above the peak recorded during World War II, in 1944'.[1]

The evidence seems to indicate that economic motives propelled these married women into the labour force, to supplement the husband's income up to certain levels. 'Data for 1951', one study concludes, 'suggest that married women tend to leave the labour force when their husband's income reaches $4,000–$5,000 a year'. Thus we see again how the availability of job opportunities combines with the propensity to enter (or leave) the labour force, and how the economic incentive seems to be the predominant one for initial entry and (in the case of married women) later exit.

The American labour force during the decade 1940–1950 was mobile enough to meet broad structural changes in the demand for labour, and expansible or contractible enough to adapt to the volume of job opportunities. Personal and institutional factors undoubtedly did impede movement in certain local labour markets and at particular times ; but the broad waves of movement did correspond to those suggested by the theoretical model.

It remains to consider whether this was a peculiarly American phenomenon, or whether the same patterns of mobility were found in Great Britain and in Western Europe during the decade. Three studies, two of them unpublished at this writing, have been made in Sweden, France, and Great Britain.[2] It is often assumed that vertical and horizontal occupational mobility are greater in the United States than in countries with an older, more stratified social structure. This needs further examination through comparative studies which test similar hypotheses in several countries. If the barriers to mobility are greater in the older countries, the theoretical model may be less applicable than it apparently is to the American labour market.

[1] Gertrude Bancroft, 'Trends in the Labor Force', in *Manpower in the United States*, William Haber *et al.* ed. (1954), pp. 138, 139.

[2] I am indebted to Dr. Gladys L. Palmer of the University of Pennsylvania for this information. The studies are : (1) Rudolph Meidner, *Svensk arbetsmarknad vid vull sysselsattning* (*The Swedish Labor Market at Full Employment*), Konjunkturinstitutet, Stockholm, 1954 ; (2) *L'Enquête pour sondage sur l'emploi*, Institut National de la Statistique et des Études Économiques, Paris ; (3) Geoffrey Thomas, *Labour Mobility in Great Britain, 1945–1949*, London, The Social Survey (mimeographed).

Chapter 21

AGGREGATE AND PARTICULAR LABOUR SUPPLY CURVES[1]

BY

GIOVANNI DEMARIA

Bocconi University, Milan, Italy

THE supply of disposable labour depends upon ten general variables :

(1) Natural population movements ;
(2) Distribution of the working population by working age ;
(3) Internal and international migration ;
(4) Productivity of the working population ;
(5) Distribution of the population by skills, industries, and labour markets ;
(6) Mobility of labour ;
(7) Labour policies pursued by the workers or imposed by the government ;
(8) Duration and intensity of work ;
(9) Disutility of work ;
(10) Remuneration for work.

We can write :

$$S_1 = F(v_1, \ldots, v_{10}).$$

If v_1 represents unit wages w,

$$S_1 = F(w, v_2, \ldots, v_{10}).$$

Let us assume that all the general variables other than the wage variable w remain constant. This is an assumption which is not always possible, since there are cases when account must be taken of changes in the disutility of work, in internal migration, and the length of the working day.

We can distinguish two basically different cases, according to whether w changes in the same manner for the whole supply of disposable labour or for one particular labour supply only, w remaining constant for all other supplies of disposable labour.

[1] Translated by Elizabeth Henderson.

I. Aggregate Labour Supply

Let us look at the first case. The question here is to establish the different levels of the supply of disposable labour for each change in w. We may then assume, at least as a first approximation, that the relative position of the various supplies of disposable labour will not change by virtue of these parallel movements of w. This is not a perfect hypothesis from the point of view of reality and logic, but without it our enquiry would become almost impossible.

We can say in this first case, given a movement of w in a certain direction, there is no reason whatever why S_1 should change in one direction or degree rather than another or, indeed, that it should change at all. There is nothing to indicate whether labour as a group will respond, say, to an increase in wages by deciding to work much more or much less, or a little more or a little less, or exactly as much as before the rise in wages. The different cases of behaviour depend, all other general variables remaining unchanged, on the utility the workers attach to the way of life which the rise in wages makes possible. This utility cannot be established *a priori* because it is conditioned not only by the utility originally attaching to the wages received before the increase in w, but also by the way of life which they attain, or can attain, through that increase. In turn, this way of life is obviously linked to the possibilities the workers have of spending their income better or less well ; hence the relative marginal utility can be higher or lower. These possibilities are in fact conditioned by the length of the working day, which can alter the workers' psychological attitude towards income and consequently also its relative utility. It is true that the marginal utility of income decreases with rising income, but its magnitude varies according to the time which is available for the spending of the income, and that time depends on the length of the working day. Let us suppose that there is an 8-hour day and that the hourly wage is 3, making a daily income of 24. The utility of this income for the workers is different from that of the same income if it were derived from working 12 hours at a wage of 2. Obviously this latter income could be spent only at most inconvenient hours, in the evening and at night ; it would purchase goods and services in little demand by themselves or their families. On the other hand, if the income of 24 were obtained by working 8 hours at a wage of 3, the workers would have better opportunities of spending it, at more convenient hours to themselves and their family. Thus, the marginal utility of the same amount of income differs according to the different conditions of working time in wich it was earned.

The different cases of behaviour can be illustrated by Fig. 1. If the workers, as a group, work only 8 hours at an hourly wage of 2, the marginal utility of an income of 16 exactly equals the disutility

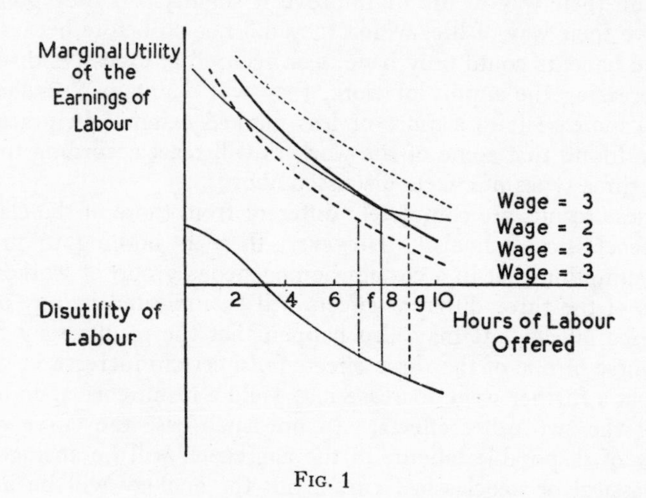

Fig. 1

of 8 work hours. If, as has been assumed, wages rise from 2 to 3, three different kinds of effect can be distinguished :

(1) Workers continue to supply the same number of hours as before, because the marginal utility of the higher income still equals the disutility of work as before, the marginal utility of the preceding portions of income being higher than before owing to a change in the psychological attitude of the workers as a result of the change in income. In this case, the effect of the wage increase on the labour supply will be zero.

(2) The workers supply more work hours, for instance 9, because the marginal utility of the higher income obtained by working only 8 hours exceeds the disutility of working 8 hours. Thus, the workers increase the daily supply of work hours to 9, which is the point where the marginal utility of the income from 9 hours' work at a wage of 3 exactly equals the disutility of working 9 hours.

(3) The workers reduce their supply of work hours, for instance to 7, because the marginal utility of the higher income that can be obtained by working 8 hours would be less than the corresponding disutility of work. Thus, the workers supply no more than 7 hours' work, which is the point where the marginal utility of the income from 7 hours' work at a wage of 3 exactly equals the disutility of working 7 hours.

In substance, this means that if the improvement of their way of life which comes within their reach through the increase in w is worth only a little to the workers in relation to the disutility of work, they will reduce S by exactly as much as will enable them to maintain their way of life or improve it slightly. If they prefer to improve their way of life, which they did not do before because the relative benefits could only have been secured at excessive disutility by increasing the supply of work, they will maintain S unchanged or will increase it to a more or less marked extent. In practice it will be found that some of the workers will react according to each of the three types of effects discussed above.

These results are completely different from those of the classical and neoclassical schools.[1] However, there is nothing to prevent the assumption that in a certain homogeneous group of workers the results of the three different effects will be indicated by any one of the three effects. It may also happen that the results may follow the course of one of the three effects for a certain increase in wages, and that a further wage increase may yield a result corresponding to one of the two other effects. In one such case the curve of the supply of disposable labour, in the aggregate, will be analogous to the classical or neoclassical curve, but the analogy will be limited to an interval. In another case, the supply of disposable labour will be represented by a vertical line. Yet another case would yield a continuously rising curve extended upwards to the right. Finally, there is the mixed case which would yield a more complicated curve than any of those mentioned.

It will not, in general, be possible to establish *a priori* what effect a wage increase will have on labour supply. It may happen that in exceptional circumstances it is possible to foresee exactly what effect a wage increase will have; but this will only happen when there is exact knowledge of the relative importance which the homogeneous group of workers attaches to the way of life which can be attained through the new income. The examples we have given are designed to show a complex of possible effects.

The conclusion which we have reached is truly a disappointment for those who might have expected a single or a simple solution. But however paradoxical it may seem, this result is in accordance both with our argument and with experience, which proves the existence of rather diverse kinds of behaviour. It is thus not an absurd result; we must, on the contrary, accept this result as the only one of general validity.

[1] In part, this has been stated by A. C. Pigou, 'Some Considerations on Stability Conditions, Employment and Real Wage Rates', *Economic Journal* (1945), pp. 346-356, and *Employment and Equilibrium* (1941).

Notwithstanding these multiple solutions, it can nevertheless be proved that among all the possible curves of labour supply, a vertical labour supply, with labour supply unchanged with changes in wages, is the most probable one from the formal point of view. Actual behaviour, when it is not known *a priori*, is closer to this labour supply curve than to any other.

II. Particular Labour Supply

Let us now examine the second case. The movement of w affects only the particular supply of disposable labour under consideration and not the rest of the labour supply. It is possible that the isolated wage change may attract into the group under consideration new recruits from other supplies of disposable labour, or this isolated wage change may cause labour to leave the group in question and join other labour forces. Apart from the indeterminateness of the behaviour of these workers who remain within the same particular labour supply in spite of a change in w (this is the indeterminateness examined in the first case) ; we now have to consider the motives which cause some workers to leave the group in question and which attract into this group other workers belonging to other supplies of disposable labour.

The theory of these motives leads in part to a second indeterminateness, but in part it can be regarded as a theory of effects which are certain *a priori* and are not indeterminable. The more the latter gain the upper hand, the less becomes the indeterminateness. Let us try to establish these two aspects in the most precise manner possible so that we can then draw a general conclusion on that basis. To do so we shall examine only the effects due to a rise in wages.

In the case of a rise in w, and on the assumption that the transfer costs are nil, the workers of other labour supplies will be inclined to swell the labour supply in question only in certain circumstances, which are those considered in the first case. There will thus be an *a priori* logical indeterminateness. But there is nothing to prevent us from asserting that part of these workers will certainly be inclined to transfer. Their number will above all depend on the costs of the transfer. The same will hold true of those workers who had retired, while indirectly some members of the family (and particularly their wives) will be induced to stay at home.

It can, therefore, be said that where the transfer costs from one labour market to another are small, the supply of disposable labour on that market will increase appreciably more than otherwise.

Other things being equal, such labour supply will tend to increase with an increase in w. In the limiting case we would even have an infinitely elastic supply of labour with respect to one single employer who could, in practice, with only a slight increase in wages, obtain any amount of labour. If the transfer costs rise, the slope of the curve will rise correspondingly. If the transfer costs are very high, or if the 'other' workers are unaware of the better conditions offered on the market in question, then the disposable supply of labour on that market will tend towards the vertical. From this we derive the highly interesting theorem of the single direction of the curve of labour supply in the case of localized changes in w. In fact, the narrower the limits within which the labour supply is localized and the lower the transfer costs, the less will be the indeterminateness of the curve itself and the more marked its singleness of direction.

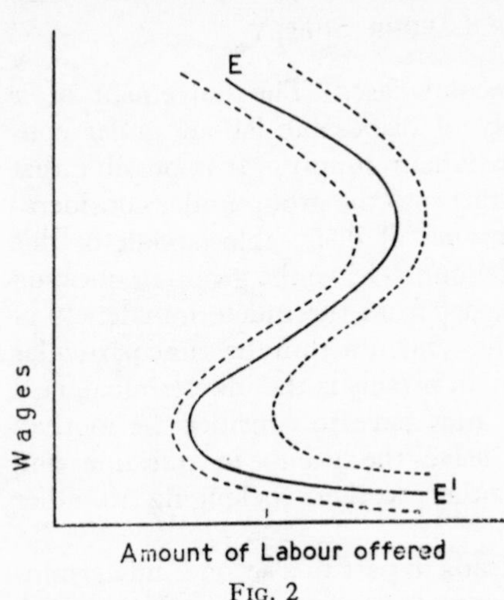

FIG. 2

If there are considerable differences in the way of life of the workers so that the schematic representation of the curve of disposable labour must formally encompass them all, then this curve will, in the second case, most likely have the structure indicated by *EE'* in Fig. 2. The dotted lines indicate the successive transpositions of *EE'* with changes in the other general variables, $v_2 \ldots v_{10}$. Thus natural population growth, immigration, a lowering of the working age and a later retiring age, growth of productive strength and skill, an increase in the rate of entry and a decrease in that of retirement, less restriction in labour supply owing to changes in the policies of labour unions, a lengthening of the working day and fewer holidays owing to the government's labour policy — all these would cause a shift of *EE'* to the left. Opposite movements in the variables would cause a shift of the curve to the right. This is, of course, only a first approximation.

If one wishes to predetermine the shape of the labour supply curve theoretically, it will be necessary to make certain definite assumptions about the movement of the general variables and their amplitude and direction ; or else, if these general variables are assumed to remain constant, such assumptions will have to be made about wages alone. In other words, we shall have to argue somewhat casuistically if we are to re-establish that old determinism which is under continuous attack by the insufficiency of our knowledge and the very nature of the facts.

In the real world the development of these effects is never perfectly continuous and proportional, so that it cannot actually be represented by near-parallel transpositions implying a simple relation with the preceding location. The intensity of the transpositions can be different at the different points of EE', to the extent of altering the mathematical form of the curves.

It follows that whenever the factors which cause the various transposition movements are sufficiently significant, they modify the structure of the transposed curves by progressively altering their original shape to an entirely different one. Whenever general factors of change intervene, it is thus somewhat improbable that the curves of labour supply will have any formal stability, unless one interferes with the most elementary data of reality and operates with pure imagination. If we are to avoid the error of the classical and neo-classical schools, we can thus not assert, apart from certain particular applications, that the curve of labour supply will necessarily be of one type only, if the other variables $v_2 \ldots v_{10}$ are also taken into consideration. Hence we derive the principle that the labour supply curves must be pluristructural in all cases in which account is taken of all the ten general variables.

We can isolate among the possible structures of the labour supply curve that which theoretically seems the most probable and most capable of being generalized. This means that we must be content with a compromise. The compromise curve of labour supply when the wage change is common to all the supply of disposable labour is a vertical line (labour supply does not change with changes in wages). When the wage change applies only to one particular collective labour supply, the compromise curve is EE' in Fig. 2. These curves are not only the most probable ones from the formal point of view, but in the present state of our knowledge they are closest to the world of observation.

PART VII

REPORT ON THE PROCEEDINGS

FIRST SESSION

SATURDAY MORNING, SEPTEMBER 4, 1954

(Discussion of Papers by Johnson and Wagner)

Professor Dunlop, opening the discussion on Mr. Johnson's paper, suggested that the latter should begin by answering a question put by Professor Reynolds : What are the main determinants of the level of money wages ?

Mr. Johnson felt that the static approach of his paper might not represent the best way of answering practical questions about money wages. Perhaps we were really interested not in the level of wages but in the direction and rate of change in wages. His own view was that to discuss the question one needed to specify a given economy at a particular point of time. A major difficulty was that countries could create money, and the money supply was therefore not a datum but an instrument of policy. So were foreign exchange rates. The question was, should one adjust money wages, the price level, or the foreign exchange rate ? Governments had changed their minds many times on such questions during the last fifteen years and could presumably go on doing so. In Britain, for example, people had moved from non-market factors like exhortation and price control towards monetary policy. One difficulty was that when one spoke of the general wage level one meant an average of the wages resulting from bargains in individual sub-markets, and one had to consider how general factors in the economy affected such bargains. The real trouble was that the world was always in disequilibrium. Sometimes disequilibrium was the result of deliberate policy ; for example, inflation could be a means of reconciling inconsistent claims to shares in the national income. There was, again, the problem that economic policy was not independently determined ; economic policies supported by individual economic units would be expressed through the political authority in a general economic policy.

Professor Myers wondered which countries had abandoned what Mr. Johnson called their 'unlimited commitment' to full employment. *Mr. Johnson* replied that he was considering European rather than United States experience. He agreed that there had been no serious rise in unemployment in Britain in 1952 ; but the government's policy change in 1951 suggested a willingness to allow unemployment if wages rose. Instead of devaluation there had been a stronger monetary policy. It was also noticeable that, before 1951, wage restraint in Britain had been linked not with unemployment but with the maintenance of the social services, though of course in an indirect way. Wage increases need not cause unemployment; they might induce reactions which could avoid unemployment. The wish for convertibility meant that greater importance was now attached to the market mechanism.

Mr. Turner pointed out that since nothing happened after the rise in the Bank Rate in 1951 one could say nothing about its effects.

M. Rottier wondered whether nothing did happen ? Might not the average unit cost of labour have fallen ? Might not the change in earnings have been less than the rise in wage rates because monetary policy led to the more efficient use of labour ?

Mr. Turner felt that one could not disentangle everything. First, there was a small increase in unemployment. Second, overtime was reduced, which lowered earnings per worker. Third, for some reason the 'annual' increases in British wage rates were the same *absolutely* and thus smaller proportionally.

M. Rottier said that he merely wanted to make the theoretical point that the way in which the Bank Rate worked may have been through making individual firms use labour more efficiently, rather than by affecting the progress of collective bargaining or the rate of increase in wage rates.

Mr. Rehn felt that the four cases set out at the beginning of Professor Wagner's paper perhaps gave too simplified a view of the problem, in just the same way as the report of six United Nations experts did, in spite of a different emotional attitude. These approaches lead to only one conclusion : if one pursues full employment there will inevitably be inflation unless there is wage restraint. But this general truth is not the whole story. Measures designed to increase employment at specific spots where employment is low mean less profit and wage inflation than with the general stimulation of demand.

Instead of merely considering *general* balance we should take more interest in *adapting* the economy, to create near-full employment in all sub-markets. A cautious policy with regard to stimulating general effective demand combined with more radical intervention at crucial points, for example, in helping people to move from sub-markets where labour was relatively abundant to sub-markets where it was scarce might mean that the government interventions needed for full employment might not be either vast or general. This was a fifth case, to be added to Professor Wagner's list, in which a fair amount of state intervention would not mean a high degree of inflation. This was not a complicated theory, but the administrative and practical problems needed studying.

Mr. Peacock asked whether Swiss experience really exemplified Professor Wagner's thesis. He wondered what had happened to the balance of payments in recent years and felt that what had happened to the Swiss economy since 1951 could be explained in terms of Keynesian economics. He also wondered why Professor Wagner said that 'price and wage controls are essential with any deliberate and consistent full employment policy, particularly if this policy is marked by public investment'. Mr. Peacock suggested two points for more general discussion, though he felt that these were more connected with full employment than with money wages. First, he wondered what was the connection between the degree of government intervention and the level of money wages. Second, he wondered what were the essential conditions for wage stability. In particular, he asked whether there was any universal proposition about the degree of unemployment needed for wage stability.

Professor Wagner replied to the points raised by Mr. Peacock. First, where did the danger of inflationary pressure begin ? Keynes said that there was no danger of inflation if there were not full employment. Once bottlenecks were met with, however, inflation began. Professor Wagner did not agree. The risk of inflation began with the initial upswing ; prices always started to rise. Therefore, he distinguished full employment resulting in a free market from that caused by a deliberate full employment policy. The latter would normally aim to stimulate private investment. Or it might be an 'anti-stagnation' policy which would regard price rises, and therefore price controls, as inevitable. Professor Wagner held to his original contention. The Keynesian formula was not a sure criterion. Prices and wages could rise before bottlenecks became manifest. On the other hand, there could be full employment without a rise in prices. Swiss experience between 1951 and 1954 had been of full employment without a full employment policy. Although there was no cheap money policy, Switzerland had cheap money. Prices, however, had not risen since 1951, proving that one could have stable prices and wages in conditions of over-employment. Thus the Keynesian formula was not valid ; there was no universally valid generalization. Professor Wagner said that Mr. Rehn had accused him of saying that in full employment inflation was always a danger. This was not a new idea of his ; all theorists stressed it. He agreed, however, that in the case set out by Mr.

Rehn, where there is government interference only at key points in the economy, there neeed be no inflation. General deflation would be accompanied by attempts to remove unemployment in any sub-market by special action. Professor Wagner agreed that this was a possible solution and perhaps a desirable one. But it would no longer be a Keynesian macro-economic policy, but one acting on particular markets or particular magnitudes.

Professor Lindahl pointed out that the case suggested by Mr. Rehn was one which appealed to many Swedes who felt that it was the only way of achieving full employment without inflation.

Mr. Peacock felt that if there was a full employment policy there was no reason why the volume of investment should not be constant or even falling. He agreed that an attack on problems in particular sub-markets was better than a general increase in effective demand, but he thought that there was here no quarrel between Keynes and the rest, or even between various types of Keynesians.

Professor Wagner still felt that Keynesians wanted to fight unemployment by a general expansion of effective demand and agreed with Mr. Rehn that it was better to attack problems in certain key sub-markets. *Mr. Peacock*, however, pointed out that Mr. Rehn had shown, in Keynesian terms, by referring to multiplier effects in the various sub-markets, how Keynesian theory could be applied to his case of a full employment policy.

Professor Reynolds wondered why things had worked out in Switzerland as they had since 1951 ?

Dr. Hansen suggested that Professor Wagner had perhaps not stated the full story. The point was surely that the supply curve of labour in Switzerland was almost infinitely elastic. There was an inflow and outflow of labour ; Switzerland exported its unemployment to Austria and Italy and imported workers from Austria and Italy when labour was scarce. This was clearly an extremely harsh full employment policy.

Professor Dupriez agreed with Professor Wagner that the number of foreign workers in Switzerland was too small to affect the situation. High wages in Switzerland, and more recently in Belgium, meant that there was no unemployment of skilled workers. They meant rapid changes in technique and also that unemployment only affected unskilled labour.

Mr. Peacock said that it might be true that there was high employment in Switzerland without any deliberate policy. What, however, was the balance of payments position ? There could be high employment and yet no price rises, because of a deterioration in the balance of payments or a change in productivity.

Professor Jöhr asked why should full employment not mean equilibrium. Some time ago no one would have thought this surprising. The foreign labour force in Switzerland was important; but it existed before 1948 and was not, therefore, a useful explanation. Technological progress had compensated for inflation. Again, the terms of trade had been favourable. Internal politics were very stable, for there was no danger of nationalization.

Mr. Rehn inquired how the distribution of income between wages and profits had changed recently, and *Professor Jöhr* replied that real wages had risen and profits were high, but perhaps there had been some shift in favour of wages.

Mr. Johnson wondered whether the right criteria were being considered. One needed to study the labour supply position in Italy and Austria as well as in Switzerland. The average amount of foreign labour in Switzerland and the average balance of payments were not relevant. But changes, for example in restrictions on the entry of labour from abroad, might help to explain the stability of employment in Switzerland.

Professor Phelps Brown thought that one might throw light on Swiss experience by looking at the pre-1914 world where no country was committed to full employment, but where none the less, in Britain, for example, unemployment seemed to have averaged less than 3 per cent during half the fifty years before 1914. The question was not, did we need extra effective demand to get full employment, but why, after arriving at full employment, did the economy fall back into a slump. The boom after 1918 broke (a) because of monetary policy, and (b) because people thought that the pre-war position was 'normal' and they were bound to return to it. There was a great difference now, especially because of Keynes, and no one expected to go back to the pre-war situation. This had preserved us from the sharp reaction of the early 1920's.

SECOND SESSION

Saturday Afternoon, September 4, 1954

(Discussion of Paper by Hansen)

M. Sellier raised two connected points about sub-markets in Dr. Hansen's paper and about the link between monetary policy and wage levels in Mr. Johnson's. Dr. Hansen's assumption of general wage stability simultaneously with disequilibrium in some sub-markets was correct only if applied to the whole working population.

The general interdependence between the various sectors was particularly clear in France where there was a considerable degree of interchange between industrial and agricultural populations.

Mr. Johnson, on the other hand, had concluded that the level of money wages depended on the quantity of money. Thus, if one considered sub-markets, the influence of monetary policy, or its absence, would often be greater in some sectors, for example, in agriculture. In France, in 1947, as a result of inflation and high prices, many people went to other sectors, commercial and professional, because of high wages, and labour left the agricultural sector. Again, policies like short-term credits for agriculture had hindered the movement of labour out of agriculture.

So monetary policy might well affect the labour force in industrial sub-markets, and also its wage, through an initial movement in other sectors. Unfortunately, M. Sellier thought, so far as Dr. Hansen's paper was concerned, it would be necessary to take account of and to measure excess supply in the agricultural sector.

M. Rottier asked what Dr. Hansen meant by a non-homogeneous market. Did he mean no movement of manpower into or out of it ? Or that wages in that market were determined separately from wages in other markets ? In formula (5) surely neither w_1 nor k_1 need be independent variables. Could not unemployment in some sectors still allow inflation in other sectors to cause inflation in the whole market ?

Mr. Johnson said it was vital to realize that Dr. Hansen's paper depended on his previous work on inflation, work which was not set out in detail in this paper. For example, Dr. Hansen's analysis was based on fixed prices and a fixed general wage level, and it traced the direction in which wages would tend to move in the sub-markets. Dr. Hansen also defined full employment as *potential* full employment ; full employment to Dr. Hansen meant that if all unemployed men were moved to available jobs there would be no unemployment. This assumed that all workers were homogeneous, which was clearly not true and was, indeed, inconsistent with the actual analysis of the labour market. Unemployment was easy to measure, but *not* the number of unfilled jobs. The fact that Dr. Hansen did not study full employment, but only *potential* full employment, was damaging only if one failed to realise that it was meant to be used for *ex ante* planning at any given point of time. Mr. Johnson pointed out that a mathematical problem arose in formula (6) of Dr. Hansen's paper. This condition for wage stability only held between period 0 and period 1. The model, as it stood, *must* mean that there would be an upward trend after period 1. The weights given to the sector where wages rose would progressively increase ; the weights of sectors where wages fall would similarly decline.

Mr. Johnson was worried by Dr. Hansen's discussion of bargaining power. Bargaining power was essentially a relation *between* groups. There was thus no need to consider separately bargaining power of labour, and that of employers. One only needed, so to speak, a measure of the *relative* strength of the two parties. For there was no need here to study bargaining power *per se* ; only its effect on wages.

Dr. Hansen's analysis did not make clear whether in the model wages were determined centrally for all markets, or whether one was only concerned with wage determination in individual markets. His central theme was important, but the discussion of bargaining was not an essential part of it. Nor was it made clear that the whole system was an *ex ante* analysis useful only in forecasting. Mr. Johnson also felt that indices of constant wages, which were obtained by using coefficients of flexibility as weights, were out of the range of useful analysis. But the paper did raise the important question of how far the movement of wages in a sub-market was related both to the degree of employment in sub-markets and also to the movement of the general wage level.

Dr. Hansen said that he had approached the question as a monetary theorist. Monetary theory had always been much concerned with money and wages, and Mr. Johnson was not quite right when he said that money wages had not often been explicitly studied by monetary theorists. In this paper, Dr. Hansen said, he had only been concerned with *changes* in money wages and not with their absolute level. To some extent, then, his paper represented 'wishful thinking' by a monetary theorist, treating money wages by methods implied in traditional monetary theory.

It was important to remember that period analysis lay behind all this ; here, however, he studied only one period. M. Sellier and M. Rottier could be answered easily if one considered what Swedish period analysis implied. By definition, the period was so short that one could always follow developments step by step, and need not consider any interdependence between such developments. M. Sellier talked of the problems of relative wages in agriculture and in industry ; the answer was that in this model the periods were so short in time that one could ignore such factors as relative wages in agriculture and industry.

In answer to M. Rottier, Dr. Hansen said that a non-homogeneous market was easily defined because one was here considering a time period which was so short that workers could not move from one job to another. Again, M. Sellier had wondered how one could measure excess demand or supply. *In principle*, of course, these concepts were measurable; there were also practical methods of measuring them, for example, by interview methods, or by inquiring at labour exchanges for information about unfilled jobs. Certainly, one ought to be able to obtain an index showing the direction of movement of the volume of unfilled jobs, though not a measure of the absolute magnitude of excess labour demand. M. Rottier had wondered whether price flexibilities in one market might not be affected by wage changes in other markets. It was quite true that this would happen, but this was only a simple model and Dr. Hansen said he had merely wanted to show the kind of weights that one would need to use. It was true also, as Mr. Johnson had said, that the analysis held only for one time period.

Mr. Johnson explained that his last point was that the relative strength of the bargainers could be assumed to depend merely on excess supply and demand, and not on complicated factors like bargaining power.

Dr. Hansen replied that he was here really concerned with 'toughness'; perhaps here the labour theorist knew more than he did. He only wanted to say that all excess supplies and demands might affect the behaviour of negotiating bodies.

Professor Dunlop suggested that it might be desirable to draw the day's discussion together by considering two related questions.

(1) Does the pursuit of a full employment policy necessarily lead to serious inflation. If not, in what circumstances would it do so?

(2) What is the relationship between changes in the general level of employment and in the general level of wages? Is a certain level of unemployment necessary for wage stability? Is there a critical level, for example, 3 per cent or 5 per cent or 10 per cent of unemployment, at which wage stability can just be achieved?

Mr. Rehn said that one could see the answer to the first question in the formula that the degree of inflationary danger was measured by the difference between the average and marginal productivity of labour. If there was little difference between the profits of marginal and intramarginal firms (or industries) there would be fewer 'provocative profits' and fewer provocative wage differences all stimulating inflation.

This helped to answer the second problem. If unemployment had only recently been overcome, the economy would not have had time to remove these inflation-provoking influences. Some of our post-war problems were not the result of high employment, but of the fact that this high employment had not 'matured'.

Professor Jöhr said that inflation could increase employment and might lead to full employment, but then this might perhaps cause more inflation. One need not, however, have inflation to increase employment, if the general conditions for investment were favourable. In the United States in 1922–1929 prices fell but there was full employment. This was a better illustration, better even than the recent Swiss example, of the fact that full employment need not imply inflation. If productivity rose, wages could be increased without rising prices.

Mr. Peacock inquired how Professor Jöhr defined inflation, to which the latter replied that he meant a rise in money flows in excess of the increase in the supply of goods. Mr. Peacock felt that we needed a definition of inflation, and thought that Professor Jöhr's definition differed at full and less-than-full employment. Professor Wagner in the morning session had run into trouble because his definition did not make it clear whether an excess of investment over savings increased output or prices. Similarly, Professor Jöhr seemed to be using inflation in two different senses. The conference had not defined either full employment or inflation, and Mr. Peacock felt that we ought to know exactly what these terms meant.

Professor Phelps Brown thought the idea that the changes in wages depended simply on the level of employment arose from a crude correlation between time series. Wages certainly had usually risen when employment was high, but profits were then high also. Low unemployment had not always meant rising wages, for example, on the British railways in the inter-war years. Professor Phelps Brown put forward three reasons why full employment might bring inflation. First, the level of demand needed to maintain employment in the least profitable sectors might impose high profits on the others. Second, public policy made management less apprehensive of cost rises and less resistant to wage claims. Third, local labour shortages caused wage rises which gave rise to wage claims elsewhere. Professor Dunlop's question was thus, really, how far the level of employment was connected with these causes of inflation.

Dr. Rothschild thought that perhaps the question could be put in another way. How much mild inflation did we need to reach full employment ? People did not like either unemployment or inflation, but since everyone felt that since inflation and full employment normally went together, a choice of evils was inevitable. Perhaps it was best to ask in what circumstances given policies and institutions would give or fail to give inflation. Professor Phelps Brown's three dangers could be kept in check by the policy of governments. Therefore, with strong trade unions, government action had to move into many fields. The real question was surely which full employment policies would, and which would not, cause inflation.

THIRD AND FOURTH SESSIONS

SUNDAY MORNING AND EVENING, SEPTEMBER 5, 1954

(Discussion of Paper by Phelps Brown)

Mr. Rothbaum raised several points on Professor Phelps Brown's paper. First, he pointed out that the capital ratio abstracted completely from changes in the qualitative structure of capital. He wondered if a money ratio like that used by Professor Phelps Brown was enough. Second, he was unsure about the validity of Professor Phelps Brown's theoretical discussion of profits. He wondered if normal profits referred to one industry or many. The idea of an average rate of profit was not close to reality. Such an idea might measure the efficiency of any management at a given time as compared with the general efficiency of management. But, whilst it might be true that entrepreneurs did not aim at maximum profits, there was no reason for supposing that they aimed at normal profits. Surely what was needed here was a discussion of a fall in all profit rates rather than in an average rate. Fourth, permanent structural changes were important. The idea of a conventional system which experienced periodic displacements might well be related to the structure of that system; for example, the problem might be connected with the differential skills of workers.

Mr. Laffer felt that conventional levels of profits did exist, but thought the change from one conventional level to another needed explaining. Perhaps a change in the conditions of entry of new firms or in the general economic climate had led to changes in these conventions.

Mr. Hague regretted that the theory of the firm had been brought up by Professor Phelps Brown since he felt that it was irrelevant to the subject under discussion. He also regretted that Professor Phelps Brown had apparently been won over by full cost pricing, for there was not often really a conventional basis. The empirical conclusions given by Hall and Hitch related to oligopoly; Mr. Andrews' study related in part to Courtaulds, a monopolist or, at least, an oligopolist. He felt that the nature of pricing policy really depended on degree of competition and monopoly in the industry in question. It was therefore both important and interesting to study how far the events noted by Professor Phelps Brown could be reconciled with market studies in the countries and periods considered. Mr. Hague said that his own main difficulty was that even where firms did attempt to follow a conventional basis for pricing individual products, there could hardly be a conventional policy relating to the profits of the whole firm, far less of the industry to which it belonged or of the economy as a whole.

Professor Marchal agreed with the evidence of inertia in the relationships considered, interrupted by periodic displacements. He could see the usefulness of the wage-income ratio when real wages changed more or less than the productivity of the whole population. He wished to comment on the first table. The pre-1914 changes were unfavourable to workers, whilst the post-war shifts were all favourable to them. Did not this suggest that we should look to a transformation in the structure of society ? For example, the post-1914 era saw the growth of trade unions, left-wing political parties, economic nationalism, and so on. *Professor Phelps Brown* agreed that one found 'faults' in the evidence, violent displacements in a short period of time. This particular displacement might well be connected with the social changes of the 1914–1918 war. He would, then, agree that non-economic factors had changed.

Professor Marchal asked whether the stability of the capital coefficient in the United Kingdom and the United States was paralleled elsewhere. *Professor Phelps Brown* answered that he did not know of any other evidence for other lands.

Professor Marchal asked how one could explain stability. *Professor Phelps Brown* replied that he could not explain it.

Professor Marchal called attention to the fact that if one group's income went up, the group changed its idea of what was a normal rate of return ; there was also an inflow or outflow of people from other groups. He instanced how, in France, commercial profits rose from 9 per cent of the national income in 1938–1939 to 11 per cent in 1945, the inflow of new workers having kept down *per capita* income. Always there was a change in the number of members of the group, which would reduce or prevent a rise in income per head.

He asked if the conventional standard of the wages of workers, or of agricultural income, was not just as important as a convention in earning profits. If this were true, there would be no autonomous theory of wages ; only a general theory of incomes, everyone striving to maintain either his standard of living or his income relative to that of other groups.

Professor Marchal asked if Professor Phelps Brown thought that a discussion of the wage/profit ratio alone was essential. Or would he agree that other shares should be considered, for example salaries and earnings in agriculture. *Professor Phelps Brown* said that the main reason for his line of argument was that in the United Kingdom agriculture was less important. But he had an uneasy conscience about leaving out salaries.

M. Rottier raised three questions. First, he felt there was not much contradiction between 'full cost' theory and profit maximization. In part, any apparent contradiction was explained if one introduced the conditions of entry to the industry. Firms might fear new entrants, or profits might be maximized not in each short period but over a succession of short periods, in the medium run. Second, Professor Phelps Brown's study covered eighty years. There was growth not only of total national product and national income per head. There must also have been a change in structure of the flows of income between sectors. In part, the explanation might be shifts of manpower to industries where the wage/income ratio was higher. Third, he queried the accuracy of empirical data for the period 1850–1900. Were any real generalizations about fluctuations over this period possible ?

Mr. Peacock thought that Professor Phelps Brown suggested that the typical market form was oligopoly. Was this a correct interpretation ? He thought that conventional behaviour was consistent with profit maximization if the market throughout the period was oligopolistic, for the entrepreneur would then be required to make judgments about his own and other firms' marginal revenue curves and about what their policies would be.

Professor Phelps Brown, in reply to the discussion, considered two points ; (a) the reliability of his statistical evidence, (b) the possibility that profits were determined by a convention.

The discussion had brought out the limitations of the wage/income ratio. It compared wage *rates* and *per capita* income, without any correction for the effects of unemployment on wage earnings. Nor did it allow for changes in the length of the working week. But his figures for the earnings/income ratio in the United Kingdom did not have these limitations. Where he used the *wage-rate*/income ratio for international comparisons, the limitations were common to all the series, and the statistical evidence was probably strong enough to take the weight which he had put on it in his paper.

On the second point, Professor Phelps Brown said that the notion of a convention had been put forward as a hypothesis to explain the observed behaviour of the rate of profit in the United

Kingdom, both its inertia and its displacement. He did not think that it implied treating all markets as oligopolistic. There were many types of market form in the world. The question was how could one explain the prevalence of a 'normal' rate of profits. He thought this convention could obtain even in highly competitive markets, if the entry of competitors into a market depended on their expectation of being able to earn a sufficient return. The criterion of sufficiency might be conventional.

But the rôle of convention in determining the rate of profit must be limited by the operation of the long-run supply price of risk capital. It was hard to believe, however, that the reactions from this side would be rapid enough to account for the observed inertia of the level of profits, nor did they easily account for its displacement. The 'conventional' hypothesis was the best explanation of these things that he could offer.

Finally, Professor Phelps Brown noted the proposal to explain shifts between profits and wages by changes in the degree of monopoly, and said this did not seem to fit the lower share of profits apparent after the first World War.

Mr. Turner put forward the general proposition that no statistical argument had any finality unless confirmed by common sense. The statistical argument of this paper was only challenged where it seemed unnecessary. The years in question were, for Britain and other European countries, years when mass trade unionism first established itself. In the United States it was not until the 1930's that mass unionism arrived. This could explain why the shift in favour of workers came later in the United States.

Second, Mr. Turner was afraid that conventional and market forces might seem to be exclusive. Yet, whilst in the first place a relationship might be formed by economic forces, it could be perpetuated by convention. Perhaps profit margins were compressed when the convention was strong and economic forces were weak, and vice versa.

Professor Kerr, having ascertained that Professor Phelps Brown did not include salaries in wages, offered an alternative explanation. The rise in the wage/income ratio might take place at the expense of salaries. The compensation/income ratio might therefore be constant. We might really need to know why manual workers gained at the expense of salaries.

Mr. Johnson said that he was not a statistician; he welcomed Professor Phelps Brown's work; nevertheless, he wanted to plead for more sophistication in the interpretation of the statistical evidence. Professor Phelps Brown sought to look at changes, inertias, and stabilities. But Mr. Johnson was not sure what these stabilities were. Several sets of phenomena might be noted and different explanations would be needed, according to the years which were taken to mark phases in the movement of the statistics. There was perhaps a need to analyse the figures to see how far movements in the statistics were cyclical and how much stability there was after the influence of cyclical factors had been removed.

If one looked at the figures for Sweden there was a sharp upswing followed by a downswing, and then a further upswing. What, then, was the trend ? Before postulating stability and putting forward elaborate theories to explain such stability, one ought to be certain that such stability existed.

Mr. Johnson pointed out that there were also difficulties and dangers in interpreting a ratio constructed from two variables, one of which included the other, especially when one was interested in the apparent stability of such ratios. If one was concerned with banks' cash ratios, the degree of stability which one found depended on whether cash or other assets was taken as the numerator. Similarly, one obtained a different idea of the stability of the consumption function if one took savings, or consumption, as the variable to be investigated. If there were any correlation between wages and income a ratio might either over- or under-state the stability according to the relation between them ; one therefore needed a theoretical model to establish standards of stability.

Professor Phelps Brown might be right, but Mr. Johnson was not convinced that there really was a problem which needed explanation.

Dr. Rothschild pointed out that, in terms of Dr. Kalecki's analysis, the fall in the degree of monopoly when Professor Phelps Brown's theory required it, namely in the 1920's, could be explained by the fact that marginal costs had risen at a time when demand was depressed.

Mr. Gasparini said that Professor Phelps Brown had pointed to the trend of the prices of primary products as a significant factor in shaping the market environment.

If, however, a long span of time were examined, as for instance by Mr. Schlote in his research on the dynamics of English foreign trade, there was evidence that from 1814 the behaviour of the terms of trade between primary and manufactured products was remarkably different in three periods of time, which were the three long waves of the Kondratieff-Schumpeter type. He thus suggested that the background of economic forces shaping the conventional element, emphasized by Professor Phelps Brown, might be traced back, at least up to 1913, to the features of a long wave. This approach might help to clarify the balancing influences working behind the ratios, where stability had been discussed.

As for the behaviour of the capital coefficient, Dr. Gasparini pointed to some provisional results of research into Italian experience which showed that the coefficient was not constant. The coefficient was about 5·5 in the period 1870–1900, where industrialization was beginning and the rate of growth of industrial production rather unstable. In 1920–1938 the coefficient dropped to about 4 and was a little higher in the post-war years.

Professor Lindahl made some brief remarks on the capital/income ratio. This could be denoted as: $k = \frac{C}{Y}$ where C = capital and Y = national income. Total capital, C, was equal to: $\frac{cY}{r}$ where cY = income from capital, and r = rate of interest. Therefore $k = \frac{c}{r}$. Though this was not Professor Phelps Brown's problem, there were useful and interesting conclusions. Take two points of time, 1 and 2, with r equal to 0·09 at period 1 and 0·06 at period 2. If k were constant and equal to 5, interest payments would represent only 30 per cent instead of 45 per cent of national income as a result of a fall in the rate of interest from 9 per cent to 6 per cent. This agreed with an estimate for Sweden, and showed that a constant capital/income ratio would be compatible with this tendency.

Professor Phelps Brown agreed with Mr. Turner's comments. He said that Mr. Johnson had called attention to the need for better criteria of stability than those of an art critic. He confessed that he had used no criteria derived from theory. On the other hand, in the period studied, the changes in the ratios had been small compared with the great changes in technique, and this was a reason for supposing that the stability was significant. Mr. Johnson was also right that there were pitfalls in comparing two terms, one of which included the other. Replying to Mr. Gasparini, Professor Phelps Brown said that he had studied the question he raised, but had not been able to find any movements in real wages of that kind.

FIFTH SESSION

MONDAY MORNING, SEPTEMBER 6, 1954

(Discussion of Papers by Rothschild and Shackle)

Mr. Meidner said Dr. Rothschild had treated real wages from a technical 'bargaining view'. He was quite right to argue that trade unions in advanced countries made bargains in terms of *real* rather than money wages, but this changed the basic assumption of wage theory.

The results of wage bargaining could be shown in three ways. First, the consequences of wage increases could be shown. Second, the need for controls would be made clear. Third, one could point to the influence of the strength of other groups. In Sweden, for example, one had not only to consider what were fair wages for the group in question but also the further consequences, resulting from the moves of other groups, for the price system in general.

Mr. Meidner thought it most important to widen the concept of bargaining and to include institutional factors. For example, in the yearly farm-price negotiations in Sweden, bargaining between the government and the farmers was pursued simultaneously with wage negotiations. The trade union was represented at these farm-price discussions, and regarded them as a basis when negotiating for wage increases with the farmers. Here, then, the same people claimed high wages and yet represented strong price-stabilizers in their other rôle. This represented a normal element of Swedish income distribution.

Mr. Meidner wondered whether one should include all such institutional environments in wage theory. If so, labour economists would become 'more institutional than the Americans'. Nevertheless, he thought it better to kill the theory rather than have a fiction that covered only part of real life.

Mr. Laffer said he would like to relate the end of Dr. Rothschild's paper to the discussion of the first day, especially the part which said that trade unions in their bargains considered not only the wage level but also broader issues like price control. This had important implications for wage theory. The discussion of the first day took the government as being 'above the battle' and choosing its objectives in abstract terms. We had taken it for granted that we should aim at some species of 'full employment without inflation'. An important development in recent years, however, was the increased power and importance of trade unions, and economic theories must take account of this. One should ask whether price stability was always in the interests of trade unions. In Australia, farm incomes had risen from about 8–10 per cent of the national income before the war to 25 per cent in the wool boom, and now stood at about 15 per cent. In these circumstances trade unions found it desirable to press for wage increases. These pushed prices up, but not enough to prevent wage earners securing some gains in real wages, at the expense largely of the unsheltered farm industries. Theories of wage determination and wage policy that neglected the interests of trade unions were of limited significance.

Professor Marchal wondered whether the recent increase in the importance of theories of bargaining did not depend on the greater importance of bargaining in the real world? He did not, however, think that wage theory could profit much from theories of games, of duopoly, and of oligopoly. These were still too general, and their observations were based on studies of the markets for goods rather than of the very specialized market for labour. On the contrary, he felt that wage theory could make contributions to the theory of oligopoly. Professor Marchal pointed out that the lower limit to wages, the subsistence minimum, varied greatly between countries and between periods, for example between modern Britain and modern India. How was this minimum determined and how was it related to changes in wage rates? We must also think of a 'wage hierarchy', including higher qualified workers. Again, one must allow for the existence of a capitalistic class and take into account not only their marginal propensity to consume but also the size of such capitalist groups.

Professor Marchal agreed with Dr. Rothschild that wage theory should represent a theory of distribution. But he thought that the distinction between the short and long period was becoming difficult to make in modern conditions. Finally he asked Dr. Rothschild whether he agreed: (1) that the theory of wages no longer had independent existence but must be merged in general distribution theory; (2) that the traditional distinction between variables and data needed to be revised to allow for the influence of institutions. Professor Marchal asked if we could rigorously maintain the dividing line between sociological and economic science or should try to combine the methods of both.

M. Sellier said that Dr. Rothschild had centred his attention on actual bargaining between workers and employers in a 'U.S.-German' model. Perhaps, however, we should consider the industrial group as a whole and study the distribution of income between this and other groups. Bargaining between employers and workers could take money from employers, but might not this money go to farmers, landlords, or tax-collectors because of consequent economic and political changes. Perhaps we needed a theory of the 'terms of trade' between the several social groups. Such a wider theory would help to show differences between bargaining of the United States type and that which took place in countries where unions were more interested in real than in money wages.

Professor Dunlop felt that we needed a theory of bargaining which was general enough to allow for varying institutional factors, and in particular for the cases where bargaining concerned the activities of firms and industries and the causes of the actions of broad social groups. The latter should apply to conditions where there really was direct bargaining between broad groups, as apparently happened in Sweden and Australia.

We needed a theory to show the effects of changes in wages on prices, of tax changes on income distribution, and so on. This theory should show the effects of social services and subsidies on the income of various groups, and should do so in a strict economic sense. Wage theory must draw on the very heart of economic analysis and not be separated from the main stream of economic theory. This procedure did not preclude sociological considerations, but merely represented an initial and different level of analysis.

Professor Wagner claimed that Professor Marchal had said that a theory of wages could not be autonomous but must consider the distribution of the national income. He himself could not imagine a theory of distribution of the national income which had not at its centre a theory of wages. How was the interdependence between the distribution of national income and the theory of wages allowed for in Professor Marchal's theory ?

Professor Marchal replied that we had long had a theory of wages in which wages were determined by bargaining between workers and employers. But there were other important factors in our complex, modern world; for example, agricultural prices. These could not be ignored, and this was where he found his relation between the two. He did not agree with M. Sellier that we must distinguish negotiations within industrial groups from those between social groups. Bargaining always becomes, ultimately, a multilateral process. M. Sellier's 'terms of trade' theory was valid, but not in more than a partial sense. For example, it ignored the fact that institutions like trade unions dealt with extra-market factors like hours of work, holiday with pay, and so on.

Professor Dupriez pointed out that while in the short period it was hard to see how trade unions could achieve more than small wage increases, if one allowed for long-period technical progress, the monopolistic action of a trade union might influence the whole economy, by, for example, increasing the direct efficiency of labour and leading to more favourable combinations of factors of production. We needed greater understanding of the actions of trade unions which favoured or hampered long-term progress.

Dr. Rothschild, replying to the discussion, concentrated on the question, 'Is economics different from sociology?' He said that he did not want to be accused of 'killing' theory. The theory might be inadequate, but we had nothing better. Nor was it enough to leave the problem to sociologists. It had long been said that each social science must first of all work out its own theory and then the various theories must be combined. But the result had been that each school's theories had been too complicated for other social scientists to understand. Therefore one could not afford to leave this problem to sociologists ; all must try to pioneer into the field. Replying to Professor Marchal, Dr. Rothschild said that one could not throw out the present theory of wages because one had no theory of distribution to take its place.

Introducing the paper by Professor Shackle, *Dr. Hansen* said that Professor Shackle took it for granted that everyone had read his previous work on expectations.[1] This led to difficulties over terminology for those who had not, in fact, read the book. Professor Shackle had entitled his paper '*The* Bargaining Process' ; but this was not an adequate title. Only some instances of the bargaining process were covered ; namely, those involving two parties. Nor had it been recognized that under an impartial chairman the process became different in an important way. The rôle of the chairman would be to 'unmask' the bargaining parties, and a clever chairman may find a quick (and different) solution. Dr. Hansen instanced the Scandinavian governments' bargaining machinery for wages which had not been studied by Professor Shackle. Dr. Hansen was troubled over Professor Shackle's conclusions where there was 'certainty'. Could not a 'certain' cocksure person be misled ? The essential factor was imperfect knowledge and foresight.

Dr. Hansen also wondered why it was assumed that the bargaining process would necessarily end. The results of abandoning the bargaining process might be so horrible as, for example, in the Korean war, that it was thought better to go on bargaining indefinitely. In economics, also, there could be an endless chain of bargaining where what one did this month could affect next month's bargaining, and so on. Dr. Hansen asked the nature of the central question of indeterminacy. What was it ? One could of course raise deep philosophical problems, but here the problem was a purely logical one.

	Complete	*Incomplete*
Static	Hicks Zeuthen Pen ?	Edgeworth
Dynamic	. .	Pen ?

[1] See G. L. S. Shackle, *Expectation in Economics* (1952).

Dr. Hansen drew up the above tabulation in which he classified economic models as being either (a) complete or incomplete; (b) static or dynamic.

A model was incomplete if there were more variables than equations, for example two variables (price and amount demanded) on one curve. This typified the Edgeworth model. Here one had indeterminacy because one could give no precise value to the variables, only a schedule. Indeterminacy, however, was also a question of what answer one wanted. A model was complete where the number of equations equalled the number of unknowns. There was only one solution and therefore determinacy in the Hicks and Zeuthen cases. Both these types of model were static. However, if there was more than one intersection point, was there indeterminacy? It might be that the model was not complete.

Dr. Hansen explained that complete dynamic theories could be determinate if the number of equations equalled the number of variables. Models might yield a 'stationary' solution or a 'moving' one. A dynamic model would explain bids over time and show if one were moving towards or away from agreement. Certainly, in such cases, the initial position might affect (a) the final result; and (b) whether the model ended in convergence or divergence. Explosive oscillations would be indeterminate in the sense that no definite results were reached, but one could still trace the path followed and to that extent the model was determinate. Perhaps the notion of indeterminacy in models of bargaining and in ordinary models differed. In the 'bargaining literature' Dr. Hansen thought a process whose result depended on the starting-point was regarded as indeterminate, but one could still tell the result. So how should 'indeterminacy' be interpreted?

Returning to Messrs. Zeuthen and Hicks as compared with Pen, Dr. Hansen said that for Hicks and Zeuthen the cutting point of the two curves gave the solution. This was typical of all static theory. Static analysis was sometimes useful in economics. So why not in bargaining? Pen, on the other hand, did not say how the final position was reached. So it was either an incomplete dynamic theory, with the central equations not given, or it was really a static theory.

Dr. Gasparini raised a question on logical versus dynamic indeterminacy. The roots of logical indeterminacy lay, partly, in the problem of integrability of the equations describing the equilibrium. However, the roots of the equations were not necessarily real, while differential equations could not always be solved and, if solved, only a type of relationship (a family of curves but not a specific curve) might be known. Indeterminacy lay also in the fact that economic forces worked in many directions, even in a static framework. This could be traced back to a problem of knowledge.

In dynamics, the indeterminacy depended on the concept of time. If changes were taking place and were shaping the economic system, one could not tell *a priori* which way the system would move. The system would move ; but one could only know on a probability basis where it would move to. If our knowledge of the future was so limited, Dr. Gasparini wondered whether unions and employers should shape their economic strategy by taking into consideration only specific issues. If economic progress were taking a new path, an attempt by unions to consider too many factors in planning their economic strategy might well affect the rate and the path of the future progress itself.

Professor Harbison said that he wanted to make a rather mundane remark about bargaining, namely, that before economists could progress much further with theoretical analysis, there was need for more information about what such bargaining was for. We needed some clear ideas, and if possible empirical knowledge, country by country, of the objectives of trade unions and entrepreneurs when bargaining occurred. Professor Harbison did not agree with M. Sellier that United States unions aimed merely at raising money wages. Safer jobs and power over union members were often objectives. Nor was M. Sellier's claim correct for German unions. The latter were much interested in gaining control over entrepreneurs. Nor could he agree that French unions were primarily interested in the purchasing power of money and income distribution. The C.G.T. had non-economic and political aims, especially where there was Communist domination. What we needed were facts about motives in bargaining, in the same way as we had wage statistics. The help of psychologists or sociologists was not needed. Such people would not first look at the facts. They would start with a preconceived framework and merely fit the facts into it. Economists made this same mistake, but probably less seriously. Professor Harbison suggested that economic theory progressed in an alternating way. First one constructed a theory ; then one looked at facts and carried out empirical study ; finally one re-examined the assumptions of one's theory and made improvements.

Professor Jöhr also considered the synthesis of economics and sociology. One needed to start from economic theory and then to introduce broader data as independent variables. There would be less danger of a difference between economic theory and reality if this were done.

Professor Jöhr felt, however, that one needed to consider yet another kind of indeterminacy. For example, the dreams of one night affect actions next day. In turn, this might affect the dreams of the following night, and so on. In this particular model, however, one could never grasp all the factors affecting (a) one's dreams or (b) one's behaviour. Professor Jöhr wondered if Professor Shackle was thinking of this kind of indeterminacy. Finally, the bargaining process was not only between employers and union. Others, the government, price control committees, and so on, took part. Similarly the leaders of a union might wish to be in a position to prove (a) that they had attained the optimum result; or (b) they had at least fought for it. Therefore, one had also to consider the position of leaders *vis-à-vis* members.

Mr. Peacock felt that one should give Professor Shackle credit for trying to discuss bargaining at a high level of abstraction, and to consider the results of his assumptions rather than assumptions themselves. It was easy enough to say that the idea of maximization was unrealistic in some cases. Perhaps the idea that unions maximized money wages was wrong but, at this level of abstraction, it had an interpretative value, even though it did not allow one to predict. Professor Harbison's remarks about the importance of non-economic factors in the United States confused ends and means. Why should a union not gain control over entry? A bargaining process should be studied as a means by which money (perhaps even real) wages could be maximized.

Professor Myers saw no reason why non-economic facts should not fit in to Professor Shackle's theory. It was hard to produce a theory to fit in with all behaviour. Mr. Peacock's analysis was too simple. The political distribution of power affected many things, and its importance might differ greatly between the United States and Sweden. Again, the behaviour of the government was not covered by Professor Shackle's theory. One needed a broad theory to cover all such points.

Mr. Turner felt that Professor Shackle's theory was self-contained. But why need there be determinacy in individual bargaining? In science, for instance, the paths of atomic particles were indeterminate, though their behaviour was determinate if one considered many particles. Why should one not here formulate a theory of the same kind, where any individual fact is untraceable but the general results are known?

M. Sellier said that he had been misunderstood. His point was not that trade unions cared only about salaries in the United States, but about other facts, too, as in France. All he had said was that the

United States unions were firm- or industry-minded while the French worker did not believe that wage bargaining could solve his problems.

Professor Shackle acknowledged the importance of Dr. Hansen's comments. He agreed that he had only considered two parties. Perhaps, however, all bargaining was in a sense 'two party'; with more than two people there might be 'atoms or molecules' of bargaining, each of which had only two parties. As an ex-civil servant, Professor Shackle agreed that the importance of an impartial chairman could not be overrated in his benefits for the 'public interest', provided only that he was acknowledged by both parties as being impartial. Dr. Hansen had also raised the vital distinction between subjective certainty and objective rightness, which was not always made in economic theory. There were countless instances in the literature of confusion arising from failure to make this distinction. Objective rightness, however, could only exist about events in the past; there could be no *ex ante* rightness about the future. Professor Shackle also wondered whether bargaining could not have a utility of its own, like gambling. Why should it not go on for ever? He thought it was better to wrangle for ever than to give up arguing and fight.

Professor Shackle said he had no time to deal with the question 'What is determinacy?' Dr. Hansen had thrown a flood of light on this point. Zeuthen, however, had only one equation for his two variables; therefore even Zeuthen's model was not strictly complete. But Zeuthen deserved credit for discovering a 'watershed'. In the past we had drawn the line too rigidly between economics and psychology. If we found indeterminacy in the models, it was our own fault for not allowing for psychological factors.

In Mr. Pen's model the forms of his functions changed during the bargaining process. Professor Shackle did not think one could have a determinate theory if the functions were not stable, but changed as the process went on. One could hardly hope to produce an equation showing how the process would develop.

SIXTH SESSION

TUESDAY MORNING, SEPTEMBER 7, 1954

(Discussion of Papers by Reynolds, Kerr, and Rehn)

Mr. Roberts said that he agreed strongly with much of Professor Reynolds's paper. But one danger of a long paper was that the author might forget at the end what he had said at the beginning;

Professor Reynolds might have made that mistake. He initially turned against comparing the development of trade union wage structures with a hypothetical wage structure that would exist under perfect competition. Yet his final conclusions made comparisons with hypothetical wage structures that would exist under perfect competition, and pointed to the possibility of considerable argument as to whether the wage structure under perfect competition represented a welfare norm. The alternative comparison suggested was with a non-union labour market.

In the United Kingdom it was extremely difficult to find a non-union labour market not influenced by collective bargaining, and it was difficult to establish control groups to measure the impact of trade unionism. Mr. Roberts felt, however, that British trade unions had not seriously distorted the wage structure. Mr. Turner had argued that changes in occupational differentials had mainly been caused by union wage policies, but he thought that Mr. Turner had over-estimated the influence of union wage policies and under-estimated economic, technical, and social, as well as historical factors. International comparisons raised enormous problems. In general, however, Mr. Roberts felt that the net effect of trade unionism on wage structures was not so great as it appeared at first sight.

In the United Kingdom the spread between wage rates and earnings was considerable, and it gave employers much scope for shaping the wage pattern within firms to suit themselves. It did not always follow that the effect of union activity would be to narrow differentials. Indeed, at present British railway unions were having second thoughts on this question.

Mr. Laffer, commenting on Professor Kerr's paper, said that it was concerned only with the direct impacts of trade unions on wage differentials and neglected their indirect effects through the government. In a country like Australia this would severely limit the usefulness of the approach, for government power in Australia was often partly a reflection of trade union power. The narrowing of area differentials in Australia had occurred mainly as a result of the principles followed by the statutory wage-fixing authorities set up by governments. Trade unions were not the only group concerned, and it would be difficult to isolate their influence. Undoubtedly, however, their pressure was an important factor in the establishment of these authorities. The obstacles to wage increases arising from interstate competition led some unions to give strong support to uniformity.

There had been no steady downward movement of occupational differentials; fluctuations occurred according to the decisions of the wage authorities. Care was needed when interpreting Australian data, as one's conclusions might be affected greatly by one's choice of years for comparison. Over a long period, a narrowing of occupational differentials seems to have occurred in two ways. Minimum wages consisted of a basic wage for unskilled workers and margins for skill, danger, etc. The key margin was that of the engineering fitter, which, in the highly integrated Australian wage structure was quickly followed by virtually all other margins. The margin of the engineering fitter had declined relatively to the basic wage, partly as a result of trade union pressure for basic wage increases, and partly as a result of principles followed by the Arbitration Court that were disliked by trade unions. At the same time there had been a tendency for the less skilled workers to secure increases in margins as a direct result of trade union pressure. The Commonwealth Government had recently announced its intention of appearing before the Arbitration Court in support of an increase in the margins of *skilled* workers. The trade unions did *not* welcome this, as they wanted an increase in all margins, including those of unskilled workers. This suggested that the Australian trade union movement was not interested in the maintenance of occupational differentials.

Finally, inter-industry differentials had narrowed in Australia from the beginning of Arbitration, and especially from 1907. This was an important effect of arbitration, which had achieved long ago for the weaker groups of workers what had only been achieved to a lesser extent in other countries under full employment. Here the Arbitration Court had given the trade unions something they could not have got for themselves.

Mr. Punekar said that his object was to furnish some Indian illustrations of the five types of wage differentials explained by Professors Kerr and Reynolds. However, he first wished to explain two peculiar features of Indian wage levels.

First, there was an absence of collective bargaining, and, instead, state regulation of wages. Before 1939 the state rarely intervened in wage matters. When war broke out, prices rose from 100 in 1939 to 218 in 1943. Many industrial disputes occurred on the issues of wages and allowances. Important disputes were then referred to adjudication. Also a 'dearness allowance' and bonus were granted quite readily by employers. Actual experience had shown that though the workers had lost in real wages, they had more faith in adjudication than in collective bargaining, because they had gained by resorting to the former method.

Another peculiar feature in India was the emergence of the

'dearness allowance' which was paid to compensate employees for the loss in real wages due to an abnormal rise in prices. Similarly the prosperity bonus was dependent on the profits of industry. The earnings of Indian workers were at present built up from three main components — the basic wage, the dearness and other allowances, and the bonus. The main fight of trade unions during the past fifteen years had been to get a bigger dearness allowance and more bonus. Comparatively little attention had been paid to basic wages.

Coming to the five types of wage differentials enumerated by Professors Kerr and Reynolds, Mr. Punekar admitted that he had not fully understood the implication of the first type, namely inter-personal differentials. The employer after all paid for the job and not for the individual; he was not much concerned whether the job was done by Mr. A or Mr. B. Professor Kerr referred to 'job selling' by a foreman and to wage discrimination by a supervisor. This was surely a personal matter between the foreman or supervisor and the worker. In so far as the worker was concerned, he was supposed to get the wage assigned for the particular job he held. Professor Reynolds referred to age, seniority, sex, and other personal characteristics, but did not develop the point. Mr. Punekar did not know whether discrimination was made because of age and seniority, as long as the particular job demanded a particular wage. Discrimination on account of sex was made and there were instances in India where male workers had been awarded not only a higher basic wage but also a higher dearness allowance. However, sex discrimination alone did not warrant a separate section on inter-personal differentials.

With inter-firm differentials one could distinguish three cases: (1) where an association of employers dealt, before an adjudicator, with a union or unions of employees; (2) where an individual employer dealt with an individual union; and (3) where wage disputes did not go to adjudication. Differentials were generally eliminated in the first case, because wages in a number of firms were jointly discussed. In cases of the second type, and more so in those of the third type, differentials were wide.

Inter-area differentials had been allowed in India, on the grounds of different standards of living in different areas. For example, minimum monthly basic wages laid down by adjudicators for the cotton mills differed as follows: Bombay City, Rs. 30; Ahmadabad, Rs. 28; Sholapur, Rs. 26; and West Bengal, Rs. 20. These inter-regional differentials were further widened by the different rates of dearness allowance. Including this allowance, monthly earnings of an Indian cotton mill worker varied from Rs. 50 in West Bengal to Rs. 103 in Ahmadabad.

The Indian difficulty in minimizing inter-occupational differentials was the lack of standardization in occupations. Except in a few cases like the cotton mills and some engineering industries, the nomenclature had not even been standardized. Craft unionism had been absent in India, with the notable exception of a powerful federation of craft unions in Ahmadabad.

Lastly, Mr. Punekar spoke about inter-industry differentials in India. He said that war-time and post-war circumstances, which had necessitated the payment of at least a starvation wage to the Indian worker, had narrowed inter-industry differentials by raising the level of wages in unorganized industries. The Minimum Wages Act, which applied to sweated industries, as well as the awards of adjudicators, industrial tribunals, and the Labour Appellate Tribunal had all contributed to reducing inter-industry differentials.

Dr. Rothschild felt that the three papers gave great satisfaction in reaching very similar conclusions although there had been no collusion. Moreover, they reached the same conclusions by different approaches. Mr. Rehn, in particular, had thrown great light on trade union motivation.

M. Brochier shared Mr. Roberts's concern over the influence of trade unions. He agreed that one must base one's own views on wage differentials between industries and occupations. But it was difficult to abstract from technical evolution. Nor was it possible to separate ideological and social factors (and power) affecting the actions of trade unions. M. Brochier felt that one ought to be conscious of the limitations imposed on our theories by the experience on which they were based. He wished to underline Professor Reynolds's discussion of the 'scope of collective bargaining units'. The important thing was the *level* at which negotiations took place. The higher the level the greater the tendency to equalization. In France unions were large, centralized, and 'general'; local trade unions had little autonomy. Negotiations took place first to settle the level of the National Minimum Wage (S.M.I.G.). Then there were negotiations for adjustments above this. The initial negotiations were particularly important, since they affected inter-firm and inter-occupational differentials. They were based, above all, on preserving marginal firms.

M. Brochier agreed that unions had little effect on inter-industry differentials. There were exceptions; for example, the printing industry. But productivity and, above all, the strategic position of the industry in the national economy were significant. A teachers' strike in France had little effect; no one cared. But with the Metro matters were quite different.

M. Rottier wondered whether in the long run, as a consequence of technological change, a comparison between the skill of, say, an engineering fitter and a labourer was meaningless. The skill differential here must be less than in 1914. If it had been significant to take the fitter/labourer ratio in 1914, the comparison should now need to be between tool-room labour and the fitter. M. Rottier said that these reports were based on United States evidence because only in the United States could one say enough about relative wages. Elsewhere we needed more information about differentials; about earnings compared with wages; about wages of men and women, and so on. The flexibility, in Britain, of the relationship between earnings and wages had been discussed already. But did it exist elsewhere? In France there was no information about earnings and wages. Though the differences there varied between industries, they remained stable within industries. But this might be the result of inflation. One could not ask intelligent questions about France, because there were not enough facts showing whether wage rates and earnings were related. *M. Brochier* replied that there were some facts. For example, the trade unions gave them.

Professor Haller noted a recent change in Germany. Formerly unions were interested in occupational differentials, now they were concerned with industry differentials. Thus, there was a tendency for inter-occupational differences to narrow, whilst those between industries widened. Mr. Rehn talked of 'equity' reducing wage differences. If, in Germany, differentials between industries grew and those between occupations fell, there was a move towards equity brought about by the nature of union organization.

Professor Dupriez mentioned a study in Belgium into inter-industry wage differences, which concluded that trade union action was not tending to bring about equality of wages between industries. Each was concerned with its own wages. This study [1] showed that inter-industry wage differentials depended mainly on the trade cycle. Industries which were not 'sheltered' paid lower wages in depression and vice versa. This was especially marked in an 'open economy' like Belgium.

Professor Kerr thought Dr. Rothschild had missed some important disagreements among the three papers. The authors did not agree about occupational and industrial wage differences. All felt that

[1] R. Dehem, 'Revenue et emploi en économie ouverte; l'expérience de la Belgique de 1913–1946', *Bulletin de l'Institut de Recherches Économiques et Sociales* (1946).

there was a major trend towards narrower occupational and industrial differences in developed areas. But did unions help this trend? Professor Reynolds, Mr. Rehn, and Mr. Turner thought that unions helped to bring equality. He himself thought that unions tended to hold up the trend. The fact was that one could explain the trend without bringing in unions. It had occurred both in Russia and in free countries, in organized and non-organized industries. It also happened in industries before unions came. Moreover, when trade unions were fully developed they held this trend back.

Mr. Rehn said that unions made wages (a) more rigid and (b) more equitable. Yet the elements of rigidity held back equity. Denmark had strong trade unions but little narrowing of differentials. Australia had also had no narrowing for thirty years. The United States had experienced still less narrowing than countries with informal craft unions. Perhaps the explanation was that though skilled workers were few in number they were influential in union councils.

Professor Reynolds thought that Professor Kerr might have over-stated the differences between them. In so far as trade unions had any effect, he himself felt that they had widened inter-industry differentials. On inter-occupational differentials the difference between him and Professor Kerr arose partly from differences in data. Professor Kerr had studied occupations over a wide field, Professor Reynolds had confined his studies within given industries. There were many reasons for narrowing occupational differences, and one need not bring in trade unions. However, in the United States, trade unions regarded this tendency for narrower differentials *within* any given industry complacently. To that extent, at least, they must take some responsibility for the narrowing of inter-occupational differences.

Mr. Rehn thought Professor Kerr and Professor Reynolds were both right. Unions did, sometimes, preserve existing wage structures, though generally they did the opposite. Everywhere, employers complained that unions destroyed the 'sound' structure of wage differentials which had previously given higher rewards for greater skill. However, though rank-and-file unionists wanted to diminish differentials, union organizers often felt that equalization could go too far. This was true both in Sweden and the United States. The drive for job-evaluation was beginning in Sweden and this seemed to be the employer's attempt to 'sell' some differentiation to unions. But Mr. Rehn thought that most unions were dominated by unskilled workers, and Mr. Turner was surely right that mass-unionism meant a narrowing of differentials.

Against this background one needed special explanation of the fact that there had been signs of some restoring of differentials during recent years. This explanation could be found in a very rapid narrowing during the 1940's because of the sudden coming of full employment and a simultaneous decrease in the size of the younger age-groups, while the older age-groups with their larger numbers of skilled people had been increasing in sizc. Thus we had got 'the full employment paradox'. The wage premium for skill had been considerably diminished at the same time as the security premium for skill (the lower unemployment risk) had disappeared with the general abolition of unemployment risks for everybody. It took some time before this (and the natural growth of population) could have any effect on the relative scarcities of skilled and unskilled workers. But when skill became more scarce there would be a reaction to the equalization trend.

SEVENTH SESSION

TUESDAY EVENING, SEPTEMBER 7, 1954

(Discussion of Paper by Rottier)

Mr. Turner said that, to judge from the day's papers, an inquirer began by collecting statistics and then reached conclusions from them. He thought that in this field statistics might be misleading. Statistical sources themselves implied definitions which were not necessarily those one wanted. The material might not be fully representative; and the method of compilation could impose a particular form of movement over time. For example, in the United Kingdom there were statistics of wage rates and earnings. Messrs. Rottier and Roberts thought that a gap between the two meant a divergence between wages agreed on in collective agreement and wages actually paid. But it followed from the nature of the published statistics that in an expansionist situation the index of earnings rose faster than that of wage rates. The explanation did not lie in the real phenomena discussed in the morning session. It was dangerous to use statistics without confidence in them and without full knowledge of their implication. One must look at 'primary facts'. Here one found a tendency for wages paid and wage rates agreed to approximate to each other. Employers observed rates; unions enforced them strictly. Therefore the narrowing of the gap between wage rates of various kinds was real.

Various causes for the narrower differences had been suggested.

But in Britain these had mainly occurred when wages were rising rapidly. At such times the prevalence of 'flat' increases had meant an automatic narrowing of relative differences; and 'flat' increases were what unions demanded. Most British unions had asked for flat, but some for *percentage* increases. What was the difference between them? The unions in Britain that had asked for flat wage increases in a time of inflation generally combined skilled and unskilled workers, and they were unions where unskilled workers could never rise to the skilled ranks, but could influence the policy of their unions. Again, they were unions which were trying to attract unskilled members. The unions asking for percentage wage increases were those where unskilled workers could become skilled, which were dominated by the skilled workers, and where either the unskilled worker *must* belong to them or the union in any case fixed unskilled rates. Union structure had thus been almost decisive in determining the policy followed. But it need not be *conscious* policy. Nor could one generalize about other countries, though perhaps it was significant that this narrowing had generally occurred under (a) rising wages, (b) mass trade unions. Perhaps it would have happened in any case, but Mr. Turner preferred to say that economic forces 'tolerated' it. Nevertheless, one had to distinguish the analysis of causation from the giving of advice on economic policy, and Mr. Turner was not sure that this had been done in the conference.

Professor Dunlop commented on percentage and flat rate differentials. One should distinguish between those situations where wages rose during periods of considerable inflation and those where rising wages reflected a rise in real income. Inter-occupational differences behaved differently in each of these cases.[1]

During war-time inflation, particularly with declines in real income, there were very strong pressures for equal flat rate changes in wages (cost-of-living bonuses), in order to make more equal the distribution of the remaining income and to offset the fact that food prices typically tended to rise most. Occupational wage differentials were thus narrowed in percentage terms, making the distribution of available goods and services among workers more equal than it would otherwise be. The war and post-war periods in many countries reflected this experience.

If real income rose, however, reflecting higher long-term productivity, occupational wage differentials typically tended to narrow a little in percentage terms, because of greater educational

[1] See *Proceedings of Sixth Annual Meeting of Industrial Relations Research Association*, December 28–30, 1953, pp. 79-82.

opportunities and because of the effects of the same sort of ideas as those which underlay progressive income taxes. Increases in real income should be distributed more equally than the existing income was.

Professor Dunlop therefore put forward the general theorem that over history one had periods of inflation and periods of rising real income. Occupational differentials tended to narrow in both periods but for different reasons and in different degrees.

Professor Shackle took up references to a 'fair' or 'equitable' wage structure in the sense both of wage rates and of wage differentials. What was the test? Some people would say that this was a value judgment; or implied a system 'fair to most', or 'fair to the majority of a disinterested and competent committee'. Professor Shackle sympathized with the idea that one could have attached a real measuring to 'fairness'. Perhaps someone in the conference would discuss the character of such a pragmatic answer to the question, What is fairness?

Was a structure fair when the ratios between wages were equal to the marginal disutilities, or to the average or the total disutility of labour? Professor Shackle did not see why one should consider marginal disutilities. But if one took average and total disutilities then one was in even deeper water. For one raised the more general problem, how does one add utilities and disutilities over time, in this case through a day's work? And yet one could have no average without a total. All this was in addition to the old problem of the measurement or interpersonal comparison of the disutility of work. One might say, then, that fairness meant a value judgment, and leave it at that. Or one might feel that it was worth thinking out a precise test of whether a wage structure was 'fair'.

There had also been references to the narrowing of differences in wages. Was it implied that this brought about 'equality' in the sense of fairness? Or were speakers referring to the other word, 'equity', a source of confusion? This ought to be an easy point to settle. Was it an Anglo-American difference? Or ought we to distinguish conceptually between a 'more equitable' and 'more equal' wage structure?

Mr. Rehn said that he knew the philosophical impossibility of defining 'equity', a word that usually needed inverted commas. He thought it was clear from his paper that he implied that equality and equity were not always the same thing. But there were hard facts behind 'the growing demand for equity'. Workers grew ever more conscious of relative wages, and 'equity-consciousness' was a great force in union behaviour. Thus the widening orbits of 'coercive comparison' and also these ideas of equity were both strong forces in determining the wage structure.

One American trade union leader had explicitly assured him equality (in this case implying equity) in the United States labour market. Big and strong unions now demanded equal wages for whole industries all over the country, thus destroying the old area-patterns and compelling other industries, which were more influenced by the local area patterns, to adapt themselves to the 'key wages' introduced from outside by these industry-wide bargains. The tendency towards equal efficiency wages thus was being established throughout the United States — notwithstanding the 'inertias' of Professors Lester and Reynolds. This was increasing the 'degree of coerciveness' in all wage comparisons. The same thing was happening in Sweden.

Professor Haller asked whether there was 'equity' for social groups, or did it exist only for persons or families? The goal of 'equity' could only exist in the sense that income had to be distributed according to certain moral criteria. One not only had to consider the disutility of work, but also the wants of the worker, and the level of intellectual satisfaction — for instance, the wish for freedom of intellectual development. The problem thus became philosophical, with no generally valid norms. All one could do would be to avoid some sorts of inequity; by job evaluation, for example.

Professor Reynolds explained that when, at the end of his paper, he had said that unions had improved the position, he was comparing differentials in imperfect competition under unions and conditions in imperfect competition with no unions. When he said that we should move in the direction expected in perfect competition, he was comparing imperfect with perfect competition. It was conceivable, of course, that the effects of unions might be worse, even, than those of imperfect, non-union, competition.

It was, however, true that the idea of perfect competition was a 'creature of the mind'. He certainly did not assert that the position under perfect competition would be the best in all circumstances. But it was an interesting and respectable thesis that it might be. Professors Simons and Machlup took perfect competition as a starting-point and showed that unions were universally bad. He only wanted to show that it was not necessary to reach the Machlup-Simons conclusion, even if one accepted their criterion of a proper wage structure.

Professor Reynolds had been interested by Professor Dunlop's suggestion that we should try to distinguish between what went on in inflation and what happened over longer periods of time. The distinction might be a little hard to make empirically except, say, during a war. Although one could say that these changes which occurred during spurts of inflation were abnormal, they were nevertheless real, and remained after the inflation ended.

Professor Shackle had raised an interesting question. What sense could one give to the word fairness or equity in a wage structure ? He himself believed that disutility was important and deserved studying. In the United States, job evaluation was widely used to measure the worth of the job, emphasizing such features as the education required, the length of training, skill, and other positive elements. Relatively less emphasis was put on fatigue, hazards, unpleasantness, etc. Perhaps the weighting needed to be reversed, with heavier weight given to the disutility elements.

Professor Kerr said that the wage slide was an extremely important phenomenon, and we were indebted to the Swedish labour economists for bringing it to our attention. It was a demonstration that market forces triumphed over efforts to control them. By studying the wage slide one could discover the extent to which the market had reached different results from the decisions of the bargaining parties.

He agreed with Mr. Turner that it was difficult to discover whether the slide existed. One could not simply take the difference between contract rates and earnings. Other factors, for instance changes in piece rates, were important too. But one could say something about the circumstances in which the wage slide was likely to appear. It was more likely when one had industry-wide or nation-wide contracts. It also occurred where unions were not particularly aggressive. In Germany, with broad contracts and an unaggressive trade union movement, there was an enormous wage slide, perhaps 25 per cent. There were three wage levels for wage setting in Germany ; first, that reached contractually by the trade unions and the employers ; second, a higher level fixed by local works councils ; and third, the actual effective rates. There was a slide up from the contract and the local agreement levels to the effective rate.

Professor Kerr said that if there was a simple solution to the problem, why should one look for a complex one ? The phenomena were universal, almost world-wide, with a narrowing of differentials as industrialization progressed. If there was that narrowing with trade unions, did one need a specific explanation when the broad explanation was adequate to the task ? Did unions tend to favour skilled workers and hold up the narrowing of differentials ? If one took all benefits into account as well as wages, a better case could be made for saying that there was favouritism to skilled workers, for example through long-service preferences, holidays with pay, retirement benefits, etc. Mr. Rehn's claim that one could show that unions had not favoured skilled workers, by citing the fact that some employers complained that the skill differential was declining, was not convincing. Employers were always prejudiced in favour of skilled workers, especially those employers with a Calvinistic background.

In Professor Kerr's own opinion there was a long-run trend towards narrowing differentials and the rigidity caused by unions could only slow up that trend. Where unions did bring about greater uniformity in wages between plants in the same area this was probably very beneficial, since it helped to create the conditions one would have in a more perfect market by eliminating or stimulating inefficient employers. Where unions were consequential they were also beneficial. But where unions gave greater stress to maintaining skill differentials they were also less consequential. It was perhaps fortunate for society that where trade unions had important effects, those effects were good ; where trade unions were unimportant, their effects were not so good.

Mr. Rehn thought one should give due credit to Mr. Levinson. He had made a comprehensive investigation, and Professor Kerr was not quite right in attributing to Levinson the view that unions had little influence on the inter-industry wage structure except in depression. Levinson had shown that in different branches of *manufacturing* industry, there had been no difference in the rate of rises between 1914 and 1947, caused by the rise in unionism. Earlier sectional minority unions had had a strong impact, but this was wiped out by later developments. Outside manufacturing, however, the position was different ; non-unionized industries had lagged behind. Levinson might be right that it was 'sympathetic pressure' inside manufacturing (representing one 'orbit of coercive comparisons') which forced non-union industries to increase wages at the same rate as in unionized trades. But apparently the 'sympathetic pressure' was less strong outside this orbit. To give another instance, in Sweden in the depression of the early 1920's wages in manufacturing industries were stable for a year after the slump started, in spite of the fact that union coverage was far from 100 per cent. In farming, with no wage agreements at all, and outside the manufacturing orbit, wages had fallen immediately. Manufacturing wages did not follow the downward trend until agreements had been renewed on lower levels. We needed further research into such sympathetic pressure. Apparently it had something to do with those factors which made wages rigid even where there were no unions. Employers had to watch employees' feelings, and if employees combined a growing demand for equity with such sympathetic pressure, this would explain many events on the labour market.

One possible research subject was differences in wage movements in unionized industries and in non-unionized industries. Some figures from post-war America tended to show a higher degree of irregularity (disparity) in the movements of wages in a number of non-unionized industries than in the case of unionized ones. This tended to suggest that unions compelled wage bargains to stick to the existing patterns. But how wide were the orbits of such an influence ? The pressure worked in both ways, not only in an upward direction, for it compelled employers to be very careful. It became a 'sin' (from an employer's point of view) to give in to an upward wage pressure if other unions would use this increase as a pattern for their demands.

EIGHTH SESSION

WEDNESDAY MORNING, SEPTEMBER 8, 1954

(Discussion of Paper by Myers)

Mr. Meidner thought one could not blame those who felt that classical wage theory, for example that of Adam Smith, was unrealistic, particularly in the way it stressed the long-run tendency for wage differences to disappear. The 'true' classics had introduced modifications, but these were peripheral. Their main line was to stress free adjustment. Imperfections consequently explained mainly the existence of unemployment. The classics did not forget the qualifications, however, they merely put them aside, with reason.

Were the results of the 6-city study [1] really contradictory to earlier findings ? According to Professor Myers, the latter had shown only a weak link between mobility and net advantages ; the 6-city study showed that workers moved in response to net advantages. But was it true that people were now more rational than they had been some years ago ? Professor Myers talked of movements similar to those in the theoretical model. What model ? Could we really assume that the movement of millions of ignorant

[1] Gladys L. Palmer, *Labor Mobility in Six Cities, A Report on the Survey of Patterns and Factors in Labor Mobility, 1940–1950*, (1954).

people resulted in the operation of an 'invisible hand'? In any case, Mr. Meidner himself did not like 'invisible hands'. Sweden had a high labour turnover, but low inter-occupational and inter-industrial mobility. In particular, the 'push motives' were stronger than the 'pull motives'. This lack of occupational mobility became more important with narrowing wage differentials. With higher mobility there was less danger of inflation.

Mr. Meidner thought Professor Reynolds was right in saying that the process of wage determination and labour mobility had only peripheral connections. If wage theory still existed at all, it had to compete with sociology and psychology. Some people did not want to hand wage theory to the other social scientists. Personally, he had found co-operation with sociologists on *mobility* useful. Wage theory needed mobility studies.

Professor Reynolds said that the 6-city study neither confirmed nor refuted earlier studies of local labour markets. Nor was it aimed at any particular theory of labour-market structure. This was not to decry the 6-city study, which was interesting and valuable. But it said little on why labour moved or on the labour market mechanism. One could put little reliance on answers to the question, 'Why did you leave your job?' Professor Myers had perhaps put his case too strongly at certain points. The large differences in mobility shown between war and non-war industries, heavy and light industry, showed in the study of the 1940's. But they proved nothing very definite about either the competitiveness or effectiveness of the labour market.

On the broad issue of the effect of the wage structure on mobility, Professor Reynolds thought that there was a relation. However, it was weaker than that in a perfect market, and its operation was different. Employed workers gave no strong indication of moving rapidly to high-wage industries. But there were also unemployed workers engaged in choosing jobs. They knew little about the market, and had only a 'reservation price'. This provided a lower limit and represented a link between differentials and mobility.

Professor Phelps Brown raised a difficulty in discovering, by field studies, the effect of wage differentials on mobility. Such studies examined a series of particular case histories, but the factors which were predominant in particular cases might be of little effect on the aggregate, because they were diverse and tended to cancel each other out. On the other hand, a factor which, though of minor influence in any one case worked in the same direction in all, might predominate in the behaviour of the aggregate. It was the particular factors, however, that people tended to remember and which questioning tended to bring out. Unfortunately, there was no way out through statistical studies of the aggregates themselves, because these analyses ran into the familiar difficulty of *ceteris non paribus*.

Mr. Peacock felt that to some extent Mr. Meidner had been unjust to the theory of 'net advantage'. As he understood it, this theory was based on pure competition, where the motivation of workers was only one element. Where Professor Myers said that a voluntary movement did not equalize the net advantages of different jobs, what weight was he putting on imperfections on the demand side as compared with those on the workers' side? Professor Myers had studied unemployment. If one considered changes in labour mobility with stable employment conditions, he suspected that imperfections in demand might then predominate.

M. Rottier wanted to defend the 'neo-classicals'. They considered only small adjustments near equilibrium; in fact, in the real world there were rarely massive transfers. It was enough for workers to know about a small range of possible jobs. Second, Mr. Meidner had thrown doubts on the link between relative wages and mobility. Why, then, was he worried that there would be little mobility of manpower if wage differentials narrowed? *Mr. Meidner* replied that at present there seemed to be a slow response to wage differentials. If one eliminated such differentials, the movement would be still less.

Professor Kerr said it was sometimes assumed that if one moved from a job with a higher to one with a lower wage, that was irrational. It might be that such a move was *more* rational than one depending only on wages. If one moved to a job with lower wages, one was likely to have thought more about the surrounding conditions.

Mr. Roberts asked whether there had been attempts to analyse the effect of institutional factors on labour mobility in the United States; for example, the effects of trade unions, seniority, and pensions schemes.

Professor Myers said that in such a short paper it was difficult to summarize the vast body of American literature on the subject. This had led to certain inconsistencies. The main point was that his own thinking had been modified as a result of the 6-city study. The 6-city study (only recently available) dealt with a longer period of time than the earlier local labour market studies. It also dealt with the war and post-war periods, when there were rapid changes in job opportunities. Generalizations from local labour market studies of New England, which had a mature and stable economy, might not apply to some of the cities in the West that were characterized by rapid expansion in the demand for labour. But the 6-city study included both some Eastern cities and also San Francisco and Los Angeles.

Despite barriers to voluntary movement, there was movement when the economy provided opportunities to move to more attractive jobs during 1940–1950. He did not know whether this movement had tended to equalize wage differentials, because there were other wartime influences. Somewhere between 50 per cent and 70 per cent of changes in jobs in this decade were voluntary, and many workers moved to better-paying jobs. The study was not designed to test the hypotheses of any model of the labour market, but did reveal some tendency to move to more attractive jobs when this was possible. Did workers choose jobs in a rational way ? Of course, said Professor Myers, some irrationality was inevitable. Workers might take the first job that appeared to be more attractive ; if they did not like this job, they might then move to another, but they could not make rational calculation of all opportunities, since they did not know about them.

Professor Myers thought there was no close relation between labour mobility and the wage determination process. Professor Reynolds had asked which model was 'confirmed' by the 6-city study. The quotation from Professor Hicks was not far from the impressions given by the 6-city study. When there was an expanding employment market, workers tended to move towards more attractive jobs, the attractions not being determined by the purely monetary advantages but by the whole nature of the job.

Professor Phelps Brown's dilemma was a real one. One could spend much time discussing the difficulties of finding out the real reasons why workers moved. Interview methods were difficult, but it was equally difficult to draw satisfactory conclusions from statistics. This was why research studies had to use the individual interview technique. A study at the Massachusetts Institute of Technology had shown very little equalization of wages through labour movement in a period of unemployment. But such conclusions about mobility tended to break down when the demand for labour increased rapidly.

Professor Myers agreed with Mr. Peacock that in full employment, with stable demand conditions, one was near the classical model, with the demand side of major importance. In answer to Mr. Roberts, Professor Myers said that some studies on these problems had been made in the United States. Professor Kerr [1] had shown that even a local labour market could break up in times

[1] 'The Balkanization of Labor Markets' in *Labor Mobility and Economic Opportunity* (1954), pp. 92–110.

of stable employment. Increased employment, as in a war, broke down gentlemen's agreements, which survived only in periods of relative stability.

NINTH SESSION

Wednesday Evening, September 8, 1954

(Discussion of Papers by Perroux and Sellier)

Mr. Rehn explained that M. Sellier presented two central theses, based mainly on French experience. In a period of inflation, when the inflation was mainly a monetary phenomenon, not very clearly connected with full employment and labour scarcity, the 'subsistence principle' dominated the development of the wage structure. The fact that the low-wage groups were being sheltered from the effects of inflation on their standard of living brought a relative rise in the wages of all low-wage groups ; that is, a narrowing of all sorts of differentials. In an extreme full-employment inflation, the demand for labour meant a special demand for highly skilled labour, and consequently at least some skill differentials grew again. This second type of inflation prevailed in France during the first post-war years. The first type prevailed in 1935–1938 and in recent years. M. Sellier's conclusion on this point was interesting and well worth further study. There was sometimes a too rough-and-ready reasoning, as if full employment were unambiguously causing equalization of differentials. One must, however, question some of the factual analysis leading up to M. Sellier's conclusions. Wage equalization in France, in 1935–1938, could not be explained as a defence of the low-wage classes against poverty through inflation, because real wages rose considerably, and the inflation was rather a secondary result of large money-wage increases. The decrease of differentials could be more naturally explained as the result of a sudden emergence of mass unionism during the Blum experiment. Unemployment was not abolished ; and this was with or without a price inflation, a situation where regulations (legal or union-bargained) would be maintained against market forces at least to a certain degree. In post-war years, on the other hand, it was not quite certain that the equalization trend was a result of the working of the principle that low-wage workers should be helped. M. Sellier had described the 'black market in manpower' and the other unregulated wage developments as something rather similar to the Swedish 'wage drift' ; further, we knew that the unions (with very few agreements in force) had little opportunity to 'police' any wage regulations or rules. Therefore, one must ask were not the increased equalization of wages as well as most of the exceptions from this trend in France since the war, generally results of market forces. Were other explanations needed ?

Mr. Rothbaum raised several problems concerning M. Sellier's methodology, and suggested alternative explanations and conclusions. On the whole, he agreed with the explanation of skill differentials. In the short run the position was explained by inflation ; only in the long run was it more complex.

In considering inter-industry differentials, one was not mainly concerned with the *average* wage in industry as a whole. The worker was concerned with the return earned by his own skill, and one needed a more useful measure. Perhaps one could use given types of labour as standards of measurement; for example, janitorial wages, though the *main d'œuvre ordinaire* was perhaps a better indicator in France. M. Sellier's analyses turned out to give an explanation of inter-personal and inter-occupational rather than inter-industry differences. These latter could be explained by factors like the sex composition of the labour force. Wage differentials between the sexes depended to some extent on differences in skill. With regional differentials, however, was not the striking fact that, in the period in question, such differentials fell so very little ?

Social insurance tended to mean that the income of labour increased in the non-wage sector. Family allowances received by a worker bore no relation to his skill, and, in a given industry, male workers might get back more than their tax payments. Female workers would get less. Regionally, social security payments led to differentials depending on different birth rates.

Mr. Rothbaum thought that inflation narrowed skill differentials, and had some effect on geographical and inter-industry differentials too. But perhaps other factors were predominant, for example, the level of employment in given regions. Regional differentials in the United States narrowed before 1945. Skill differentials narrowed later. Perhaps, then, inflation should not be blamed for all such narrowing.

Mr. Turner said that M. Sellier appeared to have 'boarded the Turner boat' on a false idea of where it went. In French printing, for example, M. Sellier attributed the large differentials to the fact that it was a craft union. Apparently in France the semi-skilled/unskilled differentials had narrowed, whilst the semi-skilled/labourer difference was still wide. In Britain it was the *latter* differential that had narrowed ; in engineering, indeed, the semi-skilled differential was sometimes greater than the skilled, because the semi-skilled rates were outside the traditional structure. In other words, the 'wage-slide' led to further distortion, not to adjustment. The explanation of this in England was probably that in a craft union, since unskilled workers could never become skilled, they were given higher wages to make amends. The French situation seemed to be different from the English, which illustrated the danger of over-wide generalization.

Mr. Turner asked a question on the French social transfers. He was not sure whether the social transfer should be added to the wage. In part, at least, it might be financed from general taxation. To this extent, it represented part of the redistribution of income. Mr. Turner wondered why Professor Perroux's figures of wages and social benefits did not agree with those of Professor Marchal. If Professor Perroux's statistics were correct, his conclusions were not justified.

Mr. Peacock said he wished to clear up a simple point. It was preferable to express wages, salaries, and benefits as percentages of personal income and not of net national product. As to whether one called such a transfer wages, Messrs Rottier or Brochier could explain the features of the tax system which made their procedure legitimate. It was interesting to note the high proportion of social benefits to total benefits, especially as compared with Britain which had gone so far with social insurance since 1939. In Britain, such benefits represented 5 to 6 per cent of personal income in 1938, and 6 per cent in 1952–1953. This figure was small compared with that in France. In 1938, much of these benefits were unemployment pay ; now most were pensions. But if, as had been done in the French papers, one was going to take account of transfers, why not include the health service or real social benefits. Sometimes benefits were monetary in one country and real in another ; therefore such uniformity would facilitate international comparison.

Professor Dunlop said that in the social sciences the comparative method often yielded great insights. We were indebted to Professor Perroux for explaining the French case. He wondered why the French economy behaved as it did ? In both these papers, reflecting the French economy, was a basic dilemma. With full employment, how could the wage system fulfil its traditional function of allocating manpower, when it might be vitiated by inflation ? Besides the prevailing full employment, six features of France seemed unique. In combination, they stated the French problem. These six factors were :

(1) Centralized wage determination.
(2) A relatively static population and labour force.
(3) No rapid increase in productivity.
(4) Little price competition which could change labour distribution.
(5) A wage structure overtaxed by a social security scheme, and small wage differentials.
(6) No fiscal and monetary policy dedicated to stop inflation.

On the one hand, if some factors changed, perhaps there would be a better situation ; on the other hand, some of these factors might be operating in other lands. Sweden, for instance, had inflation and central wage determination.

Professor Okochi said that he found traces of a pessimistic social philosophy in Professor Perroux's paper, not that this was surprising in France's present circumstances. But was there any way of a return to the market? No hint of how to choose such a path was given in Professor Perroux's paper.

Although the paper dealt with the obliteration of the wage structure, one need not consider it as representing only the French case. Other countries, Italy, and, with reservations, Japan, had suffered similarly because of too rapid political changes, inflation, strong trade unions, and Governments which were unable to exercise effective control.

Dr. Rothschild commented that Professor Perroux's paper was 'almost more than pessimistic'. Was the position really so bad, with neither a free market nor a planned economy ? Why could such a system not work with changes in, say, stocks instead of prices ? Similarly, even if there were no wage changes, could not the amounts of labour employed change ? Did we not overstress the importance of wages and other prices ? After all, in a whole economy, changes need not, proportionately, be so very large. Rigidity, coupled with an unsatisfactory economic and monetary policy was the cause of inflation.

M. Rottier agreed with Dr. Rothschild that there was perhaps no real common social outlook between Messrs Perroux and von Mises. This paper was highly pessimistic, but this disease among French economists was due possibly to the state of the French economy. It was hardly possible to deal with the French economic problem section by section ; there was much more interdependence between problems than elsewhere. One could hardly study the wage level in the French economy independently of more general problems. His own explanation was that the French working population was divided into three, nearly equal, social groups; farmers, self-employed workers in industry and commerce, and wage and salary earners. Bargaining between these three groups should be studied.

Professor Dunlop's points were not independent but closely interrelated. Which of them was most significant? Slow economic progress was to a great extent a consequence of rigidity in the structure of the labour force and of the web of government regulations. But the main trouble lay in the imperfection of markets which was due to state intervention having crystallized such rigidity into an institutional pattern.

To Dr. Rothschild, M. Rottier pointed out that for sixty years France had endured this situation without bad results. The rate of economic progress was slower than in some other western economies, but there was progress none the less. Now, however, the stresses brought about by this long-lasting rigidity suggested that the French economy was nearing a breaking-point. There was, for instance, a widening gap between the level of real wages in France and in other Western democracies.

The discrepancy between Professor Marchal's table and Professor Perroux's table on wage flows was that they used different sources. Professor Perroux had access to unpublished figures. It was also a question of definition. It was correct to include social benefits in the wage flow because all social benefits in France were financed by a tax on wage payments, which was proportional to the wage level up to a certain limit. One should distinguish sharply between the unit cost of labour to the employer and unit income to the wage earner, which were wholly different because of the big redistributive elements.

M. Brochier said that he wished to put Professor Dunlop's six points in order of priority and thus assign responsibility to certain social groups. He felt the predominant factor was the behaviour of entrepreneurs. This explained the absence of price competition, and hence the slow rate of progress. It also explained why union pressure for higher wages could not lead to higher productivity; prices were allowed to rise. The result was low wages, which in turn explained the importance of social transfers. Long-term inflation would also be linked to entrepreneurial behaviour, and profits were easily maintained. They therefore avoided the political choice, namely, on whom the burden of an anti-inflationary policy was to fall. M. Brochier said France had great political stability: governments changed often; men less often; and the essentials of policy never. One could place the responsibility on the shoulders of French entrepreneurs. The situation might change, however, through growing trade relations between France and other countries.

M. Sellier wondered whether Mr. Rehn was right. Did subsistence and skill play the part he himself assigned to them, or was there a simpler explanation in terms of the demand for labour? M. Sellier thought that both market factors and the need for a subsistence minimum had played a part. Which predominated? That was hard to establish, particularly for unskilled workers. The French labour force had swelled in some years by as many as 400,000 North African workers, which meant 5 per cent of the total labour force, and 15 per cent to 20 per cent of unskilled labour. This influx of unskilled workers led him to conclude that market forces acted against such workers.

M. Sellier thought that perhaps his 'extrapolation' did not misrepresent Mr. Turner too much. In the printing industry, the union was very strong, the most skilled men controlled entry into the profession, and thereby maintained skill differentials.

On Professor Dunlop's six points, M. Sellier pointed out that, whilst centralized wage decision making did result in rigidity, since 1950 there was the possibility of making individual collective agreements. But employers were against them, and wages were freed only when unemployment appeared and the power of labour weakened.

TENTH SESSION

THURSDAY MORNING, SEPTEMBER 9, 1954

(Discussion of Paper by Marchal)

Mr. Turner thought that Professor Marchal's general point, that the distribution of income between wage earners and others could be influenced even in the market field by political factors, was reasonable. The main difficulty lay in the wide extension that Professor Marchal gave to his theory. It would follow from his analysis that one could no longer deduce the behaviour of organizations and people from certain basic assumptions, but had to treat everything as a matter for empirical study. It would also follow that, for example, trade unions fixing wage rates would be influenced directly by taxation, social benefits, and so on. It might be possible to argue this way in terms of the French situation, but not in terms of Britain or America. For example, there was no evidence that the distribution of private income before tax in the United Kingdom had been seriously influenced by the considerable increase in direct taxation. There was no evidence that trade unions had tried to offset income taxation by changing their wage bargaining policy. How, then, did Professor Marchal make a bridge between the market 'battlefield' and the political 'battlefield'? In France, a period when wages were closely regulated in relation to social transfers had established a fairly clear association between these things in people's minds. One could argue that in Britain this level of economic consciousness had not yet been reached. Unless such a bridge were established, one had to treat the market and political fields of income redistribution as separate battlefields to which separate lines of analysis applied.

Professor Dupriez thought that, when one was interpreting the economy in general, the rôle which social transfers played was most important. Since they were now a considerable percentage of wages, one had to be clear about their incidence. He did not agree that they were important for the working of the economy when employers paid for them through contributions, and not important when they were met from general taxation. One had to distinguish between the effect on employers and that on workers. Especially in international comparisons, calculations based on *nominal* wages were unrealistic. We needed more elaborate statistical concepts adapted to the modern economy. The two main ones, Professor Dupriez thought, were the hourly cost of labour and the social wage. The first would include any costs paid by employers for one hour of labour; whatever the wage earner received otherwise the entrepreneur would ignore in deciding how much labour to employ. There would, then, be different economic effects where the social benefits came mainly from a levy on wages, from those where they were paid out of general taxes. Where they added to the wage bill, they *must* influence relative prices, for they represented part of cost, and tended to increase capital investment by making labour dearer relative to capital. Benefits met out of general taxation were paid in countries which were more interested in maintaining full employment, and which were consequently anxious that marginal firms should not have to pay part of the social security benefits.

The second concept, the social wage of workers comprised (1) money earnings, and (2) other benefits; it varied with the status of the individual. Since the net advantages of jobs became different with social security benefits, trade unions could act according to the circumstances. In a boom they would press for higher wages, since it was easy to put pressure on employers; in a slump they would try to persuade the government to increase social benefits.

Mr. Peacock thought that Professor Marchal's distinction between the initial and final distribution of income was misleading. It was often suggested that public finance lay beyond the economic decisions of the community. He asked whether Professor Marchal was saying that his view affected any attempt to allocate taxes and expenditure. Mr. Peacock said he could understand Professor Marchal if he meant that it was more hazardous to measure and allocate taxes and receipts the greater the complexity of the system. But so far as he knew, everyone who did this was aware of that fact. He did not agree that there was no awareness of the difficulties. Mr. Peacock agreed with Mr. Turner that wage negotiations might be unaffected by the direct tax system. Unions might try to maximize wages after taxes, but they also tried to affect the tax structure. Whether they succeeded, Mr. Turner was better able to say than he was himself.

Mr. Turner explained that his point was not that trade unions did not attempt to influence taxation in the interest of their members ; it was that union behaviour in the market was not affected by this. They still regarded the two fields as separate.

M. Brochier commented on the bridge between Professor Marchal's theory and traditional analysis. Professor Marchal had a useful theory which was hard to link with the traditional one. Yet need one integrate the market theory with the idea of social groups' power and reactions ? Ought one not to try to find a relationship between movements of wages on the one hand and the reactions of groups with social effects on the other. There was a link, though it was difficult to trace, between wages and social reactions. M. Brochier instanced two applications, one short run, the other long run. One ought to know the short-term market reactions which influenced social groups. Perhaps they strove to maintain the previous period's level of income. In inflation, there might be a critical size for the gap between the cost of living and wages. A big enough gap might cause strikes. In France, he thought that perhaps a gap of 5 per cent to 10 per cent would bring a strike. A second illustration was the 'scissors' between agricultural and industrial prices. Enough deterioration would bring a new market situation. This instance was, perhaps, more long-term. The relative position between groups could only affect the 'rules of the game' and this took time.

Finally, M. Brochier pointed out that between the wars there was inflation in France for a short time. Since then inflation had been permanent. The rentier had suffered, but had made no response, though he had not yet been 'assassinated'. The indexing of loans, however, begun by M. Pinay, had brought new conditions which had altered the 'rules of the game'.

M. Brochier underlined the link between Professor Marchal's theory and France. Perhaps such a theory was not necessary for countries unlike France.

M. Rottier said that he thought, when he first saw Professor Marchal's paper, that he was in a looking-glass economy. Perhaps this was the influence of French experience. He made four comments. First, a new theory should explain more than the preceding ones. This Professor Marchal did not do, unless there were very large changes. Although conditions in France had changed very much, the neo-classical theory remained relevant. Second, should one explain economic facts and problems by socio-political categories? Was not *economic* theory better? Third, was not the link between bargaining levels much more imperfect than Professor Marchal suggested? Fourth, M. Rottier raised doubts on the stability of wages *as interpreted by Professor Marchal.* Many different interpretations were possible, but none could be proved.

Professor Reynolds wished to defend Professor Marchal. He thought that one must, in the end, account for the total income of labour. The classification of 'active' and 'passive' incomes was very sensible. One could go some way in defining how far groups could defend their incomes in both these senses. He raised three points. First, was not the distinction between individuals and groups too sharp? For example, a union could fix a wage rate, but each worker could decide whether to work or not. Second, was it really true that a worker was indifferent whether he got a higher wage or paid less tax? Third, Professor Marchal suggested a single leap to a wide theory. This was a formidable task and Professor Reynolds supported the idea of 'creeping-up' by steps. One first needed a narrow theory, then a wider one. Perhaps, one needed a tailor-made theory for particular economies, such as that of France.

ELEVENTH SESSION

Friday Morning, September 10, 1954

(Discussion of Papers by Brochier and Roberts)

Professor Dupriez thought M. Brochier's synthesis of two different streams of thought was interesting. He was tempted to think that one needed to find a compromise between Professor Dunlop's ideas and the more 'political' theories of Ross and Lester. The theory of 'maximization' should be compared with explanations of how decision-making was done. The two theories were not contradictory. The action of unions must be explained because 'decision-making' implied subjective analysis.

This led to the question: which quantity was to be maximized? A trade union represented its members, and it was hard to define maximization where the interests of leaders and members might conflict. But if one took 'net advantages' as the object for maximization, one was not far wrong. On a national scale, the theory might need changing because trade unions felt a responsibility towards a government which they favoured, and, if this happened, they might not attempt to maximize anything. Just because it was hard to define maximization, one should not throw the concept overboard. But Professor Dupriez was not ready to follow Professor Dunlop to the idea of maximization for the whole union.

Professor Harbison said that Mr. Roberts had put weight on economic forces rather than on political pressure groups as the determinants of wages. He had said that the impact of unions on the wage structure had not been very great in Britain. He also drove another nail into the coffin of the 'monopoly model' of the union. Professor Harbison's own conclusion was that, in discussing the economics of unions through their impact on wages, consideration was being given only to the part of the iceberg which lay above the surface. If unions had only a minor effect on the structure and level of wages, they might have a major impact on social and political institutions. One needed to consider more facts than those covered by a theory of wage rates. The latter represented only a minor part of unionization. Broadly, unionism was a response to the total challenge of industrialization. This response was not necessarily even economic and social; it could be political and psychological as well, and an adequate theory of unionization needed to cover all these responses. If we knew all this, we would probably be better able to measure the relation of unions to wages.

Professor Harbison emphasized that taking such a broad theory did not mean neglecting either traditional or new methods of analysis. Today, more than ever, economists should become 'political economists' in the traditional sense, with realistic models subjected to rigorous analysis. Early political economy had different institutions, but it did take account of basic facts, and did not make such abstract definitions as today.

Professor Harbison thought that, in the discussion, the conference would do well to analyse the effect of unionization and trade unions on a whole economy, whether capitalist or not. For example, had unionization been a disruptive or supporting influence for American capitalism? He thought that unions were consistent with and essential to capitalism. The stronger unions were, the more respectable and less revolutionary they became. In the United States, unions might well be the 'lightning conductor' which drove to ground protests which would otherwise endanger the system. He had often told Professor Milton Friedman that the 'Friedman state' needed the support of a strong labour movement.

Professor Myers said he had been interested to see how British and French scholars tested models used in the United States. Much more empiricism was necessary. There was a need for testing the behaviour of particular unions in different economies. American economists were looking at local and regional bargaining; those in France and Sweden were concerned with nation-wide bargaining. The United States model was not general; French and British economists should pursue their studies of trade union policy in its relation to the particular structure of their own economy and unions.

Professor Robinson said the present task was to discover, first, if our models were right, and second, which factors were most important. This led back immediately to the suitability of the maximization technique. M. Brochier came near to saying that, since there was no simple aim of maximization, one should not use the technique. Professor Dupriez had said that one should find some one *synthetic* thing to maximize. But why get into such difficulties? The old-fashioned tools would deal with complex problems. In the theory of the firm, at any time in the past thirty years, we had advanced beyond the idea of maximizing short-run net revenue. A firm might maximize short-term revenue; it might be more concerned with long-term growth; or it might base its policy on moral or social views. The theory had to show how a firm chose between these many objectives. Short-run and long-run wage policies might conflict. How, for example, could one measure the marginal net product of workers in a firm with much long-lasting capital? Decision-making in a union was partly a process of reconciling objectives. One had to consider not only wages and employment, but also long-term status and long-term bargaining power. These were four obvious objectives and they could be reconciled by ordinary theory.

Professor Haller agreed that economic factors were important to United States unions. But in Europe political aims often predominated. In this situation one needed sociological tools. For example, were unions adapting *to* a situation or were they *creating* it? Professor Marchal had introduced the concept of social tension.

The active and passive groups differed between countries, but generally trade unions were in the active groups. Where trade unions were active, high wages led to high prices. These, in turn, led to higher agricultural prices and higher wages for civil servants. If, however, workers tried to control plants, industry would play its rôle in the 'social game' as a combined group.

Professor Kerr said that though there was no 'California school' or line, he wished to explain what this 'line' was ! It held that trade unions were primarily political institutions which responded both to external economic stimuli and to the external political environment. Externally the union might be concerned with economics and/or politics, but internally it was politically activated. Professor Dunlop's models were ingenious, interesting — and nonsense ! If one looked at the United States wage structure the dispersion of wage rates was much less than would be permitted by the very different elasticities of demand, etc. Unions did not respond as much as one might expect to such elasticities. Perhaps the California school had overemphasized internal political factors in the union ; for example, the importance of new and rival unionism. The two papers represented efforts to reconcile the Harvard and California 'lines'. He himself would reconcile them by saying that which one was correct depended on the question one was asking. The political model was the better model for explaining internal decision-making, but economic forces were easily the most important factor in the long run in fixing wages. In the long run political factors had little impact on wages. The union was, so to speak, operating in a 'narrow corridor' of action.

Mr. Laffer made a comment in the light of the Australian Arbitration system. Since the wage-fixing authorities determined minimum wages, the trade union merely making a 'claim', trade union leaders did not have to be 'responsible'. This made it easier for them to retain the support of their members. However, some unions took a pride in their militancy, and here Ross's argument was more important. Again, the integration of the wage system meant that the scope for changes induced by union action was narrow, as long as the margin of the engineering fitter remained unaltered. This further reduced the importance of internal politics. There was, of course, much bargaining in individual firms superimposed on the general system. Even here, politics were often unimportant as, within wide limits, workers were content with a wage somewhat above that awarded by the Arbitration Court.

Secondly, Mr. Laffer doubted how far it was useful to use the firm as a model for building up a theory of union wage policy.

With the more or less closely integrated wage structure of today, one was bound often to look beyond the individual union to the trade union movement as a whole. One must also take account of the links between trade union wage policy and general economic policy. If the Australian trade unions secured increases in wages at the expense of wool-growers, tariffs might be needed to protect the weaker import-competing industries or subsidies to assist the weaker export industries. Such issues could not be dealt with by individual unions ; political action by the trade union movement as a whole was required.

'Maximization' models were not out of the question but might be more appropriate on a national basis. For example, the trade union movement might aim at a maximum share of the national income. One thing did seem clear ; in wage theory one had to begin with some analysis of trade union interests. We needed to substitute a 'group interest' approach, perhaps with maximization as the aim of the group, for the 'general welfare' approach. We had found what the different group interests were ; we could, if we wished, work out policies which might reconcile, or effect a compromise, between these different interests. One could probably have both a short-run and a long-run analysis. In Australia the trade union movement tended to accept unpalatable decisions of the Arbitration Court because it felt that arbitration was in its long-run interest.

Professor Phelps Brown related M. Brochier's attention to historical growth to Professor Harbison's tracing of the origins of trade union action to the basic needs created by the impact of industrialization on human nature. He thought that two changes had been particularly felt by the worker in the transition from eighteenth-century society. First, he became subordinated, and his hours and his methods were prescribed to him. Second, he felt insecure, through the risk of unemployment, and also sometimes through being detached from a settled community. Trade unions met the need for support in this weakness, and arose to provide 'countervailing power'. It was not poverty that gave rise to them : wages were higher in the new factories.

But the fact that trade unions began not among the weakest wage-earners but among the strongest, the craftsmen, showed that their growth depended not on needs alone but also on their ability to act to meet those needs by creating and administering an organization. That growth might, therefore, be regarded as the result of an interplay of needs and capabilities.

For instance, clerical workers were usually late-comers to unionism, not through lack of capability, clearly, nor through lack of economic interest, but through lack of a sense of need. In recent years this sense had increased. This seemed to stem from, first, the growth in the size of the representative unit of clerical employment; second, from the lowering of the status of proficient clerical workers through the general extension of education; and, third, from the 'squeeze' of clerical incomes by manual workers. The aim of clerical unions was not to maximize anything so much as to defend a threatened status and income.

Mr. Johnson wondered what questions we wanted trade union theories to answer. On the one hand were the historical, institutional studies, considering the nature of trade unions, how they were held together, and what they did. On the other hand there were models not of evolution but of behaviour in a fixed environment. Even here there was the question whether the union should attract new members, consolidate its position, and so on. Nevertheless, one had to abstract, to build models. The analogy with the firm was instructive. Both Professor Dunlop's theory of unions and the theory of the firm had the same kind of criteria. They assumed a timeless framework. Neither had mastered dynamic problems, and both regarded the study of statics as the way of getting at dynamics.

When one looked at either the firm or the union one met with the snags mentioned by Professor Robinson, such as long-run versus short-run maximization, decision-making in uncertainty, and so on. Uncertainty could be met by convention. The fact that unions seemed to make little difference in the long run might mean that in the long run they showed considerable ability to estimate and adapt to their long-run prospects. It might mean that the theory was adequate for explaining long-run behaviour.

Unions faced three kinds of problem: they had to consider (1) member support, (2) market environment, (3) the political environment. In some cases a union's political influence might ensure that it gained its economic objectives; but one should not study only its political problems. Both macro- and micro-economics were needed. The economic aspects of its problem did not give a complete description of the union. But they did establish sufficient of the truth to produce sensible models of union behaviour. It was not fair to the early models of trade union behaviour to take them as final results. One needed such models to reveal the ultimate logic of the problem.

Mr. Rehn thought there was confusion over the word 'political'. The expressions 'political unionism' or 'political theory of unionism' had been used to say two different things without clear definitions. First, that unions influenced governments and public opinion;

second, that the behaviour of union leaders was more predictable because it was determined by internal political relations among their members rather than by strictly economic factors which one could analyse as a problem of maximization. Only the first case, which the French participants described as the French pattern of union policy, should be called political unionism. The second type, described in the writings of Ross and others, could perhaps be called 'psychological' instead of 'political' unionism.

Then one had, thirdly, Professor Dunlop's theory of 'business unionism', with unions behaving on one or another 'economic-man' pattern. Mr. Rehn felt that as a general explanation of union behaviour this was an unacceptable idea; but Professor Dunlop was superior to his theory. His facts were true, even where his theory was not. Business unionism existed where a union took 'what the traffic would bear'. Most unions, however, did not extort what they could, economically, because this would imply a degree of price differentiation for labour, inside the union as well as between unions, which would be psychologically unacceptable. They had a psychological and not an economic basis, and maximized psychological satisfactions. 'Business unions' as well as 'psychological unions' might well reach deadlock if they did not appeal to political power.

Each union claimed to increase (money) wages as much as possible for its members but rarely did it. Professor Dunlop, however, meant the opposite, namely that unions claim to be 'responsible' but really take as much as possible. But it was hard for a union to go on strike to obtain 'more and more' for workers with wages already high; they had to think of public opinion and of the sympathy or antipathy of the other unions. So, even if unions, said they were doing all they could for members, they were actually hampered by the general political and psychological situation. With growing union membership this factor became increasingly important. Once it was possible for 4 million American Federation of Labor workers to establish a profitable business unionism; but with 16 million members this was impossible. In Sweden, with nearly 100 per cent of the workers organized, this was even more clear. Every move of one union could be regarded as a possible precedent by all other unions, and this created a tendency towards self-discipline through mutual moral pressure. Countervailing power, however, was another thing, which unions had to take into account more and more, when they grew from small units doing business to big movements influencing, and being influenced by, the economy as a whole.

M. Brochier said that he was more in agreement with his critics than before the discussion. At the empirical stage, however, there was evidence both for and against maximization. But we wanted to know where it was important and where it was not. If one merely said, as at present, that it was sometimes important and sometimes not, one ruined the whole theory. What was the aim of any theory ? If it was only to explain the past, then the maximization principle was enough. In the long run, unions sought to maximize. But one wished to predict. He doubted whether, in a model explaining trade unions, maximization helped to tell what would happen.

M. Brochier replied to Professor Robinson by saying that he thought there could be no synthetic variable to maximize, but an answer in terms of maximization with diverse factors playing a part. In the short run, no one knew what objective a union would pursue. His own aim was not to destroy established ideas but to accept their validity only in some degree. M. Brochier noted, however, that everyone agreed that the higher the level of bargaining was the greater the number of political factors taken into account. There was also agreement that whilst, in the short run, politics were more important, in the long run it was economics which was predominant.

Mr. Roberts felt that Professor Harbison had been too kind. He might well have been accused of trying to have his cake and eat it. However, the discussion had brought out more clearly than before what was the basic conflict in the conference. Those interested in empirical studies were not satisfied with the 'traditional economic models'. In part, this feeling that the models were inadequate sprang from a failure to understand the assumptions of the model builders. There was, in addition, a question of semantics. Confusion arose from the meaning given to the word 'political' in Professor Ross's model of the union. But simply to substitute the word 'psychological' for the word 'political', as had been suggested, would merely make matters worse.

TWELFTH SESSION

FRIDAY AFTERNOON, SEPTEMBER 10, 1954

(Discussion of Paper by Turner)

M. Rottier made three points on Mr. Turner's paper. First, without denying the 'Turner effect', was it really so general ? Mr. Roberts did not seem quite to agree. Second, he did not think that Mr.

Turner's argument on movements of wage rates and earnings was too happy. Third, was this not really a short-term effect? In the long run, productivity and differing prosperity in various industries affected wages. Perhaps there was less room for long-term manœuvre than Mr. Turner suggested.

Mr. Roberts recognized the importance of Mr. Turner's question, but thought Mr. Turner had overstated the rôle of unions as the causal factor narrowing wage differentials. On the tendency for wage *rates* to increase by similar amounts, Mr. Roberts said that this might be true in terms of the absolute amounts gained at any 'round' of wage increases. But there were time lags between wage demands and settlements. *All* unions did *not* demand annual wage increases. Similarly, the time lags had differed. One need only look at the amounts of wage increases, and the numbers of workers concerned, to see wide variations.

Again, when considering problems of wage structures one should not consider only basic wage levels. What was most important was the total amount in the pay packet. This was what workers were interested in. In the United Kingdom the spread of 'take home' pay for adult males would be from, say, £7 to £18 a week. It would be even higher in, say, the steel industry, where there were small groups of workers receiving very high wages. No one knew the actual frequency distribution of wages in this range, but in single industries there were great disparities. If differentials were considered in this wider sense, it was obvious that other factors were at work that were more powerful than the effects of trade unions. Whilst differentials between wage rates had narrowed, this tendency had been much less evident in the case of earnings. It followed that one needed far more explanation than Mr. Turner had given to account for shifts in differentials.

Professor Phelps Brown offered some qualifications of Mr. Turner's view that the narrowing of differentials was primarily due to trade union policy. The differential between the craftsman's rate and the labourer's in building could be traced back a long way in England. For 500 years before 1914 it was usually 50 per cent of the labourer's rate, but it had departed from this in times of inflation — for example, during the Tudor inflation, the Civil War, and between 1760 and 1815 — and usually for the time being it narrowed. So the narrowing had occurred before, without the influence of trade unionism.

The extension of education was perhaps fundamental. A study [1] of rates of pay in the British Civil Service showed that the manual workers among the civil servants had about doubled their

[1] Guy Routh, 'Civil Service Pay, 1875–1950', *Economica*, August 1954.

real earnings between the late 1870's and 1950, but of the two classes with the highest educational qualifications the executive class had only held its ground, and the top class, the administrative, had had its real income halved. The explanation surely was that in the 1870's there were relatively few who could satisfy the educational requirements of the top classes, but with the extension of secondary and university education the supply had been greatly increased.

M. Sellier thought Mr. Turner's explanation of the 'motor' of wage differentials was rather like the 'tour de France'. The riders progressed because one followed another. But other factors mattered too. One must start at the beginning *and go on to the end* to get a prize. As to the speed of the race, that depended on the type of bicycle (on technical progress) and also on the particular difficulties of the road for each day. The route was the cost of living, the bicycle was productivity; finally there was the fact that all the riders pursued each other. The last fact (Mr. Turner's main explanation) seemed the least important.

Professor Dunlop approved Mr. Turner's preoccupation with points in the wage structure where change occurred. This was important for the dynamics of changes over time. He emphasized the rôle of the new firm in a tight labour market and of the industry with rapidly increasing productivity and employment.

One must study both the central tendency and the dispersion of wages. The latter had been too little stressed in Mr. Turner's paper.

Mr. Peacock said that the emphasis had been on the wage rate as the reward of the particular factor. There was also some discussion of earnings. But what importance did labour economists give to including 'fringe benefits'? In Great Britain, especially, wage restraint had narrowed differentials, but the post-war years had seen a large change in the volume of industrial pensions, financed partly from employee contribution, but largely by the employers. Such schemes had covered 1·5 million workers in 1938. They covered 6 million now. Since such schemes began with skilled workers, they were not perhaps directly relevant here. But to allow for them did mean taking the next step, from wage rates to the actual receipts of workers.

Mr. Turner said that M. Rottier had asked if the 'Turner effect' was general. That was to say, was there a connection between the earnings of workers whose pay depended on central trade union negotiations and those which were more free; for example, because of piece rates or through local agreements? How was a particular wage demand converted to a general demand? The answer, surely, was that trade union leaders faced pressure from many sources, and they always preferred to make a general demand.

Mr. Turner said that Professor Phelps Brown's instance of builders showed the persistence of a conventional relationship for long periods. Although inflation had temporarily narrowed the skill margin, it had tended to be restored until recent times. Now, the narrowing had persisted, which seemed to be connected with the development of mass unionism. With the non-manual skill margin, again, one had an element of conventional regulation. Thus it was interesting that the inter-war differential for non-manual workers had widened, *despite* growing education.

The 'margin of tolerance' permitted by economic factors was wider than was often thought. Moreover, Mr. Turner was impressed that the results of collective bargaining were similar to what one would expect in a perfectly free economy ; wages tended to be equal for the same grade of labour in different sectors of industry ; but he did not know what would happen *in the absence* of trade unions.

In studying young recruits to industry in North-West England he thought it curious that, broadly, the wages offered for non-manual workers were below those of craftsmen, which in turn were less than in some semi-skilled jobs. But people preferred non-manual jobs and then skilled jobs, perhaps because they were pleasant, but also because of their social status, which in turn depended on *past* wage relationships. If net advantages depended on *past* wages, all precision disappeared from wage theory.

M. Rottier was asked to elaborate his views on the consequences of narrow differentials in inflation. He wondered whether narrower differentials made for rigidity. There was a danger of wrong reasoning because, though British wage differentials had been reduced, there had still been much labour turnover. His point, however, was that there had not been as much movement of labour as was necessary. He agreed that the flexibility of wages in Britain between 1920 and 1939 might have been from this point of view largely accidental. But he did not think that this was a purely cyclical phenomenon. The very severity of the depression was surely a result of a long-term decline in some basic industries, and wages there might well have fallen below the subsistence level.

Mr. Rothbaum raised some general problems concerned with the reduction of skill differentials and with rigidity. Two assumptions lay behind the contention that differentials were now so small as to prevent movement. The first was that the previous set of differentials was just sufficient to attract the necessary labour supply. The second was that, as the skill differential decreased, there was a proportional decrease in attractiveness of skilled jobs. Mr. Rothbaum questioned both assumptions. On the first, he inclined more to Professor Phelps Brown's view that educational levels might be rising over time, although conventional wage relations stayed the same. Inflation might result in a sudden redistribution of labour, so that the new level of education was taken into account at one moment of time though it had been built up slowly. The new set of wage differentials thus created might well be more in conformity with real supply conditions than the previous ones.

Second, at the same time as proportional wage differentials were decreasing, absolute differentials were rising. And there was no 1 : 1 relationship between wage differentials and the attractiveness of jobs. This was partly a social and cultural phenomenon, and any maladjustments that it caused in a period of inflation might have their results only in the period that followed. Workers might, as a social phenomenon, adjust themselves to a new set of incentives, even though a given set of supply conditions remained completely unchanged.

THIRTEENTH SESSION

SATURDAY MORNING, SEPTEMBER 11, 1954

(Discussion of Paper by Demaria)

Professor Hansen felt that labour economists should be more interested than they were in amounts of labour bought and sold. They usually discussed prices, but amounts were also important. Consumer demand analysis was highly advanced, with many empirical studies. Some inspiration was to be found from it. One characteristic of demand theory was that one took the family and not the individual as the behaviour unit. If one developed a theory for the family, then the family would be conceived as able to supply several different *types* of labour. Consumer demand theory started from a utility function,

$$U = U(X_1 \ldots X_m), \tag{1}$$

and a budget restriction,

$$\Sigma px = Y.$$

If one combined this with the supply of labour, then

$$U = u(x_1 \ldots x_m, L_1 \ldots L_m), \tag{2}$$

where $L_1 \ldots L_m$ represented leisure of different types, husband's leisure, housewife's leisure, etc. The budget restriction would now be

$$\Sigma px = \Sigma W(24 - L), \text{ W being wages per hour.}$$

One could do something with this type of analysis. If one tried to reach theorems, some indeterminacy of the kind studied by Mr. Bagiotti was inevitable, as was well known in demand theory. Therefore one should turn to empirical methods and to study of the actual world.

The notion of an Engel curve was well known. It related the consumption of a given good to income. One could easily see that here Engel curves lost their meaning with a utility function like (2), because such curves needed income to be given, and it was not in this case. Nor could one use income-elasticities of demand because income and quantities of goods were determined together. Professor Myers had referred to a study where, when the family income reached $5000, the housewife stopped working. This type of case needed analysis, if the family had a function like (2) the housewife's work should be related to wage rates, not income. Traditional labour-supply theory might become most useful if developed in the way he had outlined.

Professor Shackle thought that Professor Demaria's paper led to the danger of certain linguistic traps. For there was no exact word to mean the amount of effort forthcoming. 'Supply of labour' was too vague. It might just mean people willing to work; it might mean labour actually done. Was 'travail' better than 'labour'? Perhaps we needed a review of terminology. Professor Shackle mentioned an interesting sidelight on the factors affecting the geographical mobility of labour. An Oxford study had shown that, if a man lived within a day's journey of Oxford, he was more likely to go to work in Oxford than if not. Mr. Demaria's paper was another instance of need for the real facts. Mr. Demaria agreed that the supply curve of labour was Z-shaped, but gave no reasons at all. Also, Mr. Demaria put his own 'theorem of individuality' which, Professor Shackle supposed, was related to irreversibility in English economics. Such a result was always unsatisfactory. Perhaps it was because there were not enough dimensions. Maybe ostentation of the 'Duesenberry' type was important. Mr. Demaria made no policy recommendations. He merely stated that more people stayed at home after a certain point. Perhaps governments needed to cultivate a taste for oysters and champagne in ordinary workers. Professor Shackle concluded that one must make the theory of labour supply more dynamic.

M. Sellier reported a 'picturesque example'. The Government of Madagascar, in 1890, wished to make people work. The only way in which it was able to do this was by levying a poll tax. The natives' sole money need was for cash to pay the tax.

Dr. Krelle thought it would be hard to build a theory of labour supply with the wage rate as the only variable. If the wage rate turned out to be of second-order importance only, and if other, more sociological, facts were of first-order importance, there might be no relation between the wage rate and labour supply at all. The theory of labour supply differed basically from the theory of demand, where price and income were the main determinants.

Dr. Hansen thought the difficulties were the same as in the theoretical and empirical study of consumer demand.

Dr. Rothschild agreed that one had the same problem as in consumption. He also pointed out that the disutility of work had 'Duesenberry' effects.

Mr. Peacock stressed that it was hard to define the supply of labour. One could trace the effect of taxes of differing forms and rates of progressiveness. The question of effects on incentives had been studied as a result of high income taxes. It did not follow, however, that absenteeism meant *no work*. There might be the incentive to evade the tax by doing 'odd jobs'. Professor Lewis, indeed, had said that one should not reduce the progressiveness of taxes because this would reduce the 'incentive to evade'.

M. Rottier mentioned the need to integrate the theory of the individual into that of the union. There was somewhere a gap in theory. The real point was surely the process of making united decisions. If one agreed to take the family, there might be bargaining within the family. Perhaps one did not want a model of union as a single unit. It might be composed of smaller and different-sized units.

Professor Lindahl felt that the main concern of unions was with the length of the working day, and not with the five-day week. The fight was not only on the basis of maintaining a reasonable balance between leisure and wages; it was also to raise the general wage level. It was worth remembering that when trade unions determined hours of work, individual workers might want to work longer hours but could not.

Mr. Bagiotti thought the relation between labour supply and wages was hard to analyse, first because the factors determining workers' choice between work and leisure were complex, and partly because of the formulation of the problem. The first was a question of psychology; the second meant that one had to avoid contradictions in the variables.

FOURTEENTH SESSION

SUNDAY AFTERNOON, SEPTEMBER 12, 1954

(Discussion of Paper by Krelle)

Professor Schouten said he wanted to compare Dr. Krelle's model with a simplified version of the model used at the Dutch Central Planning Bureau, and especially Dr. Krelle's conclusions about employment as a function of the money wage rate. He also wanted to draw attention to the remarkable influence which macro-economic theory had on the wage level in the Netherlands. The Netherlands had a wage stop, and nominal wages only rose if no harmful effects could be expected. The Central Planning Bureau advised the government, and the Director of the Bureau, Professor Tinbergen, advised the trade unions about the effects of a wage increase. Up to the present there had been strong confidence in the knowledge and responsibility of the Central Planning Bureau. In some way or other it had succeeded in persuading the government and the trade unions of the reliability of its magic formulae. Until 1953 it had held that there was a strong negative relation between the nominal wage level and employment. As the maintenance of full employment was a vital objective of both the government and the trade unions, the widespread faith in Professor Tinbergen's formulas explained why the wage level was kept down.

Unluckily, the model of the Central Planning Bureau was, until 1953, based on bad theory (and on the good intuition of Professor Tinbergen), and not on recent statistical inference. One bad theoretical assumption was the general supply function, or the price fixation function. This was, in the first instance, similar to that in Dr. Krelle's equation (3a). Further, it was assumed that, in the short run, income distribution between wage earners and entrepreneurs was independent of the wage level and only slightly dependent on output. In other words, an increase of the wages in all firms by 1 per cent would always be followed by an increase of 1 per cent in profit per unit of output. This proposition was based on the assumption that prices were determined by the costs of marginal firms and that there was a linear macro-economic supply curve resulting from differences of wage costs of the different firms. This could be illustrated. One could assume that

the wage sum was equal to $\frac{1}{2}(b+a)x$,
profits were equal to $\frac{1}{2}(b-a)x$,
and the national income was equal to bx.

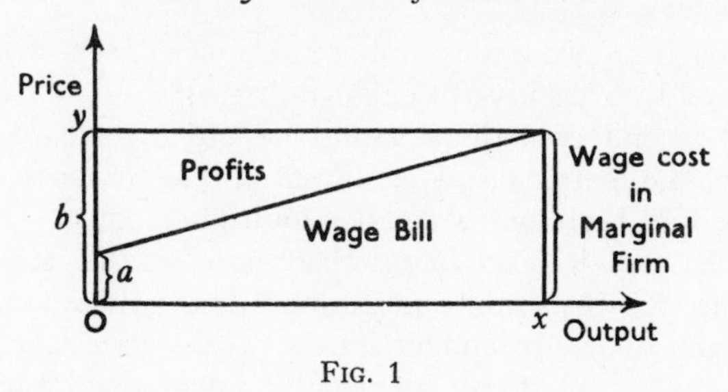

FIG. 1

In this case the wage quota of national income would be equal to

$$\frac{\frac{1}{2}(b+a)}{b}.$$

If one increased the value of a and b, by a general wage increase, income distribution would not change. The wage quota would of course decline if output rose, because of the larger value of b with constant a. According to this view it was obviously wrong to assume price flexibility equal to zero as Mr. Krelle did for the sake of simplicity.

Splitting up price increases into cost components

$$p = \bar{\lambda} p_e + \zeta p_z + \bar{\mu} p_m$$

($\bar{\lambda}$, $\bar{\zeta}$, and $\bar{\mu}$ are respectively average quotas of labour costs, profits, and imports in prices; p_e, p_z, and p_m are respectively wages, profits, and import prices per unit of output).

The Bureau had found a price fixation function according to our assumption of $p_e = p_z$, i.e. an unchanged income distribution if output were the same.

(1) $$p = (\bar{\lambda} + \bar{\zeta}) p_e + \mu p_m + \pi \gamma,$$

which was obviously different from Mr. Krelle's.

Only in recent years had statistical investigations into the formula shown that

(2) $$p = \lambda p_e + \mu p_m,$$

in which λ (the *marginal* wage quota) was more in the neighbourhood of $\bar{\lambda}$ than of $(\bar{\lambda}+\bar{\xi})$. Further, π, the price flexibility, was practically zero.

The first formula gave a very strong negative relation between the wage level and employment. But the second formula gave only a slight negative relation. In the first case, wage increases would lead to a decline of exports and to a hoarding of the marginal income of entrepreneurs. Its unfavourable multiplier effects would actually be reinforced by a positive price flexibility.

In the second case there would be no increase of profits, no hoarding of the marginal income of entrepreneurs, far less declining of exports, and therefore a smaller multiplier effect. In addition, only recently had it been found that there was no strong relation between internal costs and our export prices. These export prices were probably more dependent on the world price level. Further, the Dutch export elasticity seemed far lower than was previously assumed. So, after all, there was no relation between the wage level and employment.

Mr. Johnson said that Dr. Krelle began by reversing the problem set in the draft programme ; he set out to analyse the determination of real wages, given the money wage. Mr. Krelle's argument suggested that the real wage had a top and bottom limit and constructed a general equilibrium model, along Keynesian lines, for the determination of the real wage and the price level.

Later Dr. Krelle tackled the problem of what the money wage would have to be, given the other things, to maintain full-employment output. Mr. Johnson said, first, that he did not believe that one could have a theory of money wage determination separated from a theory of real wage determination. In various economic problems one could take the money wage level as a parameter which shifted autonomously, but one could not accept the implication that the money wage was an autonomous variable, determined by some outside forces. Second, the model itself was of a very familiar type. There were two general approaches to the construction of such models : the 'Anglo-American' and the 'Dutch' approaches. In the Anglo-American type one took substitution between home and foreign goods in consumption. In the Dutch type substitution in production was used. Dr. Krelle followed the second type which raised some logical problems. If one assumed one fixed quantitative raw material requirement regardless of how this was divided between home and imported goods, and one then assumed that its division between home and imported raw material depended on relative prices, one was in some logical inconsistency. A fixed quantity implied perfect substitutability between home and imported raw materials ; the dependence of the division on prices implied imperfect substitutability. This raised some problems, if the total situation was to be determined, and not just incremental changes.

The main question about any model was whether it was economically sensible. Dr. Krelle's model contained some startling assumptions. Both wage earners and profit earners spent a fixed proportion of their money incomes on goods, regardless of the price level. This was not valid, as Dr. Krelle admitted; the argument that it could be ignored because one was not considering business cycles was irrelevant, because one was analysing the effects of price changes. Indeed, this amounted to a 'built-in money illusion' on the part of workers and capitalists. Again, the assumption about capitalists' spending ($c_2 + s_1 > 1$) was that as capitalist income went up their spending went up much more. This was a contrast with the more orthodox Keynesian system, where there was a specific theory of investment. Government demand was also a little odd. The government had no fewer than five different types of taxes. The government was assumed to spend all the money it got, and a fixed sum besides — the budget deficit. Part of government expenditure was fixed in money terms. So, if prices went up, the government got less goods.

There were two equations, one for demand and one for price. A minor puzzle here was that fixed taxes were assumed to enter directly into the pricing process and not to fall on profits. Consequently increased output would tend to reduce prices.

There was an assumption that firms calculated their imported material costs on the basis of the price of the home-made factor. Hence material costs varied with price level. At any given output, profits varied with price, and the profit margin was constant. The elasticity of profits with respect to output was assumed to be 1. Hence, the profit margin represented a constant percentage of price whatever happened to output. The only thing left which could affect the real wage rate was those government taxes which did not vary with the price level. Constant taxes were taken out; only the specific taxes remained. So, the real wage depended entirely on the price level and not on output. The only thing that happened when the price level changed was that the government get more or less. This explained the conclusion, presented later, that real wages would only vary if there were taxes which did not change in money value with changes in the price level.

If one complicated the analysis by allowing the varying costs of internal and external materials to affect material costs, then as the money wage rate rose the real wage rate would rise too. The cost of imports would become a smaller proportion of price and the real wage would increase, whether or not there were taxes which varied with output.

Various things were wrong with Dr. Krelle's manipulation of the model: although the constant taxes were assumed to be zero, they still survived in some equations. There was also a novel conception of the meaning of flexible exchange rates. The exchange rate moved so as to keep the terms of trade constant. This was not the same thing as keeping the balance of payments in balance, unless some other special conditions were fulfilled. All the analysis of flexible exchange rates was therefore irrelevant. At other points Dr. Krelle had been misled by his own technique. Putting in simple expressions to stand for complicated ones, he got results that would not follow if properly worked out. For example, he concluded that it was possible for a change in the money wage rate to have no effect on employment if $\eta = 1$, and $\dot{T} = 0$. But, by definition, $\dot{T}$ could not be zero unless the budget surplus were equal to the total value of exports.

What happened if one allowed the relative prices of home and imported goods to affect the price level ? The effect of an increased wage rate, with a fixed exchange rate, *must* be to reduce the level of employment unless the sum of elasticities of demand of imports was sufficiently less than unity to offset the fact that rising wages transferred purchasing power from the government to workers and so increased savings. Another peculiarity in this analysis was that the answers seemed to depend on individual elasticities. In fact, they must depend on the sum of the elasticities, because the change in relative prices caused substitution in both countries between the two goods. In general, one should distrust results which depended only on one of these elasticities.

Some of Dr. Krelle's conclusions were obvious once one appreciated his original assumptions. Some conclusions were inexplicable, but they must follow from his assumptions and simplifications. Mr. Johnson said he had already explained the conclusions on wages and prices in terms of the original assumptions.

He had been rather hard on Dr. Krelle. The construction of a model of this kind meant a great deal of work, especially if one was interested in relating it to facts and trying to test it against statistics. However, if one was going to do the statistical work one had to be careful to ensure that one's model was sensible. Dr. Krelle's emphasis on having a model that could be fitted to an economy and estimated was a very good one. There was no point in multiplying models unless one was going to do something with them. But one could not construct a single model which could be fitted to all European economies ; it would surely be better to choose one particular country and to try to develop a model which conformed to its particular economic structure.

Dr. Krelle made three comments on Mr. Johnson's remarks. First, on the model itself in general, second on the usefulness of this model for the problem in question, third on the economic assumptions it implied.

First, the model was not at all 'of a very familiar type along Keynesian lines'. It originated from an extension and aggregation of a Leontief-type input-output system. Subdividing the 'final bill of goods' into private investment (I) and consumption (C), government demand (G) and exports (E), and assuming a linear technology, we get for the n goods (x) of the economy the n production equations.

$$(1) \qquad \begin{aligned} a_{11}x_1 + \ldots + a_{1n}x_n + I_1 + C_1 + G_1 + E_1 &= x_1, \\ a_{n1}x_1 + \ldots + a_{nn}x_n + I_n + C_n + G_n + E_n &= x_n. \end{aligned}$$

Denoting w the wage rate, M the amount of inputs, p_f the price of inputs in foreign currency, d the exchange rate, T the indirect taxes, Q the profits and p the prices, one had the price determination system :

$$(2) \qquad \begin{aligned} a_{11}p_1 + \ldots + a_{n1}p_n + w_1 + M_1\, p_{f1}d + T_1 + Q_1 &= p_1. \\ a_{1n}p_1 + \ldots + a_{nn}p_n + w_n + M_n p_{fn}d + T_n + Q_n &= p_n, \end{aligned}$$

(1) and (2) were a linear system of $2n$ unknowns and $2n$ equations, if all the parameters were constant and given from outside. This was the way Leontief treated the problem. Dr. Krelle's own idea was to put functions in for I, C, G, E, M, T, and Q, and to close the system thereby. Since these functions were very likely to be non-linear, he had aggregated the n sectors into one in order to facilitate the computation. He did not think that this was 'very familiar along Keynesian lines'.

Second, on the usefulness of his approach, Dr. Krelle did not deny that there was a connection between money wages and real wages. But in fact this connection was not too narrow. One could divide the theory into one part which dealt with the determination of the money wage rate, mostly institutional factors like the behaviour of the trade unions and employer associations, and a second part which dealt with the effect of changing money wages on prices, production and employment. Demands for higher wages by trade unions often had nothing to do with changes in real wages, but were due to the internal problems of trade unions, political considerations, and so on. The labour economists had elaborated some rather complicated theories of changes in the money wage rate. What was lacking now was a theory of the effects of these changes on prices, production, and employment. To connect them both into one system should, in Dr. Krelle's opinion, be a second step.

Third, he fully agreed that the functions in his system were only first approximations to reality. But every 'well behaved' function, however complex, could be approximated by a linear function in a certain neighbourhood of a starting-point. That was all he did. Others might complicate the functions as they liked. But he could not do so in this paper. The effort in computing more complicated mathematical models was very often underestimated.

As to the single functions, he thought that his consumption and investment functions were more useful than Mr. Johnson allowed. Professor Kuznets had stated, for the United States, that from about 1870 till 1954 the consumption and investment proportions averaged over the cycles were almost constant. Modigliani and Duesenberry had built a new theory of consumption on this fact. His own consumption and investment functions followed precisely these lines. They were fitted to the static nature of the system and did not contain short-run cyclical phenomena. In his own eyes the most questionable function was the profit function which made profits a function of the relative deviation from 'normal' (i.e. capacity) production. He would have been grateful for some comments.

To make $c_2+s_2>1$ was essential for a static system, and in agreement with reality in the long run. Otherwise there could be no equilibrium at all without a steady budget deficit; or, more likely, equilibrium production would be zero.

As far as he knew, price calculation in the whole world included total indirect taxes and added a profit margin. This was the idea behind the price equation. He could not see why fixed indirect taxes should be excluded from this procedure. He regretted the simplifications $\eta=1$ and $T_c=0$ which were only made to cut down the computing work to manageable limits; but he gave the rules how to correct the mistakes due to that. The same applied to the simplification of taking p instead of $p_f d$ for imports. But a calculation showed that the latter simplification was hardly of practical importance. Suppose the material input comprised 30 per cent of the total price, one-third of the material input being imported. If the deviation of internal to external prices was 10 per cent, then the mistake in the final price caused by the simplification was of the order of 1 per cent, which was surely tolerable.

The analysis about flexible exchange rates rested on the exchange rate theory originating from Gustav Cassel that a flexible exchange rate equilibrated the price levels within the country and abroad. He agreed that a theory based on the balance of trade would be nearer to reality. Nevertheless, in the long run Cassel's theory was not so wrong as to make the results meaningless. But perhaps this approach to the case of flexible exchange rates should be altered.

Finally, many experts with whom he had talked urged him to simplify the system. Mr. Johnson's criticism suggested the opposite.

FIFTEENTH SESSION

SUNDAY EVENING, SEPTEMBER 12, 1954

(Discussion of Paper by Dunlop)

Professor Lindahl considered two questions raised by Professor Dunlop's paper :

(1) What is the task of contemporary wage theory ?
(2) What is the relation between this theory and general economic theory ?

Professor Lindahl answered the first question by saying that wage theory as a special discipline dealt primarily with problems of the wage structure, problems already cultivated by so-called labour economists. This agreed with Professor Dunlop's paper, but Professor Lindahl said he would go a little further and say that the task of labour economists was not to determine the general wage level. The general wage level could only be determined in the framework of a general economic system, since it depended on factors which had to be taken as given when dealing with the wage structure ; saving and investment propensities ; changes in tastes and techniques ; monetary policy and other political factors ; the development of foreign trade, and so on. Thus he agreed with Professor Marchal that the theory of the general wage level must be integrated into general economic theory. But Professor Lindahl said he disagreed, perhaps, on how much was left to the labour economists. He thought it was more than Professor Marchal admitted.

Professor Lindahl thought the demand side of the labour market had been a little neglected in the conference. There had been no progress in discussing the rôle of employers' associations and their strategy. Again, cost curves depended on marginal productivity curves, but Professor Dunlop had pointed out that marginal productivity theory was not 'popular'.

On the relations between wage theory in this special sense and general economic theory, Professor Lindahl said that wage theory had its own *raison d'être*. We wanted to know as much as possible about the wage structure, even if we had no correct theory for the general wage level. Wage theory in this sense was a condition for developing a correct theory of the general wage level, as Professor Dunlop had shown.

The general economist must use concepts like the 'local supply of labour', 'total demand for labour', and 'general wage level'.

His 'special' wage theory should be such that his conclusions on these special points would be the best possible. But whilst the labour economist could use special theories, such as the theory of the firm and the theory of bargaining, they also needed a theory of the general wage level. What could economic theory offer ? There were two types of economic theory, (1) static and (2) dynamic. Static theory, a theory of economic equilibrium, could be used (a) for comparisons between different countries, (b) in explaining long-term development in a country, and (c) as an approximation for explaining short-run movement. With long-term problems, static economic theory could show, for example, that if the supply of labour were infinitely elastic at the subsistence wage, as in a backward country, no increase in wages was possible. Again, if supply of labour were infinitely inelastic, wages would change to the extent that the marginal productivity of labour altered. It could also set out the possible results of an increase in the supply of capital, or of technical inventions.

Professor Kerr feared that labour economists had done too little of what Professor Lindahl wanted. They had not made the necessary link with general economic theory. Professor Kerr went on to comment on Professor Dunlop's paper. He explained that, in the United States, one need only know the 'key' rates and 'contours'. If one knew 10 'contours' one knew 30 per cent of the wage structure in the United States. Professor Dunlop related his 'wage contours' to the United States. But perhaps his theory would work better in France or Australia where there might be only one contour.

Professor Dunlop had implied that, in the case of inter-industry differences in wages, the demand situation determined the wage structure, and labour supply adjusted itself to this. The supply side was under-emphasized. The 'skill-mix' was more important than conditions in the product market. Similarly, Professor Dunlop underemphasized the internal political considerations that unified the wage structure. Steel and automobile wages were tied together through trade union action. Professor Dunlop also had under-emphasized external political factors. The major contours depended on the national situation. If one party lost an election, workers might act less soberly, and so on.

Professor Dunlop had not covered some important points. He had said little about non-union wage rates and the 'wage slide'. He could tell how the contours moved but could not explain changes in the nature of an individual contour. There were serious problems in applying the theory. Any fall in employment was spread over many industries, and responses in wage rates differed considerably.

For example, lags were hard to handle. There was no 'standard' lag.

Professor Kerr wondered if this was a 'theory'. Or was it a map, which merely gave one the terrain but did so without analysing it. Indeed, he wondered if it were possible to have a 'theory' of wages, when institutions were not bound by the 'rules of the game'. Should one settle for a list of factors which were helpful in describing the 'country'?

Mr. Turner felt that there were two requirements of any theory. First, it must consider both general distribution and relative wages. Second, it must explain past history as effectively as marginal productivity theory explained the 'classical' period. It followed that we needed a general theory of income distribution. Wage theory illustrated many of the defects of a general theory. It had disintegrated on the supply side because of such sociological facts. They must now be brought in.

Professor Dunlop's contour did not mean a single given 'height' of wages; it covered a range of wages. In Britain, often, there was a tendency to uniformity because of trade unions. Cotton, for instance, had the 'uniform' list; in England the emphasis was on uniformity rather than the 'band' of wages covered by Professor Dunlop. The theory should explain both situations.

Professor Dunlop's long-run analysis also met with serious problems. In history, very low differentials were enough to get people out of agriculture — even none at all if there was a population surplus. The problem was not the same now in the 'new' countries. Factory labour was relatively highly paid, though the skill of such labour was often lower than in the Industrial Revolution. Here an external factor came in. These countries imitated the trade unions of the western world. Also public opinion, national and international, about working conditions was important.

M. Brochier thought there were advantages in distinguishing two types of 'political' theory of wages. First, there was the 'internal' type, with an elaborate decision-making process within the trade unions. Second, there was the elaborate political battle at the national level with, for example, government fixing of prices. He felt there was a need to settle the terminology and make it clear what a 'political' theory of wages implied.

The 'job cluster' developed by Professor Dunlop studied the relation between the jobs of workers in each particular wage group and the whole wage structure. It was interesting to put them together to study the short run. For instance, in the separate firm, a recession which 'laid off' workers would alter the wage structure because not all types of worker were dismissed in the same proportion.

In the long run, the analysis was harder to apply, because of changed terminology. In two periods, of the same length but ten to twenty years apart, one would find that the same word denoted a different job. It seemed that evolution changed the structure of the labour force completely. It was impossible to compare, for instance, the Renault 'job-structure' and its many conveyer belts, with De Dion Bouton. The structure of job clusters was not reliable in the long run, simply because we could not assume that 'job clusters' remained similar for long enough.

Mr. Peacock wondered whether Professor Dunlop was not making too sharp a contrast between older theory and his own. This latter was really only an extension of ordinary supply and demand analysis to allow for more complex relations than, say, bilateral monopoly. For instance, where truck drivers were employed by many firms, all drivers would be on the same contour. But discrimination was not thereby ruled out.

Professor Kerr suggested that the 'job cluster' might be re-christened the 'job family'. The father would be the 'key' rate. The other rates in the family, while the 'ages' would differ, would all move together. If the contour were denoted as M_1 any given rate M_2 could be lower or higher, but the whole complex of rates would move up or down together.

Professor Dunlop thought it less important to press the details than to think whether his views were correct on where wage theory stood in its general development, and in its link with general theory. We were concerned not with a theory relating to either the United States or France but with a whole *corpus* of ideas. What problems did labour economists expect general economists to answer for them, and vice versa.

M. Rottier pointed to two instances where the general economist wanted help. (a) He did not agree with Mr. Peacock that the key rate was a legitimate extension of general theory. The whole idea of a 'key' rate was alien to price theory. How, he asked, could an economist formulate a 'key' bargain ? (b) It was unfortunate that Professor Dunlop did not throw greater light on long-term growth. The wage structure was clearly modified by such growth. But what did the facts show ? Were wages in the expanding industry the 'key' wages for the student of economic growth ?

Professor Robinson thought Professor Dunlop had changed his mind during his paper. The historical sections considered the distinction between the general wage level and the wage structure. Later, however, Professor Dunlop seemed to say that it was useless to make this distinction and that one needed a common discussion of the two combined. If this was a correct interpretation, the idea was retrogade.

Professor Robinson thought there was an interesting analogy between wage theory and interest theory. Both were weak on the supply side. There was also no such thing as a 'general rate of interest', and it was the same with wages. One could still, however, separate the general wage level from the wage structure.

Professor Dunlop felt that the level and structure of wages were not independent, although he agreed with Professor Robinson that the distinction between level and structure was useful and basic to wage theory. The wage level rose through the process of changes at key points. Some rates moved rapidly, some slowly. We needed to know which rates moved first. We needed to discover how far a change in one rate moved others, and how the general level of wages was thus changed.

Professor Dunlop held that the tasks one allotted to wage theory, as opposed to general theory, depended on what one was interested in. In under-developed areas the wage fund theory was useful for some problems. But for the questions asked of general theorists by policy-makers in the United States or Western European countries the received doctrine was quite inadequate. For example, it could not tell us how the structure of wages was affected by differential changes in productivity, by employment changes in specified sectors, or by overtime pay. Nor could it say how wages were related to price policies either in particular industries or in general. It was to answer such questions as these that wage theory needed to be altered.

SIXTEENTH SESSION

Monday Morning and Afternoon, September 13, 1954

(Summary Discussion)

Professor Robinson, as Chairman, suggested that the position that the conference had reached was very much like the critical position in any set of wage negotiations. They had moved on from the statement of claims to an attempt to reach agreement and settlement. However, they did not want to reach agreement where there was no agreement. Where there were differences they wanted to see what was the nature of these differences. They might arise either from using different models or from making different assumptions.

The steering committee had divided the summary discussion

into three major headings, and one of the members of the conference was to lead off the discussion under each heading. The three topics were : (1) Wages and the Level of Employment ; (2) The Structure of Wages ; (3) The Impact of Organizations on Wages.

I. Wages and the Level of Employment

Mr. Peacock, opening this part of the discussion, thought that one of the results of the Round Table had been to question and to modify many of the arguments that had developed since the war about the wage-price spiral. He did not suggest, however, that the group would agree fully on policy recommendations.

If inflation were defined, in the Keynesian fashion, by reference to the inflationary gap, then in order to determine a unique level of 'full employment', one had to know the connection between the supply of labour and the level of activity. Mr. Peacock did not think there was any unique connection, at least in the short run, and he believed that post-war experience supported this view. He wished to consider how far spontaneous wage increases affected the level of money incomes, and assumed that at some definite level of money incomes prices began to rise. This was a simplification, but it was a useful starting-point.

The traditional argument, Mr. Peacock said, ran as follows. The bargaining power of labour increased with the level of employment. At the same time, the resistance to wage increases declined because of the rise in profits. In the words of Dr. Singer, this was a situation not of bilateral monopoly, but of co-operant monopoly. These conditions created larger wage incomes, and when general over-employment was reached the wage-price spiral arose.

This traditional argument had, however, to be qualified by the consideration that sub-markets might have different levels of employment, as had been suggested in the conference by Dr. Hansen. The time-factor was crucial, as wage lags might vary between industries, depending upon bargaining procedures and cost-of-living agreements. In the discussion of M. Rottier's paper it had been suggested that increases in employment might be associated with a narrowing in wage differentials, which, in turn, might have effects upon inflation.

Two policy recommendations usually followed from the traditional argument. The first was the obvious one of pressing for the wage restraint which Professor Wagner had advocated. The second was to relate wage changes to changes in productivity in the long run.

Mr. Peacock made several comments on the traditional argument. He thought that it was illegitimate to infer that wage increases were the cause of inflation or, to put it more strongly, were the main cause of inflation. For example, one could consider an equilibrium level of income, implying the equality of *ex-ante* savings and investment and the supply and demand for money. What would happen if trade unions attempted to raise wage levels ? Could one have cost-induced inflation without having demand-induced inflation ? Given no other changes, spontaneous increases in wage levels of this type would only be possible if employers were prepared to accept a redistribution of income. The income effect would then depend on the relationship between the change in the distribution of income and the marginal propensity to consume.

Such an instance of a spontaneous wage increase was, in Mr. Peacock's view, not very realistic. Certainly it was not the sort of situation that had existed in Western Europe since the end of the war. There was nothing in Europe's post-war experience which led to the conclusion that autonomous or spontaneous wage demands were the principal cause of inflation.

Apart from doubts as to the desirability of a policy of wage restraint, problems were created in maintaining such a policy for long periods of time. Post-war experience showed that wage-restraint policy could give rise to pronounced social tensions. Moreover, whilst it might be in the general interest of a society to prevent price rises immediately induced by wage increases, the particular interest of individual unions appeared to have been to raise their money wages in order to raise their real wages.

Professor Robinson asked whether it was not true that the relation between the level of wages and employment was affected by the fact that one had an advancing economy, with increasing productivity. If national income went up by about £400,000,000 a year, and if wage incomes did not go up by more than about £200,000,000 a year, there was no inflationary force on the cost side.

Mr. Peacock thought that if one was going to have a theory, and such a theory was very important for policy, one must be clear about what particular things were being held constant. Productivity was changing ; government investment policy was changing ; there were changes in the supply of money and in interest rates.

M. Rottier said he did not believe very much in the 'Rottier argument' as put forth by Mr. Peacock. The narrowing of differentials was a long-run problem. The relation of wage changes to employment was essentially a short-run one.

But he was interested in Mr. Peacock's suggestion that demand-induced inflation was a necessary condition for cost-induced inflation. Was it not possible for demand-induced inflation to start with a level of unemployment that was still fairly high? The effect of productivity was not important as an average for the whole economy, but rather in terms of productivity changes in particular industries.

Mr. Johnson felt we were in danger of taking the post-war world as the standard of reference. In most countries there was a period of substantial unemployment before the war. The level and structure of capacity had since become adjusted. There was destruction of capital during the war and a drop in the standard of living of most people. The combination of bottleneck factors and of the desire to maintain standards of living had tended to produce inflation after the war.

If, however, one took an economy which was adjusted to a higher level of demand and had a satisfactory wage structure, the problem of inflation became much less severe. An expansion to full employment was different from an expansion started at full employment.

Mr. Johnson thought that if we were to consider the relation of wages to employment as a general problem, and not just a post-war phenomenon, we needed to ask just how flexible was the structure of the economy to normal sorts of changes in demand and just how flexible was the wage structure to these changes?

As to the relation between demand-inflation and cost-inflation, if trade unions tried to raise money wage levels, and employers did not allow redistribution of income to workers, unions had to face the possibility of increased unemployment. If the government was interested in the level of employment, it would adopt policies which would not allow such unemployment to emerge. Cost-inflation might require that demand-inflation be supplied in order to maintain employment policy. We needed to concentrate on the likelihood of bottlenecks and the precise way in which wages were adjusted.

M. Sellier made the point that a consideration of equilibrium in submarkets led to the conclusion that general economic policy was very difficult to formulate. He presented three propositions in this connection: (1) There was an almost inexhaustible reserve of labour supply. Thus, in the United States, it was possible in a relatively short time during the war to find five million workers, partly out of the recruitment of family labour and partly by a shift from agriculture to industry. (2) Any addition to the labour supply led to a threat of induced inflation; but such inflation could be combated by fiscal and monetary policy if responsible officials did their jobs. (3) Countries like France were beset by old rigidities but, in the long-term adjustment, reserves of manpower and capacity were ultimately revealed.

Mr. Roberts suggested that an economy at full employment, and without inflationary pressure, might nevertheless find two factors which created inflationary pressures. These were changes in the terms of trade and changes in monetary policy derived from such changes in the external accounts. In the British economy both of these factors had operated in the past. A change in the terms of trade before the first World War had induced an atmosphere of militancy in the trade unions. After the second World War, the combination of a change in the terms of trade with a change in monetary policy had induced substantial wage demands.

Mr. Laffer said he had been asking himself how this discussion would assist a wage-fixing authority like the Commonwealth Arbitration Court in Australia. It would never ask the question: what wage increases could be granted without producing inflation? Rather would the question be: what was the capacity of the economy to pay the wages asked? The factors considered would be the effect of such increases on prices, employment, cost-of-living adjustments, and the prosperity of the farm industries.

Dr. Krelle thought the main thing to be discussed was whether there was an upper limit for wages above which inflation always set in. There might be a static connection between the price level, the wage level, and employment, so that each wage level was connected with a certain price level. But it might also be that certain levels of employment were connected with certain *increases* in the wage and price levels.

The main theoretical difficulty, in Dr. Krelle's view, was that there were several critical values which changed the relationship of employment to wages and the price level. Whether a change in the price level would lead to more or less employment could not be decided without investigating changes in the values of many other parameters. In one economy, a rise in wages and prices might lead to more employment, but in another it might lead to the reverse. One could not answer the question without going into the structure of the economy in question and finding out the parameters which determined the functioning of the whole system.

Professor Robinson wondered whether it might be profitable to spend a few moments on an important issue at this point. If we believed that there was a critical point at which increasing demand for labour pushed up wage bargains, was it close to full employment or rather remote from full employment? In the United Kingdom, both Sir Dennis Robertson and the Editor of *The Economist* apparently thought that this point was somewhere around 2½ to 3 per cent of unemployment, and that such a level was as close to full employment as they wanted to be. Others, who had analysed pre-war statistics, had put this critical level somewhere between 10 and 12 per cent of unemployment. But it was not clear whether it was safe to generalize from the pre-war experience. The pre-war economy was fairly well adjusted to long-continuing unemployment. There had been many of the phenomena of a boom in 1937, with some 10 per cent unemployed.

Professor Dupriez believed that the point at which inflationary processes arose did not depend only on labour as a disposable factor, but also on other factors of production. In a well-balanced economy one would expect a price spiral only when employment was fairly high. If there were industries which were obsolete, with non-competitive equipment and which had made little capital outlay, it was to be expected that prices there would rise sooner. In Belgium, unemployment was quite localized in parts of the country where capital equipment was insufficient.

Professor Dunlop reported that in the recent American scene there was an average money wage increase of 3 to 4 per cent per year with unemployment of approximately 4 to 5 per cent. Inflationary pressures might arise out of union demands and from general expectations of continually rising wages.

Mr. Rehn took the view that members of the conference did not speak the same language even when they used the same figures. Five per cent of unemployment in America would be equal to 10 per cent of unemployment in Sweden, since the figures were calculated differently. The English figures were more like the Swedish. In America, the percentage was calculated on the whole population, but in the United Kingdom and Sweden the figures were calculated as a percentage of workers.

Professor Robinson had put the question in terms of how high was the critical level of unemployment at which inflation began. Mr. Rehn believed we should put the question in a different way : by what methods could we make a high level of employment compatible with non-inflationary increases in wages ? Under what conditions could we approach a higher level of employment without inflation ? Mr. Rehn said that the answers to these questions depended on the level of profit margins which were necessary in order to get a particular level of employment.

Professor Robinson suggested that his question was the prior one. If one had to decide whether controls were or were not desirable, one wanted to know whether, in the absence of controls, the critical level of employment would be remote from or not very far from full employment.

Mr. Johnson thought that if the economy was generally progressing, then unions would legitimately have expectations of wage increases. The relevant measurement should be a deviation from an expected increase and not that increase itself. One should always think in terms of *increases* in productivity. There was no reason why there should not be some increase in wages with a large percentage of unemployment; such increases were a reflection of increases in productivity.

Mr. Turner believed there should be concern over the rigidity of the wage structure. Any increase in wages in one sector tended to push up the whole structure. If there was a boom in engineering, wage increases might be expected in a whole range of related industries. A wage increase in engineering would consequently affect about half the labour force. If there were a boom in chemicals, however, which did not have close links with other industries, the total effect might not be so great.

Mr. Schouten felt that Dutch experience would be of interest. In years of full employment rising productivity in the Netherlands had not led to decreased prices. Wages had been constant and profits had risen. There must be a strong deflationary situation before prices decreased.

In the next few years, Mr. Schouten expected that there would be a strong demand for increasing wages in times of full employment, but if the Dutch wage level increased, then prices would not be constant. In the Dutch economy, higher productivity did not influence prices; it led to larger profits.

Professor Robinson asked whether this result depended upon how many people were paid piece rates? If piece rates were paid, surely some increases in productivity would go into higher earnings.

Mr. Schouten replied that piece rates were not very important in his country. If the wage level increased, profits would remain constant and prices would rise by about 30 or 40 per cent of the wage increase. Unemployment had to be very large in order to give stable prices.

Professor Lindahl thought the assumptions regarding monetary and fiscal policy should be made clear. He drew a rather different dividing line between demand-inflation and cost-inflation. Demand-inflation existed, for Professor Lindahl, when there was excess demand in general. If tnere were demand-inflation, wage increases would then be said to be induced. In such circumstances, however much wages increased there would still be an excess demand for labour.

He restricted the concept of cost-inflation to an economy where there was no demand-inflation. In such an economy any wage increases would give rise to corresponding price increases. If wages were raised 10 per cent, all prices would rise 10 per cent. But this was not demand-inflation.

In the absence of inflationary policy, two measures could be adopted by the government following an increase in wages. First, the government could let the new level of wages remain ; second, the government could pursue an inflationary policy. If one had an inflationary economy, employment would increase. But such an increase in employment could not continue indefinitely. There was bound to be a break, and unemployment was the result. Consider a neutral monetary policy. Profits were not so high in this case, and therefore not important as a cause of wage increases. Wages could rise because of an increase in productivity. Employment could be rather full in this case. If there were structural causes of unemployment, they could be remedied by special measures instead of by raising the whole level of demand.

Mr. Peacock said that Professor Lindahl had just made his own point. Mr. Peacock was assuming that the supply of money was given. If wages and prices were doubled, Professor Lindahl called that neutral monetary policy. But a neutral policy was not being followed in Mr. Peacock's sense. He himself had assumed the supply of money to be given. If the supply of money, the liquidity preference function, and the marginal efficiency of capital were given, then the only way to bring about a change in the level of prices would be by a change in the distribution of income between profits and wages.

Mr. Peacock took the view that there might not be agreement about the critical level of employment at which inflation began, but there would probably be agreement about the factors which determined that level.

Professor Dunlop thought the discussion had suggested a list of factors which would influence the critical level of employment (unemployment) at which wage and price increases developed as an economic system moved from low levels to high levels of activity. These factors determined whether inflationary tendencies set in at a relatively low level of operations or at a relatively high level of employment and output.[1] These following factors must be explored in drawing any conclusions concerning the relations between employment, inflation, and wages.

[1] Contrast this approach with United Nations, Department of Economic Affairs, *National and International Measures for Full Employment* (December 1949), pp. 43-46 ; 73-75.

(1) The less unbalance there was in the structure of production, and the more evenly spread the expansion of demand, the higher the level of employment without inflation.
(2) The greater the increase in productivity and the more evenly spread the increases in productivity among sectors, the higher the level of employment without inflation.
(3) The more favourable the terms of trade, the higher the level of employment might rise without inflationary pressures.
(4) The more compressible profit margins, the higher wages might be pushed without price increases. The absolute level of profits might have an effect upon the demand of the unions for higher wages.
(5) The more adaptable or flexible the wage structure, the higher the level of employment that might be reached without inflationary developments. In a flexible wage structure, wage increases in one sector need not result in wage increases in other sectors.
(6) A policy of wage restraint adopted by trade unions or by government policy would normally raise the critical level of employment at which wages and prices rise.
(7) The response of the labour force to an increase in demand for labour would affect this critical level of employment.
(8) The methods of wage payment, including the prevalence of incentive methods of pay, would help to determine whether wages rose early or late during an expansion of employment.
(9) The more specific the direction and the impact of fiscal and monetary policies, the higher the level of employment that could be achieved without inflationary developments.

The advantage of this approach to the problem of the relation between wages and employment, in Professor Dunlop's view, was that it highlighted a variety of factors, not independent of one another, which conditioned the response of wages to changes in employment and output.

II. The Structure of Wages

Professor Dunlop, opening the discussion on the second topic, the structure of wages, said that the six papers on this subject suggested a series of observations which he summarized as follows:

(1) While there were a great many ways of classifying wage rates, the discussion had suggested a fivefold classification

of wage differentials: personal or individual wages; differentials between firms within a product market; wage differentials between industries or product groups; occupational differentials; and differentials between geographical areas.

(2) In various countries the effect of inflation had been to narrow three of these differentials: occupational, intra-industry, and inter-industry. It appeared to be an open question whether inflation had changed geographical differentials. In these various countries high levels of employment, as distinct from inflation, apparently had a marked influence in narrowing geographical, intra-industry, and inter-industry differentials.

(3) The long-run movements of wage differentials had to be distinguished from their short-term changes. Thus, in the case of occupational differentials, the long-run effects of mass education and changes in the distribution of income should be distinguished from the short-term impact of inflation.

(4) Recent years had seen a significant growth in fringe benefits or supplementary pay practices: paid vacations, pensions, family allowances, and social insurance. These payments had a marked effect upon the structure of differentials in compensation and upon relative labour costs.

(5) The movements of the level of wages and the structure of wages were not independent.

(6) Wage structures differed between countries in the way in which they responded to changes in the level of demand. This response, some of the discussion indicated, depended not only on such factors as the degree of centralization of wage decision-making, but also on differences in value judgments concerning the importance of equality and uniformity in making wage changes.

(7) There was a good deal of controversy in the discussion over the extent to which the wage structure could be used to allocate the labour force, between different firms, industries, areas, and occupations. There was need to appraise the judgment that wage differentials were not very effective in allocating the labour force in the modern world.

(8) The phenomenon of the wage slide or wage glide had attracted considerable attention. It was an interesting indication of what was going on in the wage structure of a country, but there was need to separate the independent components which constituted the difference between

contract wage rates and earnings. These factors included the effect of overtime, piece rates, personal wage adjustments, and shifts in the relative importance of firms and industries. The wage slide was frequently an indication that the market had reached different conclusions from the parties who made the formal bargains as to wage rates. The wage slide might also be an indication that wage decision-making had been divided into several parts or steps ; national bargainers set general contract rates which might later be modified as local conditions dictated.

(9) Finally, it was fruitful to look at the wage structure of a country as a whole. The wage structure frequently reflected the many attributes of an economy. The conference had considered fruitfully and rather extensively the French experience. Certain characteristics of the French economy and its wage fixing arrangements had substantially influenced the course of the French wage level and structure. Among these factors were the following : the centralized wage-setting system, the relatively stable population and labour force, the relatively small increases in productivity, the lack of competition in the international and domestic markets, the high proportion of fringe benefits, and the monetary, credit, and fiscal policies adopted over the years. Similarly, the peculiar features of the British or the American economy had influenced the wage levels and structures of those countries.

Mr. Rehn said he had tried to show that with increasing unionization there was an increase in the influence of non-market forces on wages. He called it equity. It might be called a decline in the importance of product market forces and a greater regard to human factors.

Professor Robinson asked how far the existence of wage differentials was a necessary condition for a desirable distribution of manpower. How far could this distribution of manpower be secured by means other than wage changes ? The level of employment and the expectation of regular future employment were probably more important in attracting people to particular industries than was the level of wages.

Mr. Rehn thought that another question had been raised. He asked whether equity or jobs were a more powerful influence on wages ?

Professor Robinson replied that the issue was whether equity was consistent with a given distribution of manpower. Was there some latitude within which to determine relative wage rates ? Or were relative wage rates determined by the need to distribute manpower in particular ways ?

Mr. Johnson expressed the view that it would be useful to look more closely into the function of wages in allocating the labour force. On the one hand, if all wage differentials were the same, there would be the maximum stimulus to employers to increase output of those goods which were most desired. The equality of wages would constitute the maximum incentive for the allocation of resources on the employers' side. On the other hand, if wages were set separately in each market, there would be stimulus to movement by workers. The problem was to discover the relative influence of job opportunities on the one hand and wage differentials on the other in creating movement of the labour force.

Mr. Johnson said there were two criteria for efficient allocation of the labour force. The first was through the profits of employers stimulating changes in the distribution of entrepreneurial effort. The other was through wage differentials stimulating the movement of labour. These were separate dynamic ways of inducing changes in the situation.

Mr. Turner wanted to know whether the central question was : which is the more mobile, labour or capital ? He concluded that labour was less mobile in response to wage differentials than it was in response to job opportunities. In general, capital was more mobile than labour. It followed that a system of equal wages was more likely to produce efficient labour allocation than a system of discriminatory wages.

Dr. Rothschild asked whether it was really true that capital was more mobile than labour. Did we know anything empirical about it in the short run or the long run ?

M. Rottier observed that the discussion had started with five types of wage differentials. He wondered whether the response of labour to wage differentials varied with each of these five types. Other speakers seemed to agree that there was no simple answer. *Mr. Roberts* suggested that the factors affecting the mobility of skilled workers were different from those affecting the mobility of labourers or unskilled workers, and *Professor Haller* claimed that the housing situation was an important factor affecting mobility.

Mr. Peacock thought it was interesting to consider how far there were institutional differences between countries arising from social policy. Fringe benefits had effects on mobility ; so did private pension schemes. Firms had developed many inducements to hold their labour force, and it was necessary to consider the long-run effects of all such factors.

Mr. Riches held the view that validity could be attached to the traditional analysis of the rôle of wage rates in allocating labour only if wage rates were considered to include all aspects of an occupation. Money wage rates alone might have relatively little short-run effect in moving workers. If the labour supply were to be responsive to changes in demand, the wage system had to be supplemented by training, information, allowances for travelling, and all the rest.

Mr. Rehn noted a paradox with regard to skill differentials at full employment. At less than full employment a skilled worker had an advantage over unskilled labour in having greater security of tenure. In periods of full employment, however, this advantage disappeared. Despite this, skilled workers' differentials tended to decrease at full employment. How could this be explained ? Why should not skilled workers' differentials increase in periods of full employment.

Mr. Rehn thought employers would probably like to increase wage differentials in order to get more skilled workers, but they did not do so because increased wages for skilled workers might well lead to increased wages for unskilled workers. Hence, they had to use other methods of recruiting skilled workers.

Professor Robinson felt that, in a free economy, there ought, in theory, to be a widening of differentials in conditions of full employment. Yet in practice we seemed to get the opposite effect. He suggested that in periods of depression workers moved from the contracting skilled industries into unskilled industries, and that they tended to depress wages in unskilled occupations. In times of full employment these processes were reversed and wage differentials narrowed.

Mr. Hague reported that the British radio industry had been very short of skilled workers since the war. Their supply would increase as more workers were trained. So there appeared to be no point in putting up wages ; it was a question of waiting until more skilled workers were available.

Professor Lindahl posed the following situation : Suppose there was an economy with an average annual 3 per cent increase in productivity and a 3 per cent annual increase in the general wage level, with a stable price level, and suppose that this increase in productivity was not evenly distributed among sectors. What was the appropriate monetary policy in these circumstances ? It would be simplest if the 3 per cent rise in average wages could be concentrated in the expanding sectors. There would then be a reduction in profits there, and a wage slide in these industries. If there were this adaptation of the wage level in the expanding industries, profits would be smaller, the total demand for capital would be reduced, and the monetary authorities could more easily achieve stability.

Mr. Laffer expressed the view that Australia had a rigid wage structure, but that this did not make much difference to the mobility of labour between industries and occupations. Expanding firms might raise wages a little above the average rate, which would give some flexibility. But the wage structure was more rigid than in the United Kingdom, and this did not seem to impair mobility very much.

Professor Robinson pointed out that wage differentials might reflect many different things. They might be a sign that certain sectors needed to expand and others to contract in the long run. In some economies this process of expansion and contraction was itself diminishing. Thus, in the United Kingdom, there had been a long-term decline in the proportion of the labour force in agriculture. This process of redistributing manpower from agriculture was obviously now reaching its end, and we might even be reversing the process. In this case, Professor Robinson thought that one of the reasons for the narrowing of differentials might be that the process of reallocation of labour between agriculture and industry had ended.

Professor Dunlop made two points. First, he stressed that labour was allocated by a variety of methods, not by wage differentials alone. The question was whether our wage structure, the net advantages among jobs, helped or hindered the allocation of the labour force towards that which the economy needed. It might well be that the differentials required today to perform this function were narrower, in percentage terms, than they were one hundred years ago. Second, in many countries the wage structure was determined, in the first instance, by collective bargaining, and then the market seemed to have its own way of subsequently correcting these decisions. It might not make much difference whether one had a system in which the parties to collective bargaining were immediately responsive to the market, or whether the parties who made the decisions were relatively less responsive in the first instance to the market, but recognized that the market would later make the necessary adjustments in the wage structure.

III. The Impact of Organizations on Wages

Mr. Rehn opened the third part of the discussion by observing that labour organizations were in different stages of development in various countries. The behaviour of unions might be quite different where they were a minority group from their conduct when they covered most of the labour market. Part of our difficulties in the past had arisen from a failure to distinguish the various impacts of unions according to the extent of labour organization.

Were labour organizations a disruptive force in the economy? Or were they an important conservative force in our times? Mr. Rehn indicated that it was possible to consider labour organizations from a variety of perspectives. One could approach unions from the point of view of a socially interested scientist and ask what were the tendencies in the organization. One could approach unions from the point of view of policy-makers seeking to understand union behaviour and their influence on governments. One could also approach unions from the point of view of policy-makers within the organizations themselves, seeking to explain how unions operated and made decisions.

Mr. Rehn thought that unions worked through discipline and through social and economic sanctions. They were instruments to standardize behaviour. They helped members to adapt themselves to changing conditions. He believed that a distinction should be made between the direct effect of a union upon wages within that part of the market which it had itself organized, and its secondary, more general, effects throughout the economy. When unions had become extensive they might seek to influence government economic policy in such a way that bargaining became a matter of monetary policy.

He thought this suggested a comment on the French situation. We had been told that in France there was a rigid wage policy. Wages, prices, and savings were determined by bargaining between organizations and also between organizations and the state. Might it not be quite the opposite? The organizations were always frustrated in their efforts to influence the economy. This might have the effect, from time to time, of compelling the state to adopt a sort of 'one-step inflation'. The market then decided the course of developments rather than allowing these developments to be determined by further bargaining between organizations.

Professor Kerr began the discussion on Mr. Rehn's opening remarks by developing a somewhat novel view. Unions seemed to become unimportant in the wage-fixing process when they got to be old and strong, as in Great Britain and Scandinavia, or perhaps just old, as in Germany. They might be important in other ways, in reducing the tendency of employers to control the plant. The older unions did not bring heaven, in the way their supporters expected, nor hell in the way their opponents prophesied.

As unionism got older and stronger, Professor Kerr thought it became more responsible, more concerned with the welfare of all elements in society. But did trade unions tend to become *too* responsible, so that in another sense they became irresponsible ? Did they thereby fail to do the things they might well do for society ?

As Professor Kerr saw it, in Germany the trade union movement was addicted to the 'dictatorship of the last bench', that is, the wage rate was set so low that marginal workers in marginal firms were not put out of work. An aggressive trade union movement could be a good substitute for a proper labour market.

He wondered if the trade union movement of the world might not be better off if it avoided the responsibility which economists have been exhorting it to assume, and if it remained responsible in the sense that it was responsible only to the interests of its members. Should it not leave to other groups in society the responsibility for the welfare of such groups, and work something out in bargaining ? The father of the American trade union movement (Gompers) had said that unions should have no ultimate end, but the goal should be more, more, more, and now. Might that not, in the long run, be the most responsible approach in a society which becomes progressively more rigid ? Professor Kerr speculated whether the trade union movement did not, after a time, become the opiate of the people ? Did it really do something for them ? It gave them a sense of control over destiny. It kept the populace quiet.

Professor Robinson said that these were big questions. The theoretical economist thought trade unions introduced a certain amount of monopoly into what would otherwise be nearly a free market. Was that in fact the case ? He thought the definition of a good bargain was not one in which one party or the other used monopoly power to get its way, but rather a bargain which looked like sticking. Professor Robinson could not agree with the suggestion that trade unions did not put pressure on bad firms. In the English clothing trades, the wage board set a wage which the vast majority of employers would pay. Marginal firms were made to pay that wage.

Professor Kerr replied that was what unions should do. After a while, he feared they became too responsible to do it.

Mr. Roberts thought that the ideas advanced by Professor Kerr might be applicable to the United States, but they were less applicable to the post-war United Kingdom, which was always on the verge of a balance-of-payments crisis. If the Trade Union Congress made a mistake on a large scale, it would have serious repercussions. If bargaining were on a local basis, as in the United States, the effects of any one bargain would be much less.

Mr. Johnson said that Professor Kerr's views implied a decentralization of unions. If unions were to fulfil the function he indicated, Mr. Johnson thought there was something in the suggestion that unions might become too soft.

Professor Robinson asked how far unions could succeed in pushing up real wages when they pushed up money wages. *Professor Kerr* replied that unions could raise real wages by eliminating marginal firms. Strong, aggressive unions, imposing a single wage rate, put pressure on marginal firms, but the profits earned by the stronger, more efficient, firms were saved.

M. Sellier suggested that the discussion involved a question of the level of bargaining. If there were local bargaining, there was a likelihood that the leading firm in the bargaining might be a more efficient firm. When there was a higher level of negotiations perhaps the process should not be called bargaining, but rather the 'fixation' of a price. In France this high level of negotiation led to a tacit understanding within that group of firms which had a great interest to fix a high level.

Professor Robinson pointed to an assumption which he thought underlay the discussion, namely, that unions entered negotiations on wages only at the national level, and that all other setting was in the hands of firms not controlled by the union. It was quite common for national bargaining to fix some rates and for further bargaining between local representatives of the union and the employer to fix other rates.

Mr. Johnson commented that there was a danger of over-generalizing. If one had bargaining in a very small area there might be the same sort of problem as with very highly centralized bargaining. It was not possible to say which form of bargaining exerted the greatest pressure on wages. There might be an optimum size for the area of bargaining.

Mr. Laffer reported that in Australia trade unions pressed for a general level of wages so high that they could be paid only with the support of government policy, for example, in the field of tariffs. The wage sought by the unions was not the minimum that the least efficient firms could pay. It was a high one that would drive large parts of industry out of business, except for government assistance. Professor Kerr's picture was not valid, in Mr. Laffer's view, for Australian experience.

Professor Kerr thought that, in this case, what the unions tried to do the government prevented.

Mr. Rehn indicated that, at the outset of the discussion, he had tried to indicate that there was need for some correspondence between the psychology of the members of a labour organization and rational policies, from the economic point of view, as viewed by its leaders. The most difficult task for the union leader was to pursue a rational economic policy which was contrary to the psychology of union members.

Unions tried to persuade governments to pursue economic policies that did not make it too easy for them to increase wages. In the discussions of experience in Sweden the hate word had been 'responsibility'. Swedes had written books on responsibility. In Mr. Rehn's view there was need for an economic policy which made 'responsibility' pay.

Professor Kerr urged that much could be said for rival unions. It was desirable to have two unions competing with each other, with overlapping jurisdictions. The more competition there was in union movements the greater pressure union leaders could put on employers.

Dr. Rothschild remarked that there were aggressive and competing unions in France. The Swedish trade unions did not like the word 'responsibility'. They acted, however, as if they did like it, for they had the opportunity to act through the government. If the government could not be used as an instrument by unions, then Professor Kerr was right.

Professor Robinson suggested that it was extraordinarily difficult for people engaged in wage negotiations to know exactly what they were doing. One could listen to protests of employers that any wage increase would bankrupt everybody, but one had no evidence as to precisely what would put marginal firms out of business. All negotiators could do was to push wages in a particular direction. Professor Robinson asked if the discussion was not going back on what had been said earlier in the day. If unions put pressure on employers, was there not a risk of reducing the level of employment at which inflation began ? If this doctrine, which attacked 'responsibility', were pushed too far, did we not help to create the inflation which we were seeking to avoid ?

Mr. Johnson thought there was considerable margin for squeezing more productivity out of the economy. Policies which were too tender might neglect these increases in productivity.

Professor Robinson indicated that, in the United Kingdom, wage bargains were producing an increase of prices from 6 to 7 per cent per annum. The French rate was even higher. He did not believe that in the end this was benefiting the economy as a whole, or even the wage sector of the economy. He thought there was need to consider what would happen if wage bargains were not pushed up quite so fast. He felt it did not follow that the whole of the increment went to employers. In a moderately productive economy a certain amount of improvement in technical efficiency went into lowered prices, and benefited wage earners in that way.

Mr. Rehn made the point that in an economy where political decisions determined a certain level of investment there were complications for wage policy. In full employment the bargaining position of workers was improved. But an increase in wages might not be compatible with the required division of national income between investment and consumption. Under these circumstances, the unions would have to accept other ways of creating the necessary savings, in order to maintain investment.

M. Sellier suggested that if unions were to be responsible they would need to know many things about economic policy. He thought it would be necessary for a really 'responsible' trade unionist to be in the cabinet of ministers, and perhaps be minister of finance. In France, with centralized wage negotiations, everybody was organized, which had just the same results as when nobody was organized.

Professor Dunlop drew attention to what he regarded as an important problem in the modern world : in what proportion was efficiency on the part of management stimulated by wage increases on the one hand and by price competition ? There was need for more theoretical work on the relative effects of price competition and of wage increases. Economists had a bias towards price competition. Benefits were then widely scattered throughout the system and adjustments were non-inflationary. In a world of oligopoly price competition might not be so effective a stimulus to efficiency as wage increases.

Professor Dupriez pointed out that in order to assess alternative levels of wages it was necessary to examine various implications which might conflict — the consequences on employment, on the balance of trade, for technological progress, and so on. In some cases the necessity for safeguarding employment might be more important than in others. Again, in some situations, the implications for the balance of payments might be most significant.

The discussion had been illuminated, Professor Dupriez thought, by remarks of Dr. Schouten, who had said that in the Netherlands it had been discovered that the relation between the level of wages and the level of employment was not nearly so determinate as they had for a long time supposed. Employment was a function of the level of wages only in a given state of organization and technique, and it took time to reorganize the technique and technology of the economy.

If wage policy were used to bring about a change in techniques, the wage level internally might be out of line with foreign wage levels. Unless there were some sort of bottleneck, the fixing of wages just a little above the equilibrium level might be the right type of policy. He did not say that in any country and at any time that *would* be the right policy, but he did think that in many places and at many times it *might* be the right policy.

Mr. Peacock reminded the conference that Professor Marchal's paper had created a good deal of interest, with its thesis that collective bargaining or other union action might not raise the share of union members in the national product. This led Professor Marchal to his central thesis, namely, that we took too narrow a view of wages.

Mr. Peacock found two propositions in Professor Marchal's paper : (1) the disposable income of wage earners was alterable by the political mechanism as well as by the market ; (2) social benefits were a subsidy, increasing wages. Increases in benefits through the political mechanism automatically reduced wages received from the market mechanism.

The second proposition seemed to Mr. Peacock to be a peculiar variant of the classical argument that social benefits never benefited the people who were supposed to benefit. He questioned the validity of the assumption that social benefits and wages were mutually exclusive, and doubted whether one got very far by trying to trace the effects of union action in the political field.

M. Rottier thought it was mainly a question of fact that the share of wages in the national income in France was constant — if social benefits were included. No one had ever put forward a theory explaining this fact.

M. Sellier pointed out that whilst the share of wages in the national income was rather constant, there were important changes between the pre-war and post-war distribution of the national income. There were three important and influential groups — workers, employers, and businessmen. Shareholders were not an influential group.

Dr. Rothschild wondered whether we were becoming victims of our tools. If we wanted to build an economic model of the trade union, must it have a maximization principle in it ? Trade unions never thought of maximizing anything. Would it not be better to seek a model in which the action of trade unions was determined by past wages and the wages in other industries ? These seemed to be the factors which really influenced trade union action.

Professor Robinson thought this was a basic question. Were we not prone to find a unique answer to economic problems ?

Trade unions pursued a series of objectives, which might produce one wage rate or another according to which of their objectives they were concentrating on at any given time. *Dr. Rothschild* thought it ought to be possible to build a theory, by finding out what trade unions were actually aiming at.

Mr. Johnson suggested that what we were really looking for was new formulas of behaviour. The difficulty was that we could not quantify the factors that had been suggested. Unless one could measure changes in the political environment, one could not build a model, based on this factor, which had predictive value. Nevertheless, economists who could not fit curves and quantify still had something to say. He thought it was necessary to experiment with various hypotheses. We might yet get a much better theory, even though we were not able to predict with it.

Professor Kerr said that economists had been best at prediction when they dealt with large numbers and with the long run. Few economists had been able to predict the behaviour of single units in the short run. When one tried to predict what a single decision-making unit was going to do in the short run, one was setting oneself an impossible task.

Professor Dunlop said that the concern both of Adam Smith and of Ricardo had been with the distribution of income among social groups. This reflected a particular social class structure in the society of their day. Professor Marchal was saying that French society today was structured into a different set of social groups, and he invited us to construct a theory of wages based on the power interplay among these social groups. Professor Dunlop wondered whether this was the direction that we ought to take in wage theory? Was the discussion advanced by saying that there were a lot of social groups and that they competed and produced inflation?

M. Sellier contended that Professor Marchal's point of view did not at all contradict our more precise economic analysis. As an illustration of the importance of social groups in the inter-war period in France, he pointed out that the lowering of housing rents had had effects on the level of nominal wages.

Professor Lindahl suggested that the income of a labourer could be divided into four components: (1) the money wage and benefits from the employer directly; (2) social benefits paid by the employer and included in the employer's labour cost; (3) benefits paid by the state and secured from a tax on profits; (4) benefits not related to the amount of labour supplied, such as family allowances. If we asked a labourer what he was working for he would list all these items. He got the first three elements as a reward for labour. Yet only the first two were wages, the third and fourth were income redistribution. Professor Marchal's paper had taken account of this situation.

Professor Robinson pointed out that each of Ricardo's social groups performed a different economic function: owning land, providing labour, or supplying entrepreneurship. He asked if we were being asked to substitute a new set of groups, or was it being said that each group was a complex of smaller groups? Were we asked to team up or to subdivide the Ricardian groups?

Mr. Johnson replied that we were asked by Professor Marchal to abandon the assumption that groups were internally competitive and to say instead that they were homogeneous and collective, and that they fought out distribution problems through political processes.

Mr. Riches made the point that two separate theories were needed: an economic theory of wages and distribution of income and a theory of incomes which was not necessarily economic at all, but based on political theory. Mr. Riches asked why Professor Lindahl included the third of his categories (benefits paid by the state and taken from profits tax) in wages, in the sense of a reward for work, since it was independent of whether the worker was working or not.

Professor Lindahl replied that the benefits were paid by the state, through social insurance schemes, and he regarded this as a subsidy given to employees.

Mr. Johnson asked how far the behaviour of individual labourers in collective bargaining units was influenced by their bargaining with the state. He thought that it could not make any difference to the worker whether he got more wages or more social benefits. Did he think of these as alternatives? Did social benefits influence the quality and the supply of labour?

Professor Robinson thought this was an admirable note on which to end. The discussion had been valuable if it had left everyone with a feeling that we did not yet know all the answers.

INDEX

Entries in the Index in Black Type under the Names of Participants in the Conference indicate their Papers or the Discussion on their Papers. Entries in Italics indicate Contributions by Participants to the Discussions.

Printed in Great Britain by
Lowe and Brydone (Printers) Limited, London, N.W.10